Fighter Command's Air War 1941

Fighter Command's Air War 1941

RAF Circus Operations and Fighter Sweeps Against the Luftwaffe

Norman Franks

Pen & Sword
AVIATION

First published in Great Britain in 2016 by
Pen & Sword Aviation
an imprint of
Pen & Sword Books Ltd
47 Church Street
Barnsley
South Yorkshire
S70 2AS

ISBN 978 1 47384 722 4

Typeset in Ehrhardt by
Mac Style Ltd, Bridlington, East Yorkshire
Printed and bound in the UK by CPI Group (UK) Ltd,
Croydon, CRO 4YY

Pen & Sword Books Ltd incorporates the imprints of Pen & Sword
Archaeology, Atlas, Aviation, Battleground, Discovery, Family History,
History, Maritime, Military, Naval, Politics, Railways, Select, Transport, True
Crime, and Fiction, Frontline Books, Leo Cooper, Praetorian Press, Seaforth
Publishing and Wharncliffe.

For a complete list of Pen & Sword titles please contact
PEN & SWORD BOOKS LIMITED
47 Church Street, Barnsley, South Yorkshire, S70 2AS, England
E-mail: enquiries@pen-and-sword.co.uk
Website: www.pen-and-sword.co.uk

Contents

Acknowledgements

I give sincere thanks to a number of people who have helped or advised me in the writing of this book. Many of them were men who saw action in 1941, most of whom have now left us. Fellow historians Andy Saunders, Chris Goss and Chris Shores have my respect and thanks.

This book should be read in conjunction with John Foreman's book *RAF Fighter Command Victory Claims of WW2 (Part Two)*, Red Kite, 2005, and my own *RAF Fighter Command Losses of WW2, Vol 1 (revised) 1939–41*, Ian Allan, 2008.

Prologue

Regular conferences were held at Northolt to discuss our various problems; the AOC presided and, amongst others, the leaders of the fighter wings and the bomber leaders attended. On one such occasion I raised the question of just what our purpose was in carrying out these operations. If it was to destroy the industrial potential of the various targets and so reduce the contribution of industry by the Occupied Countries to Germany's war effort I maintained that it would require a far, far greater bomber force than we had so far escorted.

If, I continued, the bombers were merely there as bait to bring up the fighters so that they could be destroyed then we should restrict our radius of activity to that which would permit us to fight without the nagging fear of running out of fuel. The mental obstacle seriously interfered with a pilot's fighting spirit and it was my opinion that we had already lost far too many first class men because these factors were not receiving sufficient consideration.

Air Vice-Marshal Leigh-Mallory looked rather taken aback at this and he turned to his Group Captain Operations, Victor Beamish, who was a very experienced and successful fighter pilot, and asked him what he thought. Victor said that he agreed with me so the AOC turned to another of his staff officers and asked his opinion. 'My answer to Kent is – we've done it!' he replied.

Although this officer had a very fine record in the First World War he had not operated in the second conflict. I was furious and was quite rude in the remarks I flung back, but it was no good: the AOC preferred the second opinion and we continued to go to Lille and lose good men, all to little purpose.

Wing Commander J. A. Kent DSO DFC, leader of the Northolt Fighter Wing in 1941.

Chapter 1

What will the New Year Bring?

T he winter weather at the end of the momentous year of 1940 curtailed air operations over Britain, and particularly southern Britain. The main achievement as far as Winston Churchill and his Government were concerned was that German forces seemingly poised across the Channel to invade this island had, at least for the time being, been prevented from doing so. The Royal Air Force had successfully denied the Germans the necessary air superiority over southern England, which was a prerequisite for any air or seaborne assault to take place. Those who gave themselves the luxury of believing that the Battle of Britain had been won, had no way of knowing that better weather in early 1941 would not herald a continuation of this Battle, and that an invasion might yet develop and take place.

History now records that no such attempt would be made even though the German Luftwaffe had every reason to assume their attacks against southern England and other parts in the north, would continue once spring began and they had recouped the serious losses incurred during the previous summer and autumn. Indeed, with the night bombing of British towns and factories now in full swing, why would their airmen think that they would not soon again be pitting themselves against the RAF's fighter pilots in order to have another try to wrest air superiority from them and dominate the skies for a sufficiently long period to allow an assault by troops, both from the air and from the sea, while bomber crews did their level best to prevent Britain's Royal Navy from spoiling the party? There was adequate evidence that the German High Command had intentions of using the massed invasion ships and barges that crammed captured French ports along the Channel coast. Hitler may have deluded himself that Britain might well surrender, or at least try to negotiate some sort of peace settlement in the circumstances, but that never happened nor was it even seriously contemplated.

Adolf Galland, a successful German fighter pilot and Kommodore of a Geschwader of fighter aircraft, who would in not so far a time, head the Luftwaffe's fighter arm, was clear in his post-war memoirs, that what was called the Battle of Britain lasted into 1941. In the early weeks of the New Year, German fighter aircraft were frequently flying *Frei Jagd* sorties over southern England, and particularly across Kent and Sussex. While these 'free hunts' were exciting for the Luftwaffe pilots and kept the local RAF fighter squadrons occupied, these incursions were no more than nuisance raids, and nothing to compare with the vast formations of bombers and fighters of August and September 1940.

Meantime, although there was still the threat of a continuation of the summer's battles, Churchill and his war council felt cheered that they had appeared to have won an important round in the war, and while blooded, were far from bowed. In the best traditions of war strategy, talk was now of the best form of defence being offence.

RAF fighter pilots had been 'taking it' for months, not only over Britain, but earlier, during the campaign in France, which led to that country falling under the control of Germany, and the British army and her air force being kicked back across the Channel. Was there now a chance of hitting back, and 'dishing some out' instead?

Viscount Trenchard, a man who had led the British air forces during the First World War, and now thought of as being the Father of the RAF, was still a man in high position and to whom many listened. Made Marshal of the RAF in 1927 at the age of 54, he was now, in 1941, aged 68, but his influence still held sway.

Trenchard had been Chief of the Air Staff in the early 1920s so he knew virtually everyone of note in the Service and although long officially retired, he was always welcomed when he turned up to give his advice and help council many of the new age of commanders who had all known him throughout their rising careers. In this way of his he had talked to Air Chief Marshal Sir Charles Portal KCB DSO MC, who had become Chief of the Air Staff in October 1940.

According to Air Marshal Sir W. Sholto Douglas KCB DSO MC, Commander-in-Chief of RAF Fighter Command following Hugh Dowding's dismissal in December 1940, Trenchard had suggested to Portal that as the major daylight assaults by the Luftwaffe seemed largely over, perhaps it was time to take the offensive. Or as Trenchard had phrased it: 'lean towards France.' As is well known, Boom Trenchard had always been of the mind to take any conflict to the enemy. Throughout World War One he had constantly advocated that the Royal Flying Corps, and then the Royal Air Force, should always operate offensively across the trenches of France and wage the aerial war above and beyond the enemy lines. Now, in WW2, the English Channel represented the trenches of the Great War, and the air war should be fought over France and the Low Countries.

The architect of Britain's defensive war against the Luftwaffe's assault had been Air Marshal Sir Hugh Dowding GCVO KCB CMG, C-in-C Fighter Command from 1936 until Sholto Douglas had taken over. Dowding and his 11 Group Commander, AVM Keith Park MC DFC, whose squadrons had taken the brunt of the Battle of Britain, had both been side-lined before the end of 1940. Their removal left something of a bad taste behind, not least amongst the fighter pilots themselves, but the move was made. 11 Group was now taken over by AVM Trafford Leigh-Mallory DSO, until then the OC 12 Group of Fighter Command. It was no secret that Park and Leigh-Mallory disliked each other, so Park's feelings can be imagined following the latter's appointment to his job, even if 'L-M' was senior to Park – by a few months. Therefore whatever occurred next was largely in the hands of Sholto Douglas and Leigh-Mallory.

One reason Park disliked Leigh-Mallory was the fact that he thought the leader of 12 Group had not supported his 11 Group fighters in the same way 10 and 13 Groups had. Leigh–Mallory had his own ideas on how to conduct his part of the Battle and had become convinced that the best way of dealing with large formations of enemy aircraft was to engage them with equally large numbers of RAF fighters. However, the nature of the Battle as seen from Keith Park's perspective was that he had to react quickly in order to engage and counter these enemy formations and didn't have the luxury of time to form up two or three squadrons, before the raiders were over the south of England – and his airfields. Leigh–Mallory, being that much further north at Duxford – well north of London – could scramble squadrons and have them form up as they headed south into 11 Group's areas.

In many ways he was right, but it just wasn't feasible to do the job properly. Often by the time the 12 Group Wing (that could use 242, 19, 616 and 310 Squadrons) had taken off, climbed and formed up, the raiders over SE England had bombed and were on their way home. If Park had scrambled something like four squadrons and for some reason had failed to engage, perhaps seeing the enemy turn back early, these four squadrons might be on the ground refuelling if another raid was reported on the way. Leigh–Mallory's favourite squadron commander, who had thus become the 12 Group wing leader, was Douglas Bader, famous for having lost both legs in a pre-war flying accident, but who, nevertheless, had rejoined the RAF and raised himself to command 242 Squadron. Leigh–Mallory saw in Bader a way to forward his Group and of course himself, by championing him and using his 'press on' attitude with their Big Wing theory.

Sholto Douglas' opinions regarding Portal's question of what he thought of Trenchard's idea were, initially, against. He doubted the value of such an undertaking. As the commander of a fighter squadron in France during WW1 he knew only too well the expense in pilots that offensive actions brought, even if it did bring air superiority, beneath which ground troops could operate more favourably. Operating over France in 1941 may gain some sort of air superiority but there were no ground troops below them now and any superiority gained would always be transitory. It would, however, show the Germans that the RAF was still raring for a fight.

Still with lingering doubts, Portal suggested Douglas collect his thoughts and write a report on how he saw the situation. Sholto Douglas did so and found to his surprise that in the final analysis his own arguments lost much of their potency. Finally, he had to admit to Portal that an offensive stance did have some merit. No sooner had the decision been made than the new policy was put in motion, in fact during December 1940, although these incursions across the Channel would, at first, be no more than pin-pricks in the form of more or less hit-and-run nuisance flights in poor weather. Initially they were code-named, appropriately, 'Mosquito' raids, but later were termed 'Rhubarbs'.

The idea was for two fighters to zip across the Channel at low level, generally when cloud cover was low and ample, so that if they ran into too much trouble they might quickly hide away in these clouds and head back to England. Before this however they were encouraged to shoot up any worthwhile ground targets they found, such as enemy troops, trucks, trains and so on, and, if extremely lucky, some wandering German aeroplane. Even an airfield, if surprise could be assured. Meantime, staff at Fighter Command Headquarters would begin to formulate a more positive way of taking the war to the enemy.

* * *

One of the first, if not the first of these nuisance attacks came on 20 December, flown by two pilots from 66 Squadron based at Biggin Hill. Flight Lieutenant G. P. Christie DFC and Pilot Officer (P/O) C. A. W. Bodie DFC made an airfield at Le Touquet their target. They successfully navigated their way there, made low level passes over the air base where they shot-up several buildings before racing away like two naughty schoolboys having raided the school tuck-shop.

George Christie was a Canadian and 'Bogle' Bodie came from Kirton, Suffolk. Both had been successful in the Battle of Britain. Christie soon returned to Canada, and was killed in a flying accident in 1942, while Bodie survived 1941 too, only to be killed in 1942 as well, again in an accident.

While it was agreed that RAF fighters would start operating over France and perhaps Belgium and Holland too, logic demanded that if going all that way, with the inbuilt dangers associated with such undertakings, there should at least be some purpose to these flights. Sholto Douglas was keen not just to let his pilots loose across the Channel on the off chance of finding trouble. There was little benefit in shooting up, say, a truck and losing a Spitfire or Hurricane, and its pilot. He was mindful too that even if a pilot was brought down and succeeded in escaping from his crashing fighter, he was lost to the Command, and although he might indeed manage to evade capture and eventually get home, the majority would end up in a prison camp.

In general terms there were two types of targets if light bombers were employed in these incursions, while being protected by several squadrons of fighters. Firstly, there would be enemy airfields and perhaps suitable factory targets to bomb, and secondly, enemy shipping along the hostile shore. Any factory within range of light bombers, which would in fact be twin-engined Bristol Blenheims, would of course be French, which had been taken over by the Germans, and were now producing materials for Germany's war effort. There would also be power stations. While the destruction of these would undoubtedly annoy French civilians whose homes would lose power, this same power was being used for the factories.

The New Year of 1941 arrived and within a week thereof came the first plan to fly an offensive operation across the Channel. By now, with Leigh-Mallory in charge of 11 Group's fighter bases, he saw that his Wing ideas could now be used to advantage. And of course, with no immediacy of combat, fighter wings could take off and form up in good order before heading out towards northern France. It was soon decided therefore, that each Sector Station, such as Biggin Hill, Kenley, Tangmere, North Weald and Hornchurch, should provide their own wing formations.

This would require someone to take command of each wing and it has to be said that at the beginning Leigh-Mallory must have sat down and penned a list of those men he thought right for the jobs on offer. To this list I have added their present or recent duties at this time, and ages.

W/Cdr F. V. Beamish DSO DFC AFC	OC RAF North Weald	37
W/Cdr H. Broadhurst DFC AFC	OC RAF Hornchurch	35
W/Cdr J. H. Edwards-Jones	OC 213 Squadron	35
W/Cdr H. W. Mermagen	ex-OC 222 & 226 Sqns	29
W/Cdr R. B. Lees DFC	OC RAF Coltishall	30
W/Cdr H. A. V. Hogan DFC	ex-CO 501 Squadron	31
W/Cdr S. F. Godden	ex-OC 3 Squadron	30
W/Cdr H. S. Darley DSO	OC RAF Exeter	27
W/Cdr R. H. A. Leigh	HQ 12 Group	29
W/Cdr H. D. McGregor	ex-CO 213 Squadron	31
W/Cdr J. Worrall DFC	Snr Controller Biggin Hill	30
W/Cdr J. W. C. Moore DFC	OC 9 Group	31
S/Ldr D. R. S. Bader DSO DFC	OC 242 Sqn & 12 Grp Wg	30
S/Ldr R. G. Kellett DSO DFC VM	OC 96 Squadron	31
S/Ldr W. M. Churchill DSO DFC	OC RAF Valley	33
S/Ldr J. R. A. Peel DFC	ex-CO 145 Squadron	29

In some ways this list embraces something of an 'old boy network' of men in whom Leigh-Mallory placed a degree of trust along with seniority and position. A number had seen exemplary service during the Battle of Britain, such as Victor Beamish, Horace Darley, Jack Worrall, Douglas Bader, Ron Kellett, Walter Churchill and Johnnie Peel. Others, while they had commanded well, had seen rather less action, and were obvious choices because of their command ability. No doubt Leigh-Mallory had yet to figure out that wing leaders, as contemplated, needed to be men with clear fighting ability and an equally tactical ability to command more than one squadron in the air.

When it came to it, the only men in this list to become active fighter wing leaders in 1941 were Bader, Beamish, Kellett and Peel, with Harry Broadhurst often leading the Hornchurch Wing whilst still commanding the Station. In the above list the average age was 30/31, whereas the list of actual wing leaders that operated in 1941 was reduced to 28/29. As a matter of interest, wing leaders in 1942 averaged 26 to 27 years of age.

The list of wing leaders actually employed in the main area of operations during 1941 were as follows:

Wing	Leader	From	Age
Biggin Hill	W/Cdr A. G. Malan DSO DFC*	March	30
	W/Cdr M. L. Robinson DSO DFC	August	23
	W/Cdr J. Rankin DSO DFC	September	27
	W/Cdr R. R. S. Tuck DSO DFC**	December	25
Kenley	W/Cdr J. R. A. Peel DFC	March	29
	W/Cdr J. A. Kent DFC AFC	July	26
	W/Cdr E. N. Ryder DFC	October	26
	W/Cdr R. F. Boyd DFC*	November	25
Hornchurch	W/Cdr A. D. Farquhar DFC	March	34
	W/Cdr J. R. Kayll DSO DFC	June	26
	W/Cdr F. S. Stapleton DFC	July	29
Tangmere	W/Cdr D. R. S. Bader DSO DFC	March	30
	W/Cdr H. de C. A. Woodhouse	August	28
North Weald	W/Cdr R. G. Kellett DSO DFC	March	31
	W/Cdr J. W. Gillan DFC* AFC	July	34
	W/Cdr F. V. Beamish DSO DFC	August	37
Northolt	W/Cdr G. A. L. Manton	March	30
	W/Cdr J. A. Kent DFC AFC VM	April	26
	W/Cdr W. Urbanowicz VM CV DFC	April	33
	W/Cdr P. Łaguna VM	May	35
	W/Cdr T. H. Rolski VM KW	July	34
Duxford	W/Cdr M. N. Crossley DSO DFC	March	28
	S/Ldr R. R. S. Tuck DSO DFC**	July	24

Before wing leaders were officially appointed, the handful of early operations were usually led by the most senior, or the most experienced squadron commander at the RAF Station that was providing the escort. Planning for the future was well under way and wing commanders (flying) would soon be appointed. Meantime HQ Fighter Command set to work to plan the first operation.

Circus No.1 – 10 January

According to Johnnie Kent, in December 1940 while still commanding 92 Squadron at Biggin Hill, it was strongly rumoured that the first full-scale operation over France would be around the 24th. However, this did not happen and eventually the first raid was arranged for 10 January 1941. Exactly when the code-word 'Circus' came into being is obscure, but one imagines someone of WW1 vintage likened the mass of aircraft to be akin to the German Flying Circuses they had seen above the trenches during 1917–18. In a report on this operation it was referred to as 'First Fighter Sweep'. The operation (that later became known as Circus Number 1) called for six Blenheim bombers from 2 Group of Bomber Command to attack an airfield, and an ammunition dump in the

Forêt de Guines, just a few miles inland from the French coast, south of Calais. The planners made the intention of the raid as: 'To harass the enemy on the ground by bombing Forêt de Guines and destroy enemy aircraft in the air, or, should insufficient or no enemy aircraft be seen, to ground strafe St. Ingelvert Aerodrome.' A report on this mission also called it the First Fighter Sweep.

The six Blenheim IVs, from 114 Squadron based at Oulton, Norfolk, had been detached to Hornchurch a few weeks earlier in anticipation of this first sortie. They took off at midday, led by Wing Commander (W/Cdr) G. R. A. Elsmie. Fighter Command put up a huge armada of over 100 fighters, Hurricanes and Spitfires, to protect them and ward off the potential of scores of German fighters who might well rise to contest the attack.

The escorting fighters were Hurricanes of 56, 242 and 249 Squadrons (North Weald), and Spitfires from 41, 64 and 611 (Hornchurch). Another three Spitfire squadrons, 66, 74 and 609 from Biggin Hill, were ordered to patrol the Channel and give cover to the force as it made its way back. All this was laid down in 11 Group's Operations Order No.17. As RAF fighters were not long-range aircraft, it was essential that other squadrons should fly out to take over the escort duties as the fuel tanks of the original escorting machines began to empty.

The bombers headed in at 10,000 feet, with 56 and 242 Squadrons close by, 1,000 feet below and to the right, while 249 Squadron was stepped up about 100 feet to the right, and 'up sun'. The three Spitfire squadrons were stepped up above the bombers and to their left with 41 Squadron as top cover at about 16,000 feet.

This force crossed out over Southend at 1219 hrs, making landfall east of Calais at 1240. The Blenheims lost height and approached the target at 7,000 feet from the south-east. Their bombs rained down on dispersal pens and huts in the wood to the south-west of Guines landing ground nine minutes later. In all, 16 x 250lb bombs and 48 x 40lb bombs dropped. Smoke from two fires began to drift skywards. The bombers headed straight back to the coast, still at 7,000 feet, raced across the Channel while losing height, then making landfall at Folkestone at 3,000 feet. All six landed safely at Hornchurch at 1329, having experienced clear and cloudless weather conditions during the entire show.

The Germans did not react. 249 Squadron reported some inaccurate anti-aircraft fire and some more accurate stuff from what was termed Bofors guns aboard four E-boats two or three miles off Calais as they flew back. The pilots reported an exceptionally quiet French countryside, and some gun posts quite deserted. Snow-covered fields and the aerodrome had no marks of any activity whatsoever. Wing Commander Beamish stirred things up a bit by machine-gunning the four E-boats, raking their decks and causing AA fire to cease. One pilot reported seeing an aircraft hit and blown out of the sky by gunfire but Circus 1 had no casualties, so if true, it must have been a hostile machine.

As Beamish levelled out and began to re-cross the Channel he spotted a Hurricane being attacked by a yellow-nosed Me109. The British fighter was already streaming glycol, and it eventually crashed into the cliffs near Dover. Its pilot, Pilot Officer W. W. McConnell baled out and ended up in hospital with a broken leg. Beamish shot the Messerschmitt into the sea and later recorded:

'... halfway over I saw bullet splashes in the sea below me. I looked to the left and saw one of our aircraft being attacked a few hundred feet above the sea. As I closed in I saw that the attacker was one of the yellow-nosed Me109s. I let him have the rest of my ammunition and saw my bullets hitting his machine. But it was not until I returned to my base that I learned I actually got my man. Two of my pilots saw him crash in the Channel.'

Sergeant M. K. Maciejowski, a Pole flying with 249 Squadron, became separated from his section and attacked two Me109s. They were at the same height as himself so he climbed above them and went for the rear machine. It turned steeply then dived vertically towards the ground as though the pilot had been wounded, and he saw the 109 hit some trees.

Meantime, two pilots of 41 Squadron, as they headed back across the French coast, acting as rear cover at 19,000 feet spotted five Me109s (yellow noses), 2,000 feet below but climbing steeply to engage the other Spitfires. Sergeants A. C. Baker and R. A. Beardsley attacked, Baker hitting one which he observed diving vertically into a layer of haze at less than 1,000 feet over the sea off Gravelines. This was also witnessed by two other pilots.

Overall the operation had been a success and the only negative comment was that with so many squadrons working at such distances apart, communications on the Group Guard radio frequency did not prove satisfactory. The only other casualty was a 74 Squadron pilot, Sergeant L. E. Freese, who ran out of fuel and was mortally injured in a crash-landing at RAF Detling.

The Germans claimed four RAF aircraft shot down. Oberfeldwebel (Obfw) Georg Schott of 2(J)/LG2, reported downing a Spitfire at 1400 hours (German time), 15 km north of Boulogne for his thirteenth victory, Feldwebel (Fw) August Dilling of Stab/JG3 a Hurricane at 1405, Oberleutnant (Oblt) Georg Michalek also of this Staffel a Hurricane in the sea off Boulogne at 1300 (one of these presumably McConnell's Hurricane). Hauptmann (Hptm.) Hans von Hahn, also Stab/JG3, claimed a Blenheim at 1435, 25 km north of Nieuport for his twelfth victory.

There is no doubt that anxious eyes had been watching the events of the day with keen interest, for Leigh-Mallory sent out a congratulatory message to everyone involved:

'Please convey to 114 Squadron that the Prime Minister and C-in-C, Fighter Command, wish to congratulate all concerned in the very satisfactory operation over France. I look forward to further operations of this kind.'

* * *

If Fighter Command's senior officers were pleased with themselves for successfully completing this first Circus operation without any great problems and with minimal losses, and a couple of claims, the euphoria was short lived. Two days later, on the 12th, 242 Squadron sent off pairs of Hurricanes on Rhubarb sorties. Squadron Leader (S/Ldr) Bader and his senior flight commander, Stan Turner DFC, found and shot-up an E-boat and a drifter. In the afternoon three more pairs took off. Two failed to return. They were both very experienced pilots, Flying Officer (F/O) W. M. McKnight DFC and Pilot Officer J. B. Latta DFC. The sections had run into Me109s and the two Canadians were shot down. Both men had been on Circus 1. Feldwebel Helmut Brügelmann of 8./JG26 claimed both Hurricanes west of Boulogne at 1515.

One man who had not been pleased about the events that occurred on 10 January was the head of the Luftwaffe, Reichsmarschall Hermann Göring. According to the diary of Oberleutnant Siegfried Bathke, Staffelkapitän of 2./JG2:

> [Tuesday] 28 January 1941. The sky is clear. Fine weather. The Kommodoren of the fighter Geschwader – including our own Hautpmann Hahn – have been summoned to see the Reichsmarschall. Apparently they have been on the receiving end of an Almighty dressing down. Firstly, on account of the poor results against British fighter escort during the (RAF) attack (10 January). Secondly on account of the lack of military bearing displayed by the fighter units (apparently noted during the visit of the Führer the previous Christmas). And lastly because of (their) general slovenliness and poor turn out. What is required is a 'spring clean' and the appointment of younger more vigorous Kommodoren and Kommandeure.

Göring obviously felt that the RAF's incursion in force over the French coast should have been repulsed with heavy losses and had probably lost a degree of 'face' with Hitler, not helped by the Führer's comments about the demeanour of his fighter pilots. Bearing in mind the later over-claiming by some German pilots, particularly, as we shall read, JG2, one has to wonder if in some way this galvanised these pilots to exaggerate their claims in order to restore their own damaged pride, and in this way, please the Reichschmarshall – and keep their jobs. It was always felt that the Germans in particular were very fastidious in confirming claims of Allied aircraft shot down, but this appears to have not been the case.

Circus No.2 – 2 February

Winter weather curtailed further operations for several days. Meanwhile, 11 Group's Operations Order No.18 was written out, dated 16 January, for Circus No.2. There was no date set for this operation, and Zero Day would be decided upon, presumably quite soon. The targets were the St Omer-Languenesse Aerodrome and the nearby landing ground at Clairmarais. St Omer was an historic base as far as the RAF was concerned, for it was to this spot where the Royal Flying Corps had located its main base almost from the start of WW1 and which became the first place hundreds of First War airmen landed when posted to France during that conflict. Now it was known to be the home of vaunted Me109 fighters. Clairmarais too had been used by the RAF in WW1.

In the event Circus 2 to St Omer did not take place in January, bad weather being the main reason for the delay. In fact Circus 2 was not mounted until 2 February, and rather than the inland target of St Omer, the coastal port of Boulogne was chosen. Operations Order No.19, dated 25 January, called for six Blenheims of 139 Squadron, again protected by squadrons of fighters, while other fighters flew a Sweep of the area and Channel. People were still very mindful of the mass of invasion barges still filling captured French ports, so there were three reasons for attacking Boulogne. Not only to bring German fighters to battle, but to hinder any thoughts of using the harbour facilities for invasion, plus denying free use of the Channel to enemy shipping.

Once the date of 2 February had been confirmed, Wing Commander W. H. Kyle led his section of Blenheims down to RAF Northolt, then set out with 601 Squadron in close escort shortly after 1300 hrs. With other fighter squadrons in attendance the bombers swept in and placed bombs on Nos. 2, 4 and 7 docks in the harbour, and flew back without loss. Very few enemy fighters were seen, but one was engaged and shot down by Flight Lieutenant W. W. Straight MC of 601.[1] This was a 109E from 1/JG3, piloted by Oberfähnrich (Obfhr) Günther Pöpel, who was wounded and crashed at Boulogne.

Hurricanes of 1 Squadron also had a brief scrap, claiming one Me109 damaged, while 74 Squadron's Spitfires, on Channel patrol, shot down two more for the loss of one pilot. The pilot was Squadron Leader E. J. C. Michelmore, a supernumerary attached to 74 since December. He had been flying No.2 to the CO, Squadron Leader A. G. 'Sailor' Malan DSO DFC. Malan and Sergeant A. D. Payne claimed the two victories, Malan seeing his crash into the outer harbour close to a dredger, while other pilots claimed a probable and a damaged. The 109s came from 1 Gruppe of LG2.

This day also saw the loss of two pilots from 605 Squadron, in an action quite separate from Circus 2. Sergeants H. W. Pettit and K. H. Jones had taken off to fly what was recorded as a Battle Climb – a test. Both men were good friends and it seems as though they decided to take a peek over the Channel. Unfortunately, they must have been picked up on German radar for suddenly they were under attack from some Me109s over the North Sea. Pettit was shot down into the sea and Ken Jones chased for some distance, became lost and disorientated. He eventually spotted an aerodrome and landed, only to find he was on the wrong side of the Channel. He quickly set fire to his Hurricane with a Very pistol, before being taken prisoner. Leutnant (Ltn)

---

1. Whitney Straight had been awarded the Military Cross for activities in Norway in April 1940. He had helped select and then clear (smooth out the ice) the frozen Lake Lesjaskog in order that fighter aircraft could operate from it.

Friedrich Geisshardt of 1.(J)/LG2 claimed a Spitfire at 1530, 40 km west of Cap Gris Nez, his eighth victory.

* * *

Circus No.3 – 5 February

Circus No.3 was slated three days later, on the 5th. This time it was to be St Omer airfield, and the force of bombers was doubled to twelve, six each from 114 and 139 Squadrons. Rendezvous over Northolt, then down to Rye to pick up their close escort, Hurricanes of 1, 615 and 302 (Polish) Squadrons. This time there were two Spitfire squadrons, 65 and 610, giving Forward Support, i.e. heading into the target area ahead of the bombers, while the Hornchurch Wing (41, 64 and 611) was to provide Withdrawal Cover. These sorts of adjustments and different tactics came with experience.

The bombers were twelve minutes late making the rendezvous (1242). Both 1 and 615 Squadrons had reached Rye at 1228 so they flew towards France independently. Likewise, the Hornchurch squadrons, who arrived over Rye at 1235 also headed off without seeing the bombers.[2] 65 Squadron had already been split up, with four Spitfires going out with 302 and 610, and the other eight going across on their own. So, the formation, rather than consisting of twelve bombers and six fighter squadrons followed by a further three, composed only the bombers, and three fighter units, plus one flight of four. The other formations consisted of three fighter squadrons, two fighter squadrons and two sections quite independent of the main body.

The weather was far from perfect and snow on the ground made it difficult to locate and pick out the aerodrome, the bombers being forced to make three runs across the area before their loads of 250lb and 40lb bombs were released from 7,000 feet. The enemy reacted, not only because one of their air bases was under attack, but the time taken to secure an aiming point allowed fighters to get into position. Twelve German fighters appeared while aircraft were still over the target area, and behind 610 Squadron.

The pilots of 610 bore the brunt of the interception and although they prevented fighters getting through to the bombers, they lost Sergeant H. D. Denchfield (PoW) shot down by Walter Oesau of Stab III/JG3. It was Oesau's fortieth victory and brought him the Oak Leaves to his Knight's Cross that he had received the previous August. Denchfield was acting as 'weaver' and had been quickly picked off by the German ace. Weavers, as the name implies, weaved behind the squadron defending the main body, but were often picked off by attacking 109s. Often they were the most

---

2. On 9 February, Wing Commander Broadhurst wrote to HQ 11 Group about this apparent failure to rendezvous by his Hornchurch Wing, saying that his pilots had been at the RV within a minute of the schedule, and seeing no aircraft, presumed that 1230 had been the leaving time and not the RV time, so had headed for France.

newly arrived and inexperienced pilots so were vulnerable. The other 'weaver' was also hit and slightly wounded. 65 Squadron also lost two pilots, Pilot Officer G. Hill (PoW) and Sergeant H. C. Orchard who was killed, but they claimed one 109 destroyed. 615 Squadron had Sergeant O. M. Jenkins shot down and killed over Calais, then two other of their Hurricanes collided over Dover. Both were Polish pilots. Pilot Officer S Czternastek did not survive, but Pilot Officer B. Wydrowski managed to bale out safely. Further losses were from 1 Canadian Squadron, losing Flying Officer R. G. Lewis, and Sergeant R. C. Jones of 56 Squadron. Lewis baled out over the sea after being shot-up by a 109 but he failed to be rescued. Jones also failed to return and was reported killed. The fight also cost 65 Squadron two pilots, but Sergeant Jones and Flight Lieutenant B. F. Finucane claimed shooting down one of the offending 109s.

The Hornchurch Wing, led by Harry Broadhurst, had crossed into France above Hardelot at 14,000 feet. Almost immediately two Me109s were spotted by 611's B Flight commander, Flight Lieutenant Barrie Heath. He attacked one and it went down to crash. In all they saw only four enemy fighters over France, Pilot Officer W. G. G. Duncan Smith helping to probably destroy one of them. 611 Squadron lost Pilot Officer H. S. Sadler who was seen to take hits and begin to go down, his canopy pushed back and the side door down. Obviously injured he must have become unconscious before he could bale out, so continued down into the sea leaving a trail of smoke and flame. Thus nine RAF fighters had been lost during the operation, and apart from Finucane's claim, only 611 Squadron managed to hit anything, putting in reports for one Me109 destroyed and another as a probable.

German fighter pilots put in several victory claims. I./JG3 five Spitfires and one Hurricane, including two for Ltn. Helmut Meckel of the 2nd Staffel, his tenth and eleventh kills. Three Spitfires and four Hurricanes by III./JG3, including three for Oblt. Peter Ostholt of the Stab (Staff) Staffel, his first confirmed claims of the war. Feldwebel Wilhelm Philipp from 4./JG26 got in on the party by claiming his eighth victory, a Spitfire near Neufchâtel at 1415. In all, twelve Hurricanes and nine Spitfires claimed – a total of twenty-one victories. Actual RAF losses were five Hurricanes and four Spitfires, including two Hurricanes of 615 that collided over Dover.

Further Sweeps were flown over the Channel after Circus 2 had returned but little was seen. Blenheims from 16 Group of Coastal Command went out to attack three destroyers that had been reported north of Calais, escorted by the Hornchurch Wing, but no ships were found and the Blenheims bombed an alternate coastal target. No enemy aircraft were seen by any of the RAF fighter pilots on these two later operations.

A full report by Sholto Douglas was sent to the Secretary of State for Air, at the Air Ministry, dated 5 February. Again it is of interest that the word Circus was not mentioned, merely referring to an offensive operation.

Circus No.3 or 4 (!) – 10 February

It is strange that although what was later referred to as Circus No.3, was flown on 5 February, as detailed above, 'another' Circus numbered No.3 was also shown as being flown on the 10th – in fact one of three flown this day. Obviously it was a confused time with these and other operations, and probably it was much later that someone decided to start a numbering system for record purposes and an error had crept in.

The first operation on the 10th called for six Blenheims of 114 Squadron, from Horsham St. Faith, to be escorted by the North Weald Wing (56, 249 and 17 Squadrons), to attack Dunkirk between 1220 and 1230. Without any interference, the bombers dropped their loads from 7–8,000 feet, being seen to fall in the tidal basin, then smoke began billowing from buildings on the dock side.

Two of the escort squadrons did not encounter hostile aircraft, but 249 was attacked by a number of Me109s, and they claimed two shot down. One enemy pilot was seen to bale out and the other Messerschmitt crashed on the beach near Dunkirk. One other 109 was claimed as a probable. 249 Squadron lost one pilot, P/O W. L. Davis, who was wounded and ended up as a prisoner, shot down by Hptm. Herbert Ihlefeld of I./LG2's Stab Staffel, for his twenty-sixth victory, although he claimed a Spitfire. German pilots preferred claiming Spitfires, just as they preferred to report being themselves shot down by a Spitfire, if in fact it had been a Hurricane!

One of the victorious RAF pilots was Micky Maciejowski of 249, who had claimed a 109 exactly a month earlier on Circus No.1. His combat report of 10 February stated:

'I was Red 2. I was flying 1,000 feet higher than the leader who was at 14,000 ft. I saw 3 Me109s attacking the formation below me. I dived down and did a steep climbing turn and delivered a ¾ stern attack with deflection with a long burst of 5 or 6 seconds. The e/a turned on its back immediately and the pilot baled out although the aircraft had given no sign of injury. I then looked around and saw a dogfight a long way above me but as I could not reach them, I dived to 700 ft and returned home.'

The German pilot may have been Unteroffizier (Uffz) Karl Ryback of I./LG2, whose 109 went into the sea. Ryback did not survive. Other pilots claiming victories this day were Sgt S. Brzeski and Sgt C. Palliser. In his log-book, 'Titch' Palliser noted a probable 109. Leutnant Adolf Steckmeyer of II./JG51 was on the receiving end of a fighter attack. Palliser recorded:

'I circled at 3,000 feet with Red 3 and saw three 109s. I picked out one and fired at about 400 yards, and saw huge pieces of his port wing fly off. I turned and saw one of our Hurricanes being attacked by a 109. I dived, giving a quarter attack to his starboard side. After two 2-second bursts half of the 109 blew up as he tried to turn away. While I was following him down, I gave one more burst, and that was the finish. I was now only 20 or 30 feet above the water.

'I followed the badly crippled 109 close to the beach, when a tracer came over my wing. I turned violently, and a 109 flashed past. I pulled the aircraft round slightly and fired at the fleeing 109, when my two starboard guns jammed. The recoil of the port cannons meant that the firing had stopped on the starboard side and my aircraft performed like a motor car skidding.

'When I straightened up, I saw Flight Lieutenant [A. G.] Lewis, a South African who was flying as Yellow 2, and had been fired at by the 109 that was on my tail. He later substantiated my claim that the pilot had been killed and had been seen to crash on the beach.'

Circus No.4 – 10 February

At the same time that Circus No.3 was put in motion, Circus No.4, six Blenheims of 59 Squadron, carried out an offensive sweep from Manston, escorted by the Kenley Wing (615 and 1 Squadrons, plus a Flight of 605 Squadron). Their target was the harbour of Boulogne, and timed to coincide with the Dunkirk raid. Perhaps the confusion over the Circus number was because 59 Squadron was part of Coastal Command (16 Group), so not part of 2 Group Bomber Command's operations.

The bombers claimed hits in the target area resulting in several large fires being started and although flak was heavy, none of the Blenheims were hit. Upon their return, the bomber crews were enthusiastic about the co-operation they had received from the fighter escort. While these two operations were in full swing, the Hornchurch squadrons, 41, 611 and 64, carried out an offensive sweep twenty minutes after the two bomb attacks, termed as a 'mopping up' mission, in order to provide cover as the bombers returned across the Channel.

Circus No.5 – 10 February

Six Blenheims, again from Coastal Command's 59 Squadron, comprised the raiding force to Circus No.5, which was targeting Calais at between 1620 and 1630 this same afternoon. Again operating from Manston, they were escorted by the Northolt Wing, 601, 303, 266 and 46 Squadrons, with Hornchurch again providing the 'mopping up' part of the scheme. Hornchurch pilots first positioned themselves above Canterbury then commenced a sweep as the attack ended. Bombs fell in the harbour, exploding amongst barges and a goods train and the rail track, as well as some harbour buildings.

Enemy reaction was slight, but Me109s did engage 601 Squadron, who lost P/O R. C. Lawson, who was seen to fall into the sea. 46 Squadron was also attacked, shooting down one Hurricane (pilot lost) with another pilot wounded. The latter, Sgt D. J. Steadman, crash-landed on a sandbank off the English coast and swam to shore. German pilots claimed two victories. Hauptmann (Hptm.) Lothar Keller, Stab Staffel

II./JG3 a Hurricane at 1742, while Herbert Ihlefeld claimed his second kill of the day, 'another Spitfire' at 1735.

There is a report by 11 Group of Fighter Command that details these three numbered Circuses (III, IV and V), although there is another reference to one action being a Roadstead Operation. Perhaps this caused confusion in the numbering sequence of these early Circus operations, especially as Coastal Command aircraft had taken part. Ordinarily, a Roadstead was an operation against shipping in the Channel, whereas all three of the day's missions had been against harbour installations at Dunkirk, Boulogne and Calais.

* * *

Group Captain C. A. Bouchier, at 11 Group HQ, wrote the report on these operations and his conclusions state:

'(i)   That these three operations were highly successful. The notable feature being, that the British forces were entirely unmolested throughout. The fighter cover provided being adequate to enable them to concentrate on the accurate bombing of the target.

(ii)   That the Germans appear now to be putting up standing patrols of fighters which is one of the objects of these operations. He still appears, however, to be reluctant to fight as a whole, but is prepared, with a height advantage, to pick off stragglers.

(iii)   That unless it is necessary for the accurate bombing of vital targets to bomb from 7–8,000 ft, it would be less of an embarrassment to our escort fighters if the bombing was carried out, in such operations as these, from a height of, say, 15,000 feet.'

It is obvious these early Circus operations were just the start of a large learning curve that was about to engulf Fighter Command and 2 Group, Bomber Command. During the Battle of Britain the previous summer, AVM Keith Park had seen that in the latter stages following heavy bomber casualties, there was no real reason to engage pure fighter sweeps, or *Frei Jagds* as they were called, for fighters on their own above England were of little danger. Therefore, he ordered his squadrons not to engage unless bombers were present. Göring, therefore, had started sending over bomb-carrying Me109s, escorted by other 109s, in order to force RAF fighters up and into combat.

Now, as 1941's offensive actions got underway, the tables were reversed and while it was an enthusiastic bunch of RAF fighter pilots that were eager to be part of a large contingent of Spitfires and Hurricanes ranging over northern France, German fighter pilots also decided that, unless there was a positive chance of making an attack, hopefully pick off a straggler, and then dive away inland, there was little reason to engage these huge formations. Rather than stick a bomb or two under a Spitfire or a Hurricane for their nuisance value, the RAF decided that twin-engined bombers going for specific targets was the best way of forcing the Luftwaffe up to a fight.

Typical of the Luftwaffe's tactic of 'sniping' at RAF fighters on patrols rather than the direct escorts, was demonstrated on 11 February while 74 and 66 Squadrons were flying a Sweep from Boulogne to Gravelines. The weather was cloudy with excellent visibility, and some flak was encountered that probably helped German fighters find the Spitfires, which were at 18,000 feet. Suddenly five Me109s dived down from cloud cover, right on the tail of 66 Squadron, and one Spitfire, whose pilot had fallen slightly back about 100 yards from the rest, was hit and went down out of control. Another pilot dived to try and identify the falling colleague but was attacked by two Me109s. Taking violent evasive action he was lucky to escape. 66 Squadron began splitting up and circling. When the two squadrons eventually returned to base, they found that a second Spitfire had failed to return. Although Fighter Sweeps, like Circuses, would continue into 1941 and later into 1942–3, there were commanders who had yet to be fully convinced about these offensive operations, especially when Britain's fighter force was still licking its wounds after 1940. Following the action on 11 February, Sholto Douglas wrote to Leigh-Mallory on the 12th:

My Dear Leigh-Mallory,

I am still not happy about these offensive sweeps. I see that we had two more pilots missing yesterday. I know, of course, that one cannot conduct offensive operations without incurring some casualties, but one does expect to get a 'quid-pro-quo' for one's own casualties in the form of enemy aircraft shot down.

Our idea was to go over the other side and leap on the enemy from a great height in superior numbers; instead of which it looks as though we ourselves are being leapt on.

I am certain that the main trouble is that we are going over too low. In the last war, when we had these big offensive sweeps, we always went over very high, with one squadron right up at the ceiling of our aircraft. I think that we ought to be doing the same now. Your top squadron should be somewhere at about 30,000 ft and there should not be too wide height intervals between squadrons; this means that your lowest squadron (with the bombers) ought to be not lower than 18,000 ft. (The enemy is patrolling at about 20,000 ft, so far as I can judge.)

Will you please have another think? In the meantime I should be glad if you will go slow on Offensive Sweeps for a day or so, while we are cogitating.

We are sending you in an official letter one or two comments on your Operation Instruction for "Circus" Operations. It is very full and thorough, but we have one or two alterations or amplifications to suggest.

On 13 February, Chief of the Air Staff, Air Chief Marshal Sir Charles Portal KCB DSO & Bar MC, wrote to Air Marshal Sir Richard Peirse KCB DSO AFC, AOC-in-C, at HQ Bomber Command, High Wycombe:

My Dear Peirse,

Thank you for your secret letter date 12th February on the subject of formation bombing in co-operation with fighter sweeps.

Before coming to the main point I would say that I cannot agree with the reflections in your para.4, namely, that these operations are desirable only if we shoot down more of the enemy than we ourselves lose, or also inflict material damage by our bombing. I regard the exercise of the initiative as in itself an extremely important factor in morale, and I would willingly accept equal loss or even more in order to throw the enemy on to the defensive, and give our own units the moral superiority gained by doing most of the fighting on the other side.

But to come to the main point I really do not see that we need incur losses as heavy as we inflict on the enemy <u>unless</u> we spoil the chances of the fighters by tying them too much to the bomber operations. We want to translate the initiative into practical terms of numbers, height and a tactical plan, and above all we must avoid falling between the two stools of fighting and bombing. If I thought that two Blenheim squadrons used against four Channel ports on fine days and with fighter support, and on other days with cloud cover, could really 'deny' these ports as invasion bases or as coast-wise shipping ports, I should be only too anxious that the fighters should conform, but I think you will agree on further reflection that this result could not, in fact, be achieved. We can certainly harass the ports and keep the enemy on the jump by light sporadic attacks, and as these also make it hard for the enemy to ignore us when we go over there, they fit in very well with the purpose of the fighter operations. I suppose that with luck the Blenheims can bomb and get away before much opposition develops, and that by varying our tactics we can ensure that he will often have to put his fighters up.

I do not like the word 'bait' and it need not be mentioned to the Blenheims. They are doing a useful job in harassing the invasion ports and at the same time they are playing an important part in our efforts to get the initiative back from the enemy. This is clearly explained in the first paragraph of your directive.

I think the best thing would be that you and Douglas to whom I am sending a copy of this letter, should discuss it between you and then, if you are not agreed or if anything is not clear, you should both come and see me about it. I would probably manage Saturday morning or Monday afternoon. Will you let me know?

To this letter, Sholto Douglas replied on the 15th:

I was very glad to get your letter of 13 February on the subject of formation Bombing in co-operation with fighter sweeps. It expresses exactly my own views on the subject.

You will be glad to know that Peirse and I had a discussion this morning with Leigh-Mallory and representatives from No.2 Group. We first of all reached agreement on the wording of the object of these operations. It reads as follows:

'The object of these attacks is to force the enemy to give battle under conditions tactically favourable to our fighters. In order to compel him to do so the bombing must cause sufficient damage to make it impossible for him to ignore them and refuse to fight on our terms.'

We also discussed a number of tactical points and reached agreement on these also. We shall not therefore have to worry you any further I hope.

* * *

Obviously there was still much to learn and absorb. In the weeks that were to follow, Fighter Command committed its forces into a war of attrition with the Luftwaffe over northern France. It was unfortunate, however, that the enthusiasm of the RAF fighter pilots often let them see what their heads wanted to see, rather than what their eyes actually saw. It was readily believed by the higher echelons of the RAF that their young pilots were clawing 'huge gaps' in the ranks of the Luftwaffe, so much so that it would not be long before the Luftwaffe would be down to its 'last fifty Messerschmitts'.

If this phrase seems familiar, one only has to refer to a similar phrase that the Luftwaffe High Command had told its fighter pilots in 1940, that (according to their intelligence reports, coloured by Luftwaffe claims) the RAF 'are down to their last fifty Spitfires.' The truth, of course, is that if claims of enemy aircraft destroyed were simply taken on face value, the losses would be horrendous and unsustainable. What was happening in reality, was that just as in World War One, if a pilot got into trouble, it was far easier to feign being hit and head down, either in a spin, or pretending to be disabled. Most sensible pilots would not follow a seemingly crippled opponent down. For one thing he would open himself up to an attack from a second hostile pilot, and for another, he would not want to sacrifice his height in the middle of a battle. Once the 'crippled' machine was clear of danger, its pilot would then level out and go home, a wiser man, and still intact.

By 1941 British Intelligence had enough information coming in from a variety of sources to know that Fighter Command was not inflicting the amount of damage on the Luftwaffe that its pilots were reporting. It was just the same for the Germans. Fighting over hostile territory, there was no way of confirming how many aircraft had actually fallen, crashed, blown up, been abandoned, or swallowed up by the sea. If on a given day the RAF Communiqués reported twenty German fighters shot down over France, the Intelligence boys would soon suspect that this was twice the actual losses. The 'powers that be' at Fighter Command must have realised this too and been well aware of the numbers game, but why did they not try to temper operations in the light of these figures? Was there any reason to go over France, lose perhaps one Blenheim and a dozen fighters, when actual German losses were, perhaps, five, even though many more had been claimed. And why were the claimants being decorated for high scores of enemy machines shot down, when they were failing to do so? It is with this background that I continue to record the operations around these Circus operations during the year of 1941.

Of course, it has also to be taken into account that many of the Battle of Britain veterans had now left front-line operations and been sent off on rest, instructing, and so on. There was now a massive influx of new and untried pilots reaching the squadrons, who, while keen to do their best, had not been given sufficient time at Operational Training Units to bring them to an operational status and mind-set. Their leaders still in combat were becoming increasingly tired and due for a rest too. Other experienced pilots were also being sent to Malta and the North African Desert.

As far as the air leaders were concerned, it was virtually World War One all over again, this time the trenches had become the English Channel, and in persisting in Trenchard's old doctrine of 'taking the war to the enemy', RAF fighter pilots were becoming the 'cannon fodder' of the present war.

Chapter 2

Step by Step

Following these initial Circus operations, there was a lull until the next one. The weather played a part, it was still the depths of winter, but the occasional Sweep was flown and a few Rhubarb sorties. The Luftwaffe pilots were still keen to press on and mounted their *Frei Jagds* over southern England whenever they could. In some ways these were like the RAF's Rhubarbs, except they preferred to go after aircraft or airfields near the coast. And they had some successes.

On 14 February, 66 Squadron was on patrol along with 64 Squadron, and were bounced by 109s. One 66 machine was shot down into the sea, two others damaged, their pilots wounded, while one 64 Squadron aircraft, also damaged, had to make a crash-landing. JG52 were the culprits, although LG2 also put in claims – a total of fifteen Spitfires between them! Perhaps these numbers would please the Reichsmarschall. The next day 66 Squadron had another pilot wounded by a roving Me109 pilot, and had to crash-land at RAF Manston. On the 17th, 91 Squadron had a Spitfire shot up by a 109 and had to crash-land near Folkestone, while on the 20th, German ace Werner Mölders, leader of JG51, surprised Spitfires of 41 Squadron on patrol and shot down two, both pilots being killed. Mölders bagged another Spitfire on the 25th, shot down off Gravelines, his fifty-ninth kill, and another pilot also claimed a victory. 611 Squadron was on an escort sortie but only lost one pilot; the 19-year-old RAF pilot never knew what hit him. RAF pilots did claim three 109s destroyed, plus a probable off Dunkirk, and JG51 did indeed suffer one pilot killed and another crash-landed.

* * *

A review of the early Circus operations had been undertaken and on 16 February Fighter Command's 11 Group HQ issued a Secret Operation Instruction, outlining how these missions were to be flown and organised. It was still very early days of course, but it is worth reading, especially in the light of how things gradually changed over the summer as more experience was gained:

CIRCUS OPERATIONS

OBJECT OF THESE OPERATIONS

1. (i)   To lay down principles which are to govern the carrying out of all air operations in which No.11 Group Fighter Squadrons are taking part in company with, Bomber aircraft supplied by either No.2 Group, Bomber Command, or No.16 Group, Coastal Command, or both. (Such operations to be known as CIRCUS 1, CIRCUS 2, etc.,)

   (ii)   By providing a clear definition of the roles of each part of the force comprising a CIRCUS; an explanation of the operational terms which will be used when issuing executive orders for a CIRCUS; and an outline of the methods which will be adopted in carrying out a CIRCUS, it is hoped to lay on a CIRCUS Operation at short notice and with a minimum of words in the executive order.

DEFINITION OF TERMS

2. (i)   <u>ZERO DAY</u> Is the day on which the operation will be carried out, and which will be communicated whenever practicable, to all concerned the evening before.

   (ii)   <u>ZERO HOUR</u> Is the time all Bomber and Fighter Squadrons (unless otherwise ordered) are to <u>Rendezvous at 15,000 feet</u> over selected places, and <u>SET COURSE FOR OBJECTIVE</u> at 180 m.p.h. indicated.

   (iii)   <u>FRENCH</u> That part of the French coastline which a CIRCUS is to cross and re-cross <u>LANDFALL</u> on their outward and return journey respectively.

INFORMATION.

3. (i)   The German Air Force in occupied territory have by day been comparatively undisturbed by offensive action on our part.

   (ii)   The initiative has been entirely theirs until recently, to be active as and when they pleased. We have been forced continually to stand on the defensive prepared at any moment to meet attacks of the enemy's choosing.

   (iii)   The German Air Force has so far been defeated in major daylight engagements against this Country, but their morale has held because they have had opportunity to recuperate at rest in their bases, where it has been unnecessary for them to be constantly on the alert against possible counter attack.

(iv)   As a result of our Circus operations to date, the Germans have now started to put up standing patrols, and these show signs of increasing with each operation. (See also paragraph 5 (vi) DISCIPLINE).

(v)   Important targets exist in certain of the enemy-occupied Channel Ports, and in addition there are also many military establishments, concentrations of supplies, and a number of aerodromes or landing grounds in northern France suitable for attack.

(vi)   Nos.2 and 16 Groups wish to take advantage of our ability to provide escorts in order to attack these targets by day.

(vii) No.11 Group require these Bombing operations to bring the enemy to action on our own terms under conditions favourable to our Fighters.

INTENTION.

4.   The object of these attacks is to force the enemy to give battle under conditions tactically favourable to our Fighters. In order to compel him to do so the Bombers must cause sufficient damage to make it impossible for him to ignore them and refuse to fight on our terms.

EXECUTION.

SELECTION OF TARGETS.

5. (i)   A.O.C., No.11 Group in consultation with A.O.C's No.2 and/or No.16 Group will select the targets, and the ZERO HOUR, after considering all Intelligence and Meteorological information available. Invariably, a secondary target will be selected and stated in the executive order. The secondary target is to be attacked only when the primary target has not been located, and to avoid the Bombers having to return with their loads of bombs.

(ii)   ALLOTMENT OF FORCES AND THEIR ROLES.

(a)   BOMBER FORCE.

The Bomber Force is required to cross the French coastline at not less than 17,000 feet. This height is not to be reduced during the actual bombing attack and withdrawal until the English coast has been regained.

(b)   ESCORT WING.

An "Escort" Wing will usually consist of three Squadrons, and is to fly in the following manner:

The "CLOSE ESCORT" Squadron is to fly at 1,000 feet above and slightly behind the higher or highest box of Bombers throughout the attack and the subsequent withdrawal to safely behind the

English coastline. They are NOT to leave the Bombers except to repel attacks actually made on the Bombers until approaching their respective Home bases. The Squadron to act as Close Escort is to be detailed by the appropriate Sector Commander.

The "ESCORT" Squadrons. The remaining two Squadrons of the Escort Wing to be known as the Escort Squadrons, are to fly one on each flank, behind, and not more than 3,000 feet and 5,000 feet respectively above the higher or highest box of Bombers. They are to engage enemy aircraft which menace the formation of Bombers.

After the attack has taken place they are to continue to escort the Bombers on their homeward journey until the French coastline has been re-crossed and the Bombers are well set on their course for home. They are then free, together with the High Cover Wing, to take advantage of the situation, and seek out and destroy enemy aircraft.

(c) HIGH COVER WING.

In certain circumstances a Wing of two or three Squadrons may be detailed as "High Cover" to the Bombers, in addition to the Escort Wing. The High Cover Wing is to fly behind the Escort Wing, and with their Squadrons stepped downwards at intervals of 2,000 to 3,000 feet from not less than 30,000 feet, and to the flanks of the Escort wing, as indicated hereunder.

Squadron	Height
Bombers	17,000 feet.
Close Escort	18,000 feet.
Lower Escort	20,000 feet.
Higher Escort	22,000 feet.
Lowest High Cover	25,000 feet.
Middle High Cover	27,000 feet.
Top High Cover	30,000 feet, or higher but in visual contact with Squadrons below.

Invariably the Leader of the High Cover Wing is to lead the lower or lowest Squadron.

High Cover Squadrons, other than the Top Squadron, are permitted to reduce height to attack enemy aircraft in the air. The Squadron flying at the top and acting as 'Above Guard' to the other Squadron or Squadrons, is to maintain a protective position above the other Squadrons, and only fight if forced to do so for the protection of the remainder.

After the bombing attack has taken place, the High Cover Wing is to continue to give cover to the Bombers and the Escort Wing during the withdrawal until the former with their Close Escort have re-crossed the French Coastline and are well set on their course for home. They are then to provide High Cover to the two Escort Squadrons of the Escort Wing, who also become free from their escort duties, to seek out and destroy enemy aircraft.

(d) <u>MOPPING UP WING.</u>

A Wing of two or three Squadrons may be detailed as a "Mopping Up" Wing. At a height of between 25,000 to 30,000 feet, and by careful timing, they are to arrive off the French Coast in an "up Sun" position, at the same time and place as the Bombers and their Close Escort Squadron will re-cross it.

Their role is to protect the Bombers and their Close Escort Squadron during their return to the English Coast, thus freeing the High Cover Wing and Escort Squadrons to enable the latter to carry out their main role of engaging enemy aircraft.

When the Bombers are safely across the Straits, the Mopping Up Wing should, if possible, sweep towards the French Coast to render assistance to the other two Wings, particularly during their homeward journey.

(iii) <u>RENDEZVOUS:</u> Is the place over which assembly of Bombers and Fighters (except the Mopping Up Wing) is to take place. Normally this is to be at 15,000 feet at one of the following places, NORTH WEALD, BIGGIN HILL or NORTHOLT.

When Rendezvous has to be made under cloudy conditions, it will be necessary for one aircraft of each Squadron taking part to obtain a Contactor Zero, in order to enable appropriate Sector Controllers to maintain their Squadrons in visual touch with each other, and to assist their Squadrons or Wings in making assembly with the Bombers. It is essential, however, that R/T silence is maintained except for "vectors" given by Controllers to enable assembly to be made. Aircraft in the air are only to break R/T silence for acknowledgments and to inform their appropriate Controllers, by means of a simple code word that Assembly has been effected.

Sector Controllers will facilitate assembly by arranging with appropriate Observer Corps Centres for the track of the Bombers from their Home Stations to the Rendezvous to be plotted on their Operations Room tables.

(iv) <u>APPROACH TO THE TARGET.</u>

The direction and method of approach to the Target will be left to the discretion of the Leader of the Bomber formation. Whenever practicable, he should endeavour to bomb without delay in formation, and at the height ordered. The Leader of the Bomber formation should realise, that an indirect course or undue circling of the target, give the enemy Fighters an opportunity to obtain the tactical advantage of height and position. Similarly, he should endeavour to turn gently on to his target in formation. Any sudden and violent turns on to the target by single aircraft make it difficult for the Close Escort and Escort Squadrons to conform without straggling and loss of cohesion, and thus, not only the Bombers, but the Fighters also, become vulnerable to attack by enemy aircraft.

(v) WITHDRAWAL AFTER ATTACK.

The direction and method of withdrawal from the Target will be left to the discretion of the Leader of the Bomber formation. He should, however, endeavour to withdraw by means of a gradual turn towards the point of re-crossing the French Coast, at the same time maintaining the same height and speed as on the Inward Journey. It is important that the speed and method of withdrawal of the Bombers is regulated so that there is no tendency to straggle, either on the part of the Bombers, or Close Escort Squadron and Wing.

On the homeward journey, all aircraft are to make for and re-cross the English Coast at one of the three Sea Rescue Boat Rendezvous, as indicated below: -

(a) From the DUNKIRK area ...   Aircraft are to make for NORTH FORELAND.

(b) From the CALAIS area ....   Aircraft are to make for DOVER.

(c) From the BOULOGNE area ..   Aircraft are to make for DUNGENESS.

Additional Fighter Cover for the withdrawal and return of our Forces after the attack, will be provided by a "Mopping up" Wing, as ordered by A.O.C. No.11 Group. (See "Mopping Up" Wing – paragraph 5 (ii)).

(vi) DISCIPLINE.

Fighter Squadrons taking part are reminded of the importance of not only maintaining visual contact with the Bombers and other Fighter formations, as applicable, but of Pilots remaining in close mutual support of each other. Fighter formations must, however, be flexible – "Hendon" formations are vulnerable.

The object of CIRCUS operations, from a Fighter point of view, is to destroy enemy Fighters enticed up into the air, using the tactical advantage of surprise, height and Sun. It is important, therefore, for all Fighters to maintain good air discipline, and only to leave their formation if ordered to do so by the formation Leader. Such orders should only be issued when an attack is to be delivered against enemy aircraft, or a particularly favourable target is sighted, under conditions where those detached to attack can be protected by the remainder of the formation.

The experience of previous Operations shows that our casualties in the past, have almost invariably been inflicted upon the "stragglers", and those Pilots who still disregard the dangers of flying alone "down Sun", without constantly turning their aircraft to left and right, and who fail to keep a sharp look-out above and behind.

Leaders of Squadron and Wing formations are to ensure that their Pilots realise the vital importance to each one of them, of not straggling, and that they themselves, endeavour to regulate their speed at all times to assist in eliminating straggling.

COMMUNICATIONS.

6. (i)　Signal arrangements and operational frequencies allotted to Wings taking part will be communicated in the "COMMUNICATIONS" paragraph of the appropriate Circus Operations Order.

   (ii)　As it is anticipated that Bombers taking part in these operations will invariably be operating from their Home aerodromes, any RECALL signal required to be passed to the Bombers in the air will be passed by Controller, No.11 Group to the Bomber Group concerned over land-line, for onward transmission by W/T.

   (iii)　Strict W/T and R/T silence is normally to be maintained throughout assembly, rendezvous and approach, except under the circumstances described in para. 5 (iii) above and in the event of enemy aircraft being sighted. As soon as the coast of France is crossed, however, on the outward journey, all Signals restrictions will be pre-warned.

7. REFUELLING.

In the event of shortage of petrol necessitating refuelling of Fighter aircraft, the forward aerodromes of MANSTON and HAWKINGE will be available for this purpose, and Servicing Parties will be pre-warned.

8. WEATHER.

CIRCUS Operations will only take place under suitable weather conditions, which will be decided by A.O.C., No.11 Group, in consultation with the Bomber or Coastal Groups or Squadrons concerned.

The Group Controller is to obtain weather forecasts for the area of the proposed operations, and in addition, on Zero Day, he is to obtain hourly weather reports, as indicated, from all Bomber and Fighter aerodromes concerned.

9. RESCUE ORGANISATION.

(i) BOATS.
    (a) The attention of all Pilots and Controllers is drawn to the Rescue Organisation as laid down in 11G/S.53/Ops, 2, dated 6th January 1941, and to the regulations for Air/Sea Rescue forwarded under even reference dated 9th January, 1941. The attention of Pilots is in particular drawn to Appendix "C" of the former. (Rendezvous Positions and Areas to be avoided if possible by Pilots in distress).

    (b) As soon as Zero Hour is known on Zero Day, the Group Staff Officer is to give advance warning to the appropriate Naval Authority that rescue boats will be required, and at the same time is to notify the Director of Sea Rescue Services. (See para. 28 of the regulations for Air Sea Rescue). He is also to notify the Rescue Service Officer at Area Combined Headquarters, at No.16 Group CHATHAM.

    (c) At Zero Hour minus 30 minutes the Group Staff Officer on the authority of the Group Controller is to request the appropriate Naval Rendezvous position.

(ii) LYSANDERS.
    (a) As soon as Zero Hour is known on Zero Day the Group Staff Officer is to request the Group Controller to consider the question of reinforcing the Lysander Aircraft in the area in which operations are to take place by Lysanders from adjacent areas. For example, when operations are taking place in the Dover Area one of the Shoreham Lysanders might be moved to Manston for the duration of the operation. At Zero Hour minus 30 minutes the Group Staff Officer, on the authority of the Group Controller, is to order the Lysander crews to an Advanced State of Preparedness.

    (b) When the Boats are ordered to Rendezvous positions the Group Staff Officer, on the authority of the Controller, is to order one Lysander to patrol the area not above 3,000 feet.

    (c) When a Lysander is ordered on patrol or search the Group Controller is to provide it with an escort of 2 Hurricanes or 2 Spitfire aircraft.

* * *

Never one to miss an opportunity to make reports was the new OC of 11 Group, AVM Trafford Leigh-Mallory. Ever since he had advocated, with the support of Douglas Bader, that fighter Wings would be more effective against German raiders, he had tried to win over others to his view. As it turned out, fighter Wings were starting to become the way forward, but they were not totally useful in the Battle of Britain, where the early interception of German bombers was paramount. This is not the place to discuss the 1940 Wing controversy, but L-M, now in charge of Fighter Command's premier Group, and being close to Sholto Douglas, gave him the opportunity to air his views again, especially as sweeps by several fighter squadrons over northern France were being tried out. On 17 February 1941, he wrote what he called a memo on the subject:

<u>Memorandum on the Employment and Training of</u>
<u>Wings and Circuses</u>

1. During the air battle in the autumn of 1940, the enemy employed mass formations of bombers and fighters with the object of destroying our fighter defence, and inflicting damage at vital points. It is probable that an even heavier scale of attack may have to be encountered in the spring of 1941. To meet these large enemy formations it is inadequate to dispatch small formations of fighters which are unlikely to succeed in stopping the enemy bombers – (though, if they are the only force available they must, of course, endeavour to do so). It is therefore necessary to meet this type of attack with large formations, which are capable of providing protection against the enemy fighter screen for those fighters whose role is to break up the enemy bomber formations and to destroy the bombers. To operate in these large formations requires careful training, and a complete understanding between the leaders of the components of such a force. It has therefore been decided to organise Wings throughout 11 Group, which will be composed of 2 or 3 squadrons. These Wings will, on occasions, operate in Circuses, which will be composed of 2 or more Wings.

2. The object of employing Wings and Circuses in offensive operations is to provide the necessary number of fighters - working in co-operation and giving mutual support – to establish air superiority over the enemy in his own country.

3. The object of employing Wings and Circuses in defence is to engage powerful enemy formations with sufficient large numbers to:

   (i)   Stop the enemy bombers reaching their objectives.
   (ii)   Break up the enemy bomber formations.
   (iii) Annihilate the enemy when the breaking up process has been achieved.
   (iv)   To have sufficient aircraft to provide protection against enemy escorting fighters to the aircraft carrying out (i) and (ii).

4. The numbers of squadrons to be used will be governed by the size and tactics of enemy formations, and the suitability of the weather. A Wing of 3 squadrons should normally suffice to deal with a mixed force of approximately 90 enemy bombers and fighters. Against larger formations, Circuses of 4 or more squadrons will be employed.

5. The task of the Sector Controller in these operations will be to give the Wing or Circus leader such information as is calculated to bring him into contact in an advantageous position if practicable – with the main enemy forces operating at the time. The method of carrying out the attack will then be left in the hands of the leader in the air.

6. To make these operations successful, it is essential that Circuses and Wings should be able to form up in the shortest possible time at the height required. Stations are to practise this at every opportunity, and to carry out frequent Circus training with the stations to which they are affiliated.

7. It is intended that each Sector should produce its own Wing, but the following will normally supply the Wings comprising Circuses:

Debden/North Weald	Hurricane Wing
Hornchurch	Spitfire Wing
Kenley	Hurricane Wing
Tangmere	Spitfire Wing

8. For the purpose of training and operations, the Debden and North Weald Wings and the Hornchurch Wing will be affiliated, and the Kenley and Tangmere Wings will be affiliated. The smooth and rapid assembly of the Wings at height will need a high standard of performance on the part of the Sector Controllers, and this will need considerable practise before active operations start.

9. Similarly, the arrangements for the starting up, taking off and the joining up of squadrons forming a Wing at the operational height and on the patrol line ordered by the Group Controller in the shortest possible time, call for a high standard or organisation on the part of the station and squadron commanders, and continual practise in control by Sector Controllers, particularly of joining squadrons up into a Wing above 10/10ths cloud.

10. It is considered a Wing policy for squadrons to fly in the same place in the Wing each time. This will not only facilitate the assembly of the Wing and Circus in the air, but squadrons will get used to carrying out their particular part of the operation. As the role of some squadrons is less attractive than others, e.g. the top Spitfire squadron which acts as above guard may have less profitable sorties, it will probably be desirable after – say – 6 operations to change the squadrons round.

11. It is often difficult to gauge the size of raids while they are still over the Channel. If a Wing has been ordered up for the interception of a large formation which subsequently turns out to be a number of small mixed raids of 20 or 30 aircraft each, then the Group Controller will order the squadrons comprising a Wing to engage separate raids.

12. If a Wing or Circus has been ordered to the interception of a powerful formation, and this formation splits before it is sighted by our Wing or Circus - as is sometimes the case - to deal with the 'splits', which may be successive. Similarly, it may be necessary to detail part of the Wing or Circus to the interception of second or third waves - which may also 'split'. All such detachments must be done before the Wing or Circus sight the enemy - afterwards it is quite impossible to persuade pilots to leave the enemy they can see, in order to intercept an enemy of whose very existence they may be dubious.

13. A great responsibility rests on the leaders of the Circus or Wing, who will often have to divide his forces on his own initiative should he see the enemy split up. It would, moreover, be economical to launch the whole of a large formation against a small number of the enemy. The leader may therefore have to make suitable detachments for such an attack - bearing in mind any information he has received from the Sector Controller as to the movement of the enemy's main forces.

14. Should the enemy revert to sending over high fighter formations carrying bombs, it will not be possible to order a Wing off to intercept as it could not reach the necessary height in time to attack. In the event of the enemy again adopting this policy, Wings would occasionally be sent up on standing patrols at about 15,000 ft, so as to be able to gain the necessary height to engage the enemy on favourable terms. These Wings will be composed of Spitfires or will have Spitfires or Hurricane IIs as the top squadron.

15. Finally, it must be borne in mind that though the squadrons of a Wing or Circus must be in visual touch, the whole formation must be flexible and loose, ready for immediate action. 'Hendon' formations may be vulnerable to enemy fighter attack and cumbersome to manoeuvre - in fact the ideal Wing or Circus formation combines flexibility with immediate readiness for action with its whole fighting strength.

While L–M's memo still reflects the experience of the autumn of 1940 while also covering the still expected resumption of another Battle of Britain in 1941, it is obvious that he is still trying to persuade people that his Big Wing theory that he had employed from Duxford during the Battle of Britain, as encouraged by Douglas Bader, was still a valid way forward. It was in fact already starting to be used for operations over France, although L–M appears to feel it was still a way of defending Britain should the Germans continue an assault when the weather improved. It is interesting that at least by this stage, the word 'Circus' appears to have been finally agreed upon in reference to offensive operations over northern France, where the new Wing ideas would be used from now on. However, Leigh-Mallory seems equally happy to call any large fighter formation a 'Circus'.

* * *

Circus No.6 – 26 February

Finally, another Circus was laid on for 26 February and this called for twelve Blenheims from 139 Squadron, with an escort of six fighter squadrons. This operation covered the period 1045 to 1416, the target being Calais. Close escort was provided by 1, 303 and 601 Squadrons (Northolt), with High Cover by 74, 92 and 609 (Biggin Hill Wing). As this formation headed out, two fighter Sweeps were sent over to the Calais-Cap Gris Nez area to fly independently of the Circus.

After making rendezvous above Biggin, the force headed out, climbing gradually until the enemy coast was reached at around 17,000 feet. One Blenheim failed to release its bombs due to an electrical failure but the other eleven bombed successfully, with explosions seen in the harbour and on the jetty, while some fell in the town. Moderate flak came up and some German fighters were spotted climbing up behind the town but they did not engage. Other fleeting glimpses of 109s were seen, 54 Squadron (covering 64 Squadron) actually making a move towards fifteen to twenty of them but the Germans immediately headed away. Sergeant H. Squire failed to get home and it was believed he had been hit by AA fire. In fact, he was claimed by Herbert Ihlefeld of LG2, near Calais, his thirtieth victory, and ended up a prisoner. 64 Squadron also encountered 109s, which they described as having dark blue upper surfaces, light blue undersides and yellow noses.

A pilot of JG51 also put in a claim for a Spitfire and the likelihood is that this was a machine of 609 Squadron, whose pilot blacked out after his oxygen mask slipped and went into a dive. When he came round he saw two Me109s to the south and thinking they might be decoys, left them well alone.

The results were fair. Bombs on targets, two Me109s claimed as probables and only one Spitfire and pilot lost. Not that the enemy made much of an attempt at intercepting the force. In fact it was generally felt that the enemy did not react until after the attack and the bombers were back across the hostile coast, so the theory that they might be forced into making standing patrols did not hold water.

Luftwaffe fighters were more active later in the day, the Stab Staffel of JG51 claiming three Hurricanes during a *Frei Jagd* across south-east Kent. They fell on 615 Squadron (easily spotted as they were leaving contrails), killing its CO, S/Ldr R. A. Holmwood, forcing another to bale out (P/O C. N. Foxley-Norris), while two more Hurricanes crash-landed (P/O D. H. Hone and Adj. G. C. Perrin of the Free French Air Force), Hone being injured. Two of these were claimed by Hptm. Hermann-

Friedrich Joppien, Kommandeur of JG51, who had around thirty victories by this time. Other claimants were Major Werner Mölders and his wingman, Oblt. Horst Geyer, who both claimed fighters near Dungeness at around the same time, although they reported them initially as Spitfires. It was Mölders' sixtieth victory.

Circus No.7 – 5 March

Wednesday, 5 March 1941, was a fine sunny day that seemed ideal for another Circus operation, and six Blenheims of 139 Squadron were assigned. This time the target was Boulogne. Escort Wing from Northolt was 601 and 303 Squadrons, High Cover was to be provided by Tangmere's 145, 610 and 616 Squadrons, and a fighter Sweep would be flown by 54, 611, 92 and 609 Squadrons - Hornchurch and Biggin Wings. Today the Luftwaffe would react.

Rendezvous with the bombers was made over Hastings at 1305 hours at 16,000 feet and heading for Boulogne, the harbour was reached at 1325, having gained another 500 feet en route. There was some haze about at lower levels but clear higher up. At least the bombing height had been increased as per Sholto Douglas's letter of 12 February to Leigh–Mallory, and the bombs were seen to fall across the inner harbour, the tidal harbour, south of Bassin Loubet, a possible hit on one end of the 'Rye' bridge. A large fire, perhaps an oil installation, began almost immediately as the bombers swung away from their run and headed for home.

The Escort Wing had reached 20,000 feet as they reached the coast and as they too headed north two Me109s approached close to 601 Squadron, but they did not break away from the bombers, showing 'commendable judgement' as the 109s sheered off without attempting to attack.

The Hornchurch squadrons, 54 and 611, while still over the Channel, sent one Section from both squadrons, off to investigate a reported eighteen enemy aircraft, which turned out to be Spitfires. Subsequently, 54 Squadron proceeded to the French coast at 30,000 feet and saw several 109s 10,000 feet below and attacked. They claimed one 109 as destroyed, and three more probably destroyed, having just one Spitfire damaged. Meantime, 611 engaged five 109s they spotted from 31,000 feet, attacked and claimed two probables and one damaged for no loss. Harry Broadhurst was leading the Wing and claimed one probable and the one damaged, with P/O Jack Stokoe claiming the one destroyed. In reality, Stokoe had not fired a shot. Having become separated in the fight, he went after a lone 109 but was then attacked by another. Stokoe skidded his Spitfire in violent evasive action, turned onto his back and saw the 109 pass below him and sent his fighter into a steep dive. Stokoe watched him go down and dive straight into the sea fifteen miles south-west of Boulogne. 2./JG51 lost Uffz. Arthur Lesch near Boulogne, while 5./JG51 claimed two Spitfires near Le Touquet. Stokoe had been with 603 Squadron during the Battle of Britain, and this was his fifth individual victory.

Meantime, the High Cover Wing, having put themselves at heights between 23–25,000 feet had not seen either the Blenheims or their escort. Orbiting the general target area the three squadrons became split up, 145 seeing nobody, 616 encountering frosting up of Red Leader's windscreen and so they also headed back. Once separated, 610 Squadron was given a course by Control and told to orbit at 30,000 feet as 'bogeys' were reported approaching from the south-east. The squadron split into pairs in line astern and engaged four Me109s some 500 feet higher. A dog-fight began and while one of the Messerschmitts was claimed as probably destroyed, four of 610 failed to get home, (one crashing at Wilmington, Sussex) with another Spitfire damaged Category [Cat] 2 [repairable at base]. Two pilots were killed, with two others taken prisoner. IV./JG51 claimed four Spitfires west of Boulogne.

This was a bit of a disaster and must have given Sholto Douglas further food for thought. Group Captain C. A. 'Daddy' Bouchier OBE DFC, writing up a report of the operation noted in his conclusions for the necessity for squadrons in a Wing to maintain contact with each other. He emphasised in particular that Wings must be in contact with each other in the target area, and there had been, seemingly, some problem between Sector and Group Controllers. The Sector controller had sent the High Cover Wing towards the French coast even though he knew it had been split up.

Bouchier also concluded: 'When our fighter squadrons were in the target areas at the heights and times ordered, serious casualties were inflicted by them on the enemy without loss to themselves, and our only losses were incurred in one squadron which, acting independently, was unwisely vectored into the target area below 30,000 feet without higher cover, with instructions to gain height in that area.'

He also remarked that in future Circus operations RAF fighters should always be able to arrive over the target area with a distinct tactical height advantage, except as regards small enemy standing patrols. (Whatever that meant?)

(It is not apparent if these reports, almost always signed by Bouchier – for the AOC 11 Group – are merely Leigh-Mallory's own words or Bouchier's, but as L-M was rarely backwards in making and signing reports, it seems obvious that L-M gave Bouchier a free hand to report on these operations.) There were some obvious misgivings about the whole operation and the following report was written up by Leigh-Mallory:

Fighter Sweep to Boulogne 5 March 1941.

1. Three Spitfire squadrons (610, 616 and 145) were ordered to leave the ground at 1230 hours and rendezvous over Hastings at 1300 hours.
2. 610 Squadron (leader – F/L Norris DFC) led the formation and was told to fly at 25,000 feet, with 616 at 26,000 and 145 at 30,000.
3. The formation circled Hastings at the right time and at the proper heights but failed to find the bomber formation or its escort fighters. After circling for about 20 minutes, leader asked Controller for instructions and said he was unable to contact 'friends' – Controller took 'friends' to mean other two

squadrons i.e.: 616 and 145, whereas of course the leader meant the bomber formation.

4. At about 1330 hours (by which time the formation had been in the air for an hour), Control vectored its three squadrons on 100° which took them out to sea towards Boulogne.

5. About mid-Channel, leader was told by Controller that bandits were approaching from south-east in his vicinity. Immediately afterwards leader sighted 4 Me109s (yellow noses) which attacked from about 500 feet higher, apparently with great determination. A dogfight ensued and the whole squadron (610) broke up and eventually 8 pilots returned to their base singly, landing between 1410 and 1430 hours. Neither the leader nor anyone else know what happened to the 4 missing pilots, who were inexperienced and the only information I was able to obtain was that one of the pilots saw 6 other 109s approach from the south after the dogfight had been going on for some time.

    In the meantime, the 2 higher squadrons (616 and 145) had lost touch with the leading squadron (610) and 616 did not see any enemy aircraft, and eventually returned to base. 145 ran short of oxygen and returned to its base at 1340 without having anything to report.

Conclusion

This whole operation seems to have been unfortunate and it was incredible that 4 109s with only 500 feet advantage in height should have been able to break up completely a squadron of 12 Spitfire IIs and presumably bring down 4 of them, and that no information can be obtained as to what happened.

Very short notice of this operation was given by Group and in fact 610 Squadron only received orders at 1215 to leave the ground at 1230 and this was the first notification the Squadron had that there was to be a sweep, and actually at that time Red Section was in the air on an operational flight. It just had time to land and refuel and took off at 1230 with the rest of the squadron.

Recommendations

1. If possible, considerably more notice should be given of a large operation of this sort so that squadron leaders can get together and discuss details. In this particular case the S/Ldr of 610 did not know there was going to be a sweep, and as a result the Wing was led by a flight commander.

2. No operational orders have been issued as to what should be done in the event of the fighter formations missing the bomber formation.

3. Squadrons are keeping too far apart, in this case – 5,000 feet between the top and bottom squadrons – with the result that they lost each other. Squadrons should not be more than 1,000 feet apart or at any rate close enough to keep in touch.

4. If possible, squadrons detailed for sweep or large scale operations should not be given operational jobs for at least an hour before the sweep commences.

5. Pilots in 610 Squadron had breakfast at 8.30 am and were not able to obtain their next meal until 6.30 pm, when they were given 30 minutes notice until 7 pm. They expect this kind of thing when there is a 'blitz' on, but it seems rather unnecessary during the present quiet times.

6. Including time from take off to 28,000 feet, pilots run short of oxygen in about one hour and consequently have often to return from patrol. Would it not be advisable for Spitfires to carry two bottles of oxygen? Super long-range PRU Spitfires now carry 3 bottles.

7. The average number of experienced war pilots in squadrons I have visited lately is five and I don't think squadrons are being allowed nearly enough training from their experienced pilots. Squadrons ought to go up and carry out surprise attacks on each other, and especially practise regaining formation after being split up. I think perhaps fighter pilots are so busy keeping formation that they are not able to keep a good enough lookout.

The only man mentioned in this report was Flight Lieutenant S. C. Norris DFC. A pre-war airman, he had been with 610 Squadron since November 1939 and had considerable combat experience. He already had six victories with others as probables. In December 1941 he went on to command a fighter squadron on Malta, and during later periods flew in Africa and then Burma, receiving a Bar to his DFC.

It might, of course, be assumed that the German pilots that caused the casualties in 610 Squadron were also top operators, but in reality, of the six pilots who claimed to have shot down Spitfires during this operation, for one it was his third kill, for four others their second and one his first.

* * *

Circus No.8 – 13 March

This Circus was again pitted against a French coastal target, namely the German airfield at Calais/Marck. 139 Squadron got the job again, six Blenheims heading out at 1100 hours escorted by 56 and 249 Squadrons from North Weald, and Northolt's Polish 303 Squadron. 56 Squadron was assigned close escort at 17,000 ft, 249 at 20,000 while the Poles had the 28,000 ft spot. Hornchurch would provide 54, 64 and 611 on the first Offensive Sweep, while Tangmere's 610, 145 and 616 Squadrons had the second.

The weather on this Thursday 13 March was clear and cloudless, with excellent visibility. The Blenheims made rendezvous over Maidstone at midday at 15,000 feet which was increased to 17,000 as they crossed the Channel. The target was reached shortly before 1300. The bombers dropped down slightly as they let go 24 x 250lb and 22 x 44lb bombs across the airfield whilst in an open box formation. A number of German aircraft were seen dispersed along the south-eastern and northern boundaries, some bombs falling amongst them. They encountered a little light flak but what did come up exploded at the bomber's height.

The escort Wing kept station with the bombers and 56 and 249 were not engaged but 303, at 28,000 feet heading in, were suddenly attacked by about half a dozen Me109s, out of the sun, from 33,000 feet. They attacked singly but when the Poles turned to engage, the 109s climbed quickly and flew off. Two further attack attempts were made but neither got close.

The Hornchurch Wing swept over the target area forty minutes after the bombing and then went inland a few miles, the three squadrons stepped up between 28 to 31,000 feet. Some 109s were seen but they were unable to engage. 64 Squadron, the highest squadron, spotted a dozen 109s at 36,000 feet. The Wing Leader warned 64's CO, S/Ldr A. R. D. MacDonnell DFC of their presence but his 'weavers' had already reported their presence. As the Wing turned north, the 109s seemed to start to follow and soon afterwards, the 109s came down in a series of short attacking dives, then swooping up again so as not to lose their height advantage. The Spitfire pilots dodged these attacks by tight evasive turns and eventually the 109s flew off. After forming up it was discovered that MacDonnell was missing.

MacDonnell in fact was shot down by Werner Mölders near the French coast, and had to take to his parachute. He came down in the sea where he was later picked up by a German E-boat to begin four years as a prisoner of war. An experienced fighter pilot, MacDonnell, although actually born in Russia, was a Scot and the 22nd Chief of the Glengarry clan, and had joined the RAF through Cranwell in 1932. During the Battle of Britain he had commanded 64 Squadron, won the DFC and had numerous victories, probables and damaged to his name. He ended up in Stalag Luft III. He was Major Mölder's sixty-second victory. Pilot Officer Campbell of 64 Squadron, ran short of fuel and had to force-land near Faversham.

Several of the other fighter squadrons had glimpses of Me109s but few engaged. 610 Squadron got into a bit of a skirmish and its pilots claimed one destroyed, one probable and one damaged without loss. However, it seems that later these claims were reduced to two probables. Although 611 did not report any combats, it is believed that one pilot was attacked and shot-up by a 109, for Sgt A. S. Darling reported damage that forced him to crash-land at Dungeness, although he was unhurt. Oberleutnant (Oblt) Hermann Staiger of 7./JG51 did claim a Spitfire for his tenth victory, about the time Mölders got MacDonnell.

In the action report, Group Captain Bouchier made the recommendation that only experienced pilots be used as squadron 'weavers' in order to protect the formation. Being a weaver was not a task that many relished and often the more junior pilots got the job, and that often resulted in them being picked off first.

There appeared to be signs that either the German fighters didn't react to these Circus operations, or they were reluctant to mix it with the RAF fighters. Seeing that these coastal targets were quickly reached by the bombers, that then bombed and headed home as fast as they could, didn't really give the 109 pilots time to take off and get to a good height before their adversaries were turning for home. There may have been Spitfires in the target area afterwards, but they posed no problem, and the Luftwaffe boys were sensible enough not to engage unless they could pick someone off and climb away before they became embroiled.

* * *

There was now a definite lull in mounting further Circus operations, in fact it was to be more than a month before the next one. Meantime, Fighter Command continued on various missions. Patrols, the odd Rhubarb, Sweeps without bombers (that were mainly ignored as a consequence) were all flown. 2 Group Blenheims were starting a series of Roadstead sorties, which to reiterate, were attacks flown against enemy shipping off the Dutch, Belgian or French coasts. German fighters still mounted fighting missions across Kent or along the south coast of Sussex, with the occasional clash with RAF fighters. German reconnaissance and bomber aircraft often tried to zip across in marginal weather too, and there were many combats, conclusive and inconclusive, off the Kent, Suffolk and Norfolk coasts with Ju88s, Do17s or He111s.

Circus No.9 – 16 April

Wednesday, 16 April 1941 was a fine but cloudy day. It had been over a month since the last Circus was flown but today, six Blenheim bombers from 21 Squadron would bomb the airfield at Berck-sur-Mer at mid-afternoon. 11 Group put up 601, 303 and 306 Squadrons as close escort – the Northolt Wing, led by W/Cdr G. A. L. Manton. It would suffer casualties.

Rendezvous was made over Northolt at 1545 and the squadrons headed directly for Berck, and bombed the aerodrome from 10,000 feet. Bombs were seen exploding amongst hangars and dispersal points, and one hangar was left smoking badly and partly demolished. As the bombers turned for home, black smoke and flame erupted from another hangar, as if an aircraft or a petrol tank had blown up. The fire could be seen by the bomber crews from ten miles out to sea. They reported no fighter or AA encounters.

306 Squadron only saw two 109s on the way in but they quickly sheered off with no attempt at engaging, while 601, flying higher and up-sun had no encounters on the way in, but as they re-crossed the French coast they began to be harassed by 109s. These mostly went for any stragglers they found but the weavers were able to turn to engage, and one Me109 was claimed shot down with another probably so. In the event only the one shot down became official, claimed by 601's CO, S/Ldr J. A. O'Neill DFC, although his machine was also hit and he was wounded by shrapnel in his left leg. He had to bale out but was picked up by rescue boat HSL 143. The Wing Leader too was

also slightly wounded and forced to crash-land near Dungeness. It was obviously a day for senior men to fly, for included in 601's party was Northolt's Station Commander, Group Captain T. N. McEvoy. He too was shot-up and wounded, being forced to crash-land at Lydd

Meantime, 303 Squadron, who had placed themselves some 5,000 feet above the bombers, were also attacked by 109s as they headed back across the Channel. They too continued to harry the Hurricanes and then two more 109s joined in. As they neared the English coast more 109s appeared and further attacks were made, which resulted in two Hurricanes being shot down into the sea, and another pilot wounded. One of the downed Hurricanes was claimed by Major Günther von Maltzahn, of the Stab Staffel of JG53 – his fourteenth victory (although he reported it as a Spitfire). Leutnant Heinz Bär and Ltn. Georg Seelman of JG51 both claimed Hurricanes. Bär would end the war with 220 victories.

The Germans over-claimed once again, for apart from the above actions, the Stab Staffel of JG51 claimed a total of four Spitfires and one Hurricane, although one Spitfire was not confirmed. Werner Mölders claimed one Spitfire and the Hurricane to make his total sixty-five.

Again Bouchier wrote 11 Group's action report, although the wounding of McEvoy was not mentioned – he shouldn't have been flying in any event! Again he reported a successful mission as regards the bombing and the Blenheims being unmolested. However, one of his conclusions says:

(iii)   That it is probable that the casualties occasioned by No.303 Squadron is some part due to the fact that close enough visual contact was not being maintained by this squadron with the lower of the two escort squadrons (No.601 Squadron), to enable No.601 Squadron to come to their assistance when they (No.303 Squadron) were being attacked.

This seems a little harsh in that 601 itself was being harried and attacked, almost losing a squadron commander, a wing leader and a station commander in the process.

* * *

It wasn't going to be a bad week overall for the Luftwaffe's fighter arm. On the 14th two Blenheims had been claimed by JG1 and JG52 although only one was lost. The following day there had been several combats over the Channel, south of Dover and the RAF had lost two 615 Squadron Hurricanes to JG51, with one pilot killed, while 266 Squadron had had three Spitfires crash-land with two pilots wounded, in a fight with JG26, in which Adolf Galland, the Kommodeur, had claimed his sixtieth and sixty-first victories, plus another unconfirmed. JG26 had slightly over-claimed, reporting four Spitfires brought down. Von Maltzahn of JG53 got his fifteenth victory on the 19th, by picking off a Spitfire of 74 Squadron on a Channel patrol.

On the 20th, JG51 and JG53 had each claimed a Spitfire over the Dover Straits, including Hptm. H-F Joppien's thirty-ninth kill, and that evening JG51 bagged another off Sheerness. 54 and 303 Squadrons had been on the receiving end, while 91 Squadron had a pilot ditch off Sandgate to swim ashore, after meeting Oblt. Wilfried Balfanz of Stab/JG51.

It would appear the RAF could get as much combat as it liked merely by reacting to Luftwaffe fighter sweeps across the Channel and into southern England, without going to the trouble of mounting Circus operations. But the RAF was being offensive and 'leaning into Europe'.

Then Circus operations were once again suspended. There were any number of anti-shipping and Roadstead missions flown over the next few weeks, across the Channel, along the Dutch coast, or as far as the Norwegian coast; several Blenheims were shot down. There was also a new type of mission being flown, code-name 'Blot'. These appear to be long-range sorties by Blenheims and fighters to targets around the Cherbourg area, with escorts provided by 10 Group fighters. One was flown on 17 April to Cherbourg docks which, along with Brest and the surrounding areas, were part of 10 Group's responsibility. Eighteen bombers were escorted by the Tangmere Wing, an 11 Group outfit, as 10 Group had yet to form its own fighter wings.

Blot II was flown on the 21st, to Le Havre, again with Blenheims escorted by Tangmere's Wing. JG2 intercepted them and Ltn. Erich Rudorffer claimed a bomber south of Jersey, but 2 Group had no losses. Meanwhile, the 21st saw further fighter action over the south coast, 74 Squadron having one pilot bale out wounded, shot down by Heinz Bär, although he claimed a Hurricane. 616 Squadron also had a pilot bale out, but over the sea, and he failed to be rescued. His victor was Ltn. Kurt Votel of JG2, south of the Isle of Wight, the German's ninth victory.

* * *

The month of May did not see a single Circus operation until the 21st. However, there was an event on the 15th that should be mentioned. With poor weather conditions Rhubarb sorties were authorised and two pilots of 303 Squadron went over, and they came across a Ju52 transport aircraft. Flight Lieutenant J. Jankiewicz and his wingman, Sergeant W. Giermer, attacked and it crashed and exploded, at Manillet, near Boulogne. While this was a welcome victory for the two Polish pilots, they had no way of knowing that aboard the aircraft was Generaloberst Ulrich Grauert, commanding Luftwaffe general of 1 Fleiger-Korps, who was killed along with the other occupants, including his quartermaster. This 52-year-old general had been decorated with the Knight's Cross.

Chapter 3

Inland

More than a month was to pass before another Circus was flown. Even so, two Circuses (10 and 11) were ordered as far back as 30 April, to be mounted on the first suitable day of good weather. It is not clear whether two Circuses were suggested to be flown in tandem, but that is what happened.

Perhaps too, the delay, wanting to be sure of good weather, was because these Circus operations were, for the first time, to go inland from the French coast, rather than attacking coastal ports or aerodromes. Obviously the air strategists wanted to raise the stakes somewhat and start encouraging the Germans to fight, and whilst sending bombers over, they may as well go for targets that would damage the enemy's ability to produce war materials, etc. Fighter Command, having been brought up to a proper strength, despite having to supply pilots and aircraft to such places as Malta and North Africa, which had helped drain the Command's numbers while still recovering from the losses of 1940, was perhaps better placed now to take on the Luftwaffe.

The first nine Circus operations had been a success as far as bombing was concerned. Each target had been hit, no bombers had been lost to either flak or fighters, and although losses among the escorts had been suffered, claims of Me109s shot down had more or less kept pace with these casualties. At least on paper.

The first day that the weather appears to have been good enough for the ordered Circuses was Wednesday, 21 May. The day began with another Blot operation, with twelve Blenheims from 101 Squadron and six from 105, taking off at 0630 hours to attack Le Havre, escorted by three fighter squadrons. Six of 101 attacked a convoy of ships near the harbour while five others went for a small ship in the harbour at Quettehou, although the bombs fell on the railhead by the docks. 105 Squadron bombed some trawlers. One bomber had its bombs hang up, so only seventeen made attacks.

Circus No.10 – 21 May

This called for eleven bombers from 21 and six from 110 Squadrons to attack the power station, benzol plant and refinery at Gosnay, three and a half miles south-west of Béthune, so some 40 miles inland from the coast. Take off came at 1547, and rendezvous was made with their escorting Kenley Wing (1,258 and 302 Squadrons), while 92 Squadron flew what was known as a 'Sphere' operation, patrolling high above the route between the coast and the target, around 35,000 feet.

As a further innovation, there would now be two squadrons (56 and 242 from North Weald) covering the German airfield at St Omer, while 303 and 306 (Northolt) would cover the airfield at Berck. Both of these locations would be further covered during the withdrawal phase, with 609 Squadron over St Omer and 145 at Berck. There would also be support from Hornchurch Wing (54, 603 and 611), while 12 Group provided three squadrons, 19, 310 and 266 to patrol between Canterbury to Dover.

The all-important weather was high cloud at 18,000 feet but ground haze up to 8,000 feet over France, with visibility of three miles. The bombers reached Gosnay without any problems and crews watched their bombs fall across the refinery causing explosions. However, 109s attacked and one Blenheim (V6390) of 110 Squadron was shot down by Fw. Otto Wessling of 9./JG3, his ninth victory. The bomber was seen falling with its port engine and turret area in flames and one wing shattered. Blenheim gunners claimed one enemy fighter shot down.

The escort squadrons all had encounters with 109s, 258 Squadron losing one Hurricane, its pilot baling out to become a prisoner. This was the first victory for Uffz. Günther Keil of 8./JG3. Two other Hurricanes were damaged, both pilots returning wounded, including the CO, S/Ldr W. G. Clouston DFC. Meantime, Oblt. Willi Stange of the same Staffel, claimed a Spitfire for his twelfth victory. 302 Squadron was attacked near St Pol by 109s, and although one was claimed as destroyed, they lost one pilot, Sgt Marian Rytka. However, he managed to evade capture in France and eventually, with the help of the Resistance, got home via Spain and Gibraltar in August. He had been in the Polish Air Force since 1935 and for his escape he was made an MBE. Commissioned he later received the DFC in 1942 but was killed in a flying accident in December of that year.

Hurricanes of 1 Squadron were engaged by a number of Messerschmitts, but fought them off, claiming two 109s destroyed and four damaged, but one pilot failed to get home. The North Weald boys lost two aircraft. They had circled St Omer and while they had seen some 109s none came close. However, on the way back, other 109s attacked, shooting down one aircraft of 56 Squadron. A pilot of 242 Squadron began circling the spot, but he was then attacked too and went into the sea. Neither pilot survived.

As aircraft began returning, 609 Squadron orbited near North Foreland at 12,000 feet and began to encounter small formations of 109s. A fight developed and while 609 claimed one shot down, one of 609's Belgian pilots, was lost. He may well have been claimed by a 109 pilot, although 609 thought his Spitfire had broken up in a high-speed dive. To add to the day's misfortunes, two aircraft of 145 Squadron collided near Tangmere and both pilots were killed.

In all, this operation cost five Hurricanes, three Spitfires and their pilots, two pilots wounded, and one Blenheim lost. Claimants for the losses inflicted during the return to England, JG51, were credited with five Hurricanes, with one going to Oblt. Erich Hohagen of the 4th Staffel, for his eleventh victory. JG3 also claimed two Blenheims!

The RAF claimed five 109s with a further eight damaged. The Biggin Hill Wing Leader, W/Cdr A. G. Malan DSO DFC, claimed one of the damaged, and he also reported seeing a 109 with rounded wing-tips, as opposed to the usual square ones. No doubt he was seeing one of the first Me109Fs that were beginning to be issued to front-line squadrons, 109Es having square wing tips.

Group Captain Bouchier again hailed the operation a success because the bombers had made a good attack on the target and it appeared several enemy aircraft had been shot down. He made no comment on RAF losses, but did say that the returning bombers and their close escort had reached the French coast five minutes before the time scheduled. That probably gave Luftwaffe pilots the extra time to gain height while the cover Wings were still back over the German airfields. This doesn't make too much sense and in any event, the main RAF losses were over the sea on the way back where the support Wings should have been ready for them.

Circus No.11 – 21 May

In the event this operation was cancelled – due to the weather. It had been planned for Blenheims to attack the airfield at St Omer/Longuenesse but that would have to wait for another day. Because the operational orders etc. had been issued under Circus 11, then cancelled, the next Circus would be number 12, but that again would mean a long wait.

In the meantime, bad weather put an end to any thoughts of further Circus operations until mid-June. Weather forecasters predicted 14 June to be a likely day and so it was decided to again attempt to mount two operations, one in the morning and one in the later afternoon. As it happened the weather deteriorated as the day progressed and so the second plan, to attack a target at Chocques, was postponed.

Circus No.12 – 14 June

The first attack ordered by 11 Group, to bomb St Omer/Longuenesse, was as far back as 27 May. It called for twelve bombers, which in the event comprised nine from 110 and three from 105 Squadrons operating out of Wattisham. Escort Wing was provided by Northolt (1, 312 and 303 Squadrons), while covering offensive patrols were laid on by Hornchurch (54 and 603) to patrol Dunkirk-Gravelines, Biggin Hill (74 and 92) for the Marquise-St Inglevert-Guines-Calais Marck areas, while a composite twelve aircraft from 145, 610 and 616 Squadrons patrolled the Straits of Dover. Weather was poor over the south-east, clear over the Channel, and variable cloud and ground haze over France.

On the way out two Blenheims had to abort and in the attack only nine of the remaining ten managed to bomb the aerodrome, explosions being observed in the south-west corner, and on the south end. The tenth aircraft had been forced back just before reaching the French coast and was not seen again. Aircraft of 9./JG26 spotted this straggler and it was shot down by Uffz. Gerhard Oemler (V6334 of 110). There were no survivors.

The Northolt Wing make no reference to the bomber turning back so presumably did not see it, for nobody was ordered to escort it back. In fact the three squadrons had little to report and only 303 Squadron was attacked by four 109s as they re-crossed the French coast, with no effect, and four more seen over the Channel were ignored.

Hornchurch pilots broke up into sections of four to patrol just off the French coast between 16–19,000 feet to cover the withdrawal. Several pairs of 109s were engaged and two were claimed shot down and two more damaged. 603 did the scoring but later they were only credited with 109s damaged. High above them the Biggin Hill squadrons at 27–32,000 feet, separated. One section of each squadron remained there making contrails so that enemy fighters could see the danger, while the other four sections reduced height to 9,000 feet. However, no enemy aircraft could be seen. As they made for home a couple of 109s were spotted but no engagement occurred.

Only 92 Squadron made any real contact. They too had left a section in the contrails height while the other two sections went down to 7,000 feet. The lower of these two was attacked by some 109s and in a brief scrap, 92's CO, Squadron Leader J. Rankin, shot one down, while another pilot claimed a damaged. III./JG26 lost Obfw. Robert Menge, an eighteen-victory ace, who was killed. One JG26 pilot, Oblt. Werner Kahse, baled out of his machine, while another, Ltn. Karl Schrader, who had been wounded, belly-landed back at base, his 109 slightly damaged. A 109 from I Gruppe also crash-landed at base without injury to the pilot.

One pilot of the high section had a burst of flak near his machine and a splinter wounded him. He rapidly began to lose height but was then spotted and attacked by a 109, a cannon shell exploding in his cockpit causing further injuries. He evaded the 109 and ejected his cockpit canopy in case he needed to bale out, but managed to reach Hawkinge where he made a successful landing. The pilot was Sgt Payne. Two other Spitfires of 92 returned with combat damage, flown by Flight Lieutenants Brian Kingcome DFC and Alan Wright DFC, both veteran fighter aces.

Bouchier in his report says that this was another successful mission, not only as regards bombing, but other than the one missing bomber that may not have been caused by enemy action, three 109s had been destroyed and another three damaged (later amended as already mentioned). He seems to ignore the four damaged Spitfires and a wounded pilot, but these were not serious casualties. He also praised the tactics of off-shore patrols although he didn't feel that fighter leaders, when reducing height to lower levels, should attempt to regain height later, especially when enemy aircraft were probably arriving on the scene. The Me109F is also mentioned for the first time officially, if only that one was destroyed and another damaged

Jamie Rankin was a pre-war airman, and an instructor during the Battle of Britain but after gaining some operational experience with 64 Squadron early in 1941, was posted to command 92 Squadron at Biggin. Unlike some former instructors thrust into combat flying, Rankin excelled. He had shared in shooting down some 109s but this was only his second personal victory. By the end of 1941 he had claimed more than a dozen, with numerous probables and damaged, and had led the Biggin Hill Wing in the autumn to win the DFC and Bar, and later the DSO. At 28 years of age, he was older than most of his contemporaries.

Circus No.14 – 16 June

With Circus No.13 postponed, the next one in date order became No.14, flown on the afternoon of 16 June. Six of 16 Group's Blenheims went for the gas works at Boulogne, with the Northolt squadrons (258, 303 and 306) flying close escort, 54 Squadron as high cover and Biggin's 74 and 92 on a supporting Sweep. It did not start well, the bombers (59 Squadron) turning up fifteen minutes late at the rendezvous and therefore twenty minutes late over the target.

The six bombers each unloaded two 500lb bombs over the target and hits were seen on a large building some 100 yards to the north of the works and on a railway line about half a mile to the north-east, although some did fall in the target area. This time however, flak and fighter opposition caused casualties.

The plan had been for the attack to be made in two sections but flak caused the bombers to come in singly and well below the 7,000 feet ordered. One was so low it even shot up a gun post. Cohesion was therefore lost. Blenheim V6386 had its observer and air gunner wounded, the starboard engine and undercarriage hit, forcing the pilot, P/O Foster, to struggle back on one engine. Only 258 Squadron tried to follow the bombers as they lost height and they could see the flak bursting amidst the attackers as well as Me109s nipping in and out. They endeavoured to attack these 109s and claimed two destroyed and one probably so. However, 258 lost P/O Dunn and another, F/Lt A. M. Campbell, baled out but was rescued (no doubt the pair were shot down by Galland and Oblt. Jürgen Westphal (his eighth). The two Polish squadrons kept their height to give cover and only one pilot of 306 got close enough to knock some pieces off a 109.

The attacking 109 pilots were from JG26 led by Oberst Adolf Galland and among his pilots were some very experienced fighter aces. 54 Squadron kept their height and although they saw a few 109s low down, remained at their cover area. 74 Squadron, flying in 'fours', patrolled a few miles inland and encountered four and then another twelve Me109Fs as they edged out and attacked. They claimed three shot down and two more as probables. The CO of 74, S/Ldr J. C. Mungo-Park DFC, claimed two of the 109s. The first one had its tail blown off by his fire, and went down in a spin. He was then himself hit by a 109 but evaded. Heading for home he was spotted by five more 109s, directed towards him, he reported, by exploding pink AA shells. The leading 109 attacked but overshot, allowing him to give the 109 a burst, whereupon the fighter burst into flames. Mungo-Park crash-landed at Hawkinge, but his Spitfire was a write-off. 92 Squadron got a warning of these Messerschmitts and then saw about fifteen of them and a fifteen-minute air battle ensued. They claimed two 109s plus two probables without loss but had great difficulty in evading the German fighters. Brian Kingcome, once free of 109s, headed for base, and saw two Blenheims heading north, and appointed himself their guardian. One was trailing smoke from one engine and it eventually ditched, the crew climbing into a dinghy. He climbed to try and give a radio fix but his R/T connections had been shot away and being low on fuel had to leave. It must be assumed that the Blenheim crew were never found.

In total, the RAF claimed about seven 109s with another nine probables and damaged, for the loss of two Hurricanes (one pilot saved) and one Spitfire pilot, plus one Blenheim.

The 109 pilots of JG26 appear to have got carried away, claiming eight Spitfires, two Hurricanes, a 'Brewster' and the two bombers. Oberleutnant Josef 'Pips' Priller (twenty-second victory) and Hptm. Rolf-Peter Pingel (eighteenth) claimed the Blenheims, while Galland claimed a Hurricane for his sixty-fourth victory. Pingel also claimed a Spitfire (nineteenth), and so too did Priller for his twenty-first. Another high-scoring pilot, Oblt. Gustav Sprick, leader of the 8th Staffel, claimed a Spitfire for victory number twenty-four. The erroneous Brewster (Buffalo) claim was the first victory of Uffz. Albrecht Held, who was destined to die in July when the wing of his 109 broke away. German losses were Gefreiter (Gefr) Karl Deitz (flying his first mission) and Ltn. Gustav Hüttner, killed. Another pilot baled out over the sea but was rescued, while another 109 was force-landed at Audembert with severe damage.

Another sortie that became embroiled in the events of the day as the operation was all but over, was an air-sea rescue (ASR) Lysander, escorted by 1 and 91 Squadrons, looking for missing pilots, and a similar mission with a He59 floatplane escorted by other 109s from JG26, also looking for downed pilots in the sea.

Flying High Cover to the sortie, 1 Squadron, warned of enemy aircraft, saw the Lysander and 91 Squadron at the same time as they saw the German rescue mission. They attacked the Germans and three of their pilots each claimed a 109, while F/Lt C. F. Gray DFC and his wingman, P/O R. N. G. Allen shared the destruction of the Heinkel (of *Seenotflugkommando* 3). 91 Squadron was bounced by enemy fighters. Sergeant Ken Charney heard his leader, P/O D. H. Gage, call a warning, and then bullets began hitting his aircraft. As Ken Charney evaded he looked back and saw a Spitfire go into the sea. 91 damaged one 109, but lost P/O Gage, while 1 Squadron also had a pilot shot down, Sgt A. Nasswetter (Czech). He was rescued from the sea but died later. Oberleutnant Martin Rysasvy, CO of JG26's 2nd Staffel, and one of his pilots, Fw. Ernst Jäckel, claimed these two victories.

Group Captain Bouchier's report mentions both the Circus and the ASR sorties, and only records two RAF pilots missing and one wounded (Nasswetter), whereas these operations had cost five fighters, with three pilots killed. To this can be added another Spitfire pilot lost from 54 Squadron in a late scramble to the area of operations, who was picked off by a 109 and baled out. He was, however, rescued by a RN launch.

Once again Bouchier recorded the operation a success due to the number of enemy fighters that had been shot down. However, he blamed the delay in arriving at the target as the reason why more 109s were not shot down, as 74 and 92 Squadrons should have been on the scene as the bombers came off target, but instead, swept over it before they arrived. All units were informed of the importance of keeping rendezvous times otherwise the whole operational planning would quickly go awry.

Circus No.13 – 17 June

The postponed Circus 13 called for another inland raid, to the Etabs Kuhlmann chemical works and power station at Chocques, which took place on the evening of the 17th. Eighteen Blenheims were required from 2 Group, but they provided six aircraft each from 110, 107, 139 and 18 Squadrons, making twenty-four in all.

Escort Wing came from North Weald's 56, 242 and 306 Squadrons, with Biggin Hill's 74, 92 and 609 acting as High Cover Wing. 11 Group was now formulating an extension to their operations, assigning a Forward Echelon Wing (Hornchurch – 303, 54, 603, 611 plus 91 Squadron), a Rear Echelon Wing (Kenley's 1, 258, and 312 Squadrons) and a Flank Offensive Sweep by the Tangmere Wing (145, 610, 616 Squadrons). Support came from one Wing each from 10 and 12 Groups, 308 and 501, and 19, 65 and 266 Squadrons. Assuming each squadron put up twelve aircraft, this made a fighter force of 164 Hurricanes and Spitfires. It might protect the bombers but would it deter the German fighter pilots from attacking? How important did the enemy think the target was to try to defend?

The weather was fine, with ground haze up to 2,000 feet, no cloud and excellent visibility. In the event there was no holding back by the Luftwaffe fighters, 306 Squadron reporting almost continuous engagements from crossing the French coast to the target. After the bombing the 109s continued to attack in groups of four or eight but this squadron succeeded in preventing any enemy fighters getting to the bombers, and while doing so, claimed three 109s destroyed and one damaged without loss.

The bombers had mixed fortunes. All of 110 Squadron bombed successfully, seeing smoke and flame around the area of the cooling towers, but only two of 107 Squadron managed to drop their loads. Leaving the target the crews reported lots of white and brown smoke. Several bombers aborted, one from 139 Squadron landed at Manston. The leader of the raid also had a problem and decided to abort but, due to a misunderstanding, three other crews broke off as well.

Four other crews saw their bombs fall 200 yards west of the target, and another three bombers turned back short of the target being unable to keep up with the main body. Of those who reached the target, all were hit by flak or fighters but all got home. Three crews of 18 Squadron saw their bombs hitting the south-west boundary where some incendiaries caused two fires. Three others saw their loads fall 200 yards to the west, while another two watched their bombs right on target. One Me109 was hit by gunners and seen to break off trailing smoke.

Meanwhile, 56 Squadron, further back and behind the bombers, was followed by three 109s not long after crossing the coast which made no effort to attack. Once the bombing had been completed, 56 turned to engage these but they immediately broke off and went away. However, on the return flight anything up to an estimated twenty Me109s began nibbling attacks upon them, using dive and zoom tactics, making it extremely difficult to get shots at the 109s, while the German pilots were successful in knocking down four Hurricanes, one of whom came over the radio to say he was landing in France. 56 lost F/Lt F. W. Higginson DFM, an exceptionally experienced fighter pilot, P/Os P. A. Harris and P. M. Robinson, plus Sgt R. D. Carvill. He was heard over the radio to say he was baling out somewhere off the French coast but was not seen again. Apart from Taffy Higginson, who in fact baled out, all were killed in this action against JG26. The 28-year-old Welshman evaded capture and made his way to the Spanish border but was discovered by Vichy French police. In 1942 he managed to escape and got back to England, where he again flew with 56 Squadron, by then flying Typhoons, where he was awarded the DFC in 1943. In 1940 he had shot down a dozen enemy aircraft.

The third escort squadron, 242, was attacked by 109s some fifteen miles short of the target but they turned away when one Flight tried to engage. Then several 109s began attacking in small groups, again using dive and zoom tactics, 242 fighting what they described as a 'rearguard action' until the French coast was re-crossed, whereupon the 109s broke off. Of the estimated forty to fifty 109s engaged, 242 claimed one destroyed, three probables and nine damaged. However, F/Lt B. A. Rogers had been killed, and two others brought down and taken prisoner. One was S/Ldr E. T. Smith, a supernumerary attached to the squadron for experience(!), the other F/O J. Bryks, a Czech pilot, who eventually ended up in Colditz Castle. The AOC later reported that the escort wing's efforts, despite the losses, made it possible for all the bombers to return home. In all, 242 put in claims for three destroyed, two probables and seven damaged. Bryks was credited with two destroyed while Pilot Officer R. D. Grassick claimed the other. He reported:

'One [109] passed immediately under me heading for the tail of the last section of bombers. I opened up full throttle but he pulled away from me. By this time I was opposite the tail end of the bombers. Just then another Me109 attacked the last section of the bombers and turned to the starboard side. I moved over and had a good 2 seconds burst at him starting from about 150 yards until he pulled away from me. I saw white smoke coming from him and he turned slowly away more to the starboard and back towards the way from which he had come. Then saw bullets hitting my wings so took certain evasive action and shook him from my tail. I then moved back to my former position near the tail end of the bombers about 500 feet above. While watching another Me109 (old type – square wing tips [an 'E']) came up to attack bombers, so I turned on to him and at about 200 yards opened fire and slowly closed in on him and saw white and black smoke pouring out and he dived steeply towards the ground, completely out of control. I then found I had another on my tail and after shaking him off saw another coming up on the bombers so turned and took a quick shot but he turned away and I saw no definite result. I resumed my original position and saw the bomber formation safely over the English coast.'

Bob Grassick, from London, Ontario, had seen action over France and Dunkirk with 242 and would receive the DFC in July 1941.

The Biggin Hill Wing had some sporadic encounters, the CO of 74 who was also Wing Leader, Squadron Leader Malan, shot down one 109, but on returning found two pilots missing, one of whom was seen to bale out over France. Both missing pilots became prisoners. Roger Boulding was one and he once told me what happened:

'I was leading one section of four and spotted a formation of Me109 climbing towards us. I radioed the sighting to Sailor who led us in a diving turn straight into them. I followed one down in a near-vertical dive but had to break off without apparently doing him major damage. At that time we had strict orders not to pursue down to low level over the other side – and Sailor was radioing us to reform. I tagged along some little while behind him, both of us using the familiar tactic of flying towards the sun in a weaving pattern so as to present a difficult target.

'I looked behind and spotted another Spitfire following me in the same fashion. Shortly afterwards Sailor began to call for someone to "look-out behind!" and to take urgent evasive action. I looked behind, saw what I thought was the same aircraft guarding my rear and began to hunt round for the one in trouble. I had just spotted a Spitfire rocking its wings violently (probably Sailor) when my aircraft was hit from behind (the armour plate behind my seat took it and saved me).

'The aileron controls went and the stick just flopped from side to side without effect. My aircraft went into a spiral dive, starting from about 25,000 feet, and I had to get out fast. I pulled the canopy release without too much trouble, undid my straps but could not get out because of the spinning so had to get my knee up and jerk the stick forward, which effectively catapulted me out. I pulled the ripcord and parachuted down from, at a guess, somewhere above 10,000 feet. The Germans had ample time to reach me when I landed and before I could stand up there were plenty of them threatening me with an assortment of weapons.'

Pilots of 92 Squadron also got mixed up with some twenty 109s, three being claimed, but the final analysis was one probable and two damaged, without loss. 609 mixed it with several 109s and claimed three destroyed for no loss.

The Forward Echelon fighters saw some action, although 603 and 611 were not involved. 54 Squadron claimed two 109s destroyed, two probables and one damaged for no loss, while 91 saw a couple of 109s but did not engage. 303 Squadron also scrapped with some 109s, claimed one destroyed and one probable. One Spitfire was hit and its pilot wounded in the leg, crash-landing back at Northolt.

The Rear Echelon squadrons patrolling mid-Channel had little contact, although three pilots in 1 Squadron saw some 109s dive through some bombers as they headed back. One pilot went after one of these and claimed it destroyed.

The Wing report claimed fifteen Me109s destroyed, seven probables and eleven damaged, while admitting the loss of nine pilots. Actual losses were four killed, five taken prisoner, plus one safe but wounded.

The Luftwaffe's JG26 had had a field-day, modestly claiming fifteen victories. Among them, Adolf Galland had claimed two Hurricanes (sixty-fifth and sixty-sixth), Pips Priller a Hurricane (twenty-third), Gerhard Schöpfel a Hurricane (twenty-third), Gustav Sprick a Hurricane (twenty-sixth), Hptm. Walter Adolph, another Hurricane (sixteenth). Oberleutnant Hans-Jürgen Westphal had bagged two Spitfires (ninth and tenth) – presumably 74 Squadron's losses, although two other pilots had claimed Spitfires, one probably being the 303 Squadron casualty.

JG26 had only one pilot killed, Fw. Bernhard Adam, shot down by a Hurricane, with another pilot crash-landing at Ligescourt.

Group Captain Bouchier's report noted the quick reaction by the Germans and the success of the RAF fighters in protecting the bombers, despite suffering losses. He remarked about the heavy casualties that had been inflicted on the German fighter force, although this appears somewhat over-optimistic. It was also apparent that German fighters were starting to engage the high cover squadrons, thereby making it impossible for them to protect the RAF squadrons at lower altitude, thus allowing other 109 pilots a better opportunity of engaging these lower squadrons. He thought that in future, it might be better for the High Cover Wing to have two squadrons from 1–2,000 feet above the Escort Wing and one or two dispersed at the same height on either flank of the bombers. The learning curve was still curving.

Some things that stand out were that the 109Fs were on the increase, their rounded wingtips and lack of tail bracing struts made them easily identifiable. Also that the yellow paint on the 109's noses was now extending back to the cockpit, or even halfway along the cockpit. A problem with the R/T was becoming more apparent when the Poles began to chatter in their native tongue, which the British pilots had no way of understanding of what was being said. This was a particular problem if the message was one of warnings of approaching danger.

Circus No.15 – 18 June

Wednesday, 18 June was another fair day with just a few scattered showers. Today, six Blenheims of 107 Squadron were to attack a hutted encampment at Bois de Licques, seventeen miles (twenty-seven km) south of Calais. There were a reported fifty army huts concealed in this wood and would be as good a target as any for a quick in-and-out sortie.

Escort Wing – Kenley – with 1, 258 and 312 Squadrons, as Cover Wing, 616, 145, 610 and 303 from Tangmere, while an Offensive Sweep would be made by Hornchurch Wing, 54, 603 and 603. 601 Squadron would make a patrol east of the Goodwin Sands while other fighters would add more support off the south-east coast of Kent.

Rendezvousing at 1800 hrs over Hastings at 10,000 feet, and setting course for the target, they had climbed to 12,000 feet by the time the target came into view. Bombs rained down which left much smoke and although flak was met, no fighters interfered.

The Close Escort had no encounters until returning over the French coast. A couple of Hurricanes had been slightly damaged by flak on the way in but now several Me109s began nibbling at the edges. 312 claimed one probably destroyed, and 258 Squadron lost a pilot, although it seems flak caused his loss rather than fighter attack. Tangmere's squadrons either saw little or had brief encounters. 610 claimed one Me109 destroyed east of Dungeness, 303 mixed it with some 109s and claimed four 109s destroyed, while 145 became split up and became embroiled with 109s and lost two pilots, both becoming prisoners. One was claimed by Galland (sixty-seventh), while Sprick got the other (twenty-seventh).

The Sweep by Hornchurch produced a fight with a number of Messerschmitts and four were claimed destroyed plus three more probably so. One went down after the attentions of Flying Officer W. G. G. Duncan Smith of 611, his first confirmed victory of an eventual nineteen. In his book '*Spitfire into Battle*', he recorded:

'We were top cover at 28,000 feet to 24 Blenheims targeted on Béthune, supported by a gaggle of over 260 fighters. A few enemy aircraft appeared over the target area but on re-crossing the coast we were bounced by about twenty-five Me109s. Turning into an attack from four of them coming in over my left shoulder I got behind the last one and opened fire. The muffled boom–boom from the cannons was a welcome new sound but the orange flash from one of my cannon shells, quite vivid as it exploded against the enemy's cockpit cover, was even more startling. Closing in, I fired a second burst but my Spitfire pitched and yawed away from my line of sight and in a split second the 109 rolled onto its back diving steeply pouring smoke from a hit in the cooling system. It was then I realised one of my cannons had stopped firing thus twisting me sideways due to the recoil from the live gun.'

Of the other support units, 609 from Biggin had a scrap with some fighters and claimed one destroyed but lost P/O S. J. Hill. He was shot up by a 109 over the Channel and although he got his crippled Spitfire almost back to the English coast, crashed into the Dover cliffs and was killed. Syd Hill had shared in 609's 100th kill back in October 1940, with F/Lt Frank Howell. JG26 made no individual credit for this Spitfire, but it was credited to the Gruppe. Thus the total loss was four pilots. JG26 suffered one 109 damaged that crash-landed at Sangatte. JG2 must have become involved in some of the action for it also had two fighters damaged, one crash-landing at St Ingelvert, the other landing in similar fashion at Morlaix.

Once again the overall report on this operation was one of success with serious casualties inflicted on the enemy. At least the RAF squadrons were virtually all now being encouraged to operate in sections of four – the 'finger four' formation. At long last the disastrous 'vics' of three were a thing of the past and pilots could operate far more effectively in fours with the two pairs covering each other and with four pairs of eyes looking out for danger, instead of one pair.

Circus No.16 – 21 June

On 20 June there was another Blot Operation, a force of 2 Group Blenheims going for Le Havre in waves. In 11 Group's area, there was almost no activity. However, the next day, Saturday the 21st, which was another fine summer day, two Circus operations were mounted. The first was for six 21 Squadron Blenheims to raid St Omer Aerodrome in the early afternoon, escorted by North Weald's squadrons, and Hornchurch and Tangmere Wings flying target support. Biggin's Wing, with a 12 Group Wing flying what was called Forward and Rear Support.

This operation was put on the schedule at a conference held at Northolt on the evening of the 20th, exactly why is not known. However, the bombers made rendezvous at noon over Maidstone at 8,000 feet and headed out on a course, Dungeness, Hardelot, St Omer/Longuenesse. On the way one bomber (V6450) began to fall back and was picked off by a 109 over the French coast, parachutes being seen. Sadly none of the three NCO crew members survived. Galland had gained his sixty-eighth victory having taken off just eight minutes earlier.

JG26's aircraft now began to engage the RAF escorts, allowing Galland to head in again towards the bombers. He shot up one, which he thought went down, but it struggled back to England in a damaged condition, the crew unhurt. Galland, having lost his wingman, was attacked by P/O B. H. Drobrinski of 303 Squadron, was hit and forced to take violent evasive action, streaming coolant. He was obliged to make a landing on Calais-Marck airfield. The reason his wingman had failed to protect his rear was that S/Ldr J. A. Kent DFC, leader of Northolt's Wing, had already shot him down. Feldwebel Bruno Hegenauer baled out without injury. It was Johnny Kent's eighth victory and 'Ski' Drobinski's third. This account of events has been written up by author and historian Don Caldwell, an expert on JG26. However, the RAF's action report indicates a different story.

The five Blenheims bombed the airfields at St Omer/Longuenesse and Fort Rouge, explosions being seen amongst hangars, buildings and dispersal areas. 242 Squadron had two Me109s slip down behind the bombers and both were attacked and damaged. The leader of 242 Squadron and Tangmere's Wing Leader, W/Cdr D. R. S. Bader DSO DFC and Norwegian Lt. H. O. Mehre were credited with these 'victories'. Bader was credited with a destroyed, and Helge Mehre the damaged. So was it Bader who shot down Hegenauer and the Norwegian who hit Galland? Mehre ended the war with six victories plus ten more enemy aircraft damaged, with the DSO DFC DFC(US) Norwegian War Cross with Swords, and became a Wing Leader. Post-war he rose to Major-General with the RNAF. Another 109 was claimed destroyed by 306 Squadron, and, as already mentioned, 303 made a claim, and another claim for a destroyed 109 on the return journey.

All fighter squadrons became engaged with Me109s and the day ended with a massive total of eleven destroyed, plus eight more probables and damaged – without loss! These included two JG26 pilots downed by 74 Squadron during the return flight, one coming down in the sea to be taken prisoner by the British, the other being chased north and shot down over Kent, again to be taken captive. The 9th Staffel also lost a pilot, Gefr Christian Knees over the sea to RAF fighters. Two other pilots from the 6th Staffel, Uffz. Otto Ewald and Obfw. Franz Lüders, flying 109Es, were shot down off Ramsgate and captured. Therefore, five Me109s appear to have been casualties, including Galland's forced landing. Galland wrote in his book '*The First and the Last*':

'... my head and right arm were hit hard. My aeroplane was in a bad way. The wings were ripped up by cannon shells. I was sitting half in the open – the right side of the fuselage had been torn away by shellfire. Fuel and coolant were streaming out. Instinctively, I broke away to the north. I noted that my heavily damaged Me, its engine now shut down, was still controllable. I was at 6,000 meters [sic] [19,500 ft] and decided to glide home. My arm and head were bleeding, but I felt no pain – no time for that. My vital parts appeared to be all right. My calm deliberations were interrupted by the explosion of the fuel tank. The entire fuselage was enveloped in flames, and burning fuel ran through the cockpit. My only thought now was escape. I pulled the canopy release – no luck! Jammed! I unbuckled my seat harness and pushed on the canopy. Too much wind resistance. There were bright flames all around me. These were the most terrible seconds of my life. In mortal fear, I pressed against the canopy with all my strength. It moved slightly, and the airstream tore it away. I pushed the stick forward, but did not clear the wreckage as I had hoped – my seat pack had caught on the edge of the cockpit. I grabbed the radio mast and pushed with my feet. Suddenly I was falling free. In my panic I grabbed the quick–release knob of my harness instead of the 'chute handle. I caught the near-fatal error in time, opened the 'chute, and floated softly to earth.'

11 Group had tried new tactics on this operation. Knowing that the bombers tended to 'tie down' the enemy fighters to the target area and along the withdrawal route, the RAF tried to take advantage of the Germans' increased tendency to press home their attacks on the bombers themselves. Therefore, Target Support Wings converged on the target area from both flanks, arriving over the target some five minutes before the bombers arrived. Good timing would ensure air superiority during the attack and then

the withdrawal. The Forward and Rear Support Wing's squadrons, at all heights from 3–18,000 feet, would be able to engage those 109s following the withdrawal forces.

Another successful operation was hailed by 11 Group especially with the number of 109s claimed, and it was thought the bomber was lost more to engine trouble than enemy action, although with another bomber shot up it was more likely to have been caused by enemy action, even if it seemed as though it had fallen behind.

Circus No.17 – 21 June

This operation was also confirmed at the Northolt Conference and called for another six Blenheims, this time to the aerodrome at Desvres, just ten minutes flying time inland from Gravelines. 110 Squadron got the job and made rendezvous over Maidstone at 8,000 feet at 1600 hours, which was four hours after Circus 16 began. Close Escort was provided by Kenley, Target Support by Biggin Hill and Tangmere, Forward Support by Hornchurch, and Rear Support by North Weald.

The bombers reached the target at 1632 having climbed to 12,000 feet and bombs were seen exploding amongst hangars and buildings. They headed back without loss. 312 Squadron in the Close Escort Wing flew two sections of four either side of the bombers with two pairs weaving, one in front and the other behind and just above, but no hostile fighters were engaged. 258 operated in sections above the Poles at 13,000 feet. The third Squadron, No.1, flew in three fours at 14,000, 14,500 and 15,000 feet, where they encountered some twenty Me109s after the bombing. In fights that followed four 109s were claimed shot down and another damaged but lost one pilot in the process, an American 'Eagle' pilot, P/O N. Moranz, who ended up as a prisoner. A Czech pilot with the Squadron, P/O V. A. Kopecky, had his Hurricane shot-up and he eventually ditched off Folkestone and was rescued. Oberleutnant Sprick claimed one (twenty-eighth) and Ltn. Hans Naumann the other (his second). Unteroffizier Heinz Carmienke and Ltn. Hans Gries of the 8th Staffel were lost in this action and Ltn. Hans-Joachim Gebertig, wounded. With No.1 Squadron was Colin Gray DFC, who had considerable experience on Spitfires over Dunkirk and during the Battle of Britain, with 54 Squadron. I met him at his New Zealand home in 1990, just as his book '*Spitfire Patrol*' was about to be published. He told me:

'Hurricanes were very different after months of flying the Spitfire. By 1941 they were alright for operations over the Channel, but they were not quick enough for our offensive actions over France. If ever we turned to see what was happening behind us it became difficult to catch up the bombers we were escorting. I recall one hectic action when acting as top cover to Blenheims bombing Desvres airfield. We were attacked by several 109s from behind and although the Squadron claimed some of them, we lost one of our American pilots, Nathanial Maranz, who was acting as my No.2. Also one of our Czech pilots, Pilot Officer Kopecky.

'Not long afterwards we were pulled out of the northern France shows, and I imagine most of the other Hurricanes units went also, or exchanged their aircraft for Spitfires. We went on anti-shipping operations and I didn't have any air combat for some months, except when I flew as a guest with 41 Squadron in mid-August and shot down a 109 near Le Havre.'

Sailor Malan (74 Sqn), leading the Biggin Hill Wing, had his three squadrons at between 15–18,000 feet over the bomber route. A single 109 was seen flying towards Boulogne which Malan shot down. Off Le Touquet six 109s were engaged, Malan downing one of these too while the rest dived away inland. 609 was not engaged until returning home and engaged four 109s claiming two destroyed and a damaged. 92 had dived to 15,000 feet to engage 109s, destroying one, with another probable. Another pilot was seen to shoot down a 109 but he was himself brought down (probably another victory to Sprick, his twenty-ninth), but baled out and was rescued unharmed. Another pilot in 74 Squadron claimed a probable. JG26 had two pilots make crash-landings at Clairmarais, their aircraft written off.

Tangmere had a few encounters. 616 and 610 saw many 109s and one section of 610 went after four of these coming up from behind and below and shot down one with another thought to be damaged. 145 Squadron claimed another 109 destroyed but had one NCO pilot slightly wounded. The pilot of this 109 was none other than the Gruppenkommandeur, Adolf Galland. Getting over his morning's shoot down, he had taken off alone, his wingman had not yet got back, and he attacked a Spitfire to the rear of 616's formation. This Spitfire went down on fire (P/O E. P. S. Brown, killed) and Galland stupidly decided to follow it down, only to be picked off by Sgt R. J. C. Grant, and baled out. New Zealander Reg Grant had been in 145 since April and this was his first victory. He would claim two more and receive the DFM before being commissioned and going to 485 (NZ) Squadron which he eventually commanded and also won the DFC. In 1944, as leader of 122 Wing, he was killed in a crash that February. His score had risen to eight. Galland suffered some injuries but was quickly back with his command. That night he was told he had been awarded the 'Swords' to his Knight's Cross with Oak Leaves, the first recipient of this high honour.

Hornchurch Wing broke into separate sections of four between 18–20,000 feet and encountered 109s, two of which were shot down, one by Canadian F/Lt E. F. J. Charles, a future wing leader. It was only his second victory but he would end the war with a score of sixteen. 603 Squadron had F/O D. Stewart-Clark shot up by Pips Priller of JG26 (twenty-fourth claim), yet despite his wounds the RAF pilot survived by crash-landing on the Goodwin Sands, his Spitfire being written off. The Rear Support Wing patrolled Dungeness to mid-Channel from 1,000 to 10,000 feet but saw nothing of enemy fighters.

Totting up the claims, the score came to fifteen Me109s destroyed, three probables and two damaged, for the loss of two pilots and three aircraft. One of the probables was credited to a Blenheim gunner.

The fighters of I Gruppe of JG2 were also called into action, arriving on the scene after the bombing. They waded in to claim a massive ten RAF aircraft and had one of their fighters shot down near Etaples, with Uffz. L. Dessoy baling out wounded. Oberleutnant Kurt Bühligen of 4./JG2 claimed three Spitfires and Ltn. Siegfried Schnell claimed two. Therefore some nine Me109s had been lost during these two operations and four damaged, with JG26 losing three pilots killed and two captured. 11 Group had claimed twenty-six victories, seven probables and six damaged. Little wonder Group Captain Bouchier in his report claimed a most successful day establishing complete air superiority with eleven and then fifteen enemy fighters shot down, for the loss of two pilots (plus two wounded) and five aircraft lost.

It had to seem to 11 Group and Fighter Command Headquarters that these Circus operations were producing good results and bringing the Luftwaffe fighters to battle. While both sides were over-claiming, Fighter Command was losing valuable pilots, not only those killed, but others brought down over France were lost to captivity. It seemed certain that Circus operations would continue, and things were about to change, a change that would make all offensive operations over northern France more of a necessity.

Chapter 4

Supporting Russia

Hitler invaded the Soviet Union at dawn on 22 June 1941, bringing war to what became more familiarly known as the Eastern Front, making northern France and Belgium, known once again as the Western Front. Support was obviously needed for the German Wehrmacht as it moved forward into Russia and Luftwaffe units were moved to the East. There was little hope of Britain being any more dangerous than it had been since the fall of France in June 1940, so all that was needed was to leave two main Jagdgruppen to oppose the RAF and its annoying incursions over the Western Front.

Therefore, JG2 became responsible for an area from Cherbourg north-east to the River Seine Estuary, while JG26 continued the defensive line from the Seine to the coast of Holland. These two units were to remain Fighter Command's main antagonists for the rest of the war.

Winston Churchill, the British Prime Minister, saw the invasion of Russia not so much an immediate problem, rather an 'ally' that would take some of the pressure from any notion Germany might still have of invading Britain, as well as taking any immediate heat off the Mediterranean and North Africa, where he was convinced Mussolini would soon be in desperate need of further German support. However, Joseph Stalin would soon be seeking help from Britain, not only by way of supplies, but also to do something to help Russia directly by hitting Germany from its rear: for the time being though little could be done. RAF Bomber Command was gradually building its forces to bomb industrial Germany but as yet these were little more than pin-pricks. Of course, there was simply no chance of opening up a 'second front' in France, which is what Stalin would have liked and was later to start demanding for.

No, for the time being, all Churchill could promise was to keep up a hostile presence over the Western Front, while continuing to support the Middle East actions, and try to keep his shipping supply lines out in the Atlantic from being overcome by submarine warfare. Daylight actions over the Western Front, Circus, Roadstead, Ramrods, Sweeps and Rhubarbs were all that could be promised in mid-1941. At least it would, perhaps, keep Germany looking over its Eastern Front shoulder and what hopefully would soon be seen as an increasing presence by Fighter Command and 2 Group of Bomber Command, while the latter's night bombing force could only move from strength to strength.

As a matter of interest, on 19 June, i.e. three days before the invasion, Churchill and his War Cabinet had been keeping a serious eye on probable developments on the Russian border, and a meeting set out the following points:

1. Enemy very sensitive about [recent] attacks in the Béthune-Lens area - so plan and develop day operations here.
2. Continue attacks on shipping in the Channel.
3. [Make] dummy preparations for invasion [into France].

Numbers 1 and 2 were achievable by normal operations, No.3 would be more one of subterfuge through other agencies. Once the invasion of Russia happened, the RAF found itself with something of a tactical role to play. If pressure in the West could be increased, it might force any German fighter squadrons sent to the Russian Front to return to defend in the West. In the event, this did not happen. JG2 and JG26 were more than capable of keeping the RAF at bay.

Circus No.18 – 22 June

This operation was flown on Sunday 22 June and of course, had nothing to do with the assault upon Russia, having already been planned and the orders sent out. It was another inland target, the marshalling yards at Hazebrouck, which called for twelve Blenheims, six each from 18 and 139 Squadrons. North Weald would provide the Close Escort squadrons (56, 242 and 303) with Target Support coming from Hornchurch (54, 603 and 611), plus Tangmere (145, 610 and 616). Forward Support Wing from Biggin (74, 92, 609), Rear Support from Kenley (1, 258 and 312), plus Hurricanes of 601 flying Low Rear Support, made a total of sixteen fighter squadrons to protect the bombers.

Bombers and fighters made rendezvous over Southend at 1530 hours, at 8,000 feet and headed out via Gravelines, although two of the bombers aborted, leaving ten to make the bomb run, most bombs being seen to hit the target with just some undershooting to the south and east. Fighters attacked the bombers and air gunners claimed two shot down and suffered no losses.

Once again the enemy fighters did not become engaged with the Close Escort Wing until the bombers were heading away from the target. An estimated fifty Me109s tried to harass the RAF fighters but it seemed they lacked determination and concentration. 56 Squadron damaged two that they engaged. 242 Squadron saw a couple of 109s trying to attack the Wing and destroyed one of them. The successful pilot was the Frenchman, Lt. Jean-Francois Demozay DFC, who had, famously, been the liaison officer with 1 Squadron in France in 1940 and having escaped to England when France collapsed, piloting a Bristol Bombay, taken fifteen British soldiers with him. He had been operational with 1 Squadron since late 1940 gaining three kills, and had now claimed his fourth, flying with 242 Squadron. The Poles of 303 Squadron waded into fifteen 109s they found waiting for the opportunity to attack the Blenheims, and claimed six destroyed and one probable.

The Hornchurch Wing was down to two squadrons upon reaching the French coast, 603 having become separated. High above the attacking force, 54 and 611 engaged a number of 109s and their pilots claimed nine destroyed, four probables and two damaged, losing just one pilot, F/O P. S. C. Pollard, shot down and killed near Dunkirk. Duncan Smith of 611 Squadron recorded:

'As the last sweltering days of June reached new heights in temperatures, we seemed to get as many as four offensive sorties a day. One afternoon, with the sun scorching through the canopy of my Spitfire, I flew with 'Polly' Pollard as the Squadron climbed steadily for North Foreland. Our task was to act as high cover to bombers whose targets were the marshalling yards at Hazebrouck. We crossed the French coast at 28,000 feet, the sun glinting on the Perspex of our cockpit hoods and long vapour trails streaming behind us. Below, I could see the stepped formations of the lower escort squadrons stretching down to the neatly packed group of twelve Blenheims with their close escort of Hurricanes, at about 12,000 ft. We called it the 'Beehive' because with individual aircraft weaving and jinking the whole affair looked like a swarm of bees.

'As we approached Hazebrouck a formation of ten Me109s, slightly below, came towards us. Eric Stapleton turned into them and started to dive; immediately the enemy formation rolled onto their backs and disappeared past the tail of the Beehive. Almost on top of the target another formation of fifteen 109s appeared below and we promptly dived for them. They saw us coming and broke into our attack. I stuck close to Polly as we waltzed around trying to get on their tails. One group of 109s then broke right with two sections after them, while Polly and I went with two others latched on to four Me109s circling across out left front. Swiftly we turned inside them and got into range. Polly called me: "Take the right 109 Charlie Two, I'll get the other."

'We were now well placed and the 109s stayed with us in a tight circle. They were staggered, the one on the right slightly above and behind the left-hand one with ourselves in a commanding position behind and a couple of hundred feet above.

'I swung my nose across closing fast and as the 109 filled the width of my windscreen I blasted into the side of his cockpit and engine. Bits flew off and thick smoke gushed; the 109 rolled slowly over and plunged vertically down. As I prepared to follow, tracers streaked past my cockpit and over the top of my propeller. I broke sharply in a right-hand climbing turn. Polly's voice hit my earphones: "Good boy, Charlie Two. Climb. I'm above."

'Wildly I looked around for Polly. Turning, I saw two Me109s flash past behind me, then above them the unmistakeable wing pattern of a Spitfire. Giving my aircraft every pound of boost I had I rocketed upwards in a tight spiral. Polly saw me coming and nosed towards me. "Did you get one, Charlie Leader?" I asked. "Think so, can't tell – had to break – attacked by six bastards."'

Moments later, the two men were battling for their lives as more 109s pounced. Duncan Smith watched as Pollard fired at one and saw it glow red and trail black smoke but the two Spitfire pilots were outnumbered and Smith saw his leader rolling over and heading down in a right spiral. However, Smith was concentrating more on one 109 that had dived beneath him and following it down closed in so he couldn't miss. Opening fire the 109 became a sheet of flame, went over and dived into the ground. Returning to base the pilots put in claims for several 109s but Pollard had not returned.

Tangmere Wing had gone to St Omer where 616 orbited before heading back via Merville. They saw an air fight in progress and joined in, claiming two victories. 610 Squadron also went inland and covered the bombers' approach. Some 109s turned up but no engagement. One pilot strafed the sand-dunes at Gravelines causing casualties at two gun posts. 145 engaged ten 109s and when three made an attack, one was claimed as destroyed.

Sailor Malan led Biggin Hill to patrol Gravelines to Berques between 16–22,000 feet. 74 went after fifteen Me109s 5,000 feet below, destroyed two and damaged a third over an airfield at Dunkirk. 609 flew higher and attacked ten 109s, claiming four destroyed and two damaged. 92 Squadron was not engaged. Nor, indeed, were the other supporting Wings.

Back at their bases and when the final tally of claims was put into Group, the numbers were impressive. Thirty-one Me109s had been destroyed, five more probably so and seven more damaged, including the two destroyed by Blenheim gunners. All this for the loss of just one pilot and aeroplane. The German fighters, the RAF reported, showed little inclination to fight. Interestingly G/Capt Bouchier thought this might be due to less experienced units having moved into the area, the more experienced ones having moved to the Russian Front. One has to wonder if British Intelligence had found any signs of JG2 or JG26 having left for the East. Otherwise, 11 Group was more than pleased with the outcome of Circus 18, and they felt sure these '… operations were having the desired effect on the morale of the enemy.'

Group and Fighter Command HQ may have felt differently had they known the extent of German losses, and amazed at the number of Luftwaffe claims. JG26 had lost one pilot killed but had claimed five Spitfires – all credited to *Experten* (aces). JG2 had claimed seven, including two Blenheims, by Major Wilhelm Balthasar, Stab/JG2 for his thirty-second and thirty-third victories – none were lost! JG2 had lost two pilots while another had force-landed his 109 at Arques badly damaged. JG26 lost Ltn. Hans Glasmacher, to Spitfire attack.

Circus No.19 – 23 June

Some readers may not be aware that until recently, RAF fighter pilots were not equipped with dinghies, their only floatation gear being their life-vests, more popularly referred to as the 'Mae West' after the well-proportioned Hollywood actress of the 1930–40s.

This would have exercised the pilots' minds as they flew across the English Channel, and more so when trying to get back again, either with a damaged aeroplane or with fuel running low. Bomber and Coastal pilots all <u>had</u> <u>had</u> access to dinghies since the war began as they were obviously required to operate over the sea, but Fighter Command had planned for either a defensive war above England, or another WW1 type fight above France. Fighter pilots were now, however, all issued with a dinghy, so at least they could, if uninjured and safely on the water, climb in out of the cold sea, hopefully to await rescue.

Rescue at this stage was mostly by motor launch, either RAF or Naval, or even the Lifeboat Service. Rescue by aeroplane was no more than Lysander or Defiant aircraft searching the wave-tops. If they spotted a man in the water, either in Mae West or dinghy, the crew was equipped to drop a smoke float and mark his position in the hope that a boat would speed out and pick him up. This would be bettered shortly with the arrival of Supermarine Walrus amphibious aircraft that could land on the sea, if the conditions were not too horrendous, and bring the downed airman home. But these life-saving seaplanes would not start to operate in this role until 1942.

* * *

Circus 19, planned for the early afternoon of 23 June, would be followed by an evening operation, Circus 20. The first was to bomb the Etabs Kuhlmann Chemical Works and power station at Chocques, the same one attacked back on the 17th. The evening raid was to bomb Mardyck airfield.

Close Escort came from Kenley, and comprised 1, 258, 312 and 303 Squadrons. Target Support came from Tangmere and Biggin. Forward Support from Hornchurch and a 12 Group (Wittering) Wing – 19, 266 and 485 (NZ) Squadron. 71 (Eagle) and 306 (Polish) Squadrons acted as Rear Support.

It was a fine day with just some thin cloud over France, but visibility was estimated at some twenty miles. Twenty-four bombers were to make rendezvous over Southend at 1300, and in the event, eleven from 105, with six each from 21 and 110 Squadrons, joined up and crossed the hostile coast at Gravelines. The target was reached at 1330 but only twenty-one Blenheims made the run-in from 12,000 feet. Bombing wasn't perfect but some hits were seen near the power station. Flak had damaged a couple of the bombers as they crossed the coast and had to abandon their attack, but no enemy fighters interfered with the mini-armada. A pilot of 6./JG2, Uffz. Karl-Heinz Rotte, claimed one bomber as his first victory. Few fighters were seen by the Escort either. 303 saw a dozen high up but effective weaving prevented the 109s from having a go. When later a couple of actions did take place, the Poles claimed eight destroyed and two probables. Sergeant Mieczyslaw Adamek claimed two, his first victories since Poland in 1939. He had seen some 109s attacking the Spitfire ahead of him and having warned this pilot, fired a long burst into the 109 whereupon it exploded and went down a mass of flames. With a 109 then behind him, he turned sharply and was able to fire into it causing much smoke to pour from it and went straight down. These 109s, he noted, had red noses. Adamek received the DFM and Bar, and the Polish Cross of Valour but was killed as a flight lieutenant in May 1944. 312 Squadron did see some 109s, later reporting that in their pilots' opinions the mission was completely dominated by Spitfires.

Tangmere had no action either but Biggin Hill's boys made a large S-shaped sweep at between 19–21,000 feet and saw some. 609 Squadron was attacked by two 109s near Hardelot, that shot-up one Spitfire. 92 fared better when engaging several 109s after leaving the target, and four were claimed shot down, plus one damaged.

Forward Support patrolled off Cap Gris Nez to Boulogne and in some small skirmishes, 611 claimed one destroyed and one probable. The 12 Group Wing also had some brief encounters - as well as some flak fire – and 19 Squadron damaged a 109 while 266 claimed one destroyed and one probable.

So, in all, 7-3-2 claims. Wing Commander P. G. Jameson DFC, leading the Wittering Wing, claimed a 109, while Jamie Rankin, CO of 92 Squadron, had bagged two; he was about to receive a Bar to his DFC. JG26 had engaged some of the Circus aircraft but only Priller and Hptm. Johannes Siefert scored. They in turn had had two pilots shot down, one crash-landing at Hesdin, but both pilots survived. Casualties not mentioned in Bouchier's report included a 92 Squadron pilot, Sgt H. Bowen-Morris, who was shot down over France seriously wounded (he lost his right arm) and taken prisoner. He was repatriated in October 1943. Also, 485 Squadron had a pilot shot down and killed off the French coast, while 616 had another bale out over the sea due to lack of fuel, but he was rescued.

Two other pilots were wounded. Pilot Officer B. M. Gladych of 303 actually collided with a 109 (he claimed three in total), forcing him to crash-land near Ramsgate, while 603's F/O W. A. Douglas returned, wounded by cannon shell fragments. As a result of this combat, Gladych was recommended for the DFC, the citation for which mentioned: '... *during a sortie over France, [he] destroyed one enemy aircraft and probably another. On a second sortie later in the day, he destroyed a second enemy aircraft but was then cut off by superior enemy forces. Whilst fighting his way back to the English coast his guns failed after they had been hit. P/O Gladych continued his fight, and collided with and destroyed yet another enemy aircraft, part of which came into his cockpit and wounded him. Although only able to see with one eye and in a semi-conscious condition P/O Gladych attempted to reach a home aerodrome; he was able to make a crash-landing, sustaining further injuries in doing so.*' This was his first recorded combat action.

Mike Gladych would become an ace (eighteen victories) flying with the RAF and USAAF later in the war, while Bill Douglas was a future wing leader and a DFC and Bar winner, who also saw considerable action over Malta in 1942.

Circus No.20 – 23 June

This second such operation of the day called for six Blenheims of 107 Squadron to hit Mardyck Aerodrome in the early evening. One bomber had to abort but the others carried on after making rendezvous with their Close Escort (242 and 303) over Maidstone at 2000 hours. Three Wings were slated for Target Support, Biggin Hill, Tangmere and Hornchurch, with Rear Support provided by Kenley.

The bombers arrived early at the rendezvous and flew on but the Hurricanes caught up with them as they crossed the English coast. No sooner had they all crossed the French coast at Hardelot than they came under flak and fighter attack. The 109s came in from every direction, virtually swamping the escorting Hurricanes and two Blenheims were shot down, although five were claimed! Leutnant Siegfried Schnell of 4./JG2 (who had just shot down a Spitfire) claimed two for his twenty-fourth and twenty-fifth victories, and then bagged another Spitfire making four kills for this action (twenty-sixth). Oberleutnant Jürgen Heppe, the Staffel leader, claimed one for his sixth. JG26's Hptm. Gerd Schöpfel, claimed the fourth one, for his twenty-fourth kill. 'Wumm' Schnell had received the Knight's Cross in November 1940 and went on to receive the Oak Leaves in July 1941 after forty victories.

Another Blenheim was badly hit and was escorted back by two of 242, and the other two bombers were forced to jettison their bomb load on a railway line they spotted and made for home, one landing at Manston. Of the two lost, one crew became prisoners, the others were all killed. It had not been a good trip for the 2 Group bombers.

The two Hurricane squadrons claimed 9-3-2 with just one of their number having to force-land at Manston. Crossing the French coast the Biggin squadrons saw fifteen to twenty 109s going down on 303. 92 Squadron attacked and shot down at least three, maybe four, with another damaged. 609 suffered from R/T problems and failed to assist 92, while 74, way up at 27,000 feet, saw little activity of any kind.

Tangmere's leader was advised by the Controller that enemy aircraft were approaching Cap Gris Nez and that there was a battle developing off Dover. He led his three squadrons in that direction, up-sun, but failed to see any 109s. Hornchurch had flown slightly inland over France where all three squadrons spread out into 'fours' as they saw several groups of 109s at varying heights above them. 611 engaged and shot down one 109, and in the fight, claimed one 109 damaged but had a pilot wounded. The Rear Support Wing saw nothing.

Other than two fighters shot up, the RAF suffered no losses, and only the two bombers failed to return. The Luftwaffe pilots of JG26 put in claims for five Spitfires, while JG2 claimed four Spitfires (in addition to the two bombers), so a total of nine. JG26 suffered no casualties while JG2 lost four pilots killed and two 109s written off in crash-landings, plus another damaged. JG26 pilot Oblt. Heinz Gotlob gained his sixth and final kill on the twenty-third, as his combat report records:

'Saw three Spitfires approaching the rear of the Staffel. My Rotte broke into this attack; the Spitfires evaded my attack by sharp turns. I climbed above them and began turning, waiting for them to break out of their circle and head to sea. However, my Rotte was itself attacked from above, and I had to dive away. After I had shaken off this attack, I saw a lone Spitfire flying in a north-westerly direction. It was still over land, at 6,000 meters [19,500 ft]. I flew after it, approaching to twenty meters without being observed.

'I then opened fire with all my weapons from behind and beneath it. The bottom of its fuselage started smoking: pieces then broke off the fuselage and wings. The plane pulled up, stalled, and fell away to the left. I saw the Spitfire hit the water – the pilot had not baled out.' Gotlob would be wounded on the 25th, but he later returned to the Geschwader as a member of the ground personnel.

Group Captain Bouchier made no comment or conclusion on his action report on the 29th, perhaps someone had finally told him that according to radio traffic, the Germans were not losing as many aircraft as 11 Group pilots were claiming. If the Germans had any similar way of gathering intelligence, what were they thinking about pilot claims? Young pilots on both sides can be forgiven for reporting things they thought they saw in the heat of combat. For instance, if a pilot of a 109 found a Spitfire on his tail, he often half-rolled and dived, increasing power as he did so. This usually produced a burst of black smoke from the exhausts that to the untrained eye might look like the start of an engine fire after a hit by .303 bullets or 20mm cannon. RAF pilots of the time could not easily follow the 109 in a similar fashion because their carburettors ceased feeding in conditions of inverted flight causing a temporary loss of power – thus allowing the fuel-injected 109's pilot to half-roll, dive, and pull away from danger.

It is well known that German fighter pilots suffered from something called 'sore throat syndrome' from wanting desperately to win the coveted Knight's Cross of the Iron Cross, a decoration worn at the throat, so claims sometimes followed an excess of enthusiasm.

Circus No.21 – 24 June

The next operation came on the 24th, and this time 2 Group put up seventeen bombers from 18, 107 and 139 Squadrons. The target was the electric power station at Commines, north-west of Lille, crossing the French coast at Dunkirk. Rendezvous at 2000 hours with the Escort Wing, Northolt's Poles – 303, 306 and 308 Squadrons – plus 71 Eagle Squadron from Martlesham, comprising the main body. The Americans, flying close to the bombers, only saw a few fleeting 109s and although one was fired at, no results were observed.

Squadrons 306 and 308 on Medium Escort similarly saw little and just one 109 was claimed hit and probably destroyed. 306 also escorted a lagging Blenheim back home. The top Squadron, 303, found six Me109s as they left the target but weaving prevented any attack. Reaching the French coast four more 109s were engaged and two shot down, one by the CO, S/Ldr W. Łapkowski. Wacław Lapkowski had fought over Poland, in the Battle of Britain and now over France. This was his last victory (his eighth). He would be lost in July.

Hornchurch followed the bombers towards Dunkirk then flew back over the Channel, and later made a sweep inland towards Lille. Some 109s turned up later and a fight developed in which 54 Squadron claimed three destroyed, one probable and two more damaged. One of the claimants was F/O E. F. J. Charles, born in Coventry but brought up in Canada. Jack Charles would become a wing leader in 1943 after commanding 611 Squadron. He would receive the DSO, DFC and Bar, and score sixteen victories, all of them fighters.

Number 611 Squadron claimed a probable while 603 also claimed a destroyed, but had two Spitfires damaged by flak. Strangely, the action report does not mention that 603 lost F/O K. J. McKelvie (killed) or Sgt D. P. Lamb wounded and force-landing at Walmer. 611 also lost F/Lt T. F. A. Buys, a Dutch pilot, who was killed, another casualty not mentioned.

Tangmere's Target Support operation followed the bombers in at 21,000 feet but saw no enemy aircraft. Heading back to the French coast, with haze and the position of the sun making cohesion difficult, the raiders headed for home. Six 109s were seen but not attacked, and they also experienced heavy flak as they crossed the coast.

Biggin Hill pilots were over the target area at 2035, but they never saw the bombers or escort. On the way out a number of small 109 formations were seen above, some up to around 30,000 feet. In total, Wing pilots thought the overall number seen was in the region of sixty. Some encounters took place and three 109s were destroyed, four probably so and two damaged.

A 12 Group Wing (19, 65 and 222 Squadrons), flying a diversion sweep along the French coast, engaged a couple of 109s and probably shot down one of them. Another formation from Kenley flew a similar sortie at between 20–25,000 feet but saw nothing of note.

Total victories claimed – nine destroyed, seven probables and five damaged for the loss of two pilots missing and one wounded. JG2 and JG26 both responded to this raid, with JG26 claiming three Spitfires, JG2 ten! Günther Sprick, leader of the JG26's 8th Staffel, gained his thirty-first, while Oblt. Erich Leie of JG2 scored twice, victories thirteen and fourteen. JG26's 9th Staffel lost one pilot killed in action while another pilot crash-landed near Wissant. JG2 lost their Gruppen-Adjutant, Ltn. Heinz Bolze, killed, shortly after gaining his fifth victory, and had another pilot wounded and his 109 written off.

Circus No.22 – 25 June

Fighter Command's 11 Group and Bomber Command's 2 Group were now in full swing as they had flown Circus operations every day since 21 June and would do so until the 28th. On 25 June Circus 22, consisting of twelve Blenheims, six each from

21 and 110 Squadrons, were to go for the Hazebrouck marshalling yards with Kenley Wing as escort, with 303 Squadron as High Cover.

Once more a small armada of RAF fighters would fill the air. One has to wonder where the dividing line was, between trying to bring the Luftwaffe to battle and scaring them off! Extra High Cover over the target would be flown by Biggin Hill, Target Support by Hornchurch, Forward Support by Tangmere and Rear Support by North Weald, which would patrol the Goodwins area. In all, sixteen squadrons were involved which, assuming all were at full strength, would mean nearly 200 fighters in the sky, although admittedly, not all clustered together.

Just minutes after midday, rendezvous was made once more over Maidstone, and having reached the target, bombed at the lower altitude of 7,000 feet. Most bombs were seen to burst in the yards, being observed to be full of railway traffic. Two rail bridges were destroyed with direct hits, one of which was across a main road. Despite the height there was no anti-aircraft fire, and no fighters were seen either.

The Escort Wing however, experienced heavy AA fire on the way out but hardly any enemy fighters showed up, although 303, at 14,000 feet, did engage four 109s and claimed two destroyed, one falling towards the sea, the other going down in flames. Biggin Hill's boys were at heights up to 30,000 feet. They found eight 109s and claimed two destroyed and possibly another, both by 92 Squadron. The successful pilots were F/Lt A. R. Wright DFC, and P/O N. F. Duke. It was Neville Duke's first confirmed victory and he would go on to claim twenty-eight (mostly in North Africa) by the war's end, winning not only the DSO but the DFC and two Bars. In his diary, Duke wrote:

'Allan and self dived down on two 109s over St Omer – couldn't catch them – going at a phenomenal airspeed. 109s pulled up vertically – blacked out and broke away just avoiding stalling. Saw Allan and 109 diving with glycol coming from the 109.

'I was attacked by two 109s from astern but saw them just in time and did a terrific turn, seeing tracer whistle past behind. Came out over Dunkirk and passed two 109s on way. Turned and saw dogfight going on near Dunkirk so went back and joined in. Sat on the tail of a 109 which was shooting at another Spit. Fired several bursts of cannon and machine-gun into him from about 50 yards range. Glycol streamed out and he started going down. Got just above him and look down into his cockpit. Pilot was crouched over stick and did not look up. Think perhaps I hit him.

'The 109 went down and crashed a few miles inland. Sped home at sea level at terrific bat. Bad AA fire from a convoy, which I came out over at 1,000 feet, and also from Dunkirk. Engine stopped just as I touched down on 'drome for lack of petrol!'

Hornchurch had joined with the main formation over Southend at between 15–18,000 feet. Some 109s were encountered near the target and 54 Squadron shot down two, one of which was destroyed. Heading back to the coast, some twenty to thirty more 109s were circling at 32,000 feet and came down. In the ensuing battle, two 109s were probably destroyed but 54 lost one pilot killed and one wounded, plus W/Cdr J. R. Kayll DSO DFC who was to have led the Wing. He became a prisoner of war. He later reported:

'I was to lead the Escort but at the last moment, Gp/Capt Broadhurst [Station Commander RAF Hornchurch] said that he would like to lead so I decided to go as his No.2. The raid was carried out successfully and the Wing headed for home but Broadhurst decided to fly back over France, detached the leading flight of four aircraft and headed west, climbing to gain height. While still climbing steeply, we were attacked by Me109s from out of the sun. Numbers 3 and 4 were shot down and did not survive [sic]. The Gp/Capt managed to get back to the UK but I was hit in the engine and lost all power. I was not able to jump as any attempt to slow down was an invitation for further attacks so I landed wheels up in a pea field between two canals and was captured hiding in a cornfield after about thirty minutes. We were an easy target and I was lucky to survive.'

Flying No.3 was Sgt John Beresford. In his mirror he spotted two 109s behind Kayll and called for a break. As he himself turned to port he found a 109 ahead of him and not having seen a 109 in front and within range before he delayed slightly to open fire, but then another 109 nailed him. A cannon shell set his Spitfire on fire and he baled out and was soon captured. Beresford's wingman, P/O K. E. Knox, was also hit and wounded but unknown to Kayll, managed to get home.

The section had been attacked by pilots of JG2, Oblt. Rudi Pflanz, Fw. Günther Seeger and the Geschwader Kommodeur, Hptm. Wilhem Balthasar, each claimed a Spitfire.

Meantime, Tangmere headed in over Gravelines, with 616 circling between St Omer and the coast at 19,000 feet. When they began to return they encountered six 109s, destroyed one, probably two more and damaged another two. 610 Squadron, warned of the approach of thirty 109s, milled around and engaged some of them, claiming one and one probable. The Wing Leader, of course, was Douglas Bader, and his wingman was Sergeant J. G. West from New Zealand. Several years ago, Jeff West wrote to me about his days with the Wing, recalling:

'I was quite happy to drop in behind Bader but on 25 June on my way home, DB suddenly stall-turned off after climbing after a 109 and I gave the EA an extra squirt for luck. On landing Douglas asked me if I had seen the pilot bale out. I said no, I was too busy catching up with him. He made me share ½ with him.'

The Messerschmitts of JG26 failed to make any effective assault but the First Gruppe eventually engaged the Tangmere fighters and claimed three. These would appear to be the three RAF aircraft that, whilst damaged in combat, each managed to get back to crash-land in England. JG26 lost one pilot and had another wounded.

Total claims by the RAF was seven destroyed, a further seven as probables and two damaged. Two Spitfire pilots failed to return. Luftwaffe pilots claimed nine, three by JG26 and six by JG2. JG2 lost one pilot (Uffz. Friedrich Otto) and another crash-landed, wounded (Oblt. Gottlob).

While Bouchier's report showed no bombers lost, one of 21 Squadron crashed on landing at Southend airfield, although the crew survived.

At 11 Group HQ's Operations Room, the Prime Minister, Winston Churchill and his wife visited with Air Marshal Sir Sholto Douglas, seeing for themselves how the operation had developed and been carried out. Whether they stayed on for the second show of the day is not known for certain.

Circus No.23 – 25 June

A second operation, Circus 23, twelve Blenheims, six each from 18 and 139 Squadrons, were tasked with an attack on St Omer Aerodrome in the late afternoon. Close Escort was North Weald's job, with 303 again as their High Cover. Extra High Cover was given to Hornchurch, while Target Support went to Tangmere and Biggin squadrons. Forward Support was provided by 12 Group while Rear Support was flown from Kenley.

Rendezvous was made above West Malling at 5,000 feet at 1600, and by the time they reached Hardelot another 1,000 feet had been added. They were met by heavy flak fire but the bombers headed for the airfield and bombed, seeing explosions among buildings and dispersal points. More heavy AA fire damaged several of the bombers, one going down in flames to crash in the target area. There were no survivors. No enemy fighters were seen by them or the escort. However, up at 9,000 feet, 303 Squadron met four 109s, claimed one as damaged but lost P/O S. Paderewski, killed.

Hornchurch also saw a few 109s but no engagement took place, although Tangmere pilots, flying between 21–25,000 feet did. The Wing Leader sent 610 after a dozen 109s at 17,000 feet and a dogfight developed, and two were shot down, plus two damaged, for the loss of one pilot, who ended up as a prisoner. Another pilot was wounded in one leg but got home. As 145 and 616 continued to the target more 109s came from above. 145 claimed two and two damaged, while 616 claimed one but lost two pilots, both killed.

Biggin Hill's squadrons at 25–29,000 feet gradually let down as the target came into view although they did not see any 109s till they were on their way out. They claimed one 109 destroyed, while P/O T. S. Wade of 92 was slightly wounded but got back. The other Support Wings had no encounters.

Fighters from JG26 and JG2 were sent up and made quick attacks on the main formation as they withdrew and two Spitfires were claimed by JG26 and a further eight by JG2 for the loss of one pilot. In total the RAF lost four pilots and one wounded. JG26 had no losses, but JG2 suffered two killed and one crash-landed. The RAF claimed a total of six destroyed and five damaged.

Circus No.24 – 26 June

Thursday, 26 June 1941 was another fair, early summer day. There was some haze over the Channel but cloud over France might be a problem. Nevertheless, a large force of twenty-eight bombers had been assigned to attack the electric power station at Commines. This was the largest raiding force thus far, but in the end the cloud prevented them pressing on. They found 10/10ths at between 9–15,000 feet and seeing this wall of cloud ahead of them as they reached the French coast, the mission was aborted, and they turned for home together with their Close Escort.

Hornchurch, the Cover Wing for the Dunkirk area, never saw the bombers so split up into sections and began to patrol Gravelines way up between 20–25,000 feet. At this height they encountered some twenty Me109s and in the fight that ensued, they claimed three destroyed, three probables and four damaged for the loss of one pilot killed.

The Tangmere squadrons also broke up, into individual squadrons, and then sections of fours. As 145 headed for the target area they ran into half a dozen 109s and shot down one but lost one pilot who was taken prisoner. 616 also engaged 109s and claimed one and another damaged, while 610, having flown some twenty miles inland encountered twenty-four 109s in loose formation at various heights. In the scrap that followed, they claimed one destroyed and two damaged for no loss.

With no message received from the Controller stating that the mission had been aborted, Biggin Hill's pilots continued to the target area way above the cloud layer and then returned towards Gravelines hoping to protect the main force, which in any event was well on its way home. 609 Squadron saw no enemy machines, while 92 and 74 became engaged with 109s and claimed three destroyed, one probable and two damaged for the loss of one pilot from 92, who became a prisoner. The other supporting Wings saw no enemy activity.

Fighter Command claimed nine 109s destroyed, four probables and eight damaged for the loss of three pilots. Despite the fact no bombers were present the Luftwaffe still scrambled to intercept – being unaware that they had turned back. No doubt the radar plotters, having detected so large a force, were misled into thinking that bombers must be present; had they realised the bombers had aborted they would probably have left well alone.

As it happened, JG26 did claim two of the RAF's losses, one by Hptm. Walter Adolph, CO of II Gruppe, for his eighteenth victory. JG2 was not very successful in forming up to engage but when they did, they managed to claim three Spitfires. However, they lost five of their aircraft with two pilots killed and one wounded.

Circus No.25 – 27 June

Friday the 27th, yet another fair day despite thick haze up to 9,000 feet, but clear blue sky above. Another attempt at a large bomber force, this time twenty-four Blenheims, six each from 18, 21, 139 and 226 Squadrons, would proceed to bomb the Fives Steel and Engineering Works at Lille. Close Escort was again flown by North Weald, Biggin's 74 and 609 Squadrons were Escort Cover, with 92 at Extra High Cover. Support Wings were provided by Hornchurch and Tangmere. 12 and 13 Groups added a Wing each as Forward and Rear Support. This was the first time 13 Group had been involved in an 11 Group Circus.

Today the bombers and their escort met over Martlesham at 2100 hours and heading out, crossed the French coast at Dunkirk, being met by some intense AA fire both to and from the target. Several bombers were hit but none lost. Bombs were seen to explode on the target and the nearby marshalling yards.

The Close Escort boys, as usual, appeared to deter enemy pilots from coming in too close and a couple that did were attacked by 306 Squadron who damaged one of them. Escort Cover Wing was at 18,000 feet and above as they approached Dunkirk. 74 Squadron was attacked by some 109s but the Squadron turned to meet them and damaged one of them seriously, however, the 'Tigers' suffered the loss of three pilots, including the CO, S/Ldr J. C. Mungo-Park DFC who was killed. The other two were both brought down and captured. Mungo-Park was a successful Battle of Britain pilot who had around a dozen victories, and was about to receive a Bar to his DFC.

Unfortunately the haze prevented 609 from being able to see 74 and therefore had no way of helping. They too were also engaged with some 109s, and damaged a Messerschmitt before re-crossing the coast. 92 Squadron, which was flying around 30,000 feet saw no sign of the enemy and after orbiting three times over the target, returned home.

The Hornchurch units were high too but could still see the flak fire as the main force went in. Only a couple of 109s were seen south of Lille and one was shot down, by F/O Jack Charles of 54. Tangmere's squadrons became rather lost being able to see little below through the haze. At one stage they saw a dozen aircraft that they took to be 610 Squadron but turned out to be green-coloured 109s. In a quick scrap one of these was probably destroyed.

The Forward 12 Group Wing saw six to eight Me109s behind and below as they crossed the French coast at 25,000 feet then they found more in loose formations. For a change the 109 pilots seemed to 266 Squadron rather keen to mix it with the Spitfires but soon went into steep vertical dives if approached too keenly. 65 and 19 Squadrons also had skirmishes and claimed one destroyed and another as a probable. One pilot attacked four 109s and shot one down before he himself was hit in the glycol tank. With his engine stopped he managed to glide across the French coast and the Channel, to crash-land at Lydd. This was Sgt D. G. S. R. Cox, a successful pilot in the Battle of Britain and one who would go on to become a wing commander with the DFC and Bar. Another pilot, however, was not so lucky and failed to return.

The Kenley Wing orbited off Calais at between 20–30,000 feet then headed for the Goodwins reducing height. Several 109s were engaged over Gravelines and one was claimed destroyed.

In Bouchier's report he gave the RAF scores by Group. 11 Group had claimed two destroyed, two probables and two damaged. 12 Group – two destroyed, one probable and four damaged. The total was four destroyed, three probables and six damaged. 11 Group had lost three pilots, 12 Group one.

Luftwaffe fighter pilots had had a busy day for in the morning Fighter Command had flown four operations before Circus 25 began. Hauptmann Pingel and his I Gruppe had engaged the main formation of this latter sortie and claimed four Spitfires without loss, but II Gruppe had lost a pilot to Spitfires and had another crash-land. During the day JG2 had claimed one Blenheim and three Spitfires for no loss. No Blenheim had been lost. Pingel and Priller had been credited with their twenty-first and twenty-seventh victories this day, Priller during the morning actions. JG2's Hptm. Balthasar was again in evidence claiming his thirty-ninth and fortieth victories, one being another 'phantom' Blenheim. This brought him the Oak Leaves to his Knight's Cross on 3 July 1941. His 'sore throat' had eased. Siegfried Schnell had claimed two Spitfires from Circus 25 to bring his personal score to thirty-one. He knew his award of the Oak Leaves was just nine kills away.

In other operations the RAF had lost three more fighter pilots. Wing Commander P. Łaguna, the Northolt Wing Leader, had been shot down by ground fire, leading 303 Squadron in a low-level strafing attack on Marck airfield. Some 109s were claimed on the ground during the run but Łaguna was hit by defensive fire, crashed and was killed. On an afternoon sweep by 19 and 266 Squadrons, three pilots were lost to 109s, one 19 Squadron pilot was captured, while 266 lost one killed and one prisoner. So in total eight fighter pilots lost, including one wing leader and one squadron commander.

* * *

In a letter to the Air Ministry from the Deputy Chief of the Air Staff dated 27 June 1941, an appendix shows the targets being considered by the RAF at this stage:

Targets in the Pas de Calais area.
Transportation Targets.

Z.437	Hazebrouck	)
Tgt map in		) Railway centres serving Calais, Gravelines
preparation	Armentieres	) and Dunkirk.
Z.184	Lille	)
Z.440	Abbeville	)

Power Plants

Z.195	Comines	Steam electric Power Station (179,000 kw) 7 miles W.N.W. of Toucoing.
Z.246	Sequedin	Steam electric Power Station (98,000 kw) 2 miles S.W. of Lille.
Z.303	Pont-à-Vendin	Steam electric Power Station (90,000 kw) 13 miles S.W. of Lille.
Tgt map in preparation	Bully	Steam electric Power Station (66,000 kw) 18 miles S.W. of Lille.
Z.302	Chocques	Steam electric Power Station (65,000 kw) 23 miles W.S.W. of Lille.
Z.283	Lomme	Steam electric Power Station (44,000 kw) 2 miles W.S.W. of Lille.
Z.301	Mazingarbe	Steam electric Power Station (78,000 kw) 16 miles S.W. of Lille.
Z.573	Labruissiere (Bruay)	Main distributing point from the industrial power stations to the ports of Dunkirk, Calais and Boulogne.

Industrial Targets in the Pas de Calais Area

Z.183	Compaigne Fives–Lille, Lille	The most important manufacturer of locomotives in France and is known to be manufacturing on German account.
Tgt map in preparation	Accumulator Tudor, Lille	The leading French manufacturer of submarine accumulators. It may now be making them for Germany, but there is no definite information on this subject.
Z.447	Kuhlmann, Hornes	Synthetic oil and methanol plant. Fischer-Tropech process. Coke ovens alongside (330,000 tons).
Z.301	Mines de Bully	Large coke oven batteries (500,000 tons Béthune, of coke per annum) synthetic nitrogen plant and small synthetic oil plant, also Bully & Mazingarbe Power Station of 66,000 kw and 78,000 kw respectively.
Z.302	Mines de Harles, Chocques	Coke oven batteries (190,000 tons) with Chocques Power Station (81,000 kw) and Marles-Kuhlmann chemical plant alongside. The latter is producing glycol which is being taken to Germany.

Z.303	Rayon & Staple Fibre Plant. Pont-à-Vendin, Calais	Produces 25% of the total French output. Manufacturing parachute material for Germany.
Z.185	Locomotive and Wagon repair and construction works at Hellemmes, S.E. of Lille	The most important works of this type in northern France. Recent photos indicate that it is being employed at maximum capacity.

* * *

Circus No.26 – 28 June

There was no let up and Circus 26 came on the 28th, twenty-three Blenheims being sent to bomb once more the electric power station at Commines – the third time this month. It was an early morning show, the bombers coming from 18, 21, 139 and 226 Squadrons, although two aborted. Close Escort went to the Polish Wing, plus 3 Squadron. Tangmere flew a Cover Wing over Dunkirk while Support Wings came from Hornchurch and Biggin. 12 Group again gave Forward Diversion Cover, Kenley the Rear Cover.

Weather was cloudy but improving, with just 3/10ths cloud at 15,000 feet. Rendezvous was made over Martlesham at 0800 hours, at 5,000 feet, the bombers originally flying in boxes of six [sic]. Eleven tons of bombs went down on the target from 7–8,000 feet and explosions were reported on the boiler house, turbine room and switch-gear building. A few bombs went astray but landed on a small factory just to the east. Flak was heavy but only one bomber was damaged.

3 Squadron weaved in pairs in close escort and while it too suffered from AA fire, no losses were suffered and no enemy aircraft seen. However, 306 Squadron, flying to the left of the bombers was suddenly attacked by four Me109s, Hptm. Schöpfel picking off P/O J. Żulikowski. As the four 109s continued their dive, Żulikowski's Spitfire was seen to go straight down and crash, so he was presumed killed. However, he survived and although captured, later managed an escape and returned to England via Spain, arriving by ship on 5 January 1942.

More 109s were engaged by 308 Squadron whose pilots claimed one in flames and another probably destroyed. 303, flying as top cover, had its rearmost section of four bounced by five 109s, whose pilots kept up harassing tactics before a more prolonged dog fight began, during which one Spitfire was shot down (P/O J. Bondar killed, claimed by Uffz. Babenz), but one 109F was claimed too. Reforming at low altitude they flew over a German airfield and one pilot opened fire on a 109 that had been mounted on a tripod and claimed to have destroyed it. Along a road they attacked a busload of German soldiers and over the coast shot up a tug. One pilot (P/O W. M. Drecki) was forced to bale out fifteen miles off Worthing but was rescued.

The Cover Wing did not see a lot, although one pilot of 145 spotted two 109s in line astern and attacked the rearmost and claimed it probably destroyed. The other two squadrons saw little and had no engagements. The Target Support Wings reached the target area around 0830 but the Hornchurch Wing saw little enemy activity. Biggin Hill saw some thirty 109s in total but most avoided combat, although two were engaged one being shot down by Sailor Malan. Diversion and Cover Wings reported little activity.

With just three aircraft and two pilots lost, it was not a bad day, especially with six 109s claimed destroyed plus a probable. The Germans suffered a severe loss by having Gustav 'Micky' Sprick of JG26 killed. All three of JG26's Gruppen had been ordered up to intercept the Circus and I Gruppe shot down one Spitfire west of Lille, which was one of the Polish losses. Meantime, Schöpfel led his III Gruppe towards Calais and got up-sun as the bombers began to withdraw, but his high staffel was engaged by Spitfires and a fight started. Sprick was attacked by a Spitfire and when he made a steep turn, a wing collapsed and the 109 plunged to the ground. This was due to structural failure, and some of the Gruppen's 109s had to be flown to Antwerp for wing replacements. Pilot Officer W. M. Drecki of 303 made head-on attacks upon two 109s and both were seen to crash, but he was hit himself and, as mentioned earlier, later baled out into the sea and was rescued. JG26 had four other 109s damaged in combat, three of the pilots being wounded. Oberleutnant Harald Grawatsch, II Gruppe's Adjutant, had to bale out of his burning 109, suffering severe injuries, resulting in a leg amputation. Three of the 109s were written off in crash-landings. Sprick had now achieved thirty-one victories and Schöpfel had claimed his twenty-sixth.

Circus No.27 – 30 June

The RAF had a break on the 29th, but Circus 27 was ordered for 30 June, involving eighteen Blenheims, ten from 18 Squadron, and eight from 139, attacking the power station at Pont-á-Vendin, north-east of Lens. The Poles from Northolt, and North Weald again got the Close Escort duty, with Hornchurch and Biggin pulling Target Support once more. Kenley, Tangmere and a 12 Group Wing had the Diversion and Rear Support tasks.

This day the RV (rendezvous) point was above the seaside town of Clacton, at 7,000 feet, timed for 1800 hours. They had gained another 2,000 feet by the time they crossed east of Gravelines, where they met heavy flak which continued more or less to the target. One Blenheim aborted but the others all dropped their bombs, five registering hits on or around the turbine building, the roof of which collapsed. Six others reported hits on the engineering works just west of the power house. Six more bombed a large factory at Haisnes, three and a half miles north-west of the primary target, securing two direct hits. All bombers returned home.

The Close Escort squadron - 242 – experienced the flak but saw no fighters. 303 Squadron saw a few 109s weaving up high but again nothing developed. 306 had two 109s try to attack the bombers but were driven off, one possibly damaged. 308 only saw a couple of 109s near the coast on the way back.

The Hornchurch Wing, at 15–18,000 feet followed the bombers to Gravelines and flew into France. Five miles inland, 603 Squadron was attacked from above by some 109s that came down in line astern, but it forced 603 to break away from the Wing and dive away. One section pulled round and went for a couple of 109s and destroyed one. The Squadron later reported that they had seen more 109s on this operation than ever before. One pilot failed to return – Sgt L. E. S. Salt – who was killed.

The other two squadrons, 54 and 611, continued to the target after circling near Merville, then split into fours. These pilots had no real encounters but reported that the German fighters appeared to be attempting to fly by or across the formation in order to entice the Wing to split up or to see if a section might detach itself and give chase.

Biggin Hill's squadrons went over at between 23–28,000 feet and although some 109s were seen there were no engagements. Only 609 was fired upon at extreme range by 109s in 'nibbling' attacks. Then a dog fight developed and 609 claimed four destroyed, with another probably so and others damaged. It was noticeable that the 109s always seemed to have a height advantage. The Wing Leader, Malan, was one of the claimants, while F/Lt P. H. M. Richey DFC bagged one and shared a probable with P/O Roger Malengreau (Belgian), before becoming separated. Paul Richey is famous as the author of *Fighter Pilot*, which concerned operations during the Battle of France in 1940. This was his tenth confirmed success. In Fighter Command's Form 'F' it recorded:

'F/Lt Richey, after linking up with other Spitfires at 16,000 ft., saw about 6 Me109Es diving in formation from above and behind. He had an ineffective engagement with one of them, then finding himself alone again, he dived for a patch of cloud at 800 ft., near Forêt de Clairmarais. At ground level he saw 2 Me109Es diving on his tail and a third opening fire from [the] starboard quarter. A violent climbing turn and side loop brought him on the latter's tail and two longish bursts with cannon and m/g caused it to half roll and dive vertically at full speed from 1,000 ft. It is impossible that it recovered. After eluding the other 2 Me109s and accurate light flak from St. Omer area, F/Lt Richey flew home alone sometimes below tree-top level.'

Of the other supporting wings, only 145 Squadron got near to an enemy fighter, which was claimed as destroyed, while a pilot in 65 Squadron knocked pieces off another. The day's total came to six destroyed, two probables and three damaged for one 'loss'. JG26 claimed one Spitfire (Sgt Salt – Priller's twenty-eighth kill), while JG2 claimed two more but had one fighter lost in a crash-landing after taking hits in combat.

For a change, Group Captain Bouchier appended a conclusion at the end of his report, saying that enemy fighters seem to be keeping a height advantage and mainly trying to decoy RAF fighters rather than mix it. Over the last few Circus operations, he said, the enemy fighters seem disinclined to press home attacks on the bombers and their close escort fighters.

Perhaps the Germans were beginning not to mind too much should damage be done to the small French targets being attacked, with the risk of losing pilots and aircraft for no real return. Attacking German airfields might produce more of a response provided they would react. Most fighter airfields were not too far from the Channel coast so the RAF bombers could reach them very quickly and soon be on their way home.

As June came to a close RAF fighter pilots must have been feeling reasonably pleased with themselves. After the struggles many of them had faced the previous summer, on the defensive, being now on the offensive and dishing it out rather than taking it, would make them feel a good deal better. Probably the more discerning, while happy to be 'dishing it out', were very aware that seats in the mess during the evenings were still emptying at an alarming rate. Often the good news that so-and-so was not only known to be alive although a prisoner, was welcome, even so the squadrons were still losing pilots.

They no doubt took comfort with the knowledge that they were knocking down the 'Hun' in equally, if not higher numbers, and while never officially acknowledged as such, the 'aces' were building up good scores of enemy aircraft shot down. However, senior officers at both Fighter Command HQ and the Air Ministry, would have been well aware that according to the radio intercepts of German communications, a different story was becoming more obvious.

It is always difficult to be precise about numbers as there are several imponderables to consider, but during January to May 1941, Fighter Command had lost something in the region of ninety-seven pilots in air actions, with another forty-one injured or wounded. Then in June more than fifty had been lost, including eighteen taken prisoner. To this must be added around a dozen pilots with varying degrees of wounds. In total, therefore, almost 150 pilots had left empty chairs in the messes and another fifty or more had been wounded.

Fighter Command had claimed around eighty-four Me109s destroyed and a further thirty-six as probably so during January to May, and in June, they estimated RAF fighter pilots had shot down over 150, plus a further sixty-four as probables. Therefore, these six months of bitter fighting over the Channel and northern France had achieved 237 Me109s claimed as destroyed, and 100 others probably destroyed.

Of course, the assumed ratio of claims to losses could not be divulged to the general public and especially not to the fighter pilots at the sharp end. It is always glib to say that air combat claims were made in good faith, and generally speaking one would agree. Yet from time to time it becomes obvious that some pilots were keen to claim anything that looked possible. One famous pilot claimed a 109 shot down in particular circumstances and said he saw it splash into the sea. We now know the identity of the

German pilot, and while he certainly dived down to evade trouble, he most certainly did not go into the sea. It was a case of saying it went into the sea in his combat report, in order to get the Intelligence Officer on the squadron to look more favourably at the claim.

Nor would it have done anyone any good to say that over-claiming went on. The man in the street was heartened that the RAF was giving the enemy a bloody nose, and the fighter pilots looking at those empty seats could at least hope that their loss had not been totally in vain. On the political front, it would have proved how successful the Germans were at shooting down Britain's young men, and the Russians, who were hoping for more support from Britain, would not have been impressed to know that the British air force was taking a hammering, so forget any immediate help from that direction.

When one thinks about these things, it becomes clear that some of the RAF aces were building up scores way above actual enemy losses. Of course they were doing their best, almost daily facing the dangers of air combat, where the best they could hope for was a slight wound or a prison camp rather than a gruesome and perhaps painful death in a blazing cockpit, or drowning in a bitterly cold English Channel. Yet they were being rewarded with medals and gaining some notoriety as national heroes. What about the fighter pilot who was not able to claim many hits on a fleeting Me109, or was being a wonderful wingman, protecting his leader? He often survived months of combat with little or no reward. But he was there – and had survived.

Chapter 5

July – and the Heavies

As July began, the Wing Leaders were:

Biggin Hill	W/Cdr A. G. Malan DSO DFC
Kenley	W/Cdr J. A. Kent DFC AFC
Hornchurch	W/Cdr F. S. Stapleton DFC
Tangmere	W/Cdr D. R. S. Bader DSO DFC
North Weald	W/Cdr J. W. Gillan DFC AFC
Northolt	W/Cdr T. H. Rolski (wef 2 July)
Duxford	W/Cdr R. R. S. Tuck DSO DFC
Wittering	W/Cdr P. G. Jameson DFC

Circus No.28 – 1 July

July began with no let up, with Circus 28 on Tuesday the 1st. The assigned target was the Kuhlmann Works and Power Station at Chocques, the same as on 17 June (Circus 13). Twelve Blenheims made rendezvous over Canterbury with their Escort Wing at 1805 hours and headed out over North Foreland. However, they had only gone a few miles before thick haze made it impossible to carry on so the raid was aborted, with the main force heading back home. One problem was that the bomber leader failed to tell the fighters. Most of the fighter squadrons involved attempted to carry on with their task but there was no reaction from the German side so everyone came back. The odd Me109 was seen taking a 'look-see' but they quickly rolled away into the haze and cloud, thankful for the chance of an 'early bath'.

Circus No.29 – 2 July

While the 1st had started fine then clouded over, the 2nd was a mainly fine summer day – even hot and sultry. Today's Circus operation would be against the City of Lille's Electric Power Station and if Fighter Command wanted a reaction, they got it.

The show began at 1150. Six Blenheims each from 21 and 266 Squadrons got the job with Northolt having the Close Escort assignment (71, 303 and 308). Cover Wing went to Biggin's usual boys, 74, 92 and 609, Tangmere's 145, 610 and 616 provided Target Support with Rear Support flown by North Weald and Kenley Wings. However, once over France the main force ran into a belt of hazy fog between 10–20,000 feet which made finding the target difficult but one bomber, running in to bomb, was attacked by three 109s, their fire wounding the pilot.

He called to the observer for help but seeing they were practically on top of the target, he first let go their bomb load, then went back to help. Meantime the gunner was returning fire and claimed to have hit one Messerschmitt. Three other bombers went for the railway junction to the south of Lille but they did not see what happened below as they were heavily engaged by six 109s. Six of the other Blenheims spotted the airfield at Merville and bombed that, explosions being seen amongst buildings and a dispersal area in the south-west corner. As they climbed away they were attacked by eight 109Fs and a running fight ensued for at least five minutes. One bomber went down trailing fire and smoke from its port engine.

As the bombers formed up and crossed out over Mardyck, a quick count found that another bomber was also missing, and on landing it was found that most of the bombers had flak damage from the defences of Lille. The missing aircraft were both from 226 Squadron, with five aircrew killed and one pilot surviving as a prisoner.

The Escort Wing was not engaged until heading away from the target and was continually attacked until almost halfway out over the Channel. 303 Squadron claimed two 109s shot down, a probable and a damaged, but lost two pilots, including their CO, S/Ldr W. Łapkowski who was killed, and Sgt R. Górecki who baled out over the sea but was rescued seventy-two hours later. 303 also had two pilots wounded but both got home. 308 was attacked near the target by an estimated sixty enemy fighters, but the Poles weaved behind the bombers to prevent the 109s getting to them. The five weavers claimed two destroyed and a probable, while the rest of the Squadron fought off other 109s to mid-Channel as well, claiming 3-1-1, but also losing two pilots. One was killed, one becoming a prisoner; another pilot returned wounded.

The Eagle Squadron was also in action over the target and another running fight commenced to way out over the Channel. Yet they stayed with the bombers fighting a gallant rear-guard action, during which they claimed three 109s plus a probable and a damaged. One American, P/O W. I. Hall, was shot down by Rolf Pingel of JG26, ending up in the famous Stalag Luft III prison camp.

Sailor Malan leading his Biggin Wing arrived over the target a few minutes before the bombers and several combats took place although his Tigers (74 Sqn) did not become especially involved. 92 Squadron, however, was heavily involved and claimed four 109s destroyed, with another damaged, and shared yet another with 74 Squadron, the latter unit losing two pilots. Both were taken prisoner. One – P/O S. Z. Krol (Polish) - also ended up in Stalag Luft III, only to be murdered by the Gestapo following *The Great Escape*, in March 1944.

The Target Support Wing had arrived at Lille by 1215. 616 Squadron immediately found a dozen 109s to the south and went off to engage them. They claimed three shot down and one damaged. One pilot, having broken away from the main battle had lost height and suddenly found himself approaching an airfield so opened fire at buildings, workshops, workmen and soldiers, finishing up with strafing a small boat as he crossed out over the coast. 610 Squadron had joined in the air battle and claimed a 109 destroyed and another damaged.

Some 2,000 feet above the fight, 145 Squadron saw the action but remained in place as top cover. On the way home they saw small formations of 109s and a couple were fired at but no claims were made. However, one Spitfire pilot failed to get home. Sergeant J. G. L. Robillard RCAF was shot down by a 109 but survived and managed to evade capture. He was escorting a man in a parachute who he thought was his CO, when the 109s intercepted him. He was later to relate in his MI9 report (a report produced for MI9 following an evader's successful return to the UK):

'We encountered Messerschmitts and I was boxed in by seven of them at 6,000 feet. I destroyed three of them, two I saw fall and French people subsequently told me that the third had fallen. I was actually trying to collide with it when a shell shot off my port wing. The aeroplane exploded and threw me out.'

Parachuting down he hid in a railway tunnel overnight and the next day met up with some Frenchmen who agreed to help him. He was taken to a farmhouse and provided with some civilian clothes before taking him to Lillers. He then met up with two British soldiers who had been at large since May 1940, and said they had actually seen the air action too, also confirming his three kills and seeing him get blown out of his exploding fighter.

After a number of adventures with French escape lines, Joseph Robillard got to Gibraltar where he was flown home in a Sunderland flying-boat in August. He was awarded the DFM. Operational again by 1942, he later saw action over Normandy in 1944. Post-war he became a Lt-Commander in the Royal Canadian Navy.

The Kenley Wing saw a number of Me109s on their way in and on their way out but saw no major actions, although one pilot did strafe German troops and some huts on a beach.

The post-operation report declared the mission as successful even though the main target was not positively attacked although a secondary one was. The report also declared that it seemed the German reaction to these intensive Circus operations was to increase the number of fighters the Luftwaffe was putting up, and by so doing it was reducing its strength in other theatres of war. We now know this was wishful thinking on the part of the RAF's top brass. The report also suggested the Germans were more likely to react when larger towns inland were attacked rather than smaller targets of perhaps less significance.

In any event Fighter Command must have been happy with the claims of Me109s shot down. The score of 21-4-7 was most encouraging, two of the twenty-one being claimed by the bomber gunners. Two Wing Leaders had scored, Malan a 109 that brought his score to around twenty-five, and a 109 by Douglas Bader (Tangmere), that brought his score to around sixteen. Wing Commander Max Aitken, the son of Lord Beaverbrook, had been flying as a guest with 610 Squadron and had claimed a 109 destroyed. However, with two Blenheims lost and eight fighter pilots missing (one was later rescued), there had been a cost.

On the German side, I./JG26 had intercepted the main force, coming down from out of the sun as the Blenheims were starting to turn for home, and managed to get into the bombers. Adolf Galland and Hptm. Rudolf Bieber each downed a bomber while other pilots claimed three RAF fighters. One German pilot baled out but it was not thought to be combat-related. The other two Gruppen also claimed fighters. It was Galland's seventy-first kill, while the American Eagle, shot down by Pingel, was his twenty-second victory. Priller had gained his twenty-ninth victory in this action, while Gerhard Schöphel scored his twenty-seventh.

Only Galland was a casualty, the Gruppenkommodeur being slightly wounded – again. JG2 had also become engaged and claimed five Spitfires shot down (and a Blenheim), but had suffered three 109 losses but no pilots, other than two wounded. One can only surmise that many of the nineteen claims by Fighter Command were actually Spitfires going down! – or 109s puffing out exhaust smoke.

Galland in fact was still recovering from his injuries received back on 21 June but had returned to his command, and this morning was preparing for a test flight. New armour had been fitted to the cockpit canopy and when slammed shut by his rigger the clearance of the hood had been reduced slightly, and the armour hit Galland's injured head, much to his discomfort. Once in the air, the alarm had started, so he joined up with his pilots and led the attack on the bombers. He wrote in his autobiography:

'I gave the order to attack and was the first to dive down through the British fighter escort on to the bombers. Flying in a shallow right bank, I fired from a distance of about 200 yards right down to ramming distance at one of the Blenheims in the first row of the formation. Pieces of metal and other parts broke away from the fuselage and from the right engine, then she went up in flames and smoke. The remnants of her were found later. I could not observe the crash because I got into a fight with the escorting Spitfires, and while I was chasing one, a second got me. Everything rattled inside my crate, my cockpit was shattered, and, what is more, my head got it again. Warm blood was running down my face. I was afraid of a black-out. I must not lose consciousness! With a great effort I succeeded in shaking off my pursuer and landed safely. My aircraft was shot up: a 20mm cannon shell had exploded on the new armour plating on top of the cockpit. At Hardinghem Hospital I had to [have my head] sewn up again. Without the armour-plating, nothing would have remained of this indispensable part of my body.'

Circus No.30 – 3 July

Thursday the 3rd was cloudy at first but cleared up to leave just haze up to 5,000 feet over the Channel, while visibility over France was perfect. The marshalling yards at Hazebrouck was to be the target for six Blenheims of 139 Squadron whose Close Escort today comprised the Northolt and North Weald Wings again.

Rendezvous was made over West Malling at 1100 and went out over Dungeness towards Hardelot. A report said that due to the sun, landmarks for the target were not picked out so the bombers went for railway sidings at St Omer but most of the bombs overshot. Heavy AA fire brought down one bomber, its three NCO crew being killed, while other aircraft received damage.

The Escort fighters saw only brief glimpses of some 109s and had one aircraft damaged by flak. Escort Cover – Tangmere – also only had brief sightings of 109s and had one pilot reported missing – Sgt D. B. Crabtree of 616 Squadron. However, he got down safely although he hurt his ankle. He set off after hiding in a hedge but ran into a German patrol and was captured. He was locked in a barn for the night, was not closely guarded, so managed to squeeze through a hole in the wall and got away. A French farmer gave him clothes and a bicycle.

Crabtree later wrote: '[A German Me109 fighter] came hurtling in and I got separated from our main body.' Seeing a lone Spitfire being attacked by several 109s he went to its assistance, claiming one shot down before his Spitfire was hit in the engine. Despite trying to get towards the coast he was attacked again and his fighter set on fire. 'I came down in a cornfield and hid in a hedge until dark. I burned my parachute but kept the dinghy, intending to get to the coast.' Finally he left his hiding place but: 'then walked smack into a German patrol of five soldiers. It was then dark. I had hurt my ankle, and pretneded that it was very bad and that I could hardly walk.' As related, the Germans finally locked him in a barn but he managed to squeeze through a hole and get away. He was looked after at a farm for a few days before being given civilian clothes, a bicycle and location to ride to where help would be available.

Being passed around he eventually arrived at Lillers where he met Sgt Joe Robillard who had been shot down on Circus 29. With some other evaders, Robillard and Crabtree eventually ended up in Gibraltar and Crabtree also flew back to the UK in a Sunderland in August, to receive a Mention in Despatches. Sadly he was killed in a civil flying accident in June 1950.

Meantime, 610 Squadron had engaged a couple of 109s and claimed one, plus another damaged. 145 Squadron saw nothing except suspected dummy aircraft on a landing ground by Calais/Marck.

The Target Support Wings had mixed fortunes. 54 Squadron saw little, 603 claimed one 109 destroyed, noting the enemy fighters evaded by climbing and diving, emitting thick black smoke during the climb and the latter part of the dive. This was smoke from the exhaust of the 109's DB601 engine when given full power, which some RAF pilots took to be the result of a damaging hit. The Biggin Hill Wing fought some 109s while covering the withdrawal of the bombers, 609 claiming one, 74 two and 92 Squadron a probable, although one 74 pilot, Sgt R. H. Cochrane, failed to return. He ended up a prisoner. Kenley Wing had little to report.

In total five 109s were claimed destroyed, one probably so plus a damaged. The cost was one Blenheim and three fighter pilots. JG2 and JG26 had engaged the 'beehive' of aircraft, claiming three Spitfires, but lost Hptm. Bieber, the man who had attacked the Blenheims with Galland the previous day. He was killed over St Omer. Rudolf Beiber was forty years of age and described as an ardent Nazi.

The most serious loss was that of the Kommodore of JG2, Hptm. Wilhelm Balthasar who went down in flames over Aire. Balthasar had, by this date, amassed a score of forty-seven victories, including the seven he achieved in the Spanish Civil War. One view is that a wing separated from his fighter, although this was probably caused by a 20mm cannon shell from a Spitfire. In fact, the CO of 609, S/Ldr M. L. (Lister) Robinson DFC, reported that the 109 he attacked lost its wing after he fired at it. There has also been a suggestion that Belgian pilot Vicki Ortmans, with 609, may have shot down Balthasar, although he was only credited with a damaged on the 3rd. Balthasar's replacement was Major Walter Oesau, posted in from commanding III Gruppe of JG3.

Micky Robinson had seen two 109s below him and went down. The 109 wingman saw the danger and dived as Micky closed in on the leader who had started a turn. The Spitfire easily turned inside it, fired, but missed. A puff of smoke showed that the German pilot had opened up the throttle to full boost – what the RAF termed as 'using one's Ha-Ha gas'. The 109 began to climb, Micky firing at great range, and suddenly the enemy fighter seemed to stop in mid-air, allowing Micky a further chance to fire from dead astern. The 109 went down half inverted, pouring out black smoke, in a left-hand spiral. He then lost sight of it but his No.4 (Sgt J. A. Hughes-Rees) watched it further and saw its wings come off and crash. It was Robinson's 10th victory and he would achieve seven more by the end of August, as Biggin Hill's Wing Leader.

Circus No.31 – 3 July

This operation followed close on the heels of the morning's outing, and the target was again the Hazebrouck marshalling yards. With rendezvous timed at 1500, it was a follow-up raid, not one organised due to the morning failure. Close Escort this time was from Kenley, with Hornchurch as the Cover Wing. Target Support, Tangmere and Biggin, with Rear Support from a 12 Group Wing (257, 266 and 401). Two Polish squadrons from Northolt formed an independent support role.

Again visibility was good despite the haze up to 4,000 feet and some very high cloud. The Blenheims went in at 10,000 feet, the bombs exploding in the town, south-west of the actual target. Some 109s edged in and one was thought to have been hit by air gunners which was last seen diving steeply.

The Close Escort was flying between 1–3,000 feet above the Blenheims and the situation was not helped when three bombers left the RV early which the main body found difficult to catch up with. Once over France Me109s could be seen either side of the formation but none approached before the target area was reached. As they flew back towards the coast, two 109s pounced, one firing at a 258 Squadron aircraft, while the other headed for a rear flanking bomber but both were driven off. One pilot in 312 Squadron claimed a 109 during a skirmish with some twenty enemy fighters.

The Cover Wing had several actions with 109s, and a couple were hit but only claimed as probables. One 109 attacked and shot down a Spitfire, its pilot taking to his parachute. However, Group Captain Harry Broadhurst, had seen the Spitfire shot down and went after the offending 109 with his Red Section, although his Number 3 and 4 could not keep up. Broadie and his wingman cut across the curve being flown by the German pilot, Red 1 opening fire whereupon the 109 dived into the ground. The two Spitfires were then attacked by two 109s and the pair broke in opposite directions, shook them off and reformed. However, the Group Captain had blacked out, completing the circle and upon recovery one 109 was in front of him, and starting an attack on his No.2. Being unable to fire in case he hit his companion, he had to wait until this 109 overshot and turned away. Broadhurst gave it a snap burst, seeing the 109's propeller jerk to a stop. His No.2 warned of more 109s approaching so they broke off and headed for the coast. They were continually harried by several 109s but managed to evade and get away.

A 54 Squadron pilot went for a 109 he saw shoot down a Spitfire and shot it down. The pilot was Canadian Flying Officer E. F. J. Charles. 603 Squadron saw some action, as their after-action report notes. Like most of the fighters on this operation, they had flown on the morning Circus and their ground crews had turned round the aircraft in less than two hours:

'Yellow 3, Sgt Neill, saw a Me109 coming towards him in a slight dive, and turned after it losing the rest of the section. He then climbed and saw a Me109 in a climbing turn. He fired at it, as it started to dive, at extreme range, no results were seen. Yellow 1 and 2, Flying Officer Prowse and Pilot Officer Falconer, dived after 5 Me109s 1,000 feet below them in echelon starboard. Yellow 1 attacked the right hand E/A which starting climbing. He closed to 350 yards and fired a short burst astern. E/A put his nose down and Yellow 1 followed, but his engine cut and E/A had drawn away to 500 yards and started climbing. Yellow 1 and 2 then at 15,000 feet, turned to port and saw an Me109F flying south near St. Omer. Yellow 1 got onto his tail. E/A climbed, Yellow 1 was catching it up and fired from 350 yards. E/A put his nose down, Yellow 1 followed but was slightly out-dived. Yellow 2 flew level waiting for E/A to climb again. E/A climbed again followed by Yellow 1, and Yellow 2 fired a five second burst from underneath Yellow 1, at E/A from 300 yards as E/A was on top of his climb. E/A then dived. Yellow 1 and 2 followed, and by this time were at 9,000 feet over Fruges. E/A then dived to 0 feet, Yellow 1 followed, and Yellow 2 stayed above. E/A then climbed, but Yellow 2 when within range was prevented from firing by his windscreen oiling up. Yellow 1 then gave E/A a final burst. Throughout this engagement E/A was emitting puffs of black smoke, mostly when climbing. These gradually increased in duration and density until E/A was last seen diving towards a wood with continuous thick black smoke. The E/A is claimed as a probable.

'Yellow 1 and 2 then went NW heading for Boulogne. They passed over Desvres, along the south perimeter of the aerodrome at 300 feet. They saw no gun posts or personnel, but about 12 'houses' with slits in the front through which they saw the airscrews of E/A. Each 'house' was between two trees which overhung the roof. They then passed a gun post on their left just north of Samer, and saw people standing about in their shirt sleeves who ran to the gun but did not fire. Then north of Alprech, they saw heavy guns and M.Gs, the guns were pointing SE. Men were inside the enclosures, 4 men to each gun. They wound the guns round and fired. M.G. bullets fell into the sea behind Yellow 1 and 2 and black flak bursts were seen accurate to a height but 200 yards behind. The apparent speed of the fusing astonished Yellow 1 and 2.'

The Yellow Section pair were H. A. R. (Harry) Prowse and J. A. R. (Hamish) Falconer. Prowse became a prisoner the next day failing to return from a Sweep in support of Circus 32, while Falconer went into the bag on 8 December during a Ramrod Operation, in a fight with JG26.

Tangmere and Biggin had some skirmishes too, the enemy tactics appearing to try tempting Spitfires to break away from the main formations and be attacked by larger groups of Messerschmitts hovering above. 609 Squadron managed to destroy one 109 (Michael Robinson's second of the day) and damage another, while 74 damaged one more. One pilot of 92 Squadron did not get back, ending up as a prisoner.

The 12 Group Wing had a problem due to one squadron becoming separated from the other two. Finding themselves alone, 266 Squadron reduced height to 21,000 feet but over France they became embroiled with a dozen Me109s. Some of these dived right through the Spitfire formation, splitting them up. The RAF pilots were already trying to avoid exploding AA shells. A dogfight started in which one German machine was claimed destroyed and three others damaged, but two Spitfires went down. One pilot was killed, the other captured. JG26 claimed four Spitfires for no loss. JG2 lost a fighter, its pilot baling out, and another 109 force-landed with combat damage; both pilots were wounded. RAF fighters claimed 6-5-5 this day, and a loss of six pilots and one Blenheim crew.

Leutnant Egon Mayer of 7./JG2 had scored twice on the 3rd, a Spitfire in the morning and another in this action, his ninth and tenth kills. Leutnant Seigfried Schnell of 9./JG2 claimed a Spitfire for his thirty-third. Mayer would achieve over 100 victories, all on the Western Front, until falling to American fighters on 2 March 1944.

* * *

Air Vice-Marshal N. H. Bottomley CIE DSO AFC, the Deputy Chief of the Air Staff, wrote to the AOC-in-C of Bomber Command at the Air Ministry, on 3 July 1941, the following two letters. [Norman Bottomley had, until recently, been SASO at HQ Bomber Command (1938–40), and OC 5 Bomber Group (1940–41)]. The AOC-in-C of Bomber Command was still Air Chief Marshal Sir Charles Portal:

Sir,

1. I am directed to refer to my letter of even reference date 27th June 1941, and to forward herewith a list of industrial establishments known to be working for the Germans in the Pas de Calais area.

2. I am to say that there are indications that the attack on these targets is likely to result in serious internal trouble, especially amongst the Communist element of the French workers, with consequent embarrassment to the Germans. There is even a suggestion that in view of the weakened German forces this unrest might develop into a revolt.

3. Such attacks are, moreover, considered to be the most profitable from the point of view of inducing the German fighters to accept combat with our own fighters.

4. These objectives are, therefore, to be regarded as having priority over those included in the appendix to my above quoted letter. [see Chapter 4]

5. I am to add that suitable leaflets, warning the French workers to keep away from factories now working for the Germans, have recently been dropped over the area in question. No restriction, therefore, is imposed on the attack of these targets, which should be delivered in strength as frequently as possible.

6. Any additions to this list will be forwarded as and when they are deemed necessary in the light of further information.

AVM Bottomley.

SECRET

Sir,

1. I am directed to refer to the daylight operations now being undertaken in the Pas de Calais area by No's 11 and 2 Groups in co-operation. The aim of these operations has up to now been to provide an opportunity for our fighters to engage and destroy the enemy fighters, and the activities of the bombers have been primarily directed to ensuring fighter combat.

2. In the light of the present strategical situation it is necessary to modify the aims of these operations. Their primary aim should now be the destruction of certain important targets by day bombing, and incidentally, the destruction of enemy fighter aircraft.

3. Although the tactical limitations of our fighter force must be given full consideration, targets are in future to be selected from the point of view of their value as bomber objectives. The fighter forces engaged are to be regarded as providing the bombers with the greatest possible freedom of action in carrying out their allotted tasks.

4. I am to say that a list of important targets within the area concerned have already been forwarded under cover of my letter of even reference, dated 27th June and 3rd July, together with an indication of priorities. I am to add that the change of aim indicated above is to be adopted with the least possible delay.

AVM Bottomley
Deputy Chief of the Air Staff

Copy to AOC-in-C, Fighter Command,
Stanmore.

No doubt this change of direction was partly to increase the pressure on the German defence forces now that Russia's Joseph Stalin was calling out for Britain to help alleviate their burdens on the Eastern Front. What Stalin really wanted was for Britain to invade France in order to divert enemy forces to the Western Front, but at this stage of the war any such plan lay years in the future.

Bottomley's letter caused Portal to ask his SASO, Air Vice-Marshal R. H. M. S. Saundby MC DFC AFC, to write to the AOC 3 Group, AVM J. E. A. Baldwin CB DSO, on 6 July, with a copy to Fighter Command HQ:

MOST SECRET

1. It is now necessary to enlarge the scope of the daylight bombing offensive with fighter escort which has previously been undertaken by No's 2 and 11 Groups. It has therefore been decided to use Stirlings for these operations.

2. The aim of these operations has, up to now, been to provide opportunities for our fighters to engage and destroy enemy fighters; the effort of the bombers being primarily directed towards forcing the enemy fighters to give battle. The primary aim is now to be the destruction of certain important targets by day bombing; the engagement of fighters being incidental to the bombing operations.

3. Although the potentialities and limitations of our fighter force must be given full consideration, you are to select targets, in consultation with AOC 11 Group, from the point of view of their value as bomber objectives and the fighter force will provide the bombers with the greatest possible freedom of action in their allotted bombing tasks.

4. A list of targets is attached as Appendix 'A' which includes a new section containing important industrial targets. These industrial establishments are known to be working for the enemy and there are indications that successful attacks on these targets may result in serious internal trouble, especially amongst the Communist elements, with consequent embarrassment to the Germans.

5. Leaflets warning French workers to keep away from factories working for Germany, have recently been dropped over the area. No restrictions, therefore, are imposed on the attack on these industrial targets which are to have first priority and which are to be attacked in strength as often as possible.

6. The use of Stirlings in daylight bombing attacks with fighter co-operation is to have first priority up to a maximum of eight sorties per day, but any not required for these operations are to be used for night bombing.

7. Detailed arrangements for these daylight operations may be made direct between yourself and AOC 11 Group. It will be necessary to arrange the approach, bombing run-up and turn away, so as to avoid throwing into confusion the large fighter formations accompanying the bombers.

Robert Saundby

* * *

At this stage it will be of interest to see what the RAF Intelligence people thought was the strength of the Luftwaffe opposition. This was an Appendix to a memo on Delegation of German-Soviet Air War:

Estimated Disposition of German Fighters on the Western Front

	Single Engine	Twin Engine	Total
Brest & Cherbourg	50	10	60
Le Havre & Dieppe	10	–	10
Pas de Calais	230/260 –	230/260	
Belgium & Holland	20	80/95	100/115
N.W. Germany	10	140/155	150/165
Norway	20	20	40
	340/370	250/280	590/650

* * *

Circus No.32 – 4 July

It was back to the Khulman Works and Power Station at Chocques again, on 4 July, with twelve Blenheims, six each from 21 and 226 Squadrons. Rendezvous with the Escort Wing (North Weald) took place over Southend at 1430 hours. Cover Wing by Biggin's squadrons, Target Support Hornchurch and Tangmere, and a 12 Group Wing as Rear Support made up the Balbo.

In tandem with this sortie, a further twelve Blenheims from 16 Group, escorted by Kenley and one squadron from Northolt, were going for the marshalling yards near Abbeville as a diversion tactic. However, the bombers and fighters failed to meet up and the diversionary bombers aborted. The fighters decided to patrol the French coast but saw nothing.

Once again the weather was good and enemy fighters were in evidence as soon as Circus 32 reached the French coast at Gravelines. The escorts kept the bombers free from attack and a good run up to the target was made. The twelve bombers aimed their bombs on target and one unloaded on a railway junction at Aire. One Blenheim of 226 was hit by flak and crashed near Dunkirk, only the navigator surviving as a prisoner.

The escorting wings were hard pressed most of the time to and from the target, 74 and 609 each losing a pilot, but claims of six destroyed, four probably so plus ten damaged were reported by the returning RAF pilots. Hornchurch failed to join up at the RV point and so headed out alone and reached the target just ahead of the main body. As the bombers appeared several Me109s began to dive down and in warding them off, claims of 8-2-2 were later made. On the way back 603 Squadron, finding themselves alone, were attacked but shot down one of the aggressors.

The Tangmere squadrons had few contacts with the enemy, only 616 having something of a scrap, claiming one probable and one damaged. Likewise, the Rear Support Wing had little to report.

The results appeared good. Scores of 15-7-14 for the loss of one bomber and three fighters looked impressive. Group Captain Harry Broadhurst, leading Hornchurch at the head of 54 Squadron, was involved in a virtual repeat of his actions the previous day. Once again he saw a Spitfire being chased by a 109. Almost at once the Spitfire trailed smoke and its pilot baled out. Broadhurst and his No.2 went after this 109 and after a short burst by the Groupie, the fighter dived into the ground. The pair were then attacked by another 109, both RAF men pulling round in opposite directions. So steep was his turn that Broadhurst blacked out, but coming too, found himself, as he had on the 3rd, right behind the 109, with his own No.2 just ahead of it. As the 109 pulled sideways, Broadhurst got in a telling burst and the 109 went down.

The enemy fighter pilots suffered the loss of JG26's Ltn. Joachim Kehrhahn, killed on only his second mission, while another pilot baled out. JG2 lost three of their fighters, with one pilot killed and another injured. Of the four claims by JG26, Priller was credited with a Spitfire as his thirtieth kill. JG2 pilots put in eleven victory claims over Spitfires, and for good measure, claimed the Blenheim as well! Leutnant Siegfried

Schnell, of 9./JG2, excelled himself, claiming and being credited with four Spitfires – victories thirty-four to thirty-seven. Twenty-five-years-old 'Wumm' Schnell was obviously keen to get his score to forty which should produce for him the *Eichenlaubs* (oak leaves) to his Knight's Cross.

Of the three missing RAF pilots, one had been killed (74 Sqn), while the two others (603 and 609) were captured. A veteran of the Battle of Britain, 609's Canadian F/O A. Keith Oglivie DFC (who had also been wounded in the left arm and shoulder) had seen considerable combat with 609. As well as six confirmed victories, his record also indicated four probables and three damaged. In March 1944 he was one of those who escaped from Stalag Luft III. Recaptured and interrogated by the Gestapo, he was lucky not to be among the fifty who were subsequently murdered.

On this day awards to fighter pilots were announced. Wing Commander Douglas Bader added a Bar to his DSO, while DFCs went to S/Ldr Ken Holden of 610, F/Lt R. D. Grassick of 242, F/O Jack Charles of 54 and W/Cdr F. S. Stapleton, Wing Leader of Hornchurch (when Broadhurst wasn't leading it).

Circus No.33 – 5 July

Although it must now be obvious to the top echelons of the RAF that casualties inflicted upon the enemy fighters over France were very much inflated, it was equally obvious they could not make this generally known. Had it been, support for these Circus operations would have floundered and the political fallout would have been considerable. They were left with little choice but to continue these operations, as well as the variety of other missions, such as Rodeos, Roadsteads, Sweeps and Rhubarbs, in order to show the Germans that they must keep looking over their shoulder while battling the Russians. Not that the Germans were any too worried at this stage of the war. Their offensive against Russia was going well, and the North African campaign, while not a sweeping success, was still going reasonably well for the Axis forces operating there.

However, the 'powers that be' insisted operations not only continue but be increased, now that summer was upon them. What they hoped to achieve, other than losing even more fighter pilots, is unclear. It was almost like the First World War, where generals continued to send thousands of men 'over the top' into barbed wire and machine-gun fire, in the hope of a victory.

Although losses amongst the 2 Group Blenheim squadrons had been comparatively light during Circus operations, a different, and bigger bait was introduced on Circus 33. Following the correspondence between Bottomley, Portal, Saundby and Baldwin, four-engined Short Stirling bombers from Baldwin's 3 Group would now be used. Just how the Stirling crews viewed this need not be asked. Bomber Command was now primarily a night-raiding force and few sorties were flown in daylight by the 'heavies'. In daylight operations the RAF's big bombers presented large targets, not only for fighters but flak gunners too, but at least their bomb loads would be heavier. It is interesting to note that while it had been suggested by Bob Saundby that up to eight sorties could be flown per day, only twice was this total achieved – or perhaps allowed by 3 Group – with individual raids generally comprising just three bombers.

The target for this first Stirling effort was again the Fives/Lille Steel and Engineering works and the marshalling yards at Abbeville, missed on the 4th. The squadron chosen for this first Stirling operation was 15 (XV) based at RAF Wyton. Two bombers would go to Lille, one to Abbeville as a diversion. Squadron Leader S. W. B. Menaul and F/Lt R. S. Gilmour would go to Lille, F/O F. Thompson RAAF and crew to Abbeville. Sidling up to the first two as Escort Wing were 258, 312, 485 and 308 Squadrons from Kenley and Northolt. Escort Cover – Hornchurch; Target Support – Biggin and Tangmere; Rear Support, 12 Group Wing (19, 257 and 401) from Coltishall. The Abbeville Stirling was escorted by North Weald and Hornchurch Wings.

The Stirlings bombed from 12,000 feet, bursts being seen on a building in the north-east corner of the factory and also on a built-up area between the target and the railway. Flak was the main problem although some Me109s did attempt to penetrate the escort. These 109s came down in a power dive from 25,000 feet and getting a shot at them was almost impossible. One Messerschmitt, however, was claimed by 485 Squadron. Similarly, the Hornchurch Wing saw a number of 109s but were unable to give combat, although one 109 was damaged. 54 Squadron lost a pilot (killed), while 308 had a pilot bale out over the Channel and later rescued.

Target Support fighters also saw any number of 109s round the edges, and only a few tried to get to the bombers, and two of these were sent away damaged. Again, enemy tactics seemed more in tune with trying to tempt fighters away from the main group, while others refused combat altogether. Tangmere too had little success but 610 claimed a 109 destroyed, while 145 claimed a probable and a damaged. 616 Squadron also lost a pilot near Lille, who was taken prisoner.

Meantime the third Stirling, dropped 18 x 500lb bombs across the target without the slightest opposition, and it and the escort all returned with nothing to report, so no enemy aircraft had been diverted from the main action. Total claims were 2-1-5 for the loss of three Spitfires and two pilots. JG26 claimed three Spitfires but possibly only two were confirmed, while JG2 claimed one also. No German fighters were lost.

Circus No.34 – 6 July

Three Stirlings of 7 Squadron were on this show on the morning of the 6th, their targets being the power plants at Yainville (F/O D. T. Witt DFC) on the River Seine and nearby Le Trait (W/Cdr H. R. Graham and S/Ldr R. W. Cox DFC) also on the Seine, near Rouen, in Upper Normandy. Kenley provided the Escort Wing, plus one squadron from Northolt, while Rear Support came from Tangmere. With such a small force it was obviously not thought to be a big event and so it proved. The force went out and back in over Beachy Head, bombs fell into the target area but were seen to either go into a river or on its banks. Just three 109s were seen, 303 Squadron claiming one probably destroyed.

Circus No.35 – 6 July

Obviously the big event on the 6th was this one, timed for the afternoon. This operation called for six Stirlings to make the raid, going back to Lille and the Fives/Lille Engineering Works. 15 Squadron provided the bombers, flying in two vics of three, led by S/Ldr S. W. B. Menaul and S/Ldr T. W. Piper respectively.

The Escort Wing was a mix. Hornchurch provided 222 Squadron, 71 and 242 came from North Weald while Northolt provided 306 Squadron. Treble-Two had recently arrived from the north and were at Manston. Cover Wing went to Biggin Hill, Target Support Wings were those of Hornchurch, Tangmere and Northolt. A 12 Group Wing of 56, 65 and 601 Squadrons were given Rear Support and a Low Support Wing – something new – was assigned to Kenley, but they were only to maintain a Readiness State unless called for.

The day was generally fine and clear with just a hint of haze, but allowing visibility to extend to twenty miles or so. The six bombers made rendezvous over Manston, then headed south to make landfall at Gravelines. Lille was reached at 1428 hours and they made their bomb run from 14,000 feet, dropping 24 x 1,000lb and 56 x 500lb bombs. Those watching their fall reported at least two and possibly three sticks registering direct hits on the target, which was left enveloped in brown/yellowish smoke. Other bombs fell onto the nearby marshalling yards and on the railway junction to the south, which caused more smoke. A couple of 109s made a brief attack, hitting and damaging one of the bombers, flown by F/Lt R. S. Gilmore DFC, in the second vic, but they were driven off by Hurricanes. Sergeant Ward, in this Stirling's front turret, damaged a 109.

In all the Escort Wing counted some twenty-five 109s and it was F/Lt C. G. Peterson of 71 Squadron that claimed the 109 – probably destroyed. This was the start of the Eagle Squadron's running fight with 109s back to the coast. Pilot Officer G. A. Daymond claimed one destroyed, while P/O W. R. Dunn probably destroyed another, shared with a 306 Squadron pilot. It was Idaho-born Chesley 'Pete' Peterson's first claim and he would go on to score seventeen times by mid-May 1943, of which eight were deemed as destroyed. By the latter date he was flying with the US 8th Army Air Force's 4th Fighter Group (two victories). 'Gus' Daymond had scored his second confirmed victory, four days after his first. From Montana, Gus would go on to be the top-scorer from all three Eagle squadrons, with seven kills. Bill Dunn would also make a name for himself, although he had already been in the news. Acting as a Lewis gunner in 1940, serving with the Seaforth Highlanders of Canada, he had helped shoot down two Ju87 Stuka dive-bombers from the ground in August 1940. Joining the RAF in December 1940 he was, remarkably, a pilot with the Eagles by April 1941 and his first victory had also been scored on 2 July. An ace with 71 Squadron, he would later fly with the 406th US Fighter Group and would score further victories in 1944.

Two pilots of 242 Squadron also claimed hits on 109s, while 222, encountering twenty Me109s at 16,000 feet damaged one. One problem the close escort found was that the second vic of bombers had lagged behind the first three by about half a mile, which made protection difficult.

The Biggin Hill Wing flew in layers from 18 to 25,000 feet, with the top squadron weaving in sections slightly ahead of the main bomber formation. They engaged in a running fight with an estimated twenty 109s and the Wing claimed three destroyed but lost three pilots. Malan claimed one of them, while Sgt W. G. Lockhart, who often flew as Malan's wingman, but today was No.2 to S/Ldr S. T. Meares (74's CO), bagged the other two. While the Circus report noted three losses, in fact four pilots of the Wing didn't get back. One of them was Lockhart, so it was other pilots that put in the two claims on his behalf. Two other 74 Squadron pilots went down, one, P/O W. M. Skinner DFM, was a Battle of Britain veteran, shot down by JG26 to become a prisoner. Bill Skinner had achieved eleven victories in the Battle (including three shared) and damaged three more. 92 Squadron had also had a pilot killed. Guy Lockhart, baled out and was taken captive but he escaped and managed to evade to Spain and eventually Gibraltar from where he was flown home in October.

(Lockhart later flew clandestine missions with Lysanders into France and received the DFC, but in 1942 he crashed and had once more to evade south and was back in England by September. He received the DSO but was not finished with operational flying for he became a Mosquito bomber pilot, receiving a Bar to his DFC, and then commanded a Lancaster squadron. Sadly he was shot down and killed by a German night-fighter in April 1944.)

Sailor Malan had decided to extract himself from the fight with the twenty-plus 109s after having become separated from his No.2 – who today was Biggin's Station Commander, Group Captain P. R. Barwell DFC – so headed down in a series of half-rolls and aileron turns. At very low level he straightened out and headed for the sea but then noticed two shadows on the ground, his and a 109. Discovering a lone 109 at 500 feet he swung in behind the German machine and shot it down. However, moments later his Spitfire took hits, three bullets actually grazing his flying helmet, ricocheting off the inside of his windscreen and into his instrument panel. A quick glance back revealed six 109s queuing up to have a go at him. By this time he had pulled into a hard turn and dropping to just 50 feet above the French countryside, evaded towards the coast, coming under much ground fire as he zipped over the beach and out to sea. Shells and bullets churned up the sea around him but he got away with it.

The pilots of 609 Squadron had also been in a fight. They had been top cover and had observed flak bursting at 20,000 feet! On the way back, two Belgian pilots, F/O J. H. M. Offenberg and P/O R. F. F. G. Malengreau were the last pair at the rear of the squadron. This was the first time they had flown together and when Jean Offenberg spotted a 109 coming in behind he called a warning, but used the wrong name. Roger Malengreau, unaware he was the target, made no move and as Offenberg watched, he saw his wingman's machine begin to trail glycol, with its engine stop. He called a 'Mayday' and summoned the rest of 609 to assist. With many Spitfires in attendance, Malengreau successfully glided across the Channel and over the English coast – at 2,000 feet – and crash-landed down-wind into a hayfield beside a road south of Deal. As other Spitfires circled, he climbed out and waved up at them, unhurt but more experienced! Jean Offenberg kept a written record of his wartime service which subsequently became the origin of the book '*The Lonely Warrior*' published in 1956. It was his journal, edited by Victor Houart. Regarding his other experiences this day, Offenberg wrote:

'We escorted four Stirlings to Albert, near Amiens. The raid was carried out without incident and we did not meet the least opposition. It was almost kid glove warfare. But I was certain that it could not continue like this and sooner or later a cloud would disclose a swarm of Messerschmitts. For a good hour we had been frolicking with impunity above their territory and nothing had happened.

'I was Blue 1, and all went well until we got over Le Touquet, when I noticed an Me109 attacking my No.4. "Blue 4, break immediately. Break, break." He broke off and I banked to port without getting excited. Yesterday in the same manoeuvre I had only managed to go down in a spin. Gently...

'The Boche dived below me. I did a roll on the way down and followed suit and we both dived almost vertically. I must get him... I must get him... He had seen me and continued in his breath-taking dive. The water rushed up towards me and I was suddenly afraid. I no longer dared to look at my air speed indicator.

'I was following him at 400 yards exactly on a line with him. We should both break our necks if we went on at that speed. The water drew dangerously close and I was afraid of a black-out. I pulled on the stick, flattened out and then for a second I saw nothing. I really had blacked-out. I have no idea how long I was in this state.

'As soon as I could see again I noticed an enormous splash in the centre of a fleet of a dozen fishing boats some miles from the French coast. The Me, in this crazy dive, had not been able to pull out and had crashed at 500 mph into the sea. I had not fired a single bullet, but Sgt Evans, my No.4, was missing. I did not think that the Messerschmitt was in a good firing position when I first spotted him.'

The Hornchurch Wing also lost a pilot over Lille – Sgt N. J. Smith – who became a prisoner. However, 611 claimed three destroyed, one of them going to F/Lt E. S. Lock, the other two to Sgt W. M. Gilmour. Eric Lock was another high-scoring veteran of the 1940 battles, having by this time achieved more than twenty victories, a DSO and a DFC and Bar. Mac Gilmour was about to receive the DFM for he had already claimed four victories plus a couple of damaged. He would later be commissioned and end the war as a squadron leader, with a DFC, and nine confirmed victories, flying in both North Africa and later, while commanding a Mustang squadron at the time of D-Day. Tangmere reached the target area and orbited it for twenty minutes as the bombers attacked. On the way back any number of 109s made half-hearted attacks on the Spitfires but never seemed to press home their assaults, which allowed the Wing to claim four 109s, one probable and one damaged for the loss of one pilot (the report said) but in fact two. One was 145's F/Lt M. A. Newling DFC, who went down over Lille and was killed. Mike Newling, was yet another Battle of Britain veteran lost to Fighter Command.

Sergeant J. A. McCairns of 611 Squadron was the other loss, crash-landing at Gravelines. James McCairns was taken prisoner and ended up in Stalag IXC. In January 1942 he managed to escape and make his way through Belgium, and eventually helped by the Resistance, got into Spain, then Gibraltar and home. He was awarded the Military Medal, and like Lockhart, later became a Lysander pilot, taking agents into France. Commissioned, he went on to receive the DFC and Two Bars for this work with 161 (Special Duties) Squadron.

The two Polish squadrons from Northolt only saw a couple of 109s, one of which tried to attack them but dived away without firing. The 12 Group Wing had nothing to report although one pilot from 56 Squadron was forced to bale out over England and was not hurt. Kenley Wing was not called upon to support the raid.

Bouchier's report noted six RAF pilots lost, although in fact there were seven, plus the Spitfire of 56 lost over England. RAF fighter pilots claimed 11-6-5, recorded as a most successful operation '…in which the target was hit with great accuracy and weight of bombs and serious casualties inflicted on enemy fighters.'

Hauptmann Rolf Pingel's First Group of JG26 had made contact with Circus 35 over Lille and battled with the Spitfires until a shortage of fuel forced a break-off over the Channel. JG26 claimed seven Spitfires and reported just two of their own fighters as damaged. JG2 was soon engaged and claimed six Spitfires for no loss. Hauptmann Walter Adolph, leader of II Gruppe, shot down one from 74 Squadron for his nineteenth victory, while Ltn. Horst Ulenberg, leader of 2 Staffel, gained his twelfth and thirteenth kills. Leutnant Paul Galland, younger brother to Adolf Galland, flying with the 8th Staffel, gained his first victory

Among JG2's claimants was Ltn. Siegfried Schnell of the 9th Staffel, who gained his thirty-eighth victory, and Obfw. Rudolf Täschner, 1st Staffel, scored twice for his thirteenth and fourteenth victories. The lack of known losses is worrying, so again the RAF pilots were a trifle over-confident in their claiming.

Circus No.36 – 7 July

With fine weather (noted as perfect with no cloud) continuing there was no let up in day operations. Circus 36 on the morning of 7 July called for a single Short Stirling bomber to bomb Hazebrouck's marshalling yards. The escort was similarly modest with Close Escort of three fighter squadrons from North Weald (2) and Hornchurch (1), while Cover was provided by two Polish squadrons from Northolt. Hornchurch's other units took on Target Support with Rear Support going to 12 Group. The object, of course, was for this operation to be a diversion for Circus 37, scheduled for a short time later.

The lone 15 Squadron bomber, piloted by P/O Stokes, picked up its escort over North Foreland at 0920 hours, proceeded to the target where 24 x 500lb bombs went down from 8,000 feet, although most fell in a nearby field. Some flak was encountered over the coast but none over the target. No enemy fighters deemed it necessary to engage.

Of the close escorts, only 303 Squadron spotted four 109s but had no chance of attacking. Hornchurch saw a few 109s they assumed were decoys and made no attempt at intercepting, and on the way home ten 109s made an attack on 603 Squadron without hurt and two more came down on them over the Channel with similar results. Hornchurch squadrons had a slight tussle with 109s and Group Captain Harry Broadhurst – hit by gunfire, began to spin down to 6,000 feet where he was engaged again and chased by six 109s off Gravelines. He turned and engaged them, claiming two shot down. The Wing only suffered one Spitfire (603) slightly damaged by flak, and Broadhurst's machine that was shot about.

The Rear Support Wing patrolled at heights from 20–24,000 feet, in fours, and saw a few 109s but did not engage. Initial claims of one destroyed and three probables were made for no loss. Pips Priller of JG26 had in fact attacked – and claimed – the Spitfire flown by Broadhurst although he got home. It should have been his thirty-second kill.

Circus No.37 – 7 July

In Bouchier's report on Circus 36, he wrote that the main object (that of diverting enemy fighters from Circus 37 which closely followed) had been successful, however, there were so few 109s seen and engaged, that one has to wonder. Most probably British radar picked up enemy aircraft being scrambled, but the Germans appear to have quickly reasoned that this might be a feint and had either ordered their pilots not to engage, or perhaps they had themselves picked up signs of another build up of aircraft across the Channel. In any event, Circus 37, which consisted of four 7 Squadron Stirlings – led by S/Ldr D. Speare - had made rendezvous with their escorts over Hastings at 1000. Their target, deemed important by Bouchier, was the Potez aircraft factory at Méaulte, south of Albert.

Crossing the coast at Berck they ran into the target at 8,000 feet and dropped 20 x 1,000lb, 39 x 500lb bombs and 940 x 4lb incendiaries. One stick of bombs went straight across the factory buildings while a second hit other buildings and part of the factory. Two more sticks went across more buildings and houses west of the factory, while the incendiaries appeared to start fires across the whole target. Smoke, debris and dust covered the area as the bombers headed north-west.

Biggin's squadrons, flying Close Escort, encountered six 109s on the return flight at 23,000 feet and a fight developed. Two 109s were claimed destroyed and two damaged. Two RAF fighters were shot down but their pilots, one each from 74 and 609, parachuted into the sea and were rescued, though wounded. Tangmere with the Support Wing task, saw some 109s but made no attacks, and all aircraft were reported back safely. However, one pilot of 145 Squadron had been wounded but managed to land back at base. His machine was so badly damaged that it was written off.

JG26 had again been in the fight and claimed four Spitfires. Priller had claimed again, number thirty-three. There had been no 109 losses. Bouchier's report mentions that the earlier diversion had helped draw off German fighters from this main attack and this, together with good bombing results, made it yet another successful operation.

Circus No.38 – 7 July

On the afternoon of this 7th day of July, a third Circus was mounted, this time three Stirlings from 15 Squadron – led by S/Ldr Menaul - would go for the Kuhlmann Power Station and Chemical Works at Chocques. Kenley would be Close Escort, Tangmere as Escort Cover, Northolt and Biggin got the Support Wing task while Hornchurch would 'Mop Up'.

Weather had continued fine throughout the day and meeting up over Rye the bombers and close escort fighters headed for France shortly before 1500. The bombs went down from 9,600 feet – 15 x 1,000lb and 42 x 500lb. A few undershot but the rest straddled the target, with a direct hit being seen on one of the cooling towers and another on one of the ammonic tanks, with others on nearby buildings. More bombs hit the power station and as the crews headed for the English Channel, the whole area behind them was enveloped in brown smoke.

Flak had been heavy on the way in and only after the bombing did a few 109s come diving out of the sun through the Kenley fighters, but they kept going so fast and so steeply they could not be engaged. Tangmere's Wing was also attacked, but again suffered no losses, although one 616 pilot had to crash-land back at Hawkinge.

The Northolt Poles all saw 109s but only 308 Squadron was engaged with any result – claiming three destroyed with another probable. The pilot claiming the probable later said he came down very low after his 109 and as it went through cloud, debris and masses of smoke were then seen rising to 2,000 feet. Biggin Hill had a scrap, 92 Squadron claiming a 109 destroyed and another damaged and 74 Squadron said they lost a pilot when jumped by some 109s, but there appears to be only the two losses that occurred on the earlier Circus 37, so perhaps a clerical error somewhere!

Hornchurch had been stepped up to 30,000 feet and made a sweep over Merville and came out over Hardelot. Only then did they spot any 109s but they quickly dived when they saw the Spitfires overhead. One pilot was chased inland by 109s but managed to evade them.

In all, the RAF claimed four 109s destroyed, one probable and one damaged. This day one Spitfire was claimed by JG26, while JG2 reported three Spitfires and two Hurricanes shot down for the loss of one pilot, Obfw. Hans Tilly. Hauptmann Hans Hahn of Stab III/JG2 claimed the Hurricanes for victories twenty-six and twenty-seven, even though no Hurricanes were lost. Leutnant Erich Rudorfer of Stab II./JG2 claimed Spitfires, kills number twenty-one and twenty-two, while Obfw. Kurt Bühlingen's claim over a Spitfire brought his score to twelve. During the day JG26 had two 109s make force-landings, while JG2 also suffered one.

As a complete aside to this day's activities, some Blenheims of 105 and 139 Squadrons flew an anti-shipping sortie to the Dutch coast. One was shot down by a flak ship and two more to fighters of JG52. One of the German fighter pilots was 43–year–old Major Dr. Erich Otto Friedrich Mix. Mix had been a pilot in WW1 and achieved three combat victories in 1918. Despite his age he had flown with JG2 during the French campaign in 1939–40 and added five more kills to his total, then a ninth during the Battle of Britain. The Blenheim on this date was his eleventh and last victory. He survived the war and died in 1971.

7 July 1941, with three Circus operations, saw the loss of just three RAF pilots wounded, but Fighter Command had claimed 7-1-4, while the Germans admitted one pilot killed and three 109s force-landed.

Something that came out of these operations was that it was suggested all support wings, particularly the rear ones, be given a definite time of withdrawal, for example, ten minutes after the bombers left the French coast. Also, that a rear support squadron be again used, flying at a very low height off the British coast. This followed the experience of Sailor Malan, who had been chased by 109s as far as Manston, while several of 74's aircraft had also been chased back and been hit by machine-gun fire. If a harassed RAF pilot thought he was in trouble he could call Control for help from the rear support squadron.

Circus No.39 – 8 July

On Tuesday, 8th July the weather continued fair, so Circus 39, with three 7 Squadron Stirlings, was mounted, led by S/Ldr R. W. Cox. The target was the Works and Power Plant north-east of Lens, and the Power Station at Mazingarbe. Kenley gave Close Escort, Biggin the Cover Wing and Target Support by Hornchurch and Tangmere. Rear Support went to Hornchurch and Northolt Wings.

Rye was again the RV point - at 0600 - and making landfall near Boulogne they were met by heavy AA fire, causing the bombers to veer down the coast and cross near Hardelot. Two Stirlings went for Lens, the other to Mazingarbe. Both those going to Lens bombed the target, the second one putting its bombs right amidst the explosions of the first. A large mushroom-shaped smoke pall rose up, edged in red flames. This was soon followed by a sheet of flame as the bombers headed away. However, only one of the two bombers returned. One had been hit by flak which damaged the starboard inner engine and the other crew reported that they had seen it receive a direct hit by German AA. Soon afterwards the Stirling went down to crash near Béthune losing its starboard wing as it fell. Only two of the seven-man crew survived as prisoners, P/O R. D. Morley and the others all perished.

The Mazingarbe bomber dropped 5 x 1,000 and 10 x 500lb bombs which mostly overshot, but one bomb did hit a gasometer which exploded in flames. As the crew looked back, smoke was rising to some 2,000 feet.

Kenley Wing protected the bombers the whole way and over the target some 109s attacked. One was shot down by 312 Squadron. On the way out several other 109s made attacks but did not press them home, but all the same, three Spitfires went down, one each from the three squadrons, 258, 312 and 485. One pilot was killed, one taken prisoner but a Czech pilot, Sgt J. Mensik, managed to evade capture. Given some civilian clothes by a farmer, he walked from the Pas-de-Calais to Paris, which took him two weeks and once there, it took him eight days to recover from it. He was then guided to Bordeaux by the end of July, then made his own way to Marseille. Staying there for two weeks he was finally guided over the Pyrenees, but he and two others, including Lockhart (74 Sqn), and F/O D. N. Forde (145 Sqn who would be shot down on 23 July) were picked up by Spanish police. In early September the British military attaché managed to secure their release. Eventually reaching Gibraltar, Josef Mensik was flown home on 21 October 1941. Sadly he was killed in a flying accident in 1943.

Biggin Hill's pilots also had skirmishes with the Messerschmitts. Soon after crossing into France one 109 dived out of the sun and fired off two white Very lights as he half-rolled over the formation. On the way home further 109s arrived and in the subsequent dogfights, one 109 was destroyed and another damaged, although two RAF pilots came down in the sea, but were rescued by ASR, one from 609, the other from 92 Squadrons. Pilot Officer Percy H. Beake was the latter, who went on to be a successful Typhoon pilot and leader, receiving the DFC.

Hornchurch had similar experiences, having any number of combats, to and from the target. Its pilots claimed five 109s destroyed, with two more probably so and four damaged. One Spitfire was damaged and its pilot crash-landed near Canterbury, a second crash-landed at base, but both men were unhurt.

Some ten 109s were claimed, plus three probables and seven damaged. One of the confirmed was by the Hornchurch Wing Leader, W/Cdr F. S. Stapleton – his third confirmed success. The RAF lost four Spitfires, two Hurricanes with three pilots missing. 3./JG2 (Specht) got one of the Hurricanes, Siegfried Schnell claimed a Spitfire for victory number thirty-nine, and JG26 claimed two Spitfires.

Circus No.40 – 8 July

It was back to the Kuhlmann Works and the Lille Power Station on this sunny afternoon, some of the RAF pilots flying for the second time this day. Squadron Leader Piper led three 15 Squadron Stirlings, making RV over Manston at 1500; the plan being for two aircraft to attack the first target, the third one the second. With the targets reached, a total of 15 x 1,000lb bombs went down but by this time extreme evasive action was in progress due to heavy and accurate AA fire. In fact, all three bombers received flak damage, although Piper's aircraft was only slightly damaged. Flying Officer Campbell's Stirling was attacked and damaged by a fighter, while P/O Needham's aircraft was badly damaged by the AA fire. As they flew north the crews could make out large columns of smoke in the target area. Only one Me109 attacked on the way back causing further minimal damage to Piper's aircraft.

All three squadrons from Hornchurch, flying Escort, had skirmishes with 109s, some being reported as having red noses. The 109s attempted to penetrate the screen to the bombers but all failed. The Cover Wing (Northolt) was also engaged without any results but 303 Squadron had two of its pilots shot down while a third returned wounded. One of the losses was its CO, S/Ldr T. A. Arentowicz, aged 31, who, like the other loss, was killed. In this fight 109s came in and made simultaneous rear-quarter attacks from both sides.

Hornchurch, flying Target Support, operated at 22–26,000 feet above the target as the bombers approached, then came down to 20,000 where they circled until the bombers were over the target. Fourteen Me109s flew across from east to west at 26,000 feet then dived in echelon on a section of 603 Squadron, flying the middle layer, and the Spitfires split up. Four other 109s attacked 611 Squadron acting as rearguard. One pilot in 603 claimed two 109s – Sgt G. W. Tabor – while other Wing pilots added a further two destroyed, two probables and a damaged. Squadron Leader R. F. Boyd DFC and Bar, CO of 54 Squadron, claimed one of these, bringing his personal score, including shares, to nineteen of an eventual twenty-one (fourteen destroyed and seven others shared). 611 Squadron had one pilot killed.

The Tangmere Wing also lost one pilot from 610 Squadron while F/Lt R. A. Lee Knight of this unit claimed a 109 destroyed. He was shortly to receive the DFC but would not survive the year. Meantime the 12 Group Diversion Wing (56, 65 and 601 Squadrons) patrolled from St Omer to Gravelines, shooting down one of two 109s they encountered. They then reduced height to maintain cover patrol and met an estimated fifty Me109s and in the combat that ensued, claimed two destroyed and one probable. One of the destroyed was claimed by the Wing Leader, W/Cdr R. R. S. Tuck DSO DFC and Two Bars. Tuck had seen considerable action over Dunkirk and throughout the Battle of Britain and this was his twenty-eighth victory, of an eventual twenty-nine, plus innumerable probables and damaged.

Only one pilot of the Kenley Rear Support Wing saw anything, having been attacked by a 109. He turned sharply and claimed to have shot it down near the Goodwins. This was P/O C. Stewart, who was to be shot down and killed three days later. Stewart's claim was one of a total of another ten 109s claimed destroyed, making twenty-one in all for the day. On this later operation three more were deemed probables and two damaged. The RAF recorded seven pilots as missing on Circus 40, thus ten missing for the day, plus two wounded. In total fourteen fighters lost or struck off.

German radar picked up the raid at 1510 and sent three Gruppen of JG26 into the air. The First Gruppe claimed six Spitfires, II Gruppe claimed three. JG2 claimed eight Spitfires for the loss of one pilot; JG26 also lost one pilot, Uffz. Karl Finke. Another pilot, Uffz. Albrecht Held, was reported to have suffered wing failure north of St Omer and also died. Hauptmann Adolph, the leader of II Gruppe, gained his twentieth victory this afternoon, while Pips Priller scored his thirty-fourth. Seigfried

Schnell of JG2 claimed his second victory of the day, making a nice round forty for his score, while Hptm. Hahn reached twenty-eight. The difference between RAF claims of 21-9-9, against three 109s actually lost defies adequate explanation! For Bouchier, he noted that this day saw yet another very successful operation.

The next day Schnell was notified of the award of the Oak Leaves to his Knight's Cross. He would continue on the Western Front until early 1944, bringing his score to eighty-seven. Posted to the Russian Front he was killed in action in February 1944 having achieved ninety-three victories. Hans 'Assi' Hahn would gain his Oak Leaves in August 1941 when his score had reached forty-two. Walter Adolph had claimed his last victory, failing to survive August 1941.

* * *

Air Vice-Marshal Norman Bottomley was still busy letter-writing. On 8 July he sent a letter to the AOC-in-C of Bomber Command:

SECRET

Enemy tactics to counter daylight sweeps

Sir,

1. I am directed to inform you that a prisoner of war who was recently under interrogation gave particulars of the tactics adopted by the enemy in dealing with daylight sweeps carried out over Northern France.

2. It appears from this interrogation that the enemy are adopting the tactics which were instituted in Fighter Command towards the end of the Battle of Britain. Special high flying 'reconnaissance' fighter aircraft examine the British sweeps as they reach the coast and report whether bombers are, or are not, present. If bombers are in the formation then fighters are instructed to engage. On the other hand if no bombers are reported the enemy fighters are instructed to avoid combat.

3. It is suggested that in order to counter this manoeuvre it might be possible on occasion for bomber formations to accompany fighter sweeps to within sight of the French coast. The bomber formation would then retire and the fighters would go on in the hope of engaging the enemy fighters sent up to intercept the formation.

4. It is requested that this tactic may be considered by the Air Officer Commanding-in-Chief, Bomber and Fighter Commands in collaboration, with a view to employing it as circumstances permit.

I am, Sir,
Your obedient Servant,
N. H. Bottomley, AVM

This tactic was introduced in due time, but rather than a bomber formation, when it was employed it tended to be a lone Blenheim from 60 Group that would be escorted from somewhere like Biggin Hill to the Kent coast around North Foreland, and then it would return, while the escorting fighters would head for the French coast.

*   *   *

In the previous chapter mention was made of Jeff West's comments to this author about Douglas Bader. He further recorded:

'When I first joined the Squadron our formation was generally twelve aircraft – two sections of three in a vic, from A and B Flights. A variation was a section of four aircraft, three in vic with the fourth flying in the box, behind and below each leader. It was found impossible to attack in either formation and we finished up with either three or four in line astern behind a leader. Naturally the leader got in the first shot and the remainder could not engage for fear of clobbering him. Once the leader broke away it was the understood thing for the No.2 to not lose touch with his No.1. After we had flown a few Sweeps, Douglas came down early one morning in his car, while the officers were still in their Mess, and we sergeants had been on Readiness for a dawn show and had not been advised of its cancellation the night before. Dogsbody[3] fixed that!

'However, he complained, in a nice way, that he could spend much more time over France looking for the Hun, if he did not have to return to base early because we were running short of fuel. He usually had plenty left with the similar tank capacity. I said to him that if he flew at the rear and had to weave furiously from side to side to see behind and below, he would find his fuel getting low, which was one of the reasons we experimented and designed the "finger four" formation, universally adopted by Tangmere [and all other fighter squadrons] in mid-1941.'

---

3. Dogsbody was Bader's call-sign in the air.

Chapter 6

Stirlings Forge Ahead

July 1941 continued with further raids by Short Stirling bombers. Not that this in itself gave any respite to the poor 2 Group Blenheim bombers, for they were heavily engaged in anti-shipping attacks, and some daylight raids such as bombing Rotterdam on the 16th (four lost). Two Blenheims were lost on anti-ship operations off Cherbourg on 14 July and three more on the 18th, then another two on the 19th off the Dutch coast, and yet another two on the 20th. It didn't end there. On 23 July six Blenheims went down to flak and fighters off the Scheldt Estuary, followed on the 30th with three lost bombing the Kiel Canal followed by four more lost against shipping off the Dutch coast. Another mass loss of Blenheims would occur on 28 August, seven lost again raiding Rotterdam.

Circus No.41 – 9 July

This operation called for three Stirlings of 15 Squadron, led by W/Cdr P. B. B. Ogilvie,[4] to attack the Synthetic Petrol, Ammonia, Alcohol, Tar and Coke plant at Mazingarbe, on the afternoon of 9 July.[5] RV with the Escort Wing (Kenley) was made over Rye at 13,000 feet at 1330. However, over France thick ground haze dictated a switch to the secondary target – the Power Station north of Béthune - where 15 x 1,000lb and 30 x 500lb bombs fell piecemeal over the target, some exploding on the northern area, others on the west, while others fell on houses to the north.

There was no sign of flak until after the bombing but it was then very heavy, and all three bombers received some damage. Fighters also attacked, and one of these was claimed by the defending air gunners.

On the way in 109s tried to get at the bombers but were thwarted by Kenley's Close Escort tactics and a pilot of 312 Squadron claimed a 109. After the bomb run more 109s came in head on, the Wing damaging one. Then a more serious assault was made by two groups of eight 109s and a dogfight broke out. One 312 Hurricane pilot baled out to become a prisoner, while the Wing Leader, W/Cdr J. R. A. Peel DFC, was forced down into the sea but was rescued. Johnny Peel had shot down a number of

---

4. W/Cdr Pat Ogilvie received the DSO and DFC, the latter for his part in attacking the German battleships at Brest, in December 1941.
5. 15 Squadron's Operational Record Book mentions Gosnay.

enemy aircraft during 1940, although he did not fly much again after this date, but the award of the DSO came in August. In response, one 109 was destroyed and another claimed as a probable.

Tangmere also suffered in this operation. The Wing, led by Douglas Bader DSO DFC, had broken up into sections of four and became embroiled in several fighter actions. Two pilots of 616 and another from 145 failed to return. The latter was killed, and one of the 616 pilots became a prisoner. However, the other one, S/Ldr E. P. P. Gibbs, who came down twelve miles east of Le Touquet, managed to evade. Edward Gibbs was a pre-war pilot who had been retained as an instructor until early 1941. After gaining experience with other squadrons he was made CO of 616 Squadron, and in the action on 9 July was to claim one 109 plus a probable. However, having then crash-landed in a field he was picked up by the Resistance and eventually got into Spain, then Gibraltar, and was flown home in September. He was flying operationally again before the year was out, and was leading the Middle Wallop Wing at the time of the Dieppe Raid in August 1942, having received the DFC and been Mentioned in Despatches.

There were seven squadrons from Hornchurch, Northolt and Biggin Hill that made up the Target Support Wings. Over the target area, one section of 611 Squadron was bounced from behind, and lost one pilot, while a second, badly damaged, managed to struggle back to crash-land on the beach near Dover. Another Section got into a scrap but they claimed a 109 destroyed and another damaged. 54 Squadron became engaged before reaching the target and engagements continued to well over the target. One Me109F was shot down, but two RAF pilots failed to return. One was taken prisoner (although he died through a bone disease in April 1942) and the other was killed.

Biggin Hill's boys reached the French coast stepped up from 25–30,000 feet and soon began to spot lurking Me109s. Three bursts of 'pointer flak' exploded from enemy coastal batteries and soon afterwards a small formation of 109s appeared. These and another group of six 109s were bounced and the Wing claimed six shot down and another probably destroyed. Jamie Rankin DFC, CO of 92, claimed one, his squadron getting all the others except one destroyed by F/Lt J. D. Bisdee of 609. John Bisdee had seen action in the Battle of Britain and this was his eighth victory. He was about to receive the DFC.

A pilot from 308 Squadron became separated and decided to head for home at low level. He came upon a lone 109 which he promptly shot down near St Omer. Other aircraft were seen by Wing pilots but no engagements resulted. All told twelve Me109s were claimed destroyed, plus one by the bombers, with three more probables and five damaged. The RAF admitted eight aircraft and seven fighter pilots lost, plus one wounded.

JG26 and JG2 had engaged the Circus just after 1400. The First Gruppe claimed four Spitfires, while III Gruppe got another but this was not confirmed. One Me109 had to make a force-landing with combat damage. JG2 claimed ten victories in this action and had one pilot killed in combat. There are no other known German losses recorded! Priller gained his thirty-fifth and thirty-sixth kills. As for JG2, Ltn. Erich Rudorffer claimed a Hurricane and a Spitfire, bringing his score to twenty-four (he probably shot down S/Ldr Gibbs). Leutnant Schnell managed to claim three Spitfires, while another up and coming ace, Ltn. Egon Mayer brought his score to twelve. Two hours after this action, Ltn. Schnell claimed to have shot down three more Spitfires, bringing his score to five for the day and forty-six overall. Would the award of his Oak Leaves sooth his 'sore throat'?

Circus No.42 – 10 July

That morning, and then later, there were two 'Gudgeon' Operations mounted, one against Cherbourg, the other to Le Havre. These operations comprised twelve Blenheims from 2 Group's 21 and 107 Squadrons, escorted by fighters from 10 Group. In effect these were 10 Group Circus missions. One Blenheim was shot down near Cherbourg on 'Gudgeon I' and all three crewmen were captured.

German fighters had reacted to these raids, eighteen bandits being picked up by radar over the sea. 1.Erg/JG2 (Ergänzungsgruppe, a unit supplying replacements for the main unit) got in amongst the raiders, Uffz. Heinz Scheibner claiming the Blenheim for his first victory. Three other pilots of the same unit also claimed their first kills – three Spitfires. A training unit, 4.(Eins.)/JFS 5 (Gruppe training unit) was also scrambled and although three pilots claimed Spitfires, only one was confirmed.

Ten Group fighters claimed five Me109s destroyed, one probable and one damaged, losing two Spitfires, with one Spitfire having Cat 2 damage, and its pilot wounded (234 Sqn). The losses were, W/Cdr M. V. Blake DFC who survived a ditching, and one other of 234 killed. Minden Blake was a successful Battle of Britain pilot and was CO of 234 and claimed two 109s before he was shot down. Exiting his downed fighter he got into his dinghy and began paddling towards England. He continued paddling for twelve hours before being spotted and rescued. Force-landing on the sea, his Spitfire immediately sank before he could get free but eventually did so. Afterwards he wrote:

'I remember seeing a seagull pass the wing tip then everything seemed to happen at once. Water flowed over me. Undid the straps and tried to get out but the parachute was holding me into the seat. The instinct was to release the parachute but I stifled the urge as the dinghy was in it. It was very dark and I realised the aircraft was over the vertical and well down, so twisted round in the cockpit and wriggled my head and shoulders out. I could see it was lighter in one direction which must be the way up. Kicked off and seemed to rise at an incredible speed. I felt like a cork as I burst out of the surface of the sea. I inflated the dinghy by turning on the CO_2 bottle and scrambled in. Fortunately it was calm but there was no land in sight. And it was dreadfully quiet. However, a slight wind began to blow me steadily north towards the Isle of Wight.'

In August 1942 Mindy Blake had a similar adventure but this time, although he paddled some five miles south of Dover, he was picked up by the German ASR service and made a PoW.

* * *

Towards midday Circus 42 was starting out, which comprised of three 7 Squadron Stirlings attacking the Khulman Chemical and Power Station at Chocques, yet again. This was the seventh visit to this target, the last being only two days earlier. The three bombers were piloted by P/O D. Witt, F/O C. V. Frazer DFC and F/O C. I. Rolfe. North Weald provided the Escort Wing with Northolt flying Cover, the Biggin Hill squadrons above them on High Cover. Hornchurch and Tangmere flew Target Support while three squadrons from Kenley and Northolt acted as Rear Support. There was 10/10th cloud over the Channel up to 1,000 feet on this Thursday, with haze up to 12,000 feet, so it was going to be a day for careful watchfulness.

The bombers made RV over Rye at 1200 hours and although the plan had been to cross the hostile coast south of Hardelot, they went in near Boulogne amidst some heavy and accurate AA fire, resulting in one Stirling being hit and falling into the sea. One parachute was seen but in the event all seven crew members of F/O Fraser's crew perished. Cecil Fraser had received the DFC in 1940 flying with 115 Squadron. Flak had scored a direct hit on the Stirling's port-inner engine which presumably ruptured a fuel tank, for almost immediately the bomber was blazing fiercely.

The other two pressed on, one bombing the Works, the other nearby marshalling yards. Pilot Officer Rolfe, who bombed the Works, had his machine hit about the tail unit by a German fighter but got back safely. However, the bomber's mid-upper gunner thought he had hit the attacking 109, despite which it followed them right across the Channel. The pilot was Hptm. Rolf Pingel, commander of JG26's First Gruppe. With his engine coughing he began to lose height, and was then set upon by Spitfires of 306 Squadron, and Sgt J Smigielski forced him to land in a wheat field near St Margaret's Bay, Kent. Pingel, who had achieved twenty-two victories during 250 combat missions became a prisoner, having delivered to the RAF its first intact example of a Me109F-2 that was quickly sent off to the Air Fighting Development Unit for evaluation, trials and mock combats. However, the Germans were soon using the F-4 model, which was a much improved version. Pingel was a very experienced fighter pilot, having gained four victories in the Spanish Civil War. In September 1940 he had been awarded the Knight's Cross. Jan Smigielski later had his claim rejected, but nevertheless he survived the war having gained the *Virtuti Militari* (Poland's highest military decoration for heroism), KW and Bar (Cross of Valour), and the British DFC. (Reports show Pingel suffered from engine trouble, and that there were no bullet holes in his 109.)

Some 109s began attacking the Escort Wing soon after crossing the coast but made no claims, the 109s just diving straight through the formation and away. One pilot of 222 Squadron did try to chase one without result but he then saw some aircraft on a landing ground at Colembert. He made a strafing run but did not see any results of his fire. However, due to the mist and cloud, most Luftwaffe fighters did not engage until the remaining two bombers and their escort were on the way home.

Escort Cover flew over the main formation and although they saw a few 109s were not engaged. High Cover ran into trouble soon after starting out, the CO of 92 Squadron found his radio on the blink so went down and landed at Hawkinge. Unfortunately two sections followed him down and also landed. There was then an alert that enemy fighters were over the Channel, so three of these Spitfires were sent off to investigate. Finding some 109s they attacked but made no claims. One Spitfire was hit by a cannon shell and the pilot, Sgt G. C. Waldron, baled out. He was later rescued by a drifter in the Estuary.

The pilots of 72 Squadron became separated from the remainder of the Wing and between Fruges and Gravelines were jumped by two formations of six 109s and two of their pilots were shot down. Extricating themselves, the others headed for the coast but one straggler was picked off by another 109. All three RAF pilots were killed. Meantime, 609 was also engaged with 109s, S/Ldr Robinson claiming one destroyed while F/Lt Paul Richey damaged another. Richey's combat report also included his observations on German pilots' tactics:

'I was Yellow One of 609 Squadron, sweeping St Omer area and Gravelines for withdrawal of our bombers from a target at Chocques. Shortly after crossing the French coast at Boulogne, sighted 109s ahead: three Me109Fs passed over formation on the left, going in the opposite direction at same height. Yellow Section turned left as EA did like-wise and circled to get on their tails. After about one circle, No.3 EA broke out of turn to the right. S/Ldr Robinson and remaining two EA flew straight, in very fast but shallow dive. I fired three bursts at left-hand aircraft at long range and saw him emit smoke which I took to be boost. I later fired again as EA climbed to [the] right, then broke away into the sun on sighting many aircraft above. (Later identified as Spitfires.) Yellow Three and Red Three both reported seeing EA I fired at with propeller almost stopped.

'Three Me109s sighted behind Yellow Section at 3,000 ft above. I led Section in a steep left-hand climbing turn as No.1 EA started to dive towards our tails. Other two EA started to dive but pulled up again as No.1 went below us and then regained his height in a steep climbing turn to the left. EA were now right above us and 2,000 ft higher. They circled as they continued to turn and then all dived very fast below and behind us in an endeavour to come up underneath our tails. This manoeuvre was foiled by turning and EA regained height. Manoeuvre repeated unsuccessfully twice more but on the third time EA continued down very fast to the ground and could not be overtaken.'

Of interest is Paul's comment that the smoke from the 109 he fired at was once again probably the result of the German pilots increasing the throttle which blew smoke from the exhaust. This (as previously explained) often led inexperienced RAF pilots into claiming something.

The Hornchurch boys flying Target Support were stepped up to 30,000 feet when they arrived over the target area at 1224. They circled for nine minutes but without sighting any opposition began to head for home. Earlier 54 Squadron had been nibbled at by some 109s and 603 and 611 had also been involved in combats. The Wing claimed five 109s destroyed but lost one pilot of 611, who was killed. Tangmere fared even worse. Crossing out over Beachy Head 616 got into fights with 109s on the way back from the target while 610, similarly engaged, had three pilots fail to return.

Rear Support saw some 109s on the way home, 306 knocking down Pingel near Dover, while 312 Squadron also claimed a probable. This brought the number of RAF claims to 11-3-4 for the loss of one Stirling and eight Spitfires. Six fighter pilots had been killed, two taken prisoner with one more wounded.

On the German side, JG26 had claimed three Spitfires, Priller gaining his thirty-seventh and thirty-eighth victories, for the loss of Pingel and two more 109s with wounded pilots, with a fourth fighter damaged. JG2 claimed ten for no loss. Among the JG2 victors were Hans Hahn, victories twenty-nine and thirty, Oblt. Rudolf Pflanz, his twelfth, Obfw. Kurt Bühelngen his thirteenth and fourteenth, Ltn. Erich Rudorffer his twenty-fifth, and Egon Mayer his thirteenth. This made a total for the day (Gudgeon I and Circus 42) of seventeen Spitfires and one Blenheim.

Among RAF pilots claiming victories was the leader of the Tangmere Wing, Douglas Bader, with one destroyed and one probable. 54 Squadron claimed two, 317 another two. The Circus claims were later reduced to 7-2-2, and Gudgeon I to 8-1-2 but this still made fifteen destroyed with actual German losses noted as only three and one damaged.

Circus No.43 – 11 July

Initially this operation, the first of three for this day, called for three Stirlings of 15 Squadron to attack the Le Trait Shipyard in the late morning. In the event this primary target was under heavy cloud cover so Piper headed for a secondary target, Z437 – Hazebrouck marshalling yards. They had an Escort Wing (Kenley) of four Spitfire squadrons with two more (from Tangmere) in Rear Support.

The weather was known not to be good, which was perhaps the reason it was allowed to proceed with fewer escort fighters, but they hit the target with 15 x 1,000lb and 22 x 500lb bombs. A few 109s were seen but there were no engagements. All-in-all, a pretty low-key affair without much opposition.

Circus No.44 – 11 July

In contrast, Circus 44 began as a diversionary mission using just one Blenheim of 60 Group acting as a decoy, with eight Spitfire squadrons from Biggin and Kenley plus a 12 Group Wing. The lone Blenheim took off from Biggin Hill at around noon, but the fighters ran into heavy cloud soon after take off and found themselves over Essex. Becoming rather lonely, the Blenheim landed at Manston and at 1430 took off again to return to Biggin.

If all this served to confuse German radar operators then it succeeded. The fighters circled Manston and later headed out for the French coast at 1435, crossing into hostile territory east of Dunkirk. As they began to sweep inland the Wing's pilots began to see many black dots heading up from the south – 109s trying to get up–sun – in order to hit the Spitfires as they flew out. Not wishing to put his back to the danger, the Wing Leader headed for Gravelines but then three more formations of 109s suddenly appeared. The first two were allowed to fly past, but the third was engaged.

A combat ensued in which six 109s were claimed destroyed, with two probables and seven damaged, for the loss of just one pilot. As the Wing headed back over the Channel three 109s were seen shadowing them. The Wing reported that there were large numbers of 109s already up when the sweep began. 485 Squadron suffered the loss according to the 11 Group report (P/O C. Stewart, killed), but 92 and 452 Squadrons also had pilots missing. Pilot Officer J. Dougall of 92 was shot down by a 109 and taken into captivity, while 452's Sgt A. C. Roberts baled out after receiving hits from a Messerschmitt. The Australian however, managed to evade capture and with the help of the French Resistance got back to England via Spain and Gibraltar, in October, along with S/Ldr E. P. P. Gibbs, mentioned earlier.[6] In all, eight 109s were claimed destroyed, with three more as probables and five damaged. Meantime...

Circus No.45 – 11 July

This operation was ordered so as to take advantage of a hoped-for scenario whereby Circus 44 had made Luftwaffe fighters respond and would now be landing to re-arm and re-fuel. Three Stirlings of 7 Squadron, led by W/Cdr H. R. Graham (later DSO DFC), were sent out to bomb the Fives-Lille Steel Works with an Escort Wing, Cover Wing, Target Support Wing and a Rear Support Wing giving escort and protection. Haze up to 15,000 feet and cloud above this to 30,000 feet did not help the raid, forcing the bombers to divert and attack the marshalling yards at Hazebrouck instead. The bombers unloaded their 15 x 1,000lb and 36 x 500lb bombs across the yards and among sheds on both sides of the target. There was no AA fire or enemy fighters in the target area.

Escort Wing comprising of 242, 71 and 306 Squadrons, similarly saw little in the way of fighters, just a few 109s south-east of Lille and a couple more that made a

---

6. Roberts came from Lismore, NSW. Unable to fly over France again, he was posted to the Far East, joining 258 Squadron. During 1943–44, he served as Air Liaison Officer with Orde Wingate's Long-Range Penetration Group (The Chindits) in Burma.

mild attempt at attacking one Section of Spitfires but were driven off. Northolt, the Cover Wing, only saw 109s on the return journey but neither side made any attempt at engaging. 303 Squadron did see a Spitfire shot down by some 109s, that appeared to be from 54 Squadron and saw a parachute open below.

Target Support from Hornchurch, on their way back too, saw four 109s dive behind the Wing and appeared to be a decoy for another ten or so that then came in overhead before wheeling round and diving onto the lower Squadron. This unit, 54 Squadron, turned to face the threat but one Spitfire was hit, caught fire and went down, its pilot baling out. One 109 was claimed as destroyed. Upon their return, 611 discovered they had a pilot missing too. This was New Zealander Sgt D. E. Fair who became a prisoner, while 54's loss was F/Lt P. M. Gardner DFC who was also captured. Peter Gardner had flown in France with 3 Squadron and then with 32 Squadron during the Battle of Britain, receiving the DFC in August 1940. He had become a flight commander with 54 in June 1941. He had eight and one shared victories.

The Tangmere Wing, also flying Target Support spotted eight 109s briefly but they went into cloud. One pilot of 616 Squadron, having problems with his oxygen supply came down to ground level and found himself over an airfield. Seeing around ten aircraft on the airfield he made a strafing run on some Ju87s and flamed two. He headed away surrounded by ground fire, and later was fired on by an E-boat off the French coast. Rear Support only saw one lone 109 over the Channel which was lost in the haze before it could be attacked.

The operation netted just one 109 and two Stukas on the ground for the loss of two Spitfires and pilots. Again the Circus was deemed a success, despite having to bomb an alternate target, and the lack of opposition was a clear indication that German fighters had been caught on the ground refuelling after the earlier raid. (If the overall strategy was to bring German fighters into combat, this particular tactic appears to have achieved the opposite.)

The day had cost 11 Group five Spitfires with their pilots missing. The Germans made claims. JG26 seven – including Priller's thirty-ninth, while Ltn. Horst Ulenberg, leader of the 2nd Staffel, got his fifteenth and sixteenth kills, while Hptm. Johannes Siefert, I Gruppe's leader, claimed his twelfth. Leader of III Gruppe, Hptm. Gerhard Schöphel, scored his twenty-eighth. One 109 was damaged but its pilot made a safe landing. JG2 claimed three Spitfires for the loss of one pilot killed over Calais. Erich Rudorffer got his twenty-sixth. Unteroffizier Valentin Nawrot was the lost pilot, from 4./JG2. Oberleutnant Siegfried Bethke, Staffelkapitän of 2./JG2, crash-landed west of Dunkirk and Uffz. Willi Morzinek's 109 was slightly damaged, after combats with Spitfires.

Circus No.46 – 12 July

On the 12th three Stirlings from 15 Squadron, led by F/Lt R. S. Gilmour, were sent to bomb the impressive ship lift at Arques near St Omer. Kenley had the Escort

Wing slot, Hornchurch the Cover Wing, while Target Support went to Northolt and Tangmere. A 12 Group Wing provided Forward Support while Northolt and North Weald drew the Rear Support.

Conditions were haze with cloud in layers up to 19,000 feet. Rendezvous with the bombers over Manston at 1000 hours and upon reaching the target the leading Stirling's bombs failed to release but the other two dropped 43 x 500lb bombs from 12,000 feet, but all overshot. The leader then tried another target – the railway line and sidings at Lumbres – and this time 22 x 500lb bombs fell on the line at Remilly Wirquin. Flak was heavy and all three bombers received some degree of damage.

The Escort Wing also recorded heavy AA fire but almost no sightings of enemy fighters. 611 Squadron was not engaged but 603 on High Cover encountered eight 109Fs that approached from the south at their height, 21,000 feet. Five of these turned and dived on 54 Squadron while the other three climbed while being chased by 603, whose pilots damaged two of them, one by the Wing Leader, W/Cdr F. S. Stapleton. At the same time six more 109s attacked them from astern and in the resulting mêlée, one 109 was claimed destroyed, probably another and damaged a third. Meantime 54 Squadron had one pilot shot down and baling out but they did damage one Messerschmitt. Sergeant F. E. Tulit became a prisoner, ending up in Kopernikus prison camp (Stalag 357).

The Northolt Wing had arrived at the target area just before the bombers and was attacked repeatedly in a series of diving attacks from both sides but they appeared not to open fire. One of these was claimed destroyed by 303 Squadron. 308 Squadron became involved as they left the area and in a dogfight claimed two 109s but lost a pilot – F/O C. Weigus, killed – whose body was later recovered from the Channel. The Tangmere boys circled the target area at 1015 at heights up to 29,000 feet. After one orbit some twenty Me109s were seen climbing in line astern. They were engaged and in a series of fights, 616 Squadron scored 1-1-4. In fact Bader claimed the lion's share with one destroyed and three damaged.

In all five 109s were claimed destroyed on this operation, with two more probables and nine damaged, for the loss of two pilots. In addition, two pilots of 308 Squadron crash-landed, one at Manston and another, running out of fuel, near Hawkhurst, Kent, but both men were uninjured.

JG2 and JG26 had opposed this operation, JG2 claiming one Spitfire north of Morlaix, but lost a fighter, its pilot baling out wounded near Hazebrouck. JG26 do not appear to have made any claims, but lost an experienced pilot, Ltn. Horst Ulenberg, who was killed over Coquelles. Ulenberg had achieved sixteen victories and had been leading the 2nd Staffel for the last ten days. Another pilot, Uffz. Gottfried Deitze, on his first combat mission, crash-landed his 109F-7 near St Omer.

Circus No.47 – 12 July

This operation, also on the 12th, comprising a lone 60 Group Blenheim, showing IFF, was sent off, hoping to confuse the enemy again as a diversion tactic, as per Bottomley's suggestion. When it reached North Foreland it returned to base with its escort of seven fighters; the hope being that they had given enemy radar sufficient 'contact' to entice fighters into the air. According to British radar, enemy fighters did rise to meet the supposed threat.

The bomber took off from Biggin Hill at 1215 hours and after it returned to base, the fighters headed back to carry out a sweep off the French coast. Squadrons from Kenley, Northolt and Biggin Hill had lots to report but this operation only claimed one Me109 shot down – 609's Micky Robinson taking the honours.

* * *

An interesting report dated 12 July, was produced by Squadron Leader Green (Air Tactics officer) and sent to Wing Commander E. S. Finch at the Air Ministry (Finch had been leader of No.63 Fighter Wing during the Battle of France in 1940):

1. I think you will be interested to read the following Circus reports, Circuses 39, 40, 41 and 42, in the light of the following remarks.
2. I have noticed that since No.3 Group have taken over from No.2 Group on the operations, certain matters of liaison have been rather inclined to be let slip.
3. To take the Circuses in order.
    Circus No.39. The close escort squadrons report: –
    (i)   There was no warning given of the Stirlings' intention to split up over the target and bomb individually with a result that the Wing Leader of the close escort Wing was in his opinion, unable to give satisfactory close escort to the bombers.
    (ii)   Bombers again crossed right over Boulogne and flew directly through very heavy AA fire.
    (iii) Bombers appear to have taken the longest route possible back over the sea to the consternation of the Kenley escort Wing.
    (iv)   There appears to be some trouble with the escort cover wing which is alleged to have drawn away at a critical period, that is when leaving the French coast. However, the leader of this Wing, G/Capt Barwell, suggests that the timing was not all that it might have been and the sun position made the withdrawal very difficult. He noted that the bombers chose to fly through heavily defended AA areas and to split up within the target area.
    Circus No.40. This operation appears to have been successful except that the Stirlings having dropped their bombs flew back at a speed so great that the close escort Wing (Hurricane II) were unable to keep up with them.

Circus No.41. Here again the close escort seemed to have been confused by the manoeuvres of the Stirling aircraft and note should be made on No.3 Group's report, where it states that no 'Friendly fighters were near at the time'.

Circus No.42. Here again the bombing force went straight through the heavily defended Boulogne area and one of the Stirlings was shot down before it had dropped its bombs or reached anywhere near the target. The weather during this operation is commented upon by every single formation and it may be of interest to note that No.72 Squadron, who were so foxed by the weather that eight of them landed at Coltishall, which is about 100 miles from their base at Gravesend. Two pilots of 222 Squadron based at Manston, force-landed in a field near Martlesham Heath, one with wheels up, and two aircraft of 54 Squadron, Hornchurch, also managed to get in at Coltishall.

4. In view of the foregoing, I think you will agree that in spite of our committed policy of bombing at all accounts the time has now come for a strong comment to be made on the following points:-

   (i)   Bombers persist in taking a route through the heaviest flak areas.

   (ii)   When the weather is as it was on Circus 42, the result so far as the fighter force is concerned could easily be achieved by employing half the effort.

   (iii) Length of trip. I have mentioned this subject to you before and perhaps you would agree to draw the attention of the Group Captain Ops, to this point. I tried to ring Wing Commander Bader at Tangmere today about this but without success.

Wing Commander Bader complains bitterly about the length of trip, they get very short of petrol, and some of our casualties have been for this reason being forced to bale out into the Channel.

One the other hand, Air/Sea Rescue seems to be getting on very well.

On the top of this report, Wing Commander Finch had written after reading it: '*I have spoken to Bomber Command Tactics and 11 Group Tactics about these points. 11 Group have been on to 3 Group about it, in fact have done so before and after every raid.*'

Unfortunately I have been unable to find a response to Finch's points.

* * *

Circus No.48 – 14 July

Number 11 Group had a day's breather, for Circus 48 did not take place until 14 July – and so therefore, did the Stirling crews. This operation called for six Blenheims to attack the Hazebrouck marshalling yards on this morning with good visibility over France above 12,000 feet but cloud above.

The Blenheims – from 21 Squadron – made rendezvous over Southend with North Weald and one squadron of the Hornchurch Wings, while the three other Hornchurch units provided Top Cover. Target Support went to Biggin and Tangmere, Kenley going for Forward Support while Debden and Kenley added one squadron each for Rear Support.

Crossing the French coast at Gravelines, they reached the target at 1034. The bombers released two dozen 250lb and 40lb bombs across the target, the majority exploding on the yards. Flak was experienced, three bombers being hit, but while some 109s were seen, none made a move against them. The Escort Wing saw a few 109s but had little to report.

Up above, the Hornchurch squadrons picked up the main formation on schedule and headed for the target. Several 109s could be seen high up in the sun but no attacks came until near the target. Four 109s flew over, and one broke downwards and attacked 603 Squadron – the top squadron – and shot down a Spitfire that went down trailing smoke. However, this 109 was reported to have been damaged. 603 continued to be nibbled at on the way back but attacks were not pressed home. 611 had also become embroiled with 109s and claimed two destroyed but they lost three pilots, two of whom it was thought, collided as both attacked a 109 simultaneously although one of the RAF pilots was seen to bale out. These were F/O P. G. Dexter DFC of 611, who was killed, and Sgt J. W. Panter of 54 Squadron, who ended up as a prisoner. 603 lost Sgt A. C. Hunter, who was wounded and also ended up a prisoner. Peter Dexter was a South African who had come to the UK in 1938 to join the RAF. During the Battle of France he had flown Lysanders. He received the DFC for an action on 21 May 1940, during a fight with Me109s in which he shot one down with his front guns while his observer got a second with the rear gun! In the Battle of Britain he moved to 54 Squadron, then to 603. He achieved some successes to become a minor ace before his loss. It was reported he was found dead in his parachute.

The Target Support Wings saw German fighters waiting for them as they crossed into France and very soon Biggin Hill squadrons became engaged in combat. As a result they failed to get to the target area, and although they claimed one 109 (by 609), they lost Sgt W. M. Lamberton of 72 Squadron, who was wounded and taken prisoner. Bill Lamberton was claimed by Pips Priller as his fortieth victory. Priller's combat reports:

'I wanted to attack two Spitfires that were high above us in the vapour trails, but my engine was acting up and it was impossible to overtake them. The Spitfires turned about and came towards us. I pulled my nose up and opened fire from about 100 meters, directly in front of them. I hit one in the cockpit and engine and its pilot baled out. I then had to dive away steeply, as I came under attack by the second Spitfire which was firing at me from very close range.'

Tangmere Wing did reach the target where they split into sections of four. One section attacked some 109s and the tail of one was literally blown off by a cannon shell hit. The pilot who achieved this was P/O J. E. Johnson of 616, thus gaining his third victory. Of the other two squadrons, just one damaged 109 was all they could claim.

The Rear Support Wing had some skirmishes but only S/Ldr P. E. Meagher, CO of 602 Squadron was able to claim a destroyed five miles south-west of Boulogne. Pat Meagher was another veteran of the 1940 French campaign during which he had flown Blenheims. Later in the war he would fly Beaufighters over Burma, winning the DSO and DFC and becoming a Group Captain.

Five Me109s had been claimed this day with three more damaged, for the loss of four pilots. JG26 had claimed three, possibly four. Apart from Priller, Hptm. Siefert had gained his thirteenth kill. Gefreiter Robert Kleinecke was shot down and killed over Marquise. Another loss this date was Ltn. Werner Roll of Ergänzunsdgruppe/JG2, shot down and wounded by a Spitfire, but this was over Cherbourg on one of two Gudgeon (numbers III and IV) operations by 10 Group. 139 Squadron lost two Blenheims to 4./JFS 5 off Le Havre and 10 Group had a Spitfire from 234 Squadron damaged but the pilot got back although he was claimed by a 1.Erg/JG2 pilot.

Circus No.49 and 50

It seems that while these two operations had also been planned for the 14th, they did not take place, but the Circus numbers remained written into the records. Circus 49 should have been a raid on Arques by three Stirlings, which were to make RV over Clacton at 1800 hours. Circus 50 was to have involved three more Stirlings in an attack on Mazingarbe, rendezvousing over Rye forty-five minutes later, but once airborne the bombers were informed that bad weather was making things difficult and both operations were aborted. The weather was indeed recorded as very cloudy and with rain.

On 16 July came a daylight low-level raid on the shipping and docks of Rotterdam. Thirty-six Blenheims took off mid-afternoon. Over the target four of the raiders were shot down by flak, two from 18 Squadron, and one each from 21 and 139 Squadrons. Of the twelve missing men, just three survived as prisoners. No doubt the Blenheim crews thought the odds or survival were rather better when on Circus operations.

There were no Circuses on the 17th either, but Fighter Command flew fighter sweeps. Despite reports that German fighters rarely reacted to RAF intrusions unless bombers were in the mix seems a little hollow, for there was much fighter versus fighter action on this day. During two sweeps, one in the afternoon and another in the early evening, Fighter Command claimed ten Me109s destroyed, three more as probables, plus a He59 seaplane destroyed. Casualties amounted to four RAF pilots killed, two taken prisoner, and another killed on a Rhubarb sortie.

The Germans claimed only a couple of Spitfires on the first encounter, one each by JG2 and JG26. JG26 lost a pilot to 'friendly' anti-aircraft fire, while JG2 had three of its 109s crash-land with combat damage. Most of the action was either over the Channel or near to the French coast, but on the second show, 308 Squadron penetrated too far into France and met around sixty Me109s. The Polish pilots fought their way out and claimed 3-2-0 but lost three pilots. Unteroffizier H-G Adam of 2./JG26 claimed one of these (his first victory), while Ltn. Julius Meimberg of JG2 claimed one, gaining his eleventh victory (of an eventual fifty-three).

Blenheims of 21 Squadron out on a Channel Stop anti-shipping sortie on the 18th lost two aircraft to AA fire and had a third so badly shot up that it was written off. Meantime an unusual mission on this day involved a lone Stirling of 15 Squadron, piloted by F/O S. D. Marshall RAAF, being tasked with an operation to Wesel using cloud cover. JG26 had been involved with the Blenheims – claiming two! – but then Fw. Ernst Jäckel spotted what he described as an unknown type, close to the sea, with four Spitfires as escort. He and his wingman made five attacks on the bomber which turned back towards Dover, while another pair of 109s engaged the fighters. Eventually the bomber hit the sea and crashed. All seven crewmen were killed. Marshall had been the yachting correspondent for the *Sydney Telegraph* in happier times. Being the first JG26 pilot to down a four-engined bomber, he received an honour trophy together with 500 *Reichsmarks*. The two Blenheims were shot down by the 3rd Staffel, while 222 Squadron flying escort lost one pilot to Obfw. Walter Mayer - his tenth victory. Jäckel's combat report stated:

'My Schwarm was covering a convoy north-west of Dunkirk. At 1115, several enemy aircraft were reported approaching the convoy at altitudes between zero and 2,000 meters [6,500 ft]. My Schwarm climbed to 2,500 meters [8,000 ft], and circled directly over the convoy. At 1120, I saw four bombers approaching the convoy from the north-west; they were flying in a single row, about three meters off the water. They were covered by about 15 Spitfires at 2,000 meters. I dived on the Spitfires and opened fire from their rear, which caused the formation to separate. I continued the dive with my Schwarm, and overtook the bombers at great speed. The lead bomber, a Bristol Blenheim, had already dropped its bombs on the convoy. As I prepared to attack one of the Blenheims, I saw a large aircraft, type unknown, somewhat farther away. It was flying at three meters altitude and had an escort of four Spitfires. I immediately turned towards this aircraft, and approached it from the right rear. The Spitfires above me disappeared. I approached the bomber but did not open fire as I wanted to identify the type. At about 200 meters range its rear turret opened fire. At 100 meters I saw the roundels on its fuselage and wings, and opened fire on the turret with my cannon. I passed close by the left side, and saw damage to the turret, the fuselage and the cockpit. I also saw that the plane had four engines.

'My wingman and the second Rotte[7] of my Schwarm also made attacks from the rear. After my second attack the rear gunner stopped firing (probably dead).

---

7. A Rotte was a two-man formation; a formation of two Rotte became a Schwarm. German fighter pilots had always flown in twos and fours, whereas the RAF had generally flown in sections of three until the more intuitive fighter leaders began to adopt a four-man section, of two pairs, begun by 616 Squadron as mentioned earlier.

The aircraft had reversed course after the first attack and now flew towards Dover, about two meters above the water. I made two more attacks and my wingman made one, while my second Rotte protected us from the Spitfires. The bomber was less than three miles south-east of Deal when I made my fifth and last attack. I closed to about 20 meters. As I prepared to make yet another attack, I saw its extended landing gear strike the water. I saw an English speed boat approaching the crash site. At that I headed home, short of fuel.'

Circus No.51 – 19 July

Finally the bad weather cleared to allow this operation to proceed normally on the afternoon of Saturday 19 July. 15 Squadron provided three Stirlings, led by S/Ldr Piper, to go for the Power Station at Lille/Sequedin. There was still some cloud around but it appeared good enough to operate in. However, the bombers failed to find the target due to these cloudy conditions so they turned back and headed for the secondary target – the Dunkirk docks.

The bombs went down from 14,000 feet, through gaps in the clouds, but on the run-in the leading bomber was seen to lurch violently and flames came from under and behind the port inner engine. The fire spread and the bomber began to lose height, apparently the pilot was making a controlled descent to allow his crew to get out. Although not seen by any of the escort, two 109s then nipped in and opened fire, following which the pilot baled out too. In the event only the pilot, Squadron Leader Piper and one Canadian crew member survived as prisoners, the other six perished.

There were plenty of scattered Me109s nipping about but the fighting became very confused due to the weather. The Escort Wing (North Weald) saw some on the way to Dunkirk but despite an exchange of fire, no claims were made. As the bombers let go their loads, four 109s dived through the Wing to engage the Stirlings and one was probably destroyed by 71 Squadron, and another damaged by 222.

Escort Cover (Hornchurch) did not see anything either until near Dunkirk on the way back, when some 109s began diving towards the bombers from height. 611 Squadron got a probable and near the coast 54 Squadron claimed one and a damaged.

Target Support (Biggin and Tangmere) were forced to operate in individual squadron formations that appeared to confuse the 109 pilots they encountered, because they were finding smaller units rather than a large Wing group. However, 72 Squadron had a pilot shot down into the Channel and was lost, while 92 Squadron also lost a pilot. The latter was Sgt G. C. Waldern RCAF, who had been rescued from the Channel on 10 July. This time his luck ran out.

Tangmere flew out over Beachy Head and were above Hazebrouck at 1345, stepped up from 25,000 feet. The Wing Leader (Bader) kept everyone together because of the cloud, putting them in echelon from north to south so they covered a wide front. They spotted some fifteen 109s operating in pairs, attacked, and claimed two destroyed and three probables. Bader and P/O H. S. L. 'Cocky' Dundas (616) shared one, while Bader got another on his own. 610 also claimed a probable, while a pilot of 145 Squadron, losing height, strafed a gun position 200 yards inland from the beach east of Dunkirk. The other Wings saw 109s but had little in the way of engagements.

In total 11 Group had claimed four destroyed, six probables and two damaged, for the loss of two pilots. Oberleutnant Christian Eikhoff, leader of JG26's 2nd Staffel, was credited with finishing off the Stirling, for his third victory. Priller and Ltn. Josef Heyarts of JG26 claimed the two Spitfires. Leutnant Heinz Rahardt of 2./JG26 was shot down and killed and another pilot was killed returning from this action. His engine suddenly stopped and in attempting a crash-landing hit a wall and burst into flames.

Circus No.52 – 20 July

Despite it being high summer the bad weather continued on 20 July with more cloud and rain. Three Stirlings of 15 Squadron, led by F/Lt R. S. Gilmour, were assigned to bomb the Hazebrouck marshalling yards this Sunday morning but the weather defeated them and they were unable to see the ground. Turning back, they jettisoned their bombs over the Barrow Deep, Thames Estuary, and went home.

602 Squadron, part of the Escort, saw some 109s but no contact was made by either side. The Hornchurch Wing also saw a few but again no engagement took place. The same was the case for the Tangmere boys. It was similar experiences that confronted the other Wings and in one brief skirmish, Northolt's Wing Leader, W/Cdr J. A. Kent DFC claimed a 109 off Gravelines, and that was that. Not a very inspiring operation, but at least there wasn't any losses – on either side! Of interest are the remarks made by Johnny Kent, former CO of 92 Squadron, and now leading the Northolt Wing, in his book '*One of the Few*'.

'[There were] two major mistakes we were making during this phase of the air war. One was that we had learned little or nothing from the German mistakes in 1940 and, like them, we tied our fighters to the bombers, their mere proximity supposedly giving protection. As we ourselves had found, a few fighters travelling fast can flash through a screen of escorting fighters, do their damage and get away while the escort is trying to accelerate and at the same time look around to see if any more of the enemy were about.

'The second mistake was really very similar in its effect to the first but, if anything, was accentuated in the operations carried out as far afield as Lille which necessitated the fighters flying slowly not only to stay with the bombers but also to conserve fuel. The fact is that one could not afford to fight on such an operation as to do so properly meant that you would have insufficient fuel to get back across the Channel. All that we could do was to defend ourselves, but by so doing one failed to give adequate protection to the bombers. This was something we had noticed with the Germans in 1940 – the fighters were loath to join combat when escorting their bombers on the more deeply penetrating raids.

The significance was not appreciated by us – or at least not by those who were more concerned with planning our operations than carrying them out.

'The advantage of speed which allowed the Spitfire to be used to its best advantage against the enemy was proven on the fighter sweeps of relatively shallow penetration. This was demonstrated with particular emphasis by the Biggin Hill Wing under the leadership of first Malan and later Rankin. The aircraft were already travelling fast when they met the enemy and so could easily catch the 109s which were shot out of the sky in large numbers with very little loss to the Biggin Wing. This could not be said of the Wings, any of them, when employed on close escort work.'

Circus No.53 – 20 July

This was also scheduled for the 20th, three Stirlings going for targets in the Forêt de Eperleques. Although the fighter escort squadrons are known, there is no reference to this operation in 11 Group's Operational Record Book, so although rendezvous was made over Rye with the bombers, this mission too must have been abandoned due to the weather.

Circus No.54 – 21 July

The weather improved to fair on the 21st. The target for three Stirlings was the Accumulator Tudor factory at Lille, with the RV point over Clacton at 0800, now designated as target Z.565 of industrial targets. 15 Squadron, led by PO Needham, again provided the bombers which crossed into France east of Dunkirk dropping 15 x 1,000 and 36 x 500lb bombs. Direct hits were observed on one large and two small buildings just to the south-west of the target, despite heavy flak which slightly damaged all three Stirlings. Sergeant P. A. Tanton had to feather his starboard outer engine, and in consequence he began to lag behind the other two Stirlings. As he neared the French coast he was attacked by a 109, and his rear gunner was slightly wounded. The starboard fuel tanks were also holed and the inner engine now stopped too. Deciding to land at Manston, Tanton found that with only the two port engines working, he could not maintain flying speed once he lowered flaps and undercarriage; he was also coming in from an unsuitable direction. Finally lining up, he was almost committed to make a belly landing but at the last moment, lowered his wheels and landed without further damage to the aircraft. Peter Tanton received an Immediate DFM.

One of two 109s that made a pass at the formation was engaged by 71 Squadron, part of the Escort Wing (485, 602, plus 71 from North Weald), while other Eagle pilots drove off four more that had edged in. 602 Squadron saw 109s above that then dived down through the Squadron. Two pilots had squirts at them but made no claims. Yellow Section was also attacked by diving 109s and one RAF pilot was shot down. This was F/Lt T. G. F. Ritchie, yet another RAFVR Battle of Britain veteran killed over France. Biggin's Escort Cover Wing had little to report but the Hornchurch squadrons (54, 603 and 611) saw several groups of 109s over St Omer. 54 Squadron was attacked but made no claims. Then another group came down and in the scrap that ensued, one 109 was claimed destroyed. Meantime, 603 went down on fifteen 109s that came in from the west, got behind them and shot down two, and damaged a third. One RAF pilot lost formation so dived to low level. He then spotted a 109F about to land at St Omer and shot it down. The Wing Leader, W/Cdr F. S. Stapleton claimed two destroyed in this action, but 603 also claimed two and a damaged, so it is not clear what the Squadron score actually was. Another Wing pilot who had gone down to ground level shot up a long line of motor transport on a road leading to St Omer and then shot a man out of the Watch Tower in the Forêt de Clairmarais.

The Tangmere Wing orbited the Forêt de Nieppe before heading for the target. On the way back they were chased by 109s and in the subsequent fight two of these were damaged. One section dived on several 109s that were attacking some Spitfires from the rear. The 109 pilots broke off the attack and one German pilot was seen to bale out although none of the Spitfires had fired. One pilot of 610 Squadron claimed a 109, one of two he chased. They were joined by three more but Sgt E. W. Merriman continued attacking all five and claimed his victory.

Results from air actions were claims of eight Me109s destroyed and five more damaged for the loss of three pilots. 609 Squadron lost one pilot killed and 611 another. On the German side, JG26 and JG2 had intercepted the raid. Seeing the bombers being set upon by AA fire, one bomber appeared to lose an engine, and was attacked by Hptm. Seifert who knocked out a second engine. Sergeant H. Taunton managed to reach RAF Manston where he landed his crippled Stirling safely. Meantime, JG26 also claimed two Spitfires in this engagement. The 602 Squadron pilot was shot down by Obfw. Walter März, his fourth victory. They lost Obgfr. Heinrich Gleixner. Meantime JG2 got in amongst the Circus aircraft and claimed five Spitfires for the loss of one Me109F. One of JG2's claims was Hans Hahn's thirty-first kill.

Circus No.55 – 21 July

During the late afternoon of the 21st, with weather continuing cloudy but fair, three more Stirlings of 15 Squadron, led by F/O Campbell, were ordered out to bomb a target at Mazingarbe, but yet again the weather defeated the attempt. No sooner had they set course for Gravelines than the huge cloud formations ahead forced the leader to order an abort.

Both the Escort Wing and Escort Cover Wings aborted too, but the Target Support Wings carried on. Biggin Hill's squadrons (72, 92 and 609) caught fleeting glimpses of the French countryside north of St Omer before spotting what might have been 109s below. One section was sent down but in the swirling cloud nothing further was seen. On the way out a couple of 109s made a half-hearted approach but did not press home their attack.

Tangmere, the other Cover Wing, orbited over France and just before 2045 saw some 109Fs pass 500 feet below heading south-west. They were attacked but the 109s turned and got stuck in, with mixed fortunes. One 109 was probably destroyed and another damaged but one pilot of 616 Squadron didn't get home, Sgt F. E. Nelson going into the Channel. A second squadron pilot, Sgt S. W. R. Mabbett, was wounded but managed to belly-land in France. He was taken to hospital but died of his injuries. Both men were victims of JG26. They had been sent to engage but with the bombers missing the German pilots assumed this was a sweep rather than a bombing raid. Nevertheless, they claimed three Spitfires for one loss. Unteroffizier Gottfried Dietz made one claim, his first, no doubt Sgt Mabbett, while the other Spitfire may not have been seen crashing into the sea. Johannes Siefert was credited with a Spitfire – kill number fifteen – while Hans Hahn of JG2 claimed another. JG2 had a pilot wounded, lost a 109 and had another damaged. Pilot Officer J. E. Johnson was on this operation and recorded in his book *'Wing Leader'*:

'Leading a section of two Spitfires, I lost my wingman on a late evening show over France. We were badly bounced and didn't see the 109s until they had opened fire. The wingman was a sergeant-pilot, a kindly farmer's son from Gloucestershire, and the next thing we heard of Mabbett was that the Germans had buried him with military honours at St Omer.'

'The bombers flew over France on every suitable day, and as the high summer wore on, so the resistance of the 109s seemed to increase and sometimes we had to fight our way to the target from the coast. One day in July we shot down Tangmere's 500th Hun, and the same fight witnessed the squadron's fiftieth victory. This was not a large squadron score since some units, including 610 Squadron, already claimed more than 100 kills, but we had got off to a poor start last autumn and our present masters seemed satisfied with our progress.'

Forward Support Wing came from 12 Group (19, 65 and 266 Squadrons), but upon crossing into France became split up due to the cloud. 19 Squadron saw several formations of 109s which they engaged, claiming one destroyed and one damaged. However, they lost two pilots killed and a third returned wounded. This operation should not have been contemplated, for the weather had already proved a problem during the morning. The day cost Fighter Command seven pilots missing (all killed) and one wounded, for little return – just a score of 1-1-3. Dundas got one of the damaged, while brother 616 pilots, Nip Heppell and Johnnie Johnson shared the probable. Douglas Bader also claimed a damaged leading his Tangmere Wing.

It was around this time that Bader received a Bar to his DSO, with Billy Burton, Ken Holden and Cocky Dundas receiving DFCs.

* * *

Summer 1941. Winston Churchill visits RAF Biggin Hill, on 11 July. Sqn Ldr M L Robinson DFC, CO of 609 Squadron, is on the left with Churchill with his back to the camera. Air Vice-Marshal Sholto Douglas, CinC of Fighter Command, slightly obscuring Group Captain P Barwell, Station Commander. On this day Barwell shot down a Me109 over France.

Hermann Göring, head of the German Luftwaffe, on a visit to his fighter boys on the Channel front. On the left is Ltn-Gen Bruno Loerzer, while on the right is Adolf Galland, commanding JG26 in 1941.

Group Captain Victor Beamish DSO DFC AFC, both Station Commander and Wing Leader of the North Weald squadrons.

Wing Commander Douglas Bader DSO DFC, leader of the Tangmere Wing in 1941, climbing out of his Spitfire. Note his initials on the fuselage, a prerogative of wing leaders during the war.

Group Captain John Peel DSO DFC, had led the Kenley Wing in 1941.

Wing Commander A G 'Sailor' Malan DSO DFC, commanded 74 Squadron in 1941. On the left is Wing Commander Pat Jameson DFC, leader of the Wittering Wing.

Wing Commander John Gillan DFC AFC, killed in action leading the North Weald Wing during a fighter sweep on 29 August 1941.

Squadron Leader Johnnie Kent DFC led both the Northolt and Kenley Wings in 1941, receiving a Bar to his DFC in October.

Sergeant H D Denchfield of 610 Squadron, shot down and taken prisoner on 5 February 1941, seen here shortly after his capture.

Sergeant J McAdam of 41 Squadron, shot down by Werner Mölders of JG51 and taken prisoner.

Two outstanding fighter pilots. Brian Kingcome DFC, (left) saw considerable action with 92 Squadron during 1940 and 1941, and Peter Simpson DFC, who flew with 111 Squadron.

The Bristol Blenheim IV, which 2 Group of Bomber Command used on the Circus operations during 1941. This aircraft (V6240) of 21 Squadron was lost during a raid on Rotterdam on 12 July 1941.

Spitfire of 74 Squadron, P7928, following its crash-landing in France, 6 May 1941. Sergeant A D Arnot became a prisoner of war.

General Ulrich Grauert, aged 52, was a Flieger Corps commander. The Ju52 transport aircraft in which he was a passenger, was shot down by Spitfires of 303 Polish Squadron on 15 May 1941, near St Omer.

Spitfire IIA (P8241) of 609 Squadron. P/O Joe Atkinson had to make a forced landing near Rochester on 17 May following combat with Me109s over Dover.

Squadron Leader Ronald Kellett DSO DFC, second from the left, whilst CO of 303 Squadron. The three Polish pilots are Flight Lieutenant J Jankiewicz, who shared in the downing of General Grauert's Ju52 in May, Squadron Leader W Lapkowski, who commanded 303 from May 1941 until he was killed on 2 July, and Flight Lieutenant F Kornicki of 315 Squadron.

Belgian pilot, R G C De Grunne, of 609 Squadron, was lost in action on 21 May 1941. He had flown for the Nationalists during the Spanish Civil War, in Italian CR32s and German Me109Bs and is reputed to have shot down 14 Republican aircraft.

Wing Commander Joe Kayll DSO DFC, leader of the Hornchurch Wing, shortly after his capture on 25 June 1941.

Spitfire R6923 of 92 Squadron, shot down off Dover on 21 June. Its pilot, Sergeant G W Aston baled out and was rescued.

A Messerschmitt 109E, recognised by its square wing-tips and bracing strut beneath the rear wing was the main opponent in 1941.

Pilot Officer N F Duke of 92 Squadron. He achieved a few victories in 1941 but later excelled in North Africa and Italy, receiving the DSO, DFC & 2 Bars.

Roger Boulding of 74 Squadron, who occasionally flew as Sailor Malan's wingman, was shot down and captured on 17 June 1941.

Wing Commander Victor Beamish with three of his Polish pilots in 249 Squadron at Northolt in 1941. From the left is Sergeant M K Maciejowski, Sergeant M Popek and Pilot Officer J J Solak. Mike Maciejowski would later win the DFM and DFC.

The Me109F model began to appear in 1941, with rounded wing-tips and no bracing struts.

P/o KROL (POLISH)
P. of W. 2.7.41.

Sgt COCHRANE
MISSING JULY 3RD 1941

SGT. LOCKHART.
MISSING 6.7.41.

SGT. HILKEN
P. of W. 27.6.41

Four other casualties of 74 Squadron. Pilot Officer S Z Krol, (PoW 2 July), Sergeant R H Cochrane (PoW 3 July), Sergeant W G Lockhart (shot down and evaded capture, 6 July) and Sergeant C G Hilken (PoW 27 June). Stanislaw 'Danny' Krol later became one of the escapees from Stalag Luft III in March 1944 (the Great Escape); he was recaptured and murdered by the Gestapo.

Two more 74 Squadron losses, were Squadron Leader J C Mungo-Park DFC, (front) (KIA 27 June) and Pilot Officer W M Skinner DFM (PoW 6 July).

Another loss from 74 Squadron on 27 June was Pilot Officer W J Sandman RNZAF, who also ended up in Stalag Luft III.

Three pilots of JG26. Hauptmann Rudolf Bieber, whose first victory was a Blenheim of 226 Squadron on 2 July, but was killed in action the following day. Hauptmann Rolf Pingel who was taken prisoner after chasing a Stirling back to England on 10 July, having achieved 22 victories (plus 4 in Spain), and Oberleutnant Josef 'Pips' Priller. By the end of July, Priller had scored 44 victories and would go on to achieve 101 by war's end.

Sergeant D B Crabtree of 611 Squadron, shot down on 3 July. Escaped and evaded, reaching England in June 1942.

Sergeant J A McCairns, captured on 6 July. However he escaped in 1942 and got back to England. He was awarded the MM and later the DFC & 2 Bars and French CdG for flying clandestine operations over occupied territory. Sadly he was killed in a flying accident in 1948 flying a Mosquito.

Another serious loss to the Luftwaffe was Major Wilhelm Balthasar of JG2. He had been credited with 7 victories in Spain and on 2 July 1941 was awarded the Oak Leaves to his Knight's Cross when his WW2 victories totalled 40. However, the next day he was shot down and killed.

Sergeant W H Lockhart became a prisoner on 7 July 1941 and evaded to return to England. He later became a Wing Commander, DSO DFC, flew with 161 Squadron and then commanded Mosquito and Lancaster squadrons but was killed in action in April 1944.

Siegfried 'Wumm' Schnell of 9/JG2 in 1941, and awarded the Oak Leaves to his Knight's Cross on 9 July. Killed in action on the Russian front in February 1944 having achieved 93 victories.

Sergeant S W R Mabbett of 616 Squadron. Shot down by JG26 on 21 July he crash landed near St Omer but died of his wounds. He became the first victory of Unteroffizier Gottfried Dietze.

In order to further entice German fighters to combat, Short Stirling bombers were employed on Circus operations in mid–1941. Here Hurricanes are part of the escort to one Stirling of 15 Squadron over France.

Adolf Galland's brother Wilhelm ('Wutz'), also with JG26. He gained his first kill on 23 July 1941, increasing this to 55 by the time he was killed over Belgium in August 1943.

Another successful pilot with JG2 was Erich Leie. He was awarded the Knight's Cross on 1 August 1941 with a score of 21 victories. He was killed on the Russian front in March 1945 having achieved 118 kills.

Egon Mayer of JG2 also received the Knight's Cross on 1 August 1940 following his 20th victory. He died over France in March 1944 with a total score of 102.

Adolf Glunz was a successful NCO pilot in 1941, firstly with JG52 and then with JG26. He received the Knight's Cross and Oak Leaves in 1943-44, ending the war with 71 victories. He is depicted here by the tail of a FW190 on which is painted his Knight's Cross and victory marks

Flight Lieutenant Eric Lock achieved 23 victories during the Battle of Britain, winning the DSO and DFC. In July 1941 he was posted to 611 Squadron, claiming three more victories but on 3 August he failed to return from a sortie over France and was last seen diving on some German troops on a road.

The legendary Douglas Bader, leader of the Tangmere Wing. Falling into German hands on 9 August 1941, his biographer perpetuated Bader's story that he had collided with a Me109 and had to bale out.

Flight Sergeant S Plzak, a Czech pilot with 19 Squadron. He was killed in action on 7 August 1941.

Flight Lieutenant L H 'Buck' Casson DFC of 616 Squadron attacked what he thought was a Me109 on 9 August that is generally believed now to have been Bader's Spitfire. He admitted this to Bader in a prison camp, having himself been shot down shortly afterwards by Gottfried Schöpfel of JG26.

Gerhard Schöpfel who flew with JG26, commanding its III Gruppe in 1941. By the end of that year he had a score of over 40, having become Galland's successor as Geschwader Kommodore on 6 December.

Wing Commander H de C A 'Paddy' Woodhouse took command of the Tangmere Wing following the loss of Douglas Bader, and received the DFC in October.

Pilot Officer J B Kremski of 308 Polish Squadron, shot down and killed by JG26 on 14 August 1941.

Hans Hahn of JG2 received the Oak Leaves to his Knight's Cross on 14 August 1941, his score having risen to 42. With a final tally of 108 victories he was captured by the Russians in February 1943.

Pilot Officer N R D Dick of 403 Squadron RCAF. Shot down by JG26 on 19 August 1941, he baled out off Dover and rescued.

Johann Schmid of JG26. He was awarded the Knight's Cross after 25 kills, on 21 August 1941, but was lost on 6 November, his wing-tip hitting the sea as he circled a downed Spitfire of 452 Squadron RAAF.

Squadron Leader W J Burnett of 408 Squadron RCAF in his Hampden on 30 September 1941.

Handley-Page Hampden bombers also made a brief appearance during Circus operations in mid-1941.

Members of 408 Squadron RCAF on 12 August 1941. Rear: P/O T W Dench, P/O R Campbell, F/L A C P Clayton DFC, W/C N W Timmerman DFC, S/L W J Burnett DFC. Front: Sgt A McMillan, Sgt J Ross, Sgt E Marshall, Sgt K McGrail, Sgt W Reinhart.

Spitfire IIA (P7308) flown by William Dunn of 71 Eagle Squadron, which he crash landed on 27 August 1941 due to battle damage. In the preceding action he had scored his 5th victory.

Bill Dunn, 71 Eagle Squadron. He was the first Eagle pilot ace.

Two successful Eagle pilots were 'Gus' Daymond and 'Pete' Peterson. Gus was to become the highest scoring pilot in 71 Squadron with seven victories while Chesley Peterson scored six plus two more with the US 4th Fighter Group in 1943.

Squadron Leader J K J Słoński-Ostoja of 306 Polish Squadron was shot down and killed on Circus 88, 29 August 1941.

Squadron Leader Jan Zumbach DFC VM KW of 303 Squadron, attacked and damaged a 'radial-engined fighter' on 13 October 1941, which would have been one of the first FW190 fighters to be met in combat.

Pilots of 609 Squadron in 1941. Pilot Officer I du Monceau, Flight Lieutenant J D Bisdee DFC, Pilot Officer R MacKenzie, Sergeant T C Rigler, with Flying Officer F H Zeigler (IO), Flying Officer 'Doc' Lawrence.

Flight Lieutenant P H M Richey DFC, flight commander with 609 Squadron 1941. He received a Bar to his DFC in August 1941.

A sergeant-pilot in 1941 with 315 Polish Squadron, Michel Cwyner scored twice prior to becoming commissioned. He later received the DFC and was still flying operationally in 1942–43 as a squadron leader with 315.

Sergeant Adolf Pietrasiak flew with 92 and then 308 Polish Squadron in 1941 and received the DFM. On 19 August 1941 he was shot down over France but evaded capture and returned to England via Spain. Returned to operations, he failed to return with 317 Squadron on 29 November 1943.

Squadron Leader Jamie Rankin, CO of 92 Squadron in 1941. He later led the Biggin Hill Wing from September that year.

Pilot Officer W C Crawford-Compton flew with 485 Squadron RNZAF. He ended the war with over 20 victories, the first three of which were scored in 1941. He received the DSO, DFC & Bar.

Squadron Leader F D S Scott-Malden DFC, saw action in 1941 with 603 Squadron before taking command of 54 Squadron in September. In 1942 he led the North Weald Wing, adding a Bar to his DFC and the DSO.

Josef Wurmheller of III/JG2 was awarded the Knight's Cross on 4 September 1941 as his score reached 21. He had achieved 102 kills by the time he was killed in a collision on 22 June 1944.

Flight Sergeant Don Kingaby DFM, 92 Squadron. In 1941 he received two Bars to his DFM, the only RAF pilot so honoured during the war. He commanded fighter squadrons in 1942/43 and was awarded the DSO.

Another successful JG2 pilot was Kurt Bühlengen who also received the Knight's Cross on 4 September, again having claimed 21 victories. His final tally was 112, but he had to endure a Russian prison camp from 1945 to 1950.

Wilhelm Philipp of JG26 ended the war with 81 victories and received the Knight's Cross in 1944.

Klaus Mietusch of 7/JG26 from September 1941. He had more than a dozen kills by October 1941. In 1943 he commanded III Gruppe of JG26 and his score had risen to 72 by the time he was killed in combat in September 1944.

Oberfeldwebel Emil Babenz if I/JG26. By October 1941 he had achieved 21 victories and was awarded the German Cross in Gold.

Walter Adolph Kommodore of II/JG26. He claimed 29 victories, including one in Spain, before he was killed in action on 18 September 1941.

Three pilots of 452 Squadron RAAF await take-off time on 20 September 1941 (Circus 100B). Sergeant K Chisholm DFM, Sergeant I Milne and Flight Lieutenant B E Finucane DFC.

Pilot Officer J H Whalen RCAF flew with 129 Squadron, claiming three victories in September 1941, as shown on the side of his Spitfire. Later he flew in Burma but was killed in action in April 1944. His DFC was announced in 1945.

American volunteer A G Donahue had been wounded in the Battle of Britain and in March 1941 was with 91 Squadron. By September he had two victories, including a Klemm training aircraft he shot down over France on the 26th. Following Japan's entry into the war he saw action over Burma (winning the DFC) before returning to 91 in 1942. He was killed in action on 11 September 1942.

Joachim 'Jochen' Müncheberg won his Oak Leaves to the Knight's Cross over Malta where JG26 had sent one of its Gruppen, awarded on 7 May 1941. Returning to France he took command of II/JG26 on 19 September. His victory total upon his return was 48. He gained his 49th on 26 August over the Dover Straits, and his 50th on the 29th. On 8 November he made it 59, with two Spitfires from 412 RCAF Squadron. He later flew in Russia and North Africa and was killed in March 1943 on his 500th mission when his score stood at 135 victories.

Squadron Leader N 'Fanny' Orton DFC & Bar had seen action in France in 1940 and in 1941 was leading 54 Squadron. Killed in action on 17 September, he had a victory tally of around 17.

New Zealander Al Deere had seen considerable action over Dunkirk and the Battle of Britain with 54 Squadron and was awarded the DFC & Bar. In 1941 he was commanding 602 Squadron. He later went on to command The Biggin Hill Wing in 1943, and was awarded the DSO.

Another notable pilot in 452 Squadron was Flying Officer K W 'Bluey' Truscott DFC. He would be lost in a flying accident in New Guinea in March 1943.

Flying Officer P W E 'Nip' Hepple was in 616 Squadron of the Tangmere Wing in 1941, during which he achieved a score of 2-2-2, and received the DFC. In 1942 he was in action over Malta.

Frenchman, Jean-Francois 'Moses' Demozay had been a liaison officer with a RAF Hurricane squadron during the French Campaign. Coming to England he served with 242 and then 91 Squadron in 1941 and had much success during the year, being awarded the DFC and several French decorations. He survived the war but was killed in a flying accident in December 1945.

Another very successful fighter pilot in 1941 was W G G Duncan Smith, flying with 611 Squadron, claiming six victories and as many probables, receiving the DFC. He continued operations during 1942, being awarded a Bar to this decoration and the DSO. He later saw combat flying from Malta and later Italy and was rewarded with a Bar to his DSO.

Flying Officer T Nowak was awarded the Polish *Virtuti Militari* flying with 315 Polish Squadron, but was shot down and killed by JG26 on 21 September 1941.

Pilot Officer E Q 'Red' Tobin was an American volunteer with the first Eagle Squadron in 1940, and shot down a German raider on the 15th of September. He remained with 71 Squadron during 1941 but was killed in action over Boulogne on 7 September, one of four Eagles lost this day.

Squadron Leader R M 'Dickie' Milne DFC, after a successful period fighting in the Battle of Britain, was posted to 92 Squadron in mid-1941, taking command in September. His action brought him a Bar to this decoration in November. In 1943 he commanded the Biggin Hill Wing until he was shot down and taken prisoner on 14 March.

Spitfire Vb (AB779) of
92 Squadron at Biggin
Hill. It was lost on
Circus 105 on 3 October
1941, its pilot, Sergeant
G E F Woods-Scawen
being killed.

Sergeant A G 'Goldie' Palmer DFM
of 609 Squadron, killed in action off
Le Touquet, 21 October 1941.

Sergeant S L Thompson RCAF, 401 Squadron,
killed in action 27 October 1941 by Adolf
Galland's JG26.

Flying Officer C D Strickland of 615 Squadron was killed on 27 October 1941, hit by ground fire during an early morning Rhubarb operation over Belgium.

Pilot Officer W M Fessler's Spitfire AA855, 71 Eagle Squadron. He too was brought down during a Rhubarb sortie on 27 October, debris from an exploding train he was strafing put his aircraft out of commission. The American pilot ended up as a prisoner.

Flight Lieutenant E P 'Hawkeye' Wells DFC RNZAF got in at the tail-end of the Battle of Britain with 41 Squadron. In 1941 he was a flight commander with 485 Squadron, where he received the DFC & Bar during the year. In 1942 he led the Kenley Wing, and in 1944 the Tangmere Wing, and awarded the DSO. He had questioned the claims of certain squadrons to Victor Beamish, but the Group Captain's loss over the North Sea in March 1942 put this on indefinite hold.

These were the last efforts of the Stirling experiment, and the C-in-C Bomber Command withdrew them at the end of the month. While their presence had brought Luftwaffe fighters up to engage, then so had Blenheims. The weather had not helped and on clear days the large Stirlings had been pretty good targets for AA fire, especially at the heights they normally flew in order to get good hits on their assigned targets. 2 Group's Blenheims would now recommence co-operating with 11 Group on Circus operations.

Circus No.56

There is some mystery about this operation. No Circus report could be found, there were no bomber losses, and no apparent fighters escorted any raid. If it was intended to mount a Circus after No.55, late on the 21st, then it was aborted before it had begun. If it was supposed to have been an early Circus for 22 July, then this too was not sent off. There were two operations on the 23rd, and six Stirlings were sent to bomb the *Scharnhorst* in La Rochelle harbour that same afternoon (which cost them one bomber) but this could hardly have been a Circus.

Circus No.57 – 22 July

Six Blenheims found themselves on the roster for a raid on Le Trait ship yard during the late morning of 22 July, yet another cloudy day. They made rendezvous with their escort over Beachy Head at 1230, Tangmere on Close Escort, Kenley doing Target Support, so a pretty limited affair with just six Spitfire squadrons in tow. They headed directly to the target, bombing north to south from 10,000 feet, many bombs bursting on sheds and slipways, bathing everything in smoke. There was no flak and no fighters.

The Close Escort similarly had no problems with the enemy, nor did the Kenley pilots. It was a cushy number and no doubt the Blenheim crews were relieved. Perhaps this was due to....

Circus No.58 – 22 July

..... an operation, billed as a diversion for Circus 57. This must have been some sort of new ploy, for although mounted as Circus 58, there were no bombers involved, just three fighter wings, sweeping Dunkirk – St Omer – Gravelines shortly after lunch.

Those involved were Biggin Hill (72, 92, 609), Hornchurch (54, 603, 611) and Northolt (306 and 308). Perhaps it was hoped that with bombers reported further to the south-west over Le Trait, the Germans would assume this operation also included bombers, and would rise to the occasion.

There was a lot of cloud over France and the Spitfires were well above 24,000 feet. Some 109s were seen below and attacked, but the German pilots wisely zipped into the cloud and disappeared. The rest of the Wing got mixed up with the Hornchurch squadrons and not being able to reform, headed home. With Hornchurch also scattered the three squadrons started to act independently.

Then 603 was suddenly confronted with an estimated forty Me109s coming from the direction of Nieuport at 22,000 feet, stepped up in two gaggles of twenty. The 109s however, flew right by and kept going, no doubt looking for bombers. A couple of Spitfire pilots attempted attacks but made no claim. On the way over one pilot had been seen to drop away off Ramsgate, probably oxygen failure. 611 Squadron saw one of the two 109 formations turning south but did not attack. The second group were spotted by 54 Squadron, and some jousting took place with each side doing little but 'sabre rattling'. However, one Spitfire pilot was lost. Pilot Officer L. J. D. Jones was last seen going down with a 109 on his tail, and he ended up as a prisoner.

Northolt's Polish pilots had skirmishes too. 306 had one pilot attacked by three 109s but they quickly climbed away as he turned to engage. Meantime, 308 Squadron, west of Dunkirk, saw eight 109s to port but when attacked they dived and flew off to the south. Not to be thwarted, the Squadron went down to almost ground level and proceeded to shoot-up an aerodrome next to a wood by Guines (one of St Omer's airfields). Every pilot joined in, giving the airfield a thorough going over, with cannon shells ripping into hangars, gun posts, buildings, personnel and some aircraft that were half-hidden beneath trees at the edge of the area. Heading back to the coast and climbing they met several 109s, and in the ensuing dogfight, the Poles claimed three or four and a probable. Still not finished the Poles shot-up a gun position on the coast and then strafed a boat they found offshore. However, two pilots did not get back, both being killed. Priller claimed one. Not to be outdone, JG2 put in claims for six victories! Hans Hahn reported he got two, his thirty-third and thirty-fourth, while Oblt. Rudi Pflanz claimed his thirteenth.

The operation report recorded claims of 4-1-2 for the RAF, at the cost of four pilots.

* * *

The month of July saw the debut of the Focke-Wulf 190 fighter, which had been expected for some weeks. Early problems with the BMW engines during tests and trials were finally overcome and the 190A-1 was cleared for service. A group of II Gruppe, JG26 pilots began to swop its Me109s at Le Bourget, Paris and gradually the whole Geschwader had received the new fighter by the beginning of September. A new era was about to begin for the German Luftwaffe.

Chapter 7

The Blenheims Return

The RAF's Blenheim squadrons hadn't been idle while 3 Group had been sending Stirlings out on Circus operations; there was always anti-shipping tasks on hand plus the occasional deep penetration missions over France or the Netherlands. However, 2 Group were now tasked to return to fly Circuses in co-operation with 11 Group.

Circus No.59 – 23 July

The Blenheims returned for two operations on the 23rd. This, the first, comprised six aircraft from 114 Squadron attacking targets at the Forêt de Eperlecques. North Weald provided Close Escort, Biggin the Cover Wing position. Target Support came from eight squadrons of the Kenley, Northolt and Hornchurch Wings.

Initial RV was over Manston at 1300 hours. Reaching the target area, a layer of 6/10ths cloud made things difficult and although bombs went down through this, only one crew saw bombs bursting on target. No enemy aircraft were seen by the crews or the Escort Wing. Neither did the Cover Wing, and their only cause for excitement was strafing two small vessels two miles off the French coast.

Kenley's pilots saw little either, although 602 Squadron saw twelve 109s diving on them in loose line astern but they did not press home their attack. Five more were seen above and one Spitfire pilot took a shot but without visible result. The Northolt pilots however, were jumped by fifteen 109s at 23,000 feet and further enemy fighters came in from behind. The Wing turned to meet the threat with 308 Squadron forming a defensive circle. A general dogfight began that gradually lost height as it drifted towards St Omer where another twenty 109s waded in.

The Poles of 306 claimed two 109s with two more damaged, but suffered casualties. Two pilots were shot down and killed, another baled out with serious wounds to be rescued from the Channel. A fourth pilot, F/O Witold Pniak, who had seen considerable action in the Battle of Britain with RAF squadrons, ran out of fuel and had to crash-land in Richmond Park, Surrey, his Spitfire having to be written-off. Hornchurch also had reactions from 109s and all three squadrons were engaged. 603 claimed one destroyed (Sgt J. Hurst) but lost a pilot, 611 claimed a probable (Sgt A. C. Leigh), while 54 Squadron got a damaged but also lost a man. In fact, 54 had P/O C. Cookson killed and P/O V. D. Page wounded, although he managed to get home, force landing near Whitstable. Vernon Page put in claims for two 109s destroyed later, and Jack Charles got the damaged.

Adolf Galland, still grounded after his wounding back on 21 June, assumed this meant combat flying, so took off on a 'test flight'. He led JG26 into some Spitfires and shot one down, while his pilots claimed another three, amongst whom Hptm. Walter Adolph scored his twenty-first and Priller his forty-third. When pilots of JG2 landed, they put in claims of fourteen - perhaps a trifle excessive!! Total RAF losses were five killed, with two wounded and two other fighters lost.

Circus No.60 – 23 July

This second operation on the 23rd had six Blenheims from 114 Squadron going for the Synthetic Petrol, Benzol plant and Power Station at Mazingarbe. North Weald got the Close Escort slot, Hornchurch the Cover, Tangmere and Biggin the Target Support while 12 Group were handed the Forward Support (266, 401 and 601) and Kenley the Rear Support.

Cloud and haze were against the operation but then, over the French coast, the leading bomber was hit in a petrol tank by AA fire, and the pilot turned back. His two wingmen turned back as well, leaving the other three to carry on alone. With difficult conditions over the target, the bombers made two runs at it before letting go their bombs from 12,000 feet. All three were hit by flak, one having to make a crash-landing on its return to base, but the crew were safe.

Due to the weather and then the bomber problems, 71 Squadron lost a section of two in cloud and they returned home. Of the ten remaining, five were sent back to escort the three aborting bombers while the other five bravely continued on. They saw a dogfight way overhead but were not themselves engaged. Cloud also caused two of 111 Squadron to collide. One pilot baled out safely, (Sgt. T. R. Caldwell) but the other was killed. Five of 111 also returned with the first three bombers, while the others also went on and also saw the dogfight above but, like 71, did not get involved.

Escort Cover reported seeing some eighty-plus Me109s high above, their three squadrons stepped up to 20,000 feet, the top squadron alone, 603, counting a bunch of twenty-plus within a thin layer of haze. From time to time several small groups of 109s dived on the Wing and although some Spitfire pilots fired at fleeting glimpses of 109s, made no claims. However, they lost two pilots, one killed, one PoW.

Tangmere, stepped up to 24,000 feet, also saw large numbers of 109s – fifty-plus – but they seemed loath to engage in combat. Of those that did come down to fight, it resulted in a number of 'terrific dogfights'. As a result, the Wing was able to claim three 109s destroyed, another probable, plus three damaged, but lost one. This was P/O D. N. Forde who, as mentioned earlier, in fact baled out and was hidden by French farm workers. With the help of Resistance workers, Derek Forde eventually crossed into Spain over the Pyrenees, later reaching Gibraltar from where he was flown home in October. Evading with him had been Sgt Lockhart and Mensik, brought down earlier in July. Forde, having seen action over Dunkirk and in the Battle of Britain, later saw action in North Africa and was awarded the DFC.

Biggin Hill's Wing was also high up and saw many 109s milling about over St Omer and dogfights began that continued back to the coast. It claimed two 109s (Paul Richey of 609 getting one) and three damaged but also lost a pilot - Sgt J. W. Perkins of 72 - who became a prisoner. A worrying note in the Wing report was that it appeared some of the 109s were able to turn inside the Spitfires, the RAF pilots not being able to turn sharp enough to fire. The 12 Group Wing got in at the end of these fights but did manage to shoot down one Messerschmitt.

The score against the 109s appears to be in the region of five destroyed, one probable and eight damaged. RAF losses came to three killed, one captured, two wounded and one evading. That evening 603 lost another pilot who was flying on an Air Sea Rescue escort. P/O H. Blackall RCAF ditched following engine trouble and although he was picked up, died later from his injuries.

Luftwaffe fighters from JG26, again led by Galland, fought the Spitfires, Galland claiming two more, bringing his personal score to seventy-three. Oberleutnant Johann Schmid got his 11th. Galland's brother Wilhelm also put in a claim but it was not upheld. JG2 were also airborne and managed to claim another *TEN* Spitfires plus *THREE* Hurricanes, making a total for them of twenty-seven for the day – and they were not finished yet! They did, however, lose two pilots killed, while JG26 lost Obgfr. Ernst Krämer to a Spitfire attack. He is reported to have baled out after colliding with a Spitfire, but he took to his parachute while going too fast and his harness ripped apart.

Galland was wounded again on this date, with yet another injury to his head, following the one received on 21 June when he had been forced to bale out. Galland, on this second occasion, had evaded his attacker and managed to land, doctors stitching him up once again. Soon afterwards he was off to meet Hitler in order for him to be presented with the Swords to his Knight's Cross and Oak Leaves.

* * *

There were other actions on the 23rd. In a late morning anti-shipping strike, two Blenheims of 18 Squadron were shot down off Den Helder by Me110s of 5./ZG76, while in the afternoon more Blenheims were out on coastal operations and 21 Squadron lost four, off the Scheldt Estuary and Ostend. Fifteen crewmen died and three were taken prisoner. JG26 claimed the latter four bombers, Walter Adolph gaining his twenty-first victory. If the Stirling crews thought they were off the daylight hook they were wrong. 15 Squadron had a machine shot down on a raid on the *Scharnhorst* at La Pallice. The bomber had been damaged by Ltn. Ülrich Adrian of JG2 and eventually crashed into the sea 50 miles out from Milford Haven. There were no survivors. (JG2 also claimed two Fortress bombers that were undoubtedly Stirlings too.) Adrian gets the credit due to identification, but the other two German pilots might just as easily have inflicted the damage on the one lost. 7 Squadron were also on this operation and at least one Stirling was attacked by three Me109s. JG2 did not suffer any losses although a rear gunner did claim two which he saw crash into the sea.

The excitement had occurred due to reports that the *Scharnhorst* had moved from Brest to La Pallice. In all this day, JG2 put in claims for twenty-nine victories while JG26 recorded ten. Total losses by the RAF for the day were fifteen, including JG2's encounter with bombers over La Pallice.

Circus No.61 – 24 July

This Thursday started operationally with another raid on La Pallice by Armstrong Whitworth Whitleys on what was named a 'Sunrise I' mission. Eighteen bombers went, bombs were seen to explode on the docks, and no RAF aircraft were lost. There was also a Gudgeon operation, the RAF and the Royal Navy combining on a pre-dawn op. to engage any enemy aircraft that reacted to it. This was followed later by Sunrise II, this time eighteen Blenheims of 2 Group, that was a diversion against Cherbourg, for a much larger raid by medium and heavy bombers. This was escorted by 11 Group's Kenley Wing of 452, 485 and 602 Squadrons.

Circus 61 was intended to be a diversion for the La Pallice raid, nine Blenheims of 16 Group's 59 Squadron going for the Hazebrouck marshalling yards, with North Weald taking the Escort Wing slot, Northolt the Cover, with Target Support going to nine squadrons from Hornchurch, Biggin and 12 Group. The weather was described as fair but with some fog, and over France 5/10ths cloud lingered at between 5–7,000 feet.

The Blenheims carried out what they recorded as high-level bombing, releasing 10 x 500, 16 x 250lb bombs, plus 28 x 25lb incendiaries. Bursts were seen on the target and on railway yards but results, other than thick smoke, could not be seen. However, as they flew off the smoke began to mingle with large fires, some noted as particularly fierce. The bomber crews also commented on the efficiency of the fighter escort, although no enemy fighters approached the raiders.

The RV over Manston at 1415 was followed by entry into France east of Dunkirk, coming back out over Mardyck. Turning back at the target 71 Squadron did see three 109s in the distance, but 111 and 222 Squadrons saw nothing. The two Polish squadrons from Northolt, 306 and 308 did not have a lucky day, with a pilot of 308 colliding with another Spitfire. P/O W. W. Chciuk became a prisoner while P/O J. Czachowski was killed. The latter pilot was from 315 Squadron but flying with 308 on this mission. Reaching the target a few 109s were seen but climbed away when the Spitfires turned in their direction. 306 also saw nine 109s that came down behind them. One pilot who was attacked dived away steeply to 3,000 feet and upon levelling out discovered a 109 in front and just below him. He opened fire and the 109 hit the ground. This was F/O S. F. Skalski who was fast becoming one of the top scoring Polish pilots. Stanislaw Skalski had seen action over Poland when the war began, then escaped to England to fly in the Battle of Britain with 501 Squadron. He had become a flight commander with 306 in the spring of 1941 and this was his first victory of the year – his fourteenth overall. He would later bring his score to twenty-four and survive the war.

Hornchurch were over France when they got a call from the Controller that the Close Escort needed help, although what help is not clear! They did head for the problem area and did see some 109s but nothing really developed until coming back. Several 109s appeared and 603 with two sections of 611 dived at them but they turned into France. Chased by the Spitfires the Wing Leader, Stapleton, claimed one destroyed and P/O W. G. D. D. Smith (Duncan Smith) damaged another; later he claimed a 109 probable.

Biggin Hill's three squadrons had as usual split into 'fours' as they crossed into France, seeing twenty to thirty 109s between 22–25,000 feet. Combats began in which two 109s were claimed destroyed, four probably destroyed and one damaged. However, they lost two pilots. One from 72 was shot down near St Omer and taken prisoner, while a 92 Squadron pilot went into the sea and was lost.

The 12 Group Wing (65, 257 and 401 Squadrons) patrolled Gravelines – St Omer – Hazebrouck – Cassel at 20,000 feet for a quarter of an hour. They saw any number of 109s way above them and several came down in pairs to attack. In the fights that followed, one 109 was claimed destroyed and two damaged. No losses were reported although one pilot, F/Lt T. A. F. 'Taffy' Elsdon DFC, of 257, suffered an arm wound but got back to crash-land his Hurricane at Hawkinge. Elsdon would later command 136 Squadron in Burma.

Claims of 5-4-4 were submitted for the loss of four pilots (and one wounded). JG26 claimed three Spitfires and two Hurricanes (although none of the latter were lost in action), Priller getting his forty-fourth and Adolph his twenty-second. II Gruppe JG2 claimed two Spitfires – and a Blenheim. No German losses are recorded.

* * *

Meantime, further along the coast this day, another main effort was being made over the Cherbourg area, and I Gruppe of JG2 were involved in the major Bomber Command raid on La Pallice and Brest – in daylight.

The Sunrise II operation mentioned earlier, had gone fairly well although one fighter pilot was lost while two 109s were claimed by 452 and 485 Squadrons. During the main attack, over 100 bombers – Wellingtons, Halifaxes and Hampdens – were subjected to flak and fighter attacks. Ten Wellingtons and two Hampdens were shot down on the Brest op. and five Halifaxes lost over La Pallice. JG2, whose I Gruppe was seeing its first major combat for some time, claimed a total of eleven Wellingtons, five Halifaxes, four Hampdens, and a Stirling(!), plus three Spitfires. Spitfires were in the escort and 152 Squadron lost two pilots, one dead, one PoW, while 485 Squadron had a pilot bale out into the sea on Sunrise II but he was not seen again. The 152 pilot killed was a Battle of Britain veteran, F/Lt E. S. 'Boy' Marrs DFC, who had scored heavily in 1940. He was just thirteen days past his twentieth birthday.

Hauptmann Karl-Heinz Krahl claimed three, a Spitfire and two Hampdens, bringing his score to eighteen. Leutnant Julius Meimberg claimed two Hampdens to reach thirteen victories, although he was also wounded in this action. However, JG2 suffered heavy losses too. Five pilots were killed, two wounded and at least another 109 damaged. Erg.Gr./JG2 also had a pilot wounded, his fighter lost. These casualties were inflicted by 501 and 316 Squadrons. Squadron Leader A. H. Boyd DFC and Bar and F/Lt J. H. Lacey DFM and Bar of 501 each claimed two. Ginger Lacey's two had actually collided as each tried to shoot him down. When the two Australian Squadrons claimed one each on Sunrise II, one was credited to F/Lt E. P. 'Hawkeye' Wells. These three pilots now had eighteen, twenty-seven and six victories respectively. 316 scored one and a damaged.

* * *

Circus No.62 - (see 7 August)

Circus No.63

Circus 63 that had been organised against Le Trait for 25 July, was also abandoned. Certainly the 'wonderful' July weather was continuing to hamper events with cloud and rain. It may have been re-scheduled for the 27th too, but it did not happen.

Circus No.64 – 27 July

This was mounted on yet another rainy day, but without a target it was in effect merely a fighter sweep by Kenley, Hornchurch and Biggin Hill. The plan had been to attack the power station at Yainville but the six Blenheims of 114 Squadron abandoned the task because of the weather. Therefore nine Spitfire squadrons headed over to France at 2030 hours, saw nothing and came home.

Earlier this day 242 Squadron were out over the Channel, escorting a Naval motor torpedo boat in the hope of attacking a reported destroyer. The Squadron found the destroyer, escorted by five E-boats but they saw no sight of the Navy boys. Over Calais they engaged some 109s, at 1340 claiming one destroyed and three probables but lost Sgt G. A. Prosser RCAF, shot down and killed by Uffz. Hans Frölich of JG26, for his fourth victory. JG26 recorded no losses. Possibly the 109 seen diving into the sea had instead been Prosser.

* * *

On the afternoon of Wednesday the 30th, 139 Squadron lost four Blenheims to the Me110s of ZG76 off the Dutch coast. All twelve men died. ZG76 claimed five in all. It was a bad day for the Blenheims, with three more lost (by 18 and 82 Squadrons) on a sweep to the Kiel Canal area – six more crewmen dead and three captured.

At the end of July the decision to end Stirling operations on Circuses was finally made by C-in-C Bomber Command. Sholto Douglas at Fighter Command HQ was not happy as he was desperate to have them in order to entice Luftwaffe fighters into battle. However, 2 Group would continue to provide its Blenheims and the CAS agreed to continue basic Circus operations during the summer.

* * *

Fighter Command's statistics for July 1941 make interesting reading. It had flown over 400 sorties on Circus operations, and claimed 161 enemy aircraft destroyed (virtually all Me109s). Fighter pilot losses totalled eighty-four killed, prisoners or missing. Adding all the other operations flown, total sorties amounted to 525, with 185 enemy machines destroyed and ninety-seven pilot casualties. Wounded pilots do not appear in this statistic. The loss of ninety-seven pilots would only be exceeded in August, by one (ninety-eight), so July had been a seriously bad month.

Rolf Pingel, who had been shot down over England on 10 July and captured had naturally been closely interrogated by the RAF's intelligence boys. While there is no suggestion here that he willingly gave more than his 'name, rank and number', the intelligence report contains some interesting comments made by him. These included the statement that he was pleased the RAF had started operating over France, because over England in 1940 many German pilots had been lost when having to bale out, whereas now, if forced to bale out, it was over their own territory. Until he was downed, he reckoned that over 100 RAF aircraft had been shot down over France while German losses had been between one fifth and one third of this number.

Pingel, when told that British claims totalled some 125 Me109s shot down, said that could not be correct as this would represent wiping out half the available fighter strength and they would not have been able to replace this number. His I Gruppe, during his pre-shoot-down period had lost just eight pilots but claimed around fifty RAF aircraft. As for the suggestion that the RAF were attempting to force the Luftwaffe to transfer fighters from the Russian front to combat the RAF daylight operations, Pingel said there was no need, because he felt that the supposed weak German opposition was a great temptation for the RAF to continue operations and thus lose pilots over France. The German intention was for the RAF to be so weakened that once Russia had been defeated, the Germans could concentrate once more against Britain, the opposition being far less than in 1940.

* * *

As August began anti-shipping sorties brought more grief. On the morning of the 1st, 107 Squadron lost two bombers, four more dead and two prisoners. The next day the CO of 82 Squadron, W/Cdr K. O. Burt DFC succumbed to ship's flak off Den Helder. His two decorated NCO crewmen also died. Burt had won his DFC in March in a similar attack and was lucky to escape being brought down. Despite severe damage to his aircraft he had brought it home on that occasion and landed safely.

Also on the 1st a Spitfire shot down another Spitfire over the Channel, killing a Canadian pilot of 242 Squadron. These things happen from time to time. The pilot responsible was an experienced fighter pilot with 602 Squadron, S/Ldr A. C. Deere DFC, who had been particularly successful over Dunkirk and during the Battle of Britain and whose score currently totalled about a dozen victories. Al Deere had only just taken command of 602, so a sad start with his new command.

On 3 August, the RAF lost one of its most successful fighter pilots, 611's F/Lt E. S. Lock DSO DFC & Bar. Eric Lock took advantage of poor weather to fly a Rhubarb sortie. He was last seen going down to strafe some soldiers he spotted near Calais and did not return. Other than a pilot of 92 Squadron being wounded during a Roadstead mission, Lock was the only loss. JG26's Oblt. Schmid of the Geschwaderstab claimed a Spitfire in the late afternoon, for his twelfth victory. Lock had shot down twenty-six German aircraft.

Wing Leaders remained largely the same for the new month of August, the only changes that would be recorded are that two Wings would have to replace their Leaders due to enemy action.

Circus Nos.65 & 66 – 5 August

The weather wasn't improving. Today 2 Group was to send out six Blenheims to bomb the airfield at St Omer-Longuenesse. The rendezvous happened over Manston at 1830 with the Escort Wings but the operation was aborted soon afterwards, just five miles from the French coast.

Circus 66 called for three Blenheims to try for this airfield again (or a target at Lille), with a RV over Manston at 2100 hours. This operation is not recorded in 11 Group's ORB, nor in the Book's appendices. The only operation this day that saw any action was Operation 'Grab' which was a combined Air and Naval operation in the English Channel to destroy a small convoy between Le Tréport and Fécamp. Two Hunt Class destroyers from Portsmouth, together with two MGBs (Motor Gun Boats) and three Blenheims from Manston were escorted by 242 and 222 Squadrons, with others standing by in case they were needed. 242 claimed to have shot down a 109 off the French coast at 1800. 242 in fact flew similar sorties on this afternoon.

To confuse the issue still further, 603 Squadron lost a pilot on this evening during a reported Circus. His body was washed ashore on the coast of Holland towards the end of the month. JG2 appears to have been responsible, pilots claiming three Spitfires! Two by Ltn. Erich Rudorffer for his twenty-ninth and thirtieth claims, and one by Hans Hahn, for his thirty-seventh. JG2 were certainly spectacular and enthusiastic scorers!

Circus No.67 – 7 August

Another attempt to bomb the St Omer-Longuenesse airfield was organised for 7 August, six Blenheims of 107 Squadron heading off at 1000 hours. Escort Wing – Kenley; Escort cover – Biggin Hill; Target Support – Hornchurch; Mopping-Up Wing – Northolt. Mopping-up was still a new term but perhaps more in keeping with what was needed, i.e. aircraft to protect the withdrawing force, especially if being pursued and having perhaps been split up.

All bombers bombed and returned safely, explosions having been noted on the landing ground and some buildings. No fighters appeared and despite heavy flak, no bombers were hit.

The close escort squadron – 452 – flew four Spitfires each side of the bombers with two pairs weaving in front of and above them. 602 Squadron put themselves 1,000 feet above and to starboard while 485 were 4,000 feet above and to port. As they approached the target 602 had eight 109s approach and one was damaged while the others broke away. Then another 109 was hit and destroyed nearer the target. All got back to the coast save one pilot of 602 who ended up a prisoner. Not mentioned in the overall report was the loss of Sgt C. S. V. Goodwin of 485 – also captured.

The Biggin Hill squadrons were under constant attack by pairs of 109s that, as usual, appeared to be trying mostly to pick off stragglers. As the Wing finally left the coast on the way back, they saw sixteen to twenty Me109s and in combats, two were probably destroyed and one damaged, for the loss of one pilot. Sergeant C. H. Howard of 92 also ended up in a PoW camp, while Sgt G. P. Hickman was forced to crash-land near Deal, injured.

Hornchurch found many 109s, at one stage approaching from the south-east, south and south-west, while 611 Squadron (Top Cover) were bounced by others. They fought it out and may have shot one down. One pilot, who had been late in taking off, was not seen again. This pilot was later reported a prisoner. Sergeant G. A. Mason, also of 611, was shot up and forced to land near Deal too, hitting a mine. He was badly injured and his Spitfire was destroyed.

So, one 109 destroyed, three probably so and two more damaged, for the loss of four pilots plus two injured. Luftwaffe pilots claimed eight Spitfires, including JG26's Galland one, Schmid two, Schöpfel one, Siefert one, and Priller one. JG26 had one pilot wounded and two machines damaged. I met George Mason once and he recalled that his relief at making the beach was rudely shattered as the mine exploded!

Circus No.62 (67) – 7 August

Circus operations planned to cover the last few days of July are anything but clear. Circus 62 was scheduled for 25 July, an attack on the Power Station at Lille that afternoon. Six Blenheims were assigned and so were the various Escort Wings, but it seems it was either aborted or cancelled. It was re-scheduled for the late afternoon of 7 August.

Six Blenheims were alerted, with all the appropriate escorts but the weather again prevented an attack. Therefore the secondary target – barges on the canal at Gravelines – were bombed, but only five dropped their loads. The other aborted with engine trouble.

The Escort Wing, from North Weald saw nothing of enemy fighters, while Kenley, as Cover, did see some 109s, two or three making passes, but there were no engagements. Biggin Hill, Target Support, however, got mixed up with several 109s at 1130. 92 Squadron got into a fight and claimed a 109 as destroyed with another damaged, achieved by F/Sgt D. E. Kingaby DFM, although it seems that he was only credited with a probable. Don Kingaby was another top scoring pilot from 1940 days with an already impressive score of more than a dozen victories plus many probables and damaged. He had just been awarded a Bar to his DFM and before the year was out he would become the only RAF man ever to receive a Second Bar in the war. Several other pilots of the Wing claimed hits on 109s, five in all. Paul Richey of 609 was attacked by what he described as 'a gaily coloured 109' whose pilot got in a telling burst into his Spitfire, smashing his glycol tank, losing most of its coolant. Spinning down away from trouble, he decided it was time to bale out but as he couldn't release the pin of his safety harness, decided he would have to make a try for home. Leaving a trail of glycol smoke, his engine overheating rapidly, he headed out to sea. However, his experience helped him bring his crippled fighter back, later deciding it had been 75 per cent skill and 25 per cent luck.

Hornchurch went into France at Le Touquet stepped up to around 30,000 feet and the top squadron – 603 – ran into eight 109s and in a quick engagement, one was claimed as a probable. As they turned back more 109s appeared behind them but they were quickly driven off. 403 and 611 had orbited east of St Omer. Heading then for the Forêt de Guines, 403 spotted four 109s coming in but they quickly dived away. Then another gaggle of sixteen were seen, and as the Canadians started to attack, the 109s all dived into cloud and haze.

Tangmere also went in over Le Touquet and headed for the original target area and encountered a number of 109s that came down from the sun on the Spitfires' starboard quarter. Once more, as the Spitfires turned to engage, the 109 pilots broke away and dived, refusing combat. There followed several hit-and-run encounters, where the 109s tried to pick off someone then dive or climb away. Some scraps developed and the Wing claimed one probable and two damaged. One pilot from 41 Squadron was seen to bale out twenty miles inland from the coast. This was F/Lt G. G. F. Draper, who became a prisoner.

Only the Rear Support Wing from 12 Group saw further combat. Heading for St Omer between 20–24,000 feet they spotted many 109s and engaged them, claiming two destroyed, with a third probably so. The Wing lost one Hurricane near Hazebrouck. Then 19 and 401 Squadrons became embroiled with further 109s and lost two more pilots.

Total losses were ten pilots for claims of 3-3-3. JG26 and JG2 engaged, Schmid of the former gaining his third victory of the day. Priller got his forty-sixth, Schöpfel his second of the day (29th), and Oblt. Josef Haiböck got one, for his eighth. Wurmheller of JG2 got his second of the day – Number 22 – and also put in a claim for a Curtiss P40 for Number 23. Hahn also claimed his thirty-eighth. Both Gruppen had 109s damaged.

The day had cost the RAF four fighter pilots killed, five taken prisoner with four injured, one of whom died of injuries after a crash-landing upon returning from a Circus, and 11 fighters.

* * *

Paul Richey, who had struggled back across the Channel, decided to write of his experiences in getting back, sending it to 'higher authority' in the hope that the contents might help others in similar circumstances to those just experienced. The following report was later reproduced in an 11 Group Tactics Memorandum, distributed by Group Captain Victor Beamish DSO DFC AFC, who by this time was at Group HQ. It should be noted that Richey refers to the operation as Circus 62.

11 Group Tactical Memorandum No.10

Special Report by Flight Lieutenant Paul Richey DFC & Bar. Circus 62 flying with 609 Squadron, attack received near St Omer. 15–20 Me109s at 25,000 feet.

(1) I was Yellow 1 of 609 Squadron taking part in Circus 62, 7 August 1941. Having failed to rendezvous with the main formation of the Biggin Hill Wing, proceeded to carry out a "SPHERE" entry into Dunkirk and flying over St. Omer with the intention of leaving France at Cap Gris Nez. 609 was top squadron, 92 middle and 72 bottom, and heights were originally from 25–28,000 feet.[8]

(2) Over St. Omer many 109s were sighted far below against cloud and 72 led by Wing Commander Robinson, attacked. 92 lost height by diving and then circled for some time, followed by 609 Squadron. If I may suggest it, I think 92's tactics were mistaken, for both height and speed were lost and nothing gained. In addition the stepped-up formations of 92 and 609 were messed up and generally confused, while the Huns were able to gain height and time and get up-sun with a good view of what was going on.

(3) I was troubled with ice on my hood and windscreen. I was also very bored and cold and was flying sloppily. While my attention was concentrated on

---

8. A 'Sphere' operation is a high altitude fighter sweep above cloud over enemy territory.

a formation above me, I was shot-up in no uncertain manner by a gaily coloured Me109 diving from behind. My glycol tank was pierced and all my glycol lost. I throttled back and went into an involuntary spin. I could see nothing but smoke, glycol, etc and could not recover from the spin which became very flat. I opened the hood to bale out but had great difficulty in removing my harness, I think because (a) I did not look at what I was doing, and (b) I was experiencing a lot of 'G'. When I got the pin out I was slowly deciding which side of the cockpit to get out. The smoke had abated and I decided to stay in and try to recover, by winding the tail trim-tab control fully forward and using considerable strength on the stick, I did so. (The tail was damaged.) I dived for cloud and the French coast, weaving, and was attacked by another 109 which I evaded by turning violently and entering cloud. My 'Mayday' was answered immediately and over the sea on Button 'D' and was given a vector.

(4)   I was unable to use the vector because of having to weave and control the aircraft. Halfway across the Straits at 1,000 feet I tried my engine and was able to use it to the English coast by cutting down boost and revs to a minimum. I had great difficulty in doing up the straps again because of instability of the aircraft which necessitated strong forward pressure on the stick, but succeeded after five minutes. I was comforted by the sight of many rescue launches and buoys and by the Hurricane low cover off the Goodwins. On a fast belly landing at Manston with a still smoking aircraft I found the fire tender very prompt. I would like to stress the following points:

   i. Slackness in the vicinity of the Huns is easy but usually fatal.

   ii. A Spitfire will last long enough without glycol and even practically without oil, if revs and boost are reduced to an absolute minimum.

   iii. The sea is much more hospitable than German-occupied territory. It is well worth risking attempting reaching it. The chances of rescue are excellent.

   iv. Do not try a slow forced landing, with damaged control surfaces.

* * *

Circus No.68 – 9 August

The weather forecast over France for this Circus to the petrol refinery at Gosnay, four miles south-west of Béthune, promised 8/10ths cumulus at 6–7,000 feet on the way in but with 10/10ths over the target. The cloud would be in layers with breaks at higher levels. Just five Blenheims of 226 Squadron were the raiding force, escorted by North Weald, Hornchurch, Kenley, Tangmere and Northolt Wings.

Rendezvous over Manston was timed at 1100 hours, but once they had reached the target the cloud cover prevented any chance of bombing and nor did the secondary target prove anymore successful and so the bombs were dropped on the estimated position of Fort Phillipe at Gravelines. Someone reported some bombs fell on land and some in the sea. Not a particularly satisfactory operation as far as the bombing was concerned.

The Escort had two or three 109s make quick attacks on the force but suffered no loss but did manage to hit and claim one destroyed and one probable. Eagle pilot P/O W. 'Bill' R. Dunn claimed the one destroyed. This was Bill Dunn's third combat victory, and if one adds two Ju87s he claimed while a ground gunner during the Battle of Britain, he reached acedom in very different circumstances to most airmen. One could say that several things were different about Bill's war. The events of 9 August prove this, as he wrote in his book '*Fighter Pilot*':

'On 9 August at 11.30 hours, while providing fighter escort for our bombers on Circus 68, I was leading White Section of A Flight. When we were about 15 or 20 miles into France my Spit's engine started to surge. Then it quit. I was left a mile and a half behind the rest of the formation, gliding down at 120 mph and planning to belly-land in a field just west of Mardyck. I fully expected to be captured by the Squareheads, to spend the rest of the war in a PoW camp.

'At 4,500 feet, just above a scattered cloud deck, I saw a Me109E some 2,000 feet above me and coming after me fast. The Kraut pilot tried to shoot me down from his higher position, but he missed. I pulled my gliding Spit's nose up sharply and fired my guns from 100 yards range, hitting the 109 squarely in the cockpit hood as it passed by me, a lucky shot. Practically on a stall, I half-rolled and, following the Hun in his dive, fired three more bursts at him from a range of about 300 yards. Luckily, my engine started up again after the half-roll, but it was running very rough without much power.

'We both went down through the clouds, then just as we broke clear, a second 109, flying under the clouds, flew between the first 109 and my Spitfire. Firing at this second enemy aircraft from 75 yards, I shot some pieces off its starboard wing. This 109 had already been shot up by someone else, since I observed that it was trailing white glycol with black smoke pouring from its engine. This second 109 went down on its back, but I did not see it crash.

'I continued to follow the first 109 down to about 900 feet, from where I saw it smash into the ground and explode in a fiery sheet of flame. With my engine giving me at least enough power to stay airborne, I decided that this wasn't going to be the day the Huns captured me. So I headed westward towards Gravelines at about 800 feet.'

Bill Dunn got back despite being a low target for many ground gunners as he flew by, and calling a 'Mayday' was soon being escorted by two Spitfires of 403 Squadron to Manston were he landed. In 1943 he transferred to the USAAF and flew with the 406th Fighter Group, ending the war with nine confirmed and three unconfirmed kills, plus twelve more destroyed on the ground.

Escort Cover was also engaged, 611 having a couple of attacks parried away, 603 were also nibbled at while 403 managed to claim a probable as other 109s lunged at them.

Target Support met 109s that came in and out of the cloud layers which developed into a series of dogfights, in which five 109s were claimed destroyed by 452 Squadron, but the Australians lost three pilots – two killed, one prisoner. F/Lt B. E. Finucane shared one with P/O R. E. Thorold-Smith, and one was claimed by P/O K. W. Truscott. Paddy Finucane also got one on his own, sharing yet another with Sgt K. B. Chisholm, while Chisholm and P/O D. E. Lewis shared one more between them.

Meantime, 602 Squadron, spotting the fight below, sent one section down to help and after a skirmish, this section decided to head for home as they had lost height and position. Some other 109s attacked as they headed north and a couple of the attackers were damaged. 485 Squadron was also part of this Escort Wing, and one of its New Zealand pilots, Sergeant J. A. 'Jack' Rae, also had problems over France like Bill Dunn. He recorded in his book '*Kiwi Spitfire Ace*':

'Such were the fuel limitations that any show, which ran over two hours, was pretty close to being marginal, and if a large proportion of the flight was at full throttle, then fuel at the show's end would be very low indeed.

'On this particular day the action had been exceedingly hectic. We had been on a Circus to Gosnay, led by Squadron Leader Marcus Knight, and were fighting our way back after protecting the bombers. I was in the lethal position of Tail-End Charlie. As each attack developed we'd turn to meet them, fight them off and reform. After one such skirmish I found myself very much alone – it was a case of turn and fight, turn and fight and slowly work myself towards the Channel.

'I finally reached the beautiful English coast in a lather of sweat and with petrol gauges that said the tanks were on empty. Suddenly, bursting through cloud I saw a very welcome sight – an airstrip right in front of me. I lined up and began to let down on the grass airfield with no runways but plenty of room. Level off, touch down, turned to taxi over to the control tower and then stopped in disbelief. Everything was ominously still. Then, horror of horrors. I could see aircraft on the ground but they were all fakes!'

Rae had landed on a dummy airfield, one of many built to deceive enemy reconnaissance aircraft, and he had been fortunate not to run into some of the obstacles that abounded. Eventually a farmer came across to him and told him where the nearest real airfield was. Despite his tanks still showing empty he took a chance, flew off and as he landed at a proper base his engine stopped.

The Tangmere Wing were also hotly engaged, 616 Squadron encountered some sixteen to twenty 109s between St Omer and the original target. One section turned to engage and claimed four of them destroyed, and one probable for the loss of two pilots. In fact, when the pilots later totted up the score it came to six and one probable, one destroyed being shared with the Wing Leader, Douglas Bader. Johnnie Johnson bagged two, Nip Heppell one, Sgt J. G. West one and the shared. F/Lt L. H. Casson DFC was one of the losses, the other being the Wing Leader; both became prisoners of war.

After the war, Bader claimed he had been attacking a 109 but had then collided with another, which sliced off his tail-plane, forcing him to bale out, minus one of his tin legs. In fact his tail had been smashed by cannon fire and no doubt Bader, not wishing to admit being bested in combat, had preferred to say he had been in a collision. In fact the story is worse than that, for it appears that Buck Casson had accidentally shot him down, believing he was lining up on a 109! While in prison camp Casson had admitted as much to Bader who was even less inclined to acknowledge this turn of events. Whatever the truth, the Wing had lost two very experienced fighter pilots, for Casson in turn had then been attacked and shot down by Gerhard Schöpfel of JG26 – his twenty-ninth victory.

The Poles (Support Wing) engaged some 109s, one squadron (306) remaining top cover as 308 and 315 went down on several pairs. 315 Squadron claimed one destroyed and three probables.

JG26 reported the loss of two Me109s with both pilots baling out, one being wounded. The Geschwader scored seven Spitfires, including Galland's seventy-fourth, Obfw. Walter Mayer's eleventh and Johann Schmid's sixteenth. RAF losses amounted to five, plus one Spitfire of 315 whose pilot had to crash-land at Little Waldingfield, Suffolk due to lack of petrol upon his return. The aeroplane was later written off. RAF claims totalled 18-12-9, 452 Squadron claiming half a dozen. 92 Squadron got four, one by Neville Duke, as described in his combat report:

'Attacked from astern by two Me109Fs at 2,000 ft over Boulogne. I saw the first one approaching to the attack and turned to the left until he was on the opposite side of the circle. I then immediately turned to the right as hard as I could. He went past me on the starboard beam and I gave him a burst from astern at 200 to 300 yards range. At this moment I saw tracer pass over my cockpit and another 109 passed me on the right. I gave him a long burst with some deflection from 50 yards rapidly increasing. The 109 went on its back and did a slow spin in this position into the cloud which was about 800 feet. I did not see it crash into the sea but do not consider it could have pulled out.

'I was shortly afterwards jumped by another two 109s just above the cloud. I ducked into cloud hoping they would give up the chase but when breaking cloud, the 109s were still there and chased me down to sea level and to within 2 to 3 miles of Dover.

'Their spinners appeared to be painted black and white. Tracer ammunition would have been a great asset as my reflector sight was u/s. I suggest some tracer be used in future.'

Bader's place as wing leader went to W/Cdr H. de C. A. Woodhouse. Paddy Woodhouse was a pre-war pilot, and although involved in non-operational duties in 1940, had joined 610 Squadron in the Spring of 1941, to gain operational experience, before taking command of 71 Eagle Squadron in June. Compared to Bader, his modest score of one destroyed plus another shared did not make him an obvious choice among the rank and file pilots, but his overall experience quickly cemented his position at Tangmere.

* * *

Fighter Command was to lose more Spitfires during a Rodeo to Hardelot in mid-to-late afternoon. JG26 again rose to the challenge, claiming six Spits and one Hurricane. Schmid made it three for the day, Galland got another for his seventy–fifth while Priller also made it two for the day, forty-fifth and forty-sixth. Schöpfel got his thirtieth, and CO of the 6th Staffel, Oblt. Walter Schneider scored twice, victories fifteenth and sixteenth – for no losses. The RAF had made claims. 92 Squadron 4-1-3, 315 Squadron 1-1-2, 111 scored a destroyed and 609 Squadron 0-1-1. Spitfires lost were five, four pilots killed (111, 403, 315 (2)). A pilot of 609 Squadron, Belgian P/O A. J. G. Nitelet, was wounded when his machine turned over upon crash-landing. He suffered serious injuries, losing his right eye, but was rescued by a farmer and he managed to evade into Spain. Alex Nitelet later became a radio operator with the French escape line, being flown back to France by Lysander in May 1942, but was captured in September. A French camp commandant released him unofficially and he was back in Spain by December.

The day's total for JG26 was fourteen of which eleven were confirmed. Anti-aircraft claimed two. Fighter Command was credited with 18-12-9, and admitted losses of ten aircraft and six pilots.

There were two senior pilots with the RAF this day. One was Group Captain F. V. Beamish DSO DFC AFC, flying with North Weald, and Wing Commander T. H. Rolski, commanding No.1 Polish Wing, having earlier led 306 Squadron. He had fought in Poland before escaping to England via France. Both were much older than the men they commanded, Victor Beamish was nearing 38, while Tadeusz Rolski would be 35 in September. Beamish, despite his rank, age and position as Station Commander, was not a man to lead from the ground and often flew operationally. He would fly often on Circuses from North Weald, and especially when the Wing Leader was lost later in August.

* * *

On the 10th, 2 Group were sent on an anti-shipping strike off Calais and ran into JG26. Two Blenheims of 226 Squadron were shot down, one falling to AA fire, although both were claimed by fighter pilots, Oblt. Walter Otte and Ltn. Paul Schauder. The 109s also got stuck into the escort, Oblt. Schmid claiming two Hurricanes (of 242 Sqn) and a Spitfire, to bring his score to twenty-one. Another pilot also claimed a Spitfire. However, only one of 242 failed to return. Obviously Schmid was anxious to acquire his Knight's Cross – which he did received on 21 August - by which time his score had increased to twenty-five. However, this 30-year-old was not destined to survive the year.

Circus No.69 – 12 August

This operation was flown in conjunction with Circus 70. Not only were these two missions a new departure by both being diversions for a major 2 Group raid by fifty-four Blenheims against Cologne's power stations at Knapsack and Quadrath, but both included, for the first time, Handley Page Hampdens from 5 Group of Bomber Command.

In the event the diversions hardly succeeded, as ten Blenheims were shot down, mostly by flak, and two more Blenheims, sent to assist the fighter escort with navigation, were also shot down. On this raid twenty-six aircrew died, ten more were captured. JG1 claimed two Blenheims, while JG26 claimed another four, including one by Galland for number 77.

Circus 69, going for the airfield at St Omer, saw six Hampdens of 408 RCAF Squadron, escorted by North Weald, with Cover provided by Debden and a third North Weald squadron. Hornchurch gave Target Support. RV was over Manston at 1015, but cloud over the target prevented any form of identification so bombs were dropped on railway lines to the south. Flak was not intense but four bombers suffered slight damage. Close Escort saw a few 109s but they did not come close. Cover Escort saw little either, despite 54 having five of its pilots abort for various reasons before reaching the French coast. Once over France some 109s came down and another 54 Squadron pilot was wounded. However, the CO, S/Ldr Newell Orton DFC and Bar, claimed two. 'Fanny' Orton had been successful during the French campaign and these victories brought his score to seventeen. 222 Squadron made claims of 1-1-1 but lost one pilot killed. Speaking to Graham Davies, who had been a flight commander in 222 Squadron in the summer of 1941, he told me:

'We were out over France regularly in the summer of 1941. We often met 109s and the flak could be pretty heavy. Often the 109s would stay clear of us but on another day we would meet more aggressive chaps who would try to get at the bombers or hope to pick off a Spitfire or two. They would dive at top speed through us and although we would give the odd one a squirt, it was difficult to hit them and we could not follow them or we'd leave the bombers open to a more determined attack.'

G. G. A. Davies had been shot down over Dunkirk in 1940, force-landing on the beach but had managed to get back to England on a boat. He fought in the Battle of Britain and in 1941 he flew around forty operations over France. In 1944 he commanded 607 Squadron in the defence of the Imphal Valley in Burma, for which he received the DFC.

The Target Support boys on the 12th were thrown into total confusion due to the bombers making a very short turn to the south over France and lost sight of them until they located them over Gravelines. Some 109s sniffed around but nothing developed.

Circus No.70 – 12 August

While Circus 69 tried for St Omer, six Hampdens of 106 Squadron from Coningsby made for the power station at Gosnay, along with Northolt, Biggin Hill, Kenley and Tangmere Wings. Unlike their colleagues, they found their target and bombed from 14,000 feet, but most of the ordnance fell 100 yards to the west of the aiming point. Again flak was a nuisance and virtually every bomber received some flak damage.

Having met at 1133 over RAF Manston, the Escort Wing trailed across with the bombers and saw almost nothing of the enemy. Biggin Hill's fighters had their Spitfires stepped up from 18–23,000 feet, but finding the top squadron of the Close Escort at a higher level than they should have been, 609 Squadron had to go up to 24,500 feet, so they were almost level with the low squadron of the Kenley Wing. Six Me109s were seen above near the coast that appeared to be waiting to pounce once the Spitfires had passed by, but nothing developed.

The Kenley Wing, flying between 25–30,000 feet headed inland some 20 miles at which time a 109 dived through the upper squadron – 602 – and picked off S/Ldr Al Deere's wingman, P/O H. J. Bell-Walker, who started down trailing smoke. He baled out lower down to become a prisoner. An Australian of 452 Squadron became detached and headed down through cloud. Coming out over Le Touquet Aerodrome he could see no aircraft on the ground so proceeded to shoot up some buildings. Coming in again – a real no-no – he met intense ground fire and was lucky to escape unharmed. The other squadron – 485 New Zealand – had some skirmishes with 109s but nothing definite. On the way back a few 109s were seen harassing some Spitfires. Some pilots attacked and one 109 was damaged but lost a pilot. He lost an arm and was taken prisoner. The Tangmere Wing saw plenty of 109s but had no close engagements. Al Deere records in his book '*Nine Lives*':

'This show witnessed my first really narrow escape since returning to No.11 Group. When at briefing the Wing Commander Flying announced the target as Lille and said that 602 Squadron would act as close escort squadron, I had a premonition that it would be rough going. I noticed 'Mitzi's' [F/L E. V. Darling] face turn white at the mention of Lille and the expressions on the faces of the other pilots in the room revealed the varying degrees of emotion caused by this announcement.

'The towering banks of cumulus cloud, interspersed with layers of thin cirrus, which covered the route to the target, confirmed my worst fears. There was a sufficient amount of cloud to make escort difficult but not enough to interfere seriously with the operation. On the other hand, conditions were ideal for defensive fighters and the strong enemy reaction was proof that the Huns thought so too. The raid had barely reached mid-Channel before R/T silence was broken by the Controller to warn us of heavy enemy activity.

'Shortly before we reached St. Omer, where the first attack developed, the escort cover fighters, and those above, were screened from view by intervening cloud banks. To make matters worse, 485 and 452 Squadrons were forced to reduce height in order to keep the bombers in view. The scene was set, action was soon to follow. The first warning of attack came in the form of a surprise yelp from Johnny Kent. "Christ! There are Messerschmitts diving through the clouds ahead of us."

'A stream of Hun fighters had broken cloud ahead of the bombers and, wheeling round to port, they lined up for an attack. I was on the port side of the bombers with my section of four and could see Johnny taking a squadron across to cut them off. Anxiously I watched two 109s, which had separated themselves from the main formation, turning in behind me for an attack and as soon as I was certain that my section was to be the target, I gave the order to break to port. With my vision greying out under the mounting 'G' loading, I pulled hard around to meet them. A menacing yellow spinner passed within inches of my wing followed closely by a second as the two attacking 109s broke up and away.'

In a fight that lasted some time, Deere's Spitfire, too, suffered a hit just as he was firing a burst into the underside of a 109.

'Too late, I felt the shock of impact on my aircraft as an unseen Hun found his target; like a crack of doom the sound of an exploding cannon shell came deafeningly through my headphones. Momentarily I panicked, but quickly realised that my aircraft was still airworthy though obviously badly damaged.'

Deere dived into cloud to escape and then began the journey home. His engine temperature began to rise, with the coolant temperature also increasing. Heading for Manston he was keenly aware of the race between reaching it or losing his engine. Making a 'Mayday' call over the sea he gradually made the English coast and then Manston hove into view. Setting his damaged fighter down was a great relief to switch off the very hot engine. However, he had forgotten to cancel the Mayday call, and aircraft were already out trying to locate a downed pilot in the water. Inspecting his aircraft he found thirty-seven bullet holes in it, in addition to the cannon shell hit in the port wing root. The top fuel tank had also been punctured and the glycol line severed. He knew he had been just moments away from an engine seizure.

Circus No.71 – 12 August

The third and last Circus of the day comprised six Blenheims going for Le Trait ship yards, preceded by a sweep by Spitfires. This being the case Close Escort was just the Kenley Wing, with Tangmere providing Cover. Two bombers failed to make it through 'formation difficulties', but the other four dropped their bombs on target. One bomb was seen to hit a ship on the southern slipway. No flak or fighters interfered with the attack.

Kenley, on their second trip of the day, rendezvoused at 1800 hours over Beachy Head and took the bombers into France. 485 Squadron was again in combat and lost their second pilot of the day – killed. Other escort squadrons saw 109s but were not engaged.

This day cost Fighter Command four pilots killed, five taken prisoner and two wounded. They claimed six destroyed, five probables and eight damaged. Oberleutnant Erich Leie of JG2 appears to have got the second New Zealander on the Le Trait show, the unit's only claim of the evening, for his twenty-fifth victory. The Germans did well in their claiming on the 12th. JG26 had twelve, including Blenheims, while JG2 managed sixteen Spitfires and two Blenheims. The Stabstaffel were on top form according to the claims – Major Walter Oesau claimed five to bring his score to ninety-two, Erich Leie got three and Fw. Günther Seeger one for his thirteenth. In addition, 4(Eins)./JFS 5 claimed four Spitfires but only had one confirmed.

It had been a long and costly day for the RAF.

Circus No.72 – 14 August

With the improved summer weather the RAF continued its multiple Circus raids, mounting two on this date. This first one called for twelve Blenheims to attack a quite different target from the normal ones – German E-boats alongside the Quay in Boulogne Harbour. These fast-moving motor torpedo boats were often active during the night hours off the British coast and their fast and deadly strikes could prove costly to ships trying to head through the Channel during darkness.

Only eleven bombers took part in fact, with six from 107 and five from 114 Squadrons setting off at 1250 pm. Kenley's 452, 485 and 602 Squadrons took on the Close Escort job, while the Cover Wing was Biggin's task, with 72, 92 and 609. Two Support Wings, Hornchurch (403, 603 and 611) and Tangmere (41, 610 and 616) comprised the rest of the escorts. Being a coastal target there was no requirement for any Wings to help 'delouse' the target. Hopefully too, any enemy fighters that rose to counter the raid would be gaining height and waiting further inland in anticipation.

Lots of summer cloud made observation difficult when the 44 x 250lb and 28 x 40lb bombs went down from 11,500–12,000 feet, but all appeared to fall close alongside the target although actual results could not be observed. All the bombers returned and if nothing else, perhaps the E-boat crews felt a little more vulnerable if the RAF were taking time and effort to attack them in port.

There was a lot of flak over the target and one Blenheim, appearing to be hit, was escorted home by two pilots from 452 Squadron. A member of 485 Squadron was slightly wounded in one leg by this flak fire. No enemy fighters were seen. Biggin's pilots too saw the flak and the cloud but no hostile fighters.

The Hornchurch squadrons at 25,000 feet and above swept as far as St Omer, inland from Boulogne and Gris Nez, but nothing stirred. Tangmere was similarly unimpressed by the non-appearance of the enemy, until 616 spotted seven Me109s about 7,000 feet below them. Being the bottom squadron, 616 dived upon them and although three pilots opened fire, made no claims. This had split up the Squadron so everyone headed out over the sea and home.

The middle squadron – 610 – also found Me109s, in fact some forty appearing, and in a brief engagement, they claimed one probable and one damaged. 41 Squadron, top cover, were dived upon by two 109s and one of them was shot off the tail of a Spitfire and claimed as destroyed. Another pilot, heavily engaged by three 109Fs succeeded in damaging one of them.

Total claims were for one 109 destroyed, one probable and two damaged, although combat reports seem to indicate a score of 2-2-2, 41 Squadron reporting 2-0-1. Two pilots failed to return, F/Lt A. L. Winskill of 41 and Sgt L. M. McKee of 616. Archie Winskill in fact was one of the claimants, so his victory was not counted until much later, when he returned to England. In fact not only Archie Winskill but also McKee, both evaded and got home.

Archie Winskill had been a pre-war Volunteer Reserve pilot and had participated at the tail-end of the Battle of Britain, during which he had the rare experience of having encountered Italian aircraft in November 1940, claiming two Fiat CR42 biplanes off the Essex coast on the 23rd, with 603 Squadron. His claim over a 109 on 14 August, was his first since that time. Having then been shot down, he was found in a slightly stunned condition by a French farmer who asked if he needed help. Saying yes please, the farmer took him to his house. No sooner had they arrived than a car turned up with two German soldiers who went and inspected the downed Spitfire. Winskill was hidden in some corn overnight. He was then turned over to a French escape line and on 5 September, met up with Sgt McKee, the other pilot who had been shot down on this day. Eventually, after some adventures, both RAF pilots arrived in Spain, then Gibraltar and Winskill got home on 23 November. McKee made it to England on 18 December. Winskill later returned to operations in North Africa, receiving a DFC and Bar. He was to retire from the RAF as an Air Commodore KCVO CBE DFC, having at one time been the Captain of the Queen's Flight. He died in 2005.

The 4th Staffel of JG26 was responsible for the two Spitfire losses, the fourteenth victory for Oblt. Hermann Segatz, while the other was credited to the Staffel as a whole. JG26 suffered no casualties.

Circus No.73 – 14 August

This early evening operation should have been for six Blenheims to attack the Shell Factory at Marquise, being escorted by North Weald, Hornchurch, Northolt and Biggin Hill Wings. In the event, however, heavy cloud at the rendezvous prevented a join-up and so the bombers turned back to base without even crossing the English coast. North Weald continued to the French coast in the hope of finding the bombers to make RV, but in the end had to turn back too.

The Cover Wing carried on into France seeing a number of vapour trails high up and then some 109s near St Inglevert. More 109s were seen over Gravelines. As the Spitfires approached some 109s began diving away while others tried to climb around behind them. One 109 did make a pass but caused no damage.

The Support Wings then met 109s and a huge scrap developed. Northolt had 306 as top cover, 308 at the bottom and 315 off to one side in the middle. As the Wing turned north, 308 and 315 went down after some 109s seen below, who in turn tried to turn in behind the diving Spitfires. The Poles screamed round towards six 109s but immediately fifteen others dived on 306 Squadron from all directions. A big fight ensued in which two 109s were claimed destroyed and another damaged by 306, but three pilots were lost, including its CO, S/Ldr L. J. Zaremba.

Meantime, 308 saw thirty-five Me109s below and to port, and the whole Squadron dived to attack claiming three destroyed, one probable and two damaged for the loss of one pilot. 315 Squadron also got in amongst the 109s, initially going down on eight they saw above a cloud layer. As they engaged, dogfights broke out and other Spitfires joined in while more 109s also appeared. The Squadron claimed eight victories, plus a probable and a damaged without loss. Afterwards the Wing reported that they had caught most of the 109s napping and none should have got away! Flight Lieutenant W. Szczęśniewski reported:

'I dived at a Me109E, opening fire at 200 yds range with one burst, slightly above and astern. Immediately thick black smoke poured out of its cockpit, and as far as I could see the cockpit was jettisoned in order that the pilot could bale out. I did not see what happened after this because I noticed another Me. coming up behind from below and slightly across me. I turned towards it, and I'm certain it did not see me because it banked and exposed the whole of the upper surface to my fire. I opened fire at 150 yds and rapidly along to point blank range 10 yds, firing all the time. The enemy aircraft simply broke up and seemed to fall into bits in the cloud. I had to pull up very sharply in order to prevent collision. I then caught sight of the leader of the Me. formation, together with another aircraft flying over my nose above me, but I was unable to fire quick enough on account of my bad position. These two aircraft disappeared. I rejoined the formation, landing at Northolt at 1825 hrs, and claim one e/a destroyed, and one probably destroyed.'

The Squadron Intelligence Officer later noted that he had fired 700 rounds of .303 bullets but no cannon shells. The pilot had omitted to press the cannon button! Władysław Szczęśniewski failed to return from Circus 110 on 8 November, and became a prisoner. By that date he was commanding the Squadron.

The Biggin Hill Wing crossed into France penetrating to about fifteen miles inland, also to the St Omer area. A large number of 109s were seen in various formations and Sailor Malan kept his fighters up-sun of them. Finally, 72 Squadron moved to attack but the 109s merely moved off to avoid combat. The Spitfires returned without loss.

Total claims over the German fighters amounted to thirteen destroyed, two more as probables and four damaged for the loss of four RAF pilots. The Polish Wing had attacked the Third Gruppe of JG26 and had shot down two 109s, one pilot being killed, the other taking to his parachute suffering injuries. The Third Gruppe was the only unit engaged, losing just two pilots, so the Poles' claims were rather optimistic to say the least. Of the Pole's four losses, all were killed, one being S/Ldr Jerzy Zaremba, the CO of 306 Squadron.

Amongst the claimants were Oblt. Walter Schneider (his seventeenth), Ltn. Robert Unzeitig (fifth), Ltn. Erwin Biedermann (third), while Ltn. Heinz Schenk gained his first. Not wanting to be left out, JG2 also claimed four Spitfires, three of which were confirmed. Schnieder and Schenk of the 6th Staffel of JG26 were flying their new Focke-Wulf 190s, but none of the Polish pilots reported seeing a new type of fighter in this combat. It would not be long before everyone discovered the Germans had a new aeroplane at the front.

One of the successful Polish pilots was Jan Falkowski of 315. In his book *With the Wind in my Face* (privately published in 1967) he wrote:

'We were south of Calais when I spotted, some 17,000 feet below us, about 25 or 30 German aircraft. Petro [S/Ldr S. Pietraszkiewicz] ordered the attack and we dived. We were in an advantageous position – much higher than the enemy and in the sun where we couldn't be seen. As we went in, 306 was tackling between eight and twelve Germans.

'I picked out an Me109 and opened fire, never stopping until I saw his tail flying into pieces. Then I saw black smoke and he spun to the ground. Having despatched my German, I turned back to the squadron. I saw Sgt. Malczewski shoot down an Me., Petro bagged one … It was quite a sight.

'On return to base, we learned that we had shot down thirteen enemy aircraft altogether, my squadron alone accounting for eight without any losses. But 306 Squadron, which had fought above us, had had a stiffer engagement and had lost three pilots. One was its commander.'

According to Falkowski:

> 'The Polish Wing received a flood of congratulations, including personal messages
> from the Secretary of State for Air, and the Air Officer Commander-in-Chief
> Fighter Command. The AOC No.2 Bomber Group sent his hearty thanks to the
> Wing, for the Poles had intercepted and destroyed German fighters sent out to
> attack the British bomber formation which, as a result, was able to bomb with
> accuracy the power stations which were its targets that day.'

He was wrong about the success of the bomber raid of course. One wonders too what
the 'back room boys' in air intelligence thought about it all. It would not be long before
German intercepts asking for replacement Me109s would suggest the losses suffered
by JG26 (or even JG2) were far, far lower than thirteen. (It also appears that this total
was later amended upwards to 16-3-5 by Fighter Command.)

In 315 Squadron's Intelligence Officer's Form 'F' report the comment was made:
'The opinion of all pilots is that the enemy aircraft were completely surprised, lost
their heads [the German pilots that is], and each one adopted the suave *qui peur*
attitude. There were no attempts at co-ordinated escape, which possibly confirms the
fact that the Squadron had just broken cloud and was not yet properly under control.'

Chapter 8

Summer at Last – Well, Almost

The fickle summer weather had hindered many operations during the first half of August 1941 but in the second half it improved somewhat although summer showers were often in attendance. Fighter Command was now well into the swing of things as far as Circus operations were concerned and although the obvious dangers of combating German fighters over France occurred on virtually every occasion, there was to be no let up.

To many it was like a summer cricket season, with everyone gung-ho to get to grips with the Luftwaffe fighters, but in reality, for those who were able to look deeper into things, there seemed to be far more empty chairs in the Mess at dinner time, and it could only be hoped that the enemy fighter pilots were also giving sideways glances to their own empty chairs. The problem, of course, was that they didn't have the number of empty chairs the RAF fighter pilots imagined.

Circus No.74 – 16 August

Two more operations took place on this day. With the failure on the 14th, 2 Group put up another six Blenheims in the late morning to try again to bomb the Shell Factory at Marquise. The weather was a bit better, fair but with showers and 5/10ths cloud. This time it was aircraft from 82 Squadron and RV was made over the seaside town of Hastings at 1230. Escort Wing came from North Weald, Cover Wing from Hornchurch, Support Wings were those of Northolt and Biggin Hill, while a Mopping-up Wing was provided by Kenley.

Bombs were released at 1244 from 10,000 feet through gaps in the cloud, the same cloud that obscured results although it was thought most fell slightly south-west of the target hitting a railway junction. No fighters turned up to interfere but flak was heavy. One bomber was hit and set on fire; however, the fire was ably put out by the air gunner. A second bomber was also damaged by shellfire while two crew members of a third were slightly wounded by shrapnel.

The Close Escort squadrons (71, 111 and 222) had nothing to report, nor did the Cover Wing, although they did see six Me109s some way off. However, the Northolt boys got into the action. At 22,000 feet over St Omer, 306 Squadron saw fifteen 109s in three small formations and climbing towards them. The Poles dived and began to mix it with the German fighters, claiming six 109s destroyed. They lost one pilot who was seen to bale out over Cap Gris Nez, and believed to have been picked up by

German ASR. Two pilots, forced down during the fight, spotted a landing ground near Boulogne and proceeded to shoot it up, and strafe a party of soldiers. The other two Polish units, 308 and 315, remained above to give protection and were not engaged.

Some dozen Me109s were seen by the Biggin Hill Wing as they swept the St Omer area but did not make contact. One pilot, whose windscreen frosted up, went down and suddenly met a 109 at 1,000 feet which he fired at and claimed as damaged.

Heading over the coast, the Mopping-Up Wing (452, 485 and 602) saw several groups of 109s and as the time came for the Spitfires to head north, single 109s made attacking passes four times and fire was returned but neither side scored any hits. 602 Squadron spotted eight 109s at 27,000 feet which turned in behind them and then made a dive past the Spitfires. Two sections followed but made no claim. However, one pilot did not return. 485 Squadron saw six 109s making vapour trails way above but they did not come down. Another 109 came in and it was fired at, the RAF pilot seeing it go down in an uncontrolled vertical spin.

The missing Pole was indeed reported a prisoner later but the 602 Squadron pilot was killed. JG26 had the action with 602 Squadron and actually claimed four Spitfires, which was a bit excessive. There were a lot of German claims on the 16th and some recorded times seem a little suspect.

Circus No.75 – 16 August

This same Saturday an evening operation against the German airfield of St Omer/ Longuenesse needed six bombers which were supplied by 21 Squadron. RV with the Close Escort Wing (Kenley) was made above Hastings at 1800 hours, with Cover being down to Biggin Hill, Target Support by Tangmere and Northolt, with Forward Support being flown by Hornchurch.

The cloud that had been a problem for Circus 74 had now cleared, certainly over the target where the sky was clear with perfect visibility. 24 x 250 and 24 x 40lb bombs went down, bursts being seen across the aerodrome and along its northern boundary. There was no sign of enemy aircraft, either on the ground or in the air. Of interest is the comment by the Close Escort Wing that the Blenheim's camouflage was so good it had been difficult to maintain visual contact with them.

The Escort Wing squadrons had very mixed reports. 602 Squadron saw some 109s above and climbing into the sun but no attack came. However, 452 Squadron saw around fifty Me109s, all operating in small formations and on re-crossing the French coast, eight 109s attacked from behind and a dogfight broke out. Apparently 452 not only shot down six enemy fighters, but they also saw them crash into the Channel. This battle had caused the Spitfires to lose height and they headed for home at zero feet. 485 Squadron saw just one Me109 but failed to see the battle going on overhead before 452 dived.

Biggin Hill's squadrons, flying between 16–21,000 feet, also had some action. 72 and 609 had fights, initially with eight 109s that came down from the sun. 72 destroyed one as did 609 but the latter had one pilot fail to return – later reported killed. One pilot of 72 who had lost a lot of height, strafed a German sound detector near Gris Nez while another shot-up gun posts on the beach near Hardelot.

Two pilots in the Support Wing also shot up gun posts near Boulogne while others had indeterminate scraps with 109s. Tangmere's 610 Squadron claimed a damaged. Northolt's three Polish squadrons all saw combat but had little in the way of claims. The CO of 315, S/Ldr Stanislaw Pietraszkiewicz, had some difficulty with his R/T just as a warning of 109s was made. Believing he saw something to his left he broke away and became separated from his pilots. He then spotted seven 109s, got behind one and opened fire as he rapidly overtook it. The 109 broke up and went down.

Hornchurch crossed the French coast at 1822 and immediately saw two 109s coming from the south at 23,000 feet. Red Section of 603 went for them and shot one down. More 109s began to sniff around but every time the Wing made an attempt to engage the 109s dived away.

Total kill claims for this operation came to ten destroyed and one damaged, for just one loss. Hauptmann Adolph of JG26 claimed one Spitfire, victory number twenty-three, while JG2 reported having shot down another four. JG26 lost one pilot to a Spitfire. He was hit and baled out but his harness had been damaged and gave way as his parachute opened. Two other 109s got home damaged. JG2 had one pilot make a crash-landing near Calais and another 109 sustained slight damage while making a wheels-up landing at Moorsele airfield. The RAF's adjusted total for the day was 19-3-4, for the loss of four Spitfires.

It certainly seems as if the Australians of 452 Squadron were a little over-zealous in their claims, attempting to obtain confirmation by stating that their victims were seen to crash into the sea. Flight Lieutenant B. E. Finucane DFC claimed two, Sgt K. B. Chisholm two more, P/O K. W. Truscott one, while Sgts E. B. Tainton and A. R. Stuart claimed one each which in fact makes seven in all. The Irishman Paddy Finucane and Aussie 'Bluey' Truscott were certainly starting on a mission to see who could score the most victories and perhaps this made them over keen to claim. No doubt this also rubbed off on the other pilots in the Squadron. Finucane had now been credited with fourteen victories, including shares, while Truscott had achieved his second, but by the end of the 'shooting season' Finucane would have raised his score to twenty-six, Truscott to eleven. The story goes that later in 1941, S/Ldr E. P. 'Hawkeye' Wells, once he became CO of 485 Squadron, was actually suggesting to G/Capt Victor Beamish, that 452's claims should be investigated, but before Beamish could agree or not, he was lost over the North Sea. Certainly feelings were running high between the Australians and the New Zealanders at the time. Al Deere refers to this in his 'Nine Lives':

'I was most interested to hear Bill's [Hawkeye] views on the present operations and particularly to discuss with him my frustrated efforts to get near enough to the Hun fighters. "Frankly, Al, I fail to see how many of the squadrons shoot down the numbers they claim. On a very great number of operations, 485 Squadron has been on the same show, and in the same area of sky, and none of us has seen more than a few stray Messerschmitts. It always mystifies me, therefore, to find on landing that a particular squadron has destroyed a large number of enemy fighters when we were in spitting distance of that squadron throughout the operation. I have, in fact, reported my beliefs to the Station Commander."

"'It certainly worries me, Bill," I said, "602 Squadron is breaking about even at the moment and, as for me, I just cannot seem to get decisive results. As you know, we have had more than our share of close escorts as a squadron and that, perhaps partly explains the reason. Mind you, I defy anyone to get results on close escort duties, unless he is an exceptional shot, and damned lucky into the bargain." "I agree" said Bill. "It's difficult whatever the task, and the Kenley Wing has had more than its share of the less fruitful ones.'"

Al went on to write how difficult it was regarding claims and confirmations. He said that in most cases there was no intention on the part of the pilot to mislead; it was more a case of imagination, fired by the excitement of battle, causing him to dream up a picture in his mind which, in the process of telling, became so real that what started as a probable victory now became an enemy aircraft destroyed. He also realised there were definite cases of exaggeration but the offenders were usually taken to task by their fellow pilots. The RAF he was sure over-claimed, but not nearly to the same extent as the Germans.

Victor Beamish said he would look into it. Whether he did is not known to this author, and when Beamish was lost in early 1942, that appeared to be an end to the matter.

Circus No.76 – 17 August

After the euphoria of the 16th, this Sunday operation was very much a non-event. Six Blenheims from 139 Squadron set off at 0620 for an attack on the Le Havre docks. Having made RV with the escorts over Tangmere, the bombers headed out, losing one bomber soon after RV, but over the Channel the leader's starboard engine cut out and his followers overshot. By the time the pilot had got his engine going again, the other four bombers had turned back too, thinking the show was not proceeding. The escorting Wings were ordered to abort a few miles from the French coast.

Circus No.77 – 17 August

In some records this operation was also to take place on the same day as Circus 76, a raid on the power station at Gosnay. There is even mention of six Blenheims being assigned along with the various escorting fighter Wings, with a RV above Manston at 0900 hours. However, there is no entry in 11 Group's ORB, nothing in the Appendices, and nothing noted in 2 Group's ORB, so we must assume that this too was cancelled and the circus number not re-used. There was a Roadstead operation that evening that cost the lives of two Hurricane pilots from 242 Squadron (JG2 claimed four Hurricanes of course). 242 claimed two 109s, and F/Lt F. D. S. Scott-Malden of 603 claimed another. JG2 lost one pilot and had another wounded, with a third having to make a crash-landing at Berck-sur-Mer.

Circus No.78 - 18 August

Nine Bristol Blenheims, five from 226 and four from 110 Squadrons, went for the Fives-Lille Engineering Works this Monday afternoon, escorted by North Weald's 71, 111 and 222 Squadrons, Covered by Hornchurch's 403, 603 and 611 Squadrons, with Target Support provided by Biggin and Tangmere (72, 92, 609 and 41, 616, 610). Kenley drew the Cover Withdrawal slot (452, 485 and 602) while Rear Support was taken by 12 Group's 56, 65 and 121 Squadrons.

Despite a discouraging 10/10ths cloud up to 6,000 feet over southern England, once nearing France this became 4/10th to 5,000 feet, then clear up to a layer of cirrus at 30,000 feet above France itself. The bombers and close escorts were to meet over Manston at 10,000 feet at 1430 but failed to do so. However, all nine raiders carried on and bombed at 1501 from 8,000 feet. Photographs confirmed hits on the north end of the Works, but all aircraft were hit to some degree by heavy flak fire. One Blenheim of 110 Squadron struggled back towards Wattisham but eventually crashed off Lowestoft, with all three aboard being lost.

With the failure of the rendezvous, 71 and 222 orbited hoping for something to happen but only 111, who had become separated from the other two squadrons, met up with the bombers and acted as escort throughout the mission. No doubt due to the cloud, Hornchurch also failed to meet up and after waiting around for thirty-five minutes, set out for the French coast. They did see seven enemy fighters but no engagements took place. 92 lost a pilot.

Biggin Hill's pilots saw the bombers with just one escorting squadron and joined up although 72 Squadron lost position and became separated. Eventually small numbers of 109s began to turn up but again nothing developed into actions. Tangmere, at 21,000 feet and above, headed for Lille and seeing fifteen Me109s near Hardelot, the top squadron – 41 – broke away to engage. Several dogfights ensued in which one 109 was probably destroyed and four damaged, but at the cost of two pilots. One was reported killed and the other a prisoner, although there is a suggestion they may have collided. Nevertheless, JG2's Obfw. Josef Wurmheller claimed two Spitfires for his twenty-fifth and twenty-sixth victories, while Ltn. Walter Höhler of JG2 probably got the 92 Squadron Spitfire, bringing his score to five.

Withdrawal Cover made no contact with the enemy while 12 Group had some action, claiming 1-1-1 without loss. Neither JG26 or JG2 reported any losses.

Circus No.79 – 18 August

This operation was postponed, probably because of the weather that caused problems for Circus 78.

Circus No.80 – 18 August

By the late afternoon the weather had improved to 'fine' with good visibility and just 2/10ths cloud over France. Just five of the six Blenheims from 18 Squadron carried on to attack the Shell Factory at Marquise this afternoon, with Northolt flying Close Escort, Kenley as Cover Wing, Hornchurch taking Target Support and Biggin Rear Support.

Despite the better weather, all the bombs were seen to over shoot by at least 200 yards, but perhaps it was the heavy flak that accompanied the bombers from Gravelines to the target that put them off. One bomber was hit and although the pilot got back across the Channel, he brought back his dead air gunner. The machine finally crash-landed north-east of Rye, injuring pilot and observer.

Northolt's 308 Squadron was the only unit of the Close Escort to make a satisfactory rendezvous over Dungeness at 1800 hours and took the bombers across alone. Over France some twenty Me109s were seen above and some others below but they made no attempt to engage the Poles. The other two squadrons orbited for some minutes before aborting the show.

Kenley Wing likewise saw nothing of the main formation so carried out a Sweep on their own. Arriving in the target area they found four 109s above but no engagement was made, and on the way back another four 109s made a sudden attack from out of the sun but failed to capitalise on their chances. Hornchurch Wing was also unable to find any enemy fighters over France and just one quick pass by two 109s also caused no hurt to the Spitfires.

Only Biggin Hill's 609 Squadron was able to make any claims. The Wing began orbiting Hardelot when they spotted some 109s towards Le Touquet, then another twenty could be made out over Boulogne with others hovering around Calais. 609 became embroiled in a fight and claimed two 109s destroyed and one probably so. The two destroyed were by Belgians, F/O V. M. M. Ortmans and P/O Y. G. A. F. D. DuMonceau. Vicky Ortmans was an experienced fighter pilot, having flown in the Battle of Britain with 229 Squadron, and was always in the action during 1941. This was his sixth confirmed victory. The probable was scored by P/O D. A. Barnham but may not have been confirmed as such. Dennis Barnham was later to operate successfully over Malta and wrote of his experiences in the book *One Man's Window.*

Circus No.81 – 19 August

This show became known as 'Operation Leg'. When W/Cdr Douglas Bader had been shot down on 9 August, he had lost one of his tin legs whilst baling out of his Spitfire over France. It was arranged that the Germans would accept delivery of a replacement but the RAF decided it would be dropped during a normal raid, and 18 Squadron got the job. Six of their Blenheims would be going for the power station at Gosnay, probably the raid that was to have been made on the 17th. However, the 19th was going to prove an arduous Tuesday.

Close Escort today was flown by the Tangmere Wing, with Cover being provided by Kenley. Target Support came from Northolt and Hornchurch, while Biggin Hill got the Rear Support position. The summer weather had still to make an appearance, for today there was 10/10th cloud at 8–10,000 feet with large masses of cumulus cloud up to 20,000, plus storm clouds over the target area. RV was made over Manston at 1030 and the bombers proceeded via Dunkirk to St Omer where Bader's parcel was parachuted down. However, cloud made it impossible to see the target so the bombers returned without dropping their ordnance. On the way in all the bombers had received some flak damage and on the way out cloud forced them all down to 1,000 feet before they broke cloud.

Tangmere stayed with the bombers all the way, saw just a few fighters, but as they seemed disinclined to come close there were no combats. Of the Cover Wing, 452 Squadron had one aircraft damaged by two cannon shells from a quick diving pass by a 109 and he had to return home wounded. As the Squadron headed back at 29,000 feet they were continually sniped at by 109s and two pilots were lost, claimed by JG2, and killed. 485 claimed one fighter destroyed and another probable. 485 also lost a pilot to JG2 on the way back, but pilots claimed 1-1-1 during several combats. 602 Squadron had a fight but neither side scored any decisive hits. Paddy Finucane claimed the destroyed, while he and Truscott also claimed a probable each, the damaged being upgraded.

The Poles from Northolt were stepped up from 22–27,000 feet and upon crossing into France a red star shell burst near their formation and five minutes later some fifteen 109s dived on them before splitting into two groups, one climbing the other diving. 308 Squadron followed the climbing bunch but to no avail. One pilot went down on the diving lot and claimed one destroyed. 306 Squadron, when attacked, went into a defensive circle and one pilot shot down a 109 that pulled right across him. The three squadrons had become split up due to the cloud and the third unit, 315, did not get into the action. The claim by 306 was made by S/Ldr Stanislaw Skalski.

The lion's share of the combats went to the Hornchurch squadrons, up at between 28–32,000 feet. 611 Squadron had a fight above Poperinghe with ten Me109s and chased them off, but 403's Canadians, in the same area, claimed 4-1-2 for the loss of one pilot, then shot down a fifth over the Channel. The lost pilot became a prisoner. Another pilot, P/O N. R. D. Dick, who claimed three victories (but may have only been credited with two), was himself hit over the sea and had to bale out but was rescued. He was shot down by Oblt. Harry Koch of JG26, his seventh victory. Norman Dick's report:

'I was Yellow 4, 403 (Canadian) Squadron, on circus 81. When at 26,000 ft North of St. Omer I sighted 15/20 e/a heading N/W below at 15,000 ft and Squadron Commander ordered us to attack. Whilst diving I saw an Me109F attacking Yellow 3 from behind and fired a 2-second burst at 400 yards range, but missed and e/a took evasive action by half-rolling to port. I was flying then at 24,000 ft in a northern direction and made a sharp right-hand climbing turn and pulled up. I then saw 3 Me109Fs in line abreast above flying east at 26,000 ft. I fired a 7-second burst from 250 yards range at centre one and thick black smoke poured from its belly

'I saw tracers strike cockpit and fuselage, a further 2-second burst was then given at 75 yards range and e/a blew up and spun down vertically in flames.

'The other two e/a then dived away towards the south. I was then alone and could see none of our aircraft and was about to turn for home when I sighted 6 Me109s in sun, 2,000 ft above me at 24,000 ft flying N/W in loose formation. I made for cloud cover and when making the coast near Gravelines I saw a Spitfire at 1,000 ft above me at approx. 18,000 ft being attacked from rear quarter starboard side by one Me109F.

'I pulled my nose up and fired a 4-second burst into his belly at 150 yards range. Shortly after, black smoke and flames came from his belly and he was last seen diving to starboard with flames coming from his belly. I then saw another e/a below at 15,000 ft and used up the rest of my ammunition with a 2-second burst at 350 yards range, but did not see result, although I think I hit him.

'During this time I was attacked on port and starboard side by 2 e/a. My starboard wing tip was struck by 3-cannon shells and broke off. The port wing was also hit by cannon. On making a left-hand turn I found a cannon shell had struck the base of my control column, rendering my right aileron useless and being unable to straighten out I used heavy right rudder to pull her up.

'When at 6,000 ft I see-sawed for cloud cover and was again attacked from astern. The radiator panel was hit and also my reflector sight and the cockpit filled with smoke. I yanked the emergency cockpit cover, which blew off. On my port side I saw another Me109F 1,000 yards away about to attack. I went down in a slow left-hand dive and lost 3,000 ft. As I recovered from the dive, I saw e/a turn for France. I levelled out and found engine failing, so I used the hand pump and injected fuel to keep going. When at 2,500 ft over Channel I found myself losing control and on sighting the Cliffs of Dover I realised I could not make land, and jettisoned my helmet.

'From 2,500 to 2,000 ft I called Mayday on button 'D'; and at 1,800 ft, baled out clear from port side of aircraft. My parachute opened easily. Whilst floating down I inflated my Mae West. On the way down I lost one flying boot and my revolver. As my feet touched the water, I tried to release the parachute, but I missed hitting the release. I was dragged 2 or 4 feet below the surface and then managed to release myself.

'I pulled the Dinghy towards me and partially inflated it by giving one full turn, then being exhausted I hung on to the dinghy and when on top of a high wave I saw 6/7 Spitfires orbiting me and also a Rescue Boat approaching which reached me about 10 minutes later.'

The pilots of 603 Squadron found twenty Me109s heading in their direction and one section was detached to engage, while the rest kept cover at 30,000 feet. Flight Lieutenant Scott-Malden destroyed one, Sgt D. F. Ruchwaldy another, while others claimed two probables and a damaged for no loss. This was Desmond Ruchwaldy's second victory, having bagged his first three days earlier. By the end of 1941 he would have achieved a score of 2-2-3, and later, with 129 Squadron in 1943 brought his total to 7-3-6, having been awarded in the meantime, the DFM and then the DFC. Flying Mustangs in 1944 he shot down a number of V1 flying-bombs. Sadly he was killed in a flying accident two weeks after VE-Day. 609 Squadron damaged two 109s but lost one Spitfire. The Belgian, Vicki Ortmans, came down in the sea but was rescued later.

Total victory claims for this operation was ten destroyed, six probables and eight damaged, for the loss of four pilots and seven fighters. Adolf Galland had scored his seventy-ninth kill and Hptm. Siefert his eighteenth, but JG26 had suffered casualties. Two 5th Staffel pilots were shot down and killed, one baling out but opening his parachute while going down too fast, snapped his harness and he fell to his death. A 3rd Staffel pilot also went into the Channel after the fight with Kenley Wing. JG2 claimed a total of nine Spitfires. Among the claimants, Ltn. Erich Rudorffer got three, bringing his total to thirty-four, and Oblt. Rudolf Pflanz two more bringing his war total to twenty-one. Someone also claimed a Blenheim but none were lost.

Circus No.82 – 19 August

This late afternoon mission was to attack the marshalling yards at Hazebrouck with six Blenheims of 107 Squadron making up the raiding party. North Weald was to fly Close Escort, Northolt the Cover Wing, with Tangmere and Hornchurch giving Target Support. Withdrawal Cover Wing would be provided by Biggin Hill. The morning cloud had gone leaving a clear sky over France, the sun making a slight ground haze, otherwise visibility was excellent.

With a successful RV over Southend at 1800 hours, the bombers were releasing their bombs thirty-four minutes later from 12,000 feet. A number of direct hits were recorded leaving much smoke while buildings to the north and south were seen to be hit. Flak scored hits on four bombers but they all got back.

Fighters that attacked the main formation on the way out were engaged by 71 Squadron that claimed two damaged, but one Eagle pilot was shot down into the sea. He baled out but was not rescued; the body of P/O V. W. Olsen eventually being washed ashore on the coast of Holland some weeks later. Treble-Two Squadron, the middle squadron, was also attacked and although one pilot claimed a probable, a Czech pilot, Sgt R. Ptáček, was shot down by Johannes Schmid of JG26 (victory number twenty-four) and baled out.

Rudolf Ptáček had just been firing into a 109 that had begun to trail smoke when he was hit from behind. He brought his crippled Spitfire down to crash-land with a dead engine near Rubrouck, north-east of St Omer. Setting his Spitfire on fire, he headed away but on looking back he saw the fire had gone out. Before he could go back, two German soldiers turned up. Moving away, he was taken in hand by some Frenchmen, and he later met the nurse who had helped Douglas Bader to get away from the hospital in St Omer. Being able to speak fluent French, the Czech had no trouble buying a train ticket to Lille, then went to an address he had been given during an escape lecture back in England. This became the start of his trek south and he was back home via Spain and Gibraltar by 5 January 1942. Sadly he was shot down again in March of that year and did not survive.

Treble-One Squadron also engaged 109s, claimed two but lost three pilots and had another wounded at the hands of JG26. One pilot was killed and two taken prisoner. 111's CO, S/Ldr J. S. McLean who made the claims, was 29-years-old and a pre-war pilot. In September he would lead the North Weald Wing. He retired from the RAF as a Group Captain OBE DFC on 19 August 1960, exactly 19 years after this action. The Wing Leader, J. W. Gillan DFC AFC, also put in a claim for another 109 destroyed. John Gillan was famous for a record-breaking flight in a Hurricane on 10 February 1938. Having flown from Northolt to Turnhouse (Edinburgh) he refuelled before heading back to Northolt, this leg taking just forty-eight minutes, helped by a tail wind! His squadron (111) had been the first to be equipped with the Hawker Hurricane.

The three Polish squadrons of the Northolt Wing crossed the French coast at Mardyck at 1826, stepped up from 17 to 21,000 feet. Eight Me109s dived on 308 Squadron from out of the sun some fifteen miles inland but no engagement developed. Not long afterwards twelve Me109s made a similar warlike approach but again nothing happened. On the way back Sgt E. Watolski's Spitfire developed engine trouble and he was forced to take to his parachute, coming down in the Channel, but was rescued.

A similar scenario met 306 Squadron, with 109s approaching but making no real attempt to engage. 315, the high squadron, was also attacked by four Me109s some ten miles inland, but this time the Polish pilots got stuck in and claimed three 109s shot down but one of their own failed to return. The missing pilot was Sgt A. Pietrasiak who was officially with 308 Squadron although, for this operation, it has to be assumed he was flying with 315.

Adolf Pietrasiak baled out of his crippled Spitfire, hurting his leg in the process. He was lucky enough to get help from the Resistance although he had to remain with a doctor for a while who attended his injured leg. Eventually he was passed along, ending up in Gibraltar where he was sent back to England by ship early in January 1942. He later received the DFM (as well as the Polish *Virtuti Militari*) and was Mentioned in Despatches. He had been in action during the French campaign and his companions confirmed that he shot down a 109 before he was himself brought down, this bringing his score to seven destroyed and four others shared. Unhappily, just like Ptáček of 222 Squadron above, (whom he met soon after being picked up by the Resistance) he was to lose his life later in the war (29 Nov 1943), having returned to 308 Squadron.

Tangmere's Target Support squadrons headed out over Beachy Head and into France at Hardelot, starting with 41 Squadron at 25,000 feet with 610 and 616 above. All three saw 109s but no serious encounters ensued although 616 became split up as some Messerschmitts dived at them. Seven Spitfires came home in formation while the other five returned separately, having claimed just one 109 as damaged.

Up at between 28–30,000 feet the Hornchurch Wing had encountered four 109s but they evaded two sections of 603 Squadron that tried to engage them. Various other enemy fighters were seen but all evaded contact for the most part, but eventually 611 Squadron got into a scrap and claimed two 109s for no loss. One of the 109s might have been that flown by Obfw. Willy Vierling, who is known to have crashed from high altitude over Cassel.

The Biggin Hill Wing arrived in the target area at 1834 to provide withdrawal cover. They saw many 109s but had no engagements.

The final tally was seven 109s destroyed, one probable and five damaged for the loss of eight RAF pilots missing. JG26 and JG2 had been involved in these actions and apart from Oblt. Schmid's victory over Ptáček of 222 Squadron, Galland had claimed one of 111's losses, and Hptm. Siefert another. Galland had also shot down the 71 Squadron Hurricane, and these two kills made it three for the day, and brought his personal score to eighty-one. Leutnant Sternberg had shot down one of the Polish losses. JG2 made a modest single claim for a Spitfire and two of their 109s sustained slight combat damage.

The two operations this day had cost the RAF thirteen Spitfires, two Hurricanes with another seven Spitfires damaged. This resulted in the loss of five pilots killed, four taken prisoner, two missing but evading capture, two wounded, and three more rescued from the sea after baling out. A revised claim total by Fighter Command raised the estimated German losses to twenty destroyed, eight probables and one damaged. German losses amounted to five pilots killed.

* * *

While this latter operation was in progress, further north Blenheims of 114 Squadron had left West Raynham to fly an anti-shipping strike, and were intercepted by Me110s from 5./ZG76, whose pilots shot down three of them. Of the nine aircrew, only one survived as a prisoner. Among the losses was 114's CO, W/Cdr J. L. Nicol DSO.

The next day, the 20th, this German Staffel ran into Spitfires that were escorting Blenheims in an attack on Alkmaar Aerodrome, Holland. The 110s were also covered by Me109s and the German aircraft came onto the scene as the RAF formation was heading away from the Dutch coast. In a fight that ensued, 66 Squadron lost two Spitfires to ZG76, one pilot killed, one taken prisoner. A pilot of 1.Erg/JG3 also claimed a Spitfire. ZG76 lost one aircraft to 152 Squadron, and 56 Squadron also claimed a 110. 66 Squadron claimed a 109 probably destroyed, and the CO, S/Ldr A. S. Forbes DFC claimed a 109 with Sgt Green.

Also on the 20th, JG2 claimed two Spitfires during two engagements, but Fighter Command suffered no casualties.

Circus No.83 – 21 August

Circus 83 called for six Blenheims of 88 Squadron to bomb the chemical works at Chocques this Thursday morning, the bombers taking off from Swanton Morley at 0805. Kenley got the Close Escort job, with Biggin Hill flying Cover. Target Support went to eight squadrons from Hornchurch, North Weald and Tangmere, while Rear Support was given to Northolt.

Once over France the main formation ran into 10/10ths cloud at 5,000 feet with just a strip of clear weather along the coast. Because of this cloud the bombers were unable to locate the target so they released their bombs on a 'last resort target' – the railway lines between St Omer and Watten. Five of the Blenheims let go 20 x 250lb bombs but results went unobserved. The sixth bomber brought its load home.

The RV with the bombers over Manston did not go to plan, 71 Squadron arriving a couple of minutes late and failed to link up, so were ordered to go home. 485 and 602 did meet up and proceeded with the escort and although half a dozen 109s tried to engage, they failed. Up above the Biggin Hill pilots saw the 109s too but there was no reason to go down to engage as the 109s began to depart. Only 92 Squadron became embroiled, having become separated from the Wing during a turn near Gris Nez and were heavily engaged by more 109s out over the coast. Although one 109 was probably destroyed, the Wing lost one pilot from 92 and one from 609. Another pilot from 92, P/O P. L. I. Archer, received leg wounds during the combat but got home.

The Hornchurch squadrons were stepped up to 28,000 feet and went into French airspace at 0911 but although they spotted the bombers, they became separated as they tangled with some 109s. 403 Squadron had a brief encounter that cost them one aircraft, its pilot becoming a PoW. 603 became embroiled with four more and had one pilot wounded. He baled out off the English coast and was rescued by two soldiers, all three then being picked up by a launch. Heading back, the rest of the Wing got into scraps, probably destroyed one fighter and damaged five others. JG26 claimed four Spitfires, JG2 another four.

Circus No.84 – 21 August

Circus 83 had been laid on as a diversion to Circus 84, but as it didn't start till six bombers of 18 Squadron took off at 1330, the term 'diversion' seems to have been a misnomer. Despite, or perhaps because, the morning raid on Chocques had failed, this sortie was to be a return to that target.

North Weald got the Close Escort, with Cover from Hornchurch. Target Support went to Biggin, Tangmere and Northolt, while a 12 Group Wing patrolled south of Gravelines. One bomber aborted the raid and again the target was not reached due to cloud. However, 109s were once more able to get above the raiders and Oblt. Kurt Ebersberger's 4th Staffel of JG26 came down on the Tangmere Wing and shot down four Spitfires in quick succession, the Staffelführer claiming one for his eleventh kill.

Flight Lieutenant   D. Crowley-Milling DFC was one of the four lost, coming down near Ergny. Two others were brought down to become prisoners, the fourth being killed. Denis Crowley-Milling had been with Douglas Bader's 242 Squadron during the Battle of Britain, but he was another of those fortunate enough to evade long enough to be picked up by the French Resistance and eventually he returned home by ship having travelled to Spain and then Gibraltar from whence he sailed on 1 December 1941, arriving in Plymouth on the 21st. He went on to receive a Bar to his DFC and, in 1943, the DSO. He later became Air Marshal Sir Denis KBE.

The Canadians of 403, on their second operation of the day, were also hit badly, losing their CO, S/Ldr B. G. Morris RAF, and an American, Sgt C. E. McDonald, who both become prisoners. 92 Squadron also lost a pilot as he took off for this operation from Biggin Hill. In other operations this day, 130 Squadron lost two pilots to Erg./JG53, one killed and one taken prisoner, during an anti-shipping mission, and 65 lost two more on a fighter sweep, again one killed and one prisoner.

Total RAF losses for the day were six killed, five taken prisoner, three wounded and one missing but evading. Fourteen fighter aircraft were lost with two more with Cat.2 damage, while total claims only amounted to one destroyed, ten probables and six damaged. JG26 had one pilot killed, Fw. Adolf Garbe, who, having baled out, had his parachute catch on the 109's tail, dragging him to his death. JG26 claimed a total of ten Spitfires, while JG2 put in claims for another eight for a single loss.

* * *

There were no Circuses on the 22nd but the Tangmere Wing flew a Sweep and destroyed two 109s, one falling to F/Lt C. F. Gray DFC, a very experienced New Zealand pilot, his score being around eighteen at the time. The other victory went to F/Lt C. R. Bush, another New Zealand Battle of Britain veteran.

Colin Gray was a guest this day with 41 Squadron, as he recalls in his book *Spitfire Patrol* (Hutchinson, 1990). He was with 1 Squadron who had arrived at Tangmere in July. On this day … 'I managed to persuade Nobby Fee, who commanded a Spitfire squadron in the Wing, to let me go on a sweep with them. Nobby's squadron, No.41, was led on this occasion by Douglas Bader's replacement[9] and I flew as his number two for a sweep of the Le Havre area. The weather was fine but quite cloudy, and at

---

9. Wing Commander H. de C. A. Woodhouse AFC.

10,000 feet east of Le Havre Aerodrome we came across a Messerschmitt 109 diving down through the clouds. He did not seem to have seen us, so I followed him down and pumped in all my ammunition at fairly close range. His starboard wheel and flap fell down amidst much smoke, and the aircraft finally crashed on the southern boundary of the airfield just as three other 109s were taking off. Having no ammunition left and as the rest of the squadron had disappeared in the clouds, I did not stay around to see what they were after.'

I once spent a morning with Colin Gray at his New Zealand home, and having some years earlier done the same in England with his wartime pal, Al Deere, I felt honoured to have met and spent time with both these famous Kiwi aces.

It is thought that Circus operations had been planned for 23 August, but in the event flying was virtually non-existent due to adverse weather, until the 27th. However, on the 26th a late-evening raid on St Omer's satellite airfield at Wizernes was intercepted by JG2 and Hptm. Schmid claimed one Blenheim shot down, although it returned badly shot up but safe. Not so fortunate were Blenheims that were on anti-shipping sorties to Heligoland. Six failed to return, either shot down by flak or by Me109s of JG52.

Further south Fighter Command flew sweeps and anti-E-boat missions, losing two pilots killed.

Circus No.87 – 26 August

There was obviously some reason that the next two Circus operations were put in motion out of numerical sequence because of some delay in mounting Nos.85 and 86, which will be seen below for 27 August. Circus 87 called for six Blenheims of 18 Squadron to attack St Omer airfield at Longuenesse on this late Tuesday afternoon.

Rendezvous was made over Hastings, at 1800 hours with the Kenley Wing as Close Escort and Biggin Hill giving cover. Target Support this time was by Tangmere and Hornchurch, while Northolt took on Forward Support and North Weald Rear Support. Weather over the target was clear of cloud giving good visibility, although cloud tended to be worse further inland.

Bombs went down on the airfield at 1821, hits being seen on buildings and across the main landing ground, plus a hit on a camouflaged hut. The bombers experienced no opposition, although AA fire did probe for the bombers on the way back, and three 109s were also encountered. All three came in but only the last of them scored hits on one Blenheim which hit the turret as well as damaging the hydraulic landing gear. None of the crew was injured. This damaged bomber had to make a crash-landing at base.

The Kenley squadrons became split up and 602 remained over mid-Channel before returning to base. In this case 485 Squadron took the close escort position and although several 109s came up behind, no attacks developed. 452 Squadron saw the bulk of enemy fighters – they estimated around fifty – and had some action in which two 109s were claimed destroyed, one falling to F/Lt A. G. Douglas, a Welshman flying with this Australian outfit. It was his first victory. 'Pinky' Douglas had been in the RAF since 1928 but had not managed to get himself posted onto operations till early 1941. After gaining a second victory in September he took command of 403 Squadron RCAF and in 1942, 401 Squadron RCAF.

Biggin Hill had encounters with 109s, trying unsuccessfully to chase several. Somehow in the mêlée one pilot of 92 Squadron was shot down and killed. All the other squadrons had some sort of encounter with 109s, 603 Squadron making a couple of claims, while 611 Squadron also lost a pilot. Oberleutnant Joachim Müncheberg of 7./JG26 claimed one for his forty-ninth victory. Sergeant A. E. Gray ended up in Stalag Luft VI. JG2 pilots put in claims for four Spitfires, Josef Wurmheller being credited with his twenty-eighth and twenty-ninth kills. The Circus Report noted a total of 1-2-3 claims but was later adjusted to 3-1-2, for the loss of two pilots.

Circus No.85 – 27 August

Number 11 Group cut the orders for this operation on 22 August and as it was set to be a diversion for Circus 86, the delay in putting this into motion is why both are out of chronological sequence. Blenheim crews of 139 Squadron were briefed to RV over Rye to start the diversion, and although cloudless over the town and the sea, the bombers became split up. Three arrived at 0645, some thirty minutes before the appointed time and three minutes later a fourth bomber arrived, followed soon afterwards by a fifth. Instead of remaining over Rye in order to meet their escort, the five bombers headed north-east towards Manston via Hawkinge.

Their Escort Wing, from Northolt, arrived a few minutes before the arranged time and, unable to find the Blenheims, continued to search around until 0705, when they headed out towards France. Over the Channel they saw Spitfires returning from France and turned to give cover, but this allowed two Me109s to make a sudden attack. Pilot Officer Z. Radomski was hit and badly wounded, being forced to make a crash-landing at Deal, losing an arm.

Kenley, the Cover Wing, arrived over Rye and saw a number of aircraft but no bombers, so headed south in the hope of picking up the main formation somewhere near the target. Instead they became embroiled in a number of dogfights with, some estimated, to have involved up to 100 enemy fighters. 452 Squadron claimed three 109s for no loss; Finucane claiming two. In fact P/O R. E. Thorold-Smith was also credited with two, so the Aussie squadron may have claimed four in total. 485 was continually dived upon by some thirty Me109s from the sun and in taking evasive action became split up. Heading for home the pilots were still harassed by 109s but they only lost one pilot, who baled out too low near Calais and was killed.

Target Support – Tangmere – had its three squadrons stepped up to 21,000 feet but by the time they crossed into France the top squadron was at 30,000. All pilots saw

109s but other than 41 Squadron, who claimed one destroyed and two damaged, there were no engagements.

Another 41 Squadron pilot, having also become separated was flying back across the Channel and saw eight 109s circling, apparently awaiting a chance to pounce on any returning aircraft from the Circus. He stayed well clear.

The Biggin Hill Wing arrived over Hazebrouck at 0658, the top squadron flying at 27,000 feet. 609 Squadron called in the warning that 109s were in the sun and the Wing Leader, Micky Robinson, turned the aircraft towards them. Many 109s could be seen in twos and fours but none came near enough to engage, presumably because the German pilots saw no bombers below, so decided there was no real need to attack the Spitfires. However, on the way out, some 109s were seen below and in an attack two were destroyed, one by Robinson and one by his French wingman, Lt. M. Choron FFAF (Free French Air Force).

According to Group Captain Bouchier he was unable to understand, given the good weather conditions, just why the bombers and fighters did not meet up as planned. However, he thought the overall objective was achieved in that enemy fighter reaction seemed quite extensive. Reports he had seen indicated some fifty Me109s had taken to the air and by the time Circus 86 arrived on the scene (see below) enemy activity had subsided to inland patrols.

It appears seven Me109s were claimed destroyed, with another probable and three more damaged. However, six fighter pilots had failed to return and one had been wounded. One more had baled out and been rescued from the Channel. JG26 claimed seven Spitfires and had one 109 shot down but its pilot survived, while an Ergänzungruppe 109 also crashed, again its pilot surviving.

Circus No.86 – 27 August

The idea of this operation, which had been scheduled to take place fifty-five minutes after Circus 85, was to get German fighters into the air and as they began to land back at their bases, this second Circus would be heading out, its target being the Lille Power Station. For this, twelve Blenheims were chosen, but in the event only nine from 18 Squadron flew the mission.

Variable cloud from the French coast to some eight miles inland, where it cleared gave excellent visibility, some Spitfire pilots reporting that they could see Lille as they crossed into France. Rendezvous was successful with the Escort Wing (North Weald) and the Cover Wing (Hornchurch) while a 12 Group Wing acted as Rear Support.

The day continued to be jinxed as this time, instead of crossing into France where planned, the bombers went in west of Dunkirk, missing the spot by twenty miles. What made it worse was that the bomber crews did not realise their navigation error and carried on as if they had crossed east of Dunkirk. Subsequent course changes brought them to St Omer from where they headed south and then east to Béthune, and finally south again to the Albert-Amiens area. By this time they realised that they were some fifty miles south-south-west of Lille and so had to head north-west, crossing out of France near Boulogne where flak damaged four of the Blenheims. As an effort it was totally wasted.

The Close Escort Wing stayed with the bombers but fared worse. 402 Squadron lost a pilot as they headed out to sea on the way home, while another pilot collided with a Spitfire of 222 Squadron. The Canadian baled out and was not recovered, while the body of the New Zealander from 222 was later washed ashore at Dunkirk where he was buried.

The Eagle pilots of 71 Squadron fought off eight Me109s and claimed two destroyed the victorious pilot being wounded in the right leg and foot. This was P/O W. R. Dunn who had thus become the first ace of the Eagle Squadron as a result of his double victory. 403 Squadron apparently confirmed Bill Dunn's claims, reporting seeing both 109 pilots baling out. We have read about him earlier.

Hornchurch pilots flew their escort cover but no doubt due to conflicting courses 611 became separated and linked up with four of 54 Squadron to fly towards Lille as briefed. Meantime, 403 Squadron who found itself over Albert-Amiens saw thirty 109s at 24,000 feet which were attacked by 603 Squadron, claiming two probables and one damaged. One of the successful pilots in 603 was Flight Lieutenant Wilfred Duncan Smith DFC who had only recently joined this Squadron from 611. Today had been his second trip with 603, the first had been the previous evening. After the mix-up with the bombers, 603 was attacked by several 109s. Duncan Smith reported:

'I was flying as Green 1 in Squadron formation when on the return journey north of Amiens we encountered upwards of 6 e/a at our own height. I turned starboard to engage these and attacked an e/a from head-on but saw no results. I then turned to port and dived to engage an Me109E which was manoeuvring to fire at a Spitfire. I opened fire at 150 yards on a fine quarter closing to 100 yards astern. Pieces flew off the e/a and it looked like Perspex splinters whereupon e/a rolled over to port and dived away steeply. I turned to follow but lost sight of him. After this I climbed up and rejoined the bomber escort which was some distance to the west.'

Smith's wingman, Flying Officer R. V. L. Griffiths saw his leader going after the 109 but also spotted a 109F about to attack him. He pulled up under this fighter and fired, blowing away part of the fuselage beneath the cockpit area. The 109 curved down and away. Now alone, Griffiths flew to catch the bombers but then saw two 109s with the same idea. He opened fire on the leading German but his fire hit the second one! Seeing bits fly off its starboard wing, it half-rolled and went down. Back at base he claimed a probable and a damaged.

Smith did not mention in his report that after his engagement he had been badly hit but managed to get back across the Channel to make an emergency landing at RAF

Manston. On his approach he ran out of fuel but managed to glide down and land. He would end the war with a DSO DFC and Bar, with a score of almost twenty kills.

The Wing Leader, F. S. Stapleton, and a pilot of 403, saw three 109s shoot down a Spitfire from 611 Squadron. These 109s were then engaged and two were shot down east of Boulogne, before heading out over the Channel. The WingCo claimed one.

With the 12 Group Wing not seeing any appreciable action, the fight ended and the bombers and remaining fighters headed for home. Four Me109s had been claimed destroyed, with two more probably so with another damaged. The RAF had four pilots missing, but two others returned wounded, while another had also been wounded and forced to bale out over the sea. Luckily he was rescued.

JG2 had been in action against this Circus, JG26 having been on the ground after the earlier fight. They claimed a modest three victories but recorded no losses – at least no pilots killed. Two of the victorious pilots had been Josef Wurmheller, who reported his thirtieth victory, while Ltn. Egon Mayer scored his twenty-first. Known as 'Sepp', Wurmheller was about to receive the Knight's Cross following his twenty-fourth victory. He would later command JG2's Third Gruppe and score over 100 kills before colliding with his wingman shortly after D-Day 1944. Mayer had received his Knight's Cross four days earlier, 23 August 1941. Oberleutnant Müncheberg attained his forty-ninth victory, downing Sergeant A. E. Grey of 611, who became a prisoner.

This day's actions had cost the RAF eleven Spitfires and two Hurricanes, with another six fighters damaged. Seven fighter pilots had died, three taken prisoner and a further four wounded. An amended claim figure against the Luftwaffe was 11-3-5.

* * *

A Rhubarb sortie on the 28th cost 41 Squadron the life of one of its pilots near Le Havre, while a night strike against Morlaix airfield resulted in one Hurricane pilot of 247 Squadron being brought down and taken captive. Who shot down the 41 Squadron machine is unclear but 4.(Eins)/JFS 5 managed to claim nine Spitfires! One pilot reported three shot down, and two other pilots claimed two each.

Eighteen Blenheims of 21, 88 and 226 Squadrons were sent to bomb shipping in Rotterdam docks from low level. While at least two large cargo ships were hit and some damage was done to dock installations, seven bombers failed to return – mostly to AA fire - while another crashed on take off. In all, sixteen aircrew died, and five became prisoners. Leutnant Hans Möller of 6./JG53, claimed two (perhaps three) of the Blenheims, and this Staffel also claimed two others. No doubt there was some interesting discussions between the Luftwaffe and the flak units!

12 Group of Fighter Command made a sweep to Rotterdam but were bounced by other Me109s of 6./JG 53, losing three Spitfires. Two pilots of 19 Squadron were shot down, including the CO, S/Ldr W. J. Lawson DFC, who was killed, and F/Lt W. Cunningham DFC, taken prisoner. Both were Battle of Britain veterans. 152 Squadron also had a pilot brought down and captured.

Circus No.88 – 29 August

This operation began just after 0600, with six Blenheims of 139 Squadron assigned to bomb the marshalling yards at Hazebrouck – the 11th time this target had been chosen for attention. There was lots of cloud over the Channel, up to 20,000 feet, but this was much less over France and totally clear over the target. Kenley got the Close Escort position, Northolt's Poles the Cover slot, while Support Wings were provided by Hornchurch, Biggin and North Weald. Just one Hornchurch squadron – 402 – got the Rear Support task.

The bombing operation was knocked into a cocked hat as the Blenheims reached the French coast at Hardelot. Heavy flak was experienced and the leading bomber was hit which damaged the bomb-release gear causing most of his ordnance to drop. This was taken by the other crews to mean they should drop too. The farce was followed by all six bombers heading for the target where the leader's one remaining bomb was dropped into the yards. Fortunately all the bombers returned safely.

The Escort Wing took the bombers in and although several 109s were sighted none attacked until they were coming back. One section of 485 Squadron became involved with three 109s, one of which was destroyed and another claimed as a probable. One Australian was hit and baled out, but was rescued. 602 had a brief exchange with several 109s short of the target but neither side did any damage to the other.

The Poles were attacked by up to thirty Me109s and as dogfights developed the Wing became broken up. 306 Squadron claimed one destroyed, and despite reporting later that they were heavily outnumbered, 308 Squadron damaged three, while being chased almost to mid-Channel. 315 Squadron claimed two destroyed. Each squadron lost a pilot of whom, two were killed and one became a prisoner. 306 lost its CO, S/Ldr J. Słoński-Ostoja – killed. He was 31-years-old and had fought in Poland before escaping to England via Romania and France. He had taken command of 306 just fifteen days earlier, following the loss of S/Ldr Jerzy Zaremba on 14 August.

Hornchurch squadrons became separated because the top lot, 54 Squadron, were in thick cloud at 30,000 feet and decided to abort. 603 and 611 continued on into clear sky and had some 109s shadowing them for a while. Then a pair of 109s attacked 603, but were driven away.

The Biggin Hill boys also became separated while climbing through cloud, and radio silence had to be broken once over the French coast in order to get everyone back together. Heading for the target, the Spitfires arrived three minutes before the bombers and German vapour trails could be seen above at 35,000 feet while more 109s were located down-sun of the target. Once battle commenced, the Wing claimed 3-2-4 for the loss of one pilot of 72 Squadron who was killed.

The North Weald Wing had been briefed to patrol five miles out from Dunkirk above 20,000 feet but due to cloud were forced to fly well below this height. Twenty Me109s came down and attacked 111 Squadron, being led by the Wing Leader, W/Cdr J. W. Gillan. He was hit in the first pass and went down. His death was later confirmed. He was 34-years-old. Initially Gillan came over the R/T to confirm he had been hit but was alright. Presumably he was either hit again, or the damage to his Spitfire was more severe than he imagined. The other squadrons were not engaged, although 222 Squadron was requested to give cover to an ASR Lysander, sent out to look for Gillan. Landing back at Manston the squadron refuelled and went out again, but found no sign of the missing wing leader. However, 402 Squadron RCAF on Rear Support also assisted an ASR launch to a downed pilot who was rescued but this was Sgt L. P. Griffiths of 485 Squadron.

Total enemy fighters claimed came to seven destroyed, three probables and eight damaged for the loss of five pilots missing. JG26 and JG2 had been engaged with this Circus. JG26 claimed three Spitfires one being Müncheberg's fiftieth victory. Oberleutnant Hermann Seegatz had shot down the 72 Squadron machine for his fifteenth kill. However, they lost Uffz. Werner Hetzel who crashed near Hazebrouck. JG2 initially claimed four Spitfires but later one was accredited to Müncheberg. JG26, that had started to convert to the new Focke-Wulf 190 fighters, suffered the first loss of a 190. Leutnant Otto Schenk was hit by German AA fire and was killed crashing on the beach south of Dunkirk. Josef Wurmheller of JG2 scored his thirty-first victory.

Peter Göring, nephew of Hermann Göring, crash-landed his Me109 near Hazebrouck the following day and was slightly injured. He was on a combat sortie but it is not clear if his fighter had been damaged by enemy action, suffered engine trouble, or if it was merely pilot error.

On other operations, 19 Squadron was out searching for their CO (Lawson), lost off the Dutch coast the previous day, in case he had come down and was in a dinghy. They did not find him but enemy fighters found the Spitfires off Goeree Island. Amazingly the Me110s of 6./ZG 76 shot down four, all the pilots being killed. One of the German pilots was Ltn. Martin Drewes, who became a successful night-fighter pilot, receiving the Knight's Cross and Oak Leaves. The 110 pilots in fact claimed seven in all. All the RAF pilots could claim were four 110s damaged.

Circus No.89

This was an operation that was planned and scheduled for 30 August but in the event did not take place. Twelve Blenheims were to have attacked the shipyards at Le Trait, after making a rendezvous over Biggin Hill at 0700, but it was then cancelled.

Circus No.90 – 31 August

The day began with 10 Group conducting a Gudgeon operation, a force of Blenheims attacking Lannion Aerodrome, escorted by five fighter squadrons. The raid was completed without interference from the Germans.

Circus 90 was virtually a repeat of the abandoned Circus 85 on this Sunday morning, with six Blenheims alerted. In reality this was mounted as a diversion for Circus 91.

The target was to have been the St Omer airfield, 21 and 82 Squadrons providing the bombers. They crossed out over Rye at two minutes past midday and were crossing the French coast twelve minutes later but cloud prevented the target being seen so the bombs went down on the railway line just west of Audruicq, SE of Calais. Heavy flak accompanied the bombers but all returned unharmed.

The Northolt Wing escorted the bombers, although one 306 machine had a problem and had to be escorted back by two other Spitfires. The Kenley Cover Wing saw a few 109s but had no engagement, but Tangmere's 616 Squadron had a scrap with some 109s, Sgt R. D. Bowen claiming one and damaging a second. Biggin Hill, one of the Support Wings, also became embroiled in a fight and 92 Squadron claimed one destroyed (by the CO, S/Ldr Jamie Rankin), with another probable plus two damaged. One of the latter went to P/O N. F. Duke. It was Neville Duke's last combat action over France for he was soon posted to North Africa where he would become one of the most successful fighter pilots operating over the desert and later Italy, receiving the DSO, DFC and two Bars.

Total claims for this operation came to a modest 1-2-3 for no loss.

Circus No.91 – 31 August

Twelve Blenheims, six each from 18 and 114 Squadrons, headed off at 1153 hours, their target being the power station at Lille, so virtually another repeat, this time of Circus 86. Only eleven aircraft bombed the target, but cloud prevented seeing any results. The twelfth bomber had R/T trouble so it bombed the railway line east of Dunkirk. No hostile fighters were seen but heavy flak was encountered.

The Escort Wing (North Weald), Cover Wing (Hornchurch) and Rear Support (12 Group Wing) all saw enemy fighters but no real engagements occurred, although one pilot of 54 Squadron became separated and was spotted being chased by six 109s. This was F/Lt R. Mottram, whose death was later confirmed. Roy Mottram was another very experienced fighter pilot, having flown with 92 Squadron during the Battle of Britain.

Leutnant Jakob Augustin of 8./JG 2 claimed his fourth victory two miles north of Merville at 1434 (German time). Mottram is buried in Merville's Communal Cemetery.

Circus No.92 – 31 August

This raid was put on because Circus 89 had been cancelled, so the target was again the shipyards at Le Trait. It was also the third Circus of the day. Six Blenheims of 139 Squadron took off at 1755 hours and met up with their escort over Beachy Head at 1830, this being the Tangmere Wing that provided the fighters. It was a pretty low-key affair for other than Tangmere's 41, 129 and 616 Squadrons, only two Kenley Wing Squadrons (452 and 602) went too, as Rear Support.

The formation found haze right up to 8/10,000 feet although it was clear above, and the bombers had no problem in finding the target at 1906 which they bombed from 8,500 feet. Two of the 24 x 250lb bombs were seen to explode on a shed by the slipway, four more overshooting but the remainder fell on the western slipway. Only one lone Me109 was seen, flying west at 8,000 feet.

Other 109s were seen by the escorts and during a short engagement, one Spitfire went down in flames and in return, one 109 was claimed as a probable. The downed pilot was Sgt P. Hind of 41 Squadron, who was destined to die in captivity on 8 July 1942. Other than this, the operation was quiet and all the bombers returned.

The 109s of JG2 had intercepted this raid and claimed two Spitfires. Major Walter Oesau claimed his over Rouen at 2007 for his ninety-sixth victory, and Fw. Günther Seeger claimed his one minute later for kill number sixteen. Oesau had already received the Knight's Cross with Oak Leaves and Swords after eighty victories. He had flown in Spain, over England and would shortly leave for the Russian Front. In mid-1943 he would return to the west to command JG2 and later JG1. He was the third German fighter pilot to attain 100 victories but would die in combat in May 1944. Seeger had been flying with JG2 since early 1940, and would see later action over the Mediterranean with JG53. He ended the war with the Knight's Cross and fifty-six victories.

Chapter 9

Thoughts from the Top

Circus Operations during August 1941 had been much reduced from July, mainly due to the adverse weather conditions prevailing, yet Fighter Command had flown a recorded 321 operational missions, claimed 100 German fighters destroyed, and lost seventy-two pilots, either killed, missing or taken prisoner. Don Caldwell, historian of JG26's operations, noted ninety-eight Spitfires and ten Hurricanes lost, (although a more accurate count makes these totals 105 and 18) while JG26 and JG2 had lost thirty of its fighter aircraft – to all causes. Therefore, if the RAF and Fighter Command were still hopeful that a war of attrition would eventually pay dividends, things were not going exactly to plan.

Although the RAF fighter pilots were claiming Me109s shot down in good numbers, the intelligence network must have been receiving information indicating a much lower loss rate by the Germans via 'Y' Service interceptions. This Service monitored German radio traffic and the Bletchley Park people would be de-coding this traffic almost on a daily basis. German quartermasters needed to replace lost aeroplanes for their units and if the unit requested replacements, it suggested that either that unit had lost the same number of machines on operations, had others lost in flying accidents, or had aircraft sufficiently damaged to warrant replacement. Certainly, a significant contradiction existed if RAF pilots claimed twenty Me109s destroyed in one day while German quartermasters were only requesting four replacements.

In his book '*Years of Command*', Sholto Douglas referred to the book by Denis Richards and Hillary St. George Saunders, '*Royal Air Force 1939–45*'), which stated:

'The objectives were manifold. To destroy enemy machines in the air or on the ground. To shoot up and bomb airfield buildings, ports and communications – all these were within their province. The chief motive underlying the offensive, however, was not so much to cause direct damage as to force the enemy to maintain strong air defences in the West. At the same time powerful moral advantages would accrue as our pilots grew accustomed to exercising the initiative, and as the enemy became thoroughly imbued with the idea of our superiority in the air'.

Sholto Douglas subsequently remarked:

'But in speaking of the results achieved during the first six months – up until the time of the German attack on Russia on the 22nd of June 1941 – Richards is too inclined to pour cold water on what we were able to achieve, and I cannot agree with his reference to "… the completely ineffective mass sweeps at high level by fighters without bombers". This is overlooking altogether the tremendous value of the experience alone which was gained by our pilots. All too often the need for a severely objective approach by the official historians is inclined to smother features of what is being written about in a fashion that drains the events of their true colour.

'In his official history of this period, Basil Collier speaks about the sorties flown by our early and smaller, formations of fighters accompanying our bombers in their attacks on targets just across the Channel. "… but neither their value as targets nor the readiness of the Germans to lose fighters in defending them could be defined in terms convincing to all schools of thought." he wrote. And regarding the lack of any outstanding results from these early sweeps, Collier states: "The operations failed, therefore, to achieve their primary object, though the part they played in developing qualities which stood our pilots in good stead on other occasions deserved to be remembered." These pallid summaries of their work must strike some lively sparks in the minds of those pilots who actually flew on the operations.

'Of the overall results of the offensive sweeps up to June 1941, Collier concludes: "On any reckoning the operations cannot, therefore, be judged more than moderately successful if a quantitative standard is to be applied to them. On the other hand, their moral value is generally held to have been substantial." That is such a cursory dismissal of the work of our air crews. From the point of view of Fighter Command these were major fighter operations, involving at times large numbers of squadrons, and if the results were not spectacular, by a "quantitative standard" they were nevertheless very effective.

'After the Germans attacked Russia in June 1941, it became of even more importance that we should keep up the pressure over France and so prevent the enemy from moving their Air Force in any large numbers to the Eastern front. At about this time, Trafford Leigh-Mallory wrote to me pointing out that our casualties in the sweeps were becoming such that he doubted if they were paying off. After thinking that over I wrote to the C.A.S. [Portal] and asked for a review of the whole idea of our operations out over France. As had happened when I had expressed my doubts before, the answer that I got from Portal was a balanced and wise appreciation of the whole situation. The important point that he emphasised was one that Leigh-Mallory and I had already discussed: the value of our offensive operations in helping the Russians.'

* * *

Writing about Fighter Command in his book of that title, Peter Barnes, who retired from the RAF as Air Marshal Sir Peter Wykeham KCB DSO OBE DFC AFC, records the following, and includes how Fighter and Bomber Commands initially had differing views of the Circus idea following the first two:

'There was an immediate inquest at Bentley Priory, and the Prime Minister asked for a report. Apart from the detailed misfortune of the missed rendezvous, it appeared, to everyone's embarrassment, that Bomber and Fighter Commands had different ideas regarding the intention of the "Circus" operations. The former had given the objective as:

'... to deny the enemy the use of the nearer ports as invasion bases or as bases for his coastwise shipping and to put him on the defensive in the narrow waters. The secondary aims are to force him to put his fighters into the air and to accept combat under conditions tactically favourable to our fighters.

'Fighter Command, however, understood that the purpose was:

"To bomb selected targets, and to take advantage of the enemy's reaction to shoot down his fighters under conditions favourable to our own fighters."

'Neither was quite compatible,' continued Sir Peter, 'with that of the Air Ministry, which was that the bombers were only needed to make the enemy come up and fight and that after dropping their bombs they should get away at once. C-in-C Bomber Command [ACM Sir Richard Peirse], however, did not take kindly to the idea that his squadrons should be used as bait, and a meeting had to be held between the two Commands before an agreed intention could be produced, as follows:

'The object of these attacks is to force the enemy to give battle under conditions tactically favourable to our fighters. In order to compel him to do so, the bombers must cause sufficient damage to make it impossible for him to ignore then and refuse to fight on our terms.'

This at least cleared the decks, but it appears that everyone was assuming that the Germans would allow the RAF to 'fight on their terms' or 'on conditions favourable to the RAF'. These phrases that became well used were more or less wishful thinking. As the Germans found in 1940, close escort sorties handicapped fighters whilst they defended their bombers over England. So too the close escort squadrons of Fighter Command over France, which forced extra cover squadrons to be employed to cover them. Squadrons given the close escort role knew how restricted it made them. In any event, the Germans dictated their own conditions of combat and if a situation did not look favourable, they simply refused to engage.

* * *

By mid-1941, Sholto Douglas at Fighter Command HQ must have been getting some intelligence reports on his desk and must have been wondering as to actual German losses, but he could probably guess. Yet he was still endorsing recommendations for decorations and awards to his pilots for achieving victories in air combat. On 29 August he wrote to Air Chief Marshal Sir Wilfred Freeman KCB DSO DFC and Air Ministry:

My Dear …………,

1. I want you to consider the future policy during the next few weeks in regard to our offensive sweeps.

2. We started these sweeps of course, some time before Russia entered the war – in fact we made our first sweep last January. But we have intensified our efforts very considerably since the entry of Russia into the war, with the object of doing our bit towards drawing the pressure off the Russian Front. At present, Leigh–Mallory and I aim at having two large sweeps on every fine day. This, I think, is about the most that the squadrons of No.11 Group can do over a prolonged period of fine weather.

3. When we first started these sweeps they were a spectacular success. For the first few weeks we shot down considerably more enemy fighters than we lost ourselves. The enemy became largely demoralised and we were right on top. This position, however, has changed during the past month or six weeks. Whether or not the enemy has increased the number of his fighters in occupied territory I cannot say. The Intelligence people say that he has not done so. My 'fighter boys' say that he has. The reason for the discrepancy however, may well lie in the fact that, taught by experience, the enemy has vastly improved his RDF [radar] warning system of reporting the movements of our fighters after they come into visual contact with his observer corps. We hear the German fighters receiving their instructions in the air about the approach of our main force when the latter are still over British territory. In the course of the battle over occupied territory we frequently hear the enemy giving accurate information to his fighters about the whereabouts and direction of flight of our own patrols. (Sometimes on the other hand, his information is wide of the mark.) The consequence of this improvement of the enemy's defence organisation is that a large proportion of his fighters are brought into the battle from the right direction and at the right height to give him the greatest possible tactical advantage. This does not happen of course on every occasion but it does quite frequently.

4. Then again, there is no doubt that the quality of the German pilots has improved. The majority of German fighter pilots that my 'fighter boys' were meeting three months ago were described by the latter as 'OTU boys'. The 'OTU boys' however, have now learnt a good deal in the hard school of experience, while there is no doubt – in fact this is confirmed by Intelligence Reports – that the enemy has drafted a considerable number of experienced pilots into fighter units in the Pas de Calais area, either from the Russian Front, or more probably, by combing his training schools in Germany.

5. The result of all this is that the battle is now much more even. On occasions we have lost more of our fighters than we have shot down of the enemy's – on one or two occasions, very considerably more. The balance is probably still slightly in our favour, but it is, as I say, more or less even. In fact, considered

purely from the parochial Fighter Command point of view, this particular view has ceased to pay dividends.

6. What I want to ask you, therefore, is how long ought we to continue with these offensive sweeps to give the fighter boys a 'jolly' and some practical training, and to keep their spirits and morale up? It will also annoy the Hun and keep him on his toes if he never knows when we are going to put over another fighter sweep. At the present time, however, he knows that, if the day is fine enough, we are bound to do a sweep sooner or later.

7. How long then should this policy of intensive sweeps continue? I take it that the answer is – at the present rate until the Russian Front stabilises and the intensity of the warfare dies down on the Eastern Front. If this is the answer, then I would likewise have the best possible estimate of when that will be (one sees such varying estimates). Since my plans with regard to the change round of squadrons, replacements of aircraft and pilots from O.T.U.'s, re-equipment of squadrons, etc., depend to some extent on the answer to this question.

8. I am afraid this is rather a rambling letter, but what it boils down to is this: -

(a) Do you agree that, if and when the Russian Front stabilises, we should reduce the intensity of our offensive operations over occupied territory? We should of course continue periodical sweeps at irregular intervals, but we should definitely 'take as much of the war as we wish'.

(b) If the answer to this question is 'yes', can I have the best estimate available of when that date will be?

9. There is one more point about these sweeps which has to do with our conversation yesterday. We quite definitely find that, if we send fighters <u>alone</u> to do a sweep, or fighters with a small force of bombers (e.g. three Blenheims), the Hun will not come in and 'mix it'. He hangs about high up round the outskirts of the fighter wings, waiting for some inexperienced pilot to straggle, or for 'flak' to cause the formation to open out. He then takes a quick dive at any of our fighters which have become isolated; has one squirt, and goes diving straight on down to the ground. In this way he is able to pick off a proportion of our fighters with very small chance of loss to himself. It is only if we can hit him really hard in a place that he values (e.g. the Lille Steel Works) with an adequate bomber force that he will really come in and 'mix it', and try to shoot the bombers down or spoil their bombing run. It is only when he does this that our fighter wings have a chance of getting a really good bag. That is why I am so keen for you to let me have a sufficient number of bombers, preferably heavy bombers, for these offensive sweeps. If you don't, then I am afraid that, so long as the enemy adopts his present

tactics, our own losses and the enemy's, are liable to be much on a par, and at times we shall lose more than we shall shoot down.

10. I should be grateful therefore if you would consider this aspect of the problem also and let me have your views.

Yours,
(Sholto Douglas)

While this letter was being digested by the Air Ministry, Trafford Leigh-Mallory, who had obviously received a copy, quickly put pen to paper and became busily engaged in writing a Memorandum to all who mattered, about his Group's results and his thoughts about the possible future conduct of Circus operations. This was sent out on 5 September 1941.

MEMORANDUM BY AOC NO. 11 GROUP ON THE
RESULTS OF "CIRCUS" OPERATIONS, AND
RECOMMENDATIONS FOR THEIR FUTURE CONDUCT.

1. Since it became possible to start regular offensive sweeps over FRANCE on the 14th June 1941, we have averaged two to one aircraft destroyed in our favour – without taking into account "probably destroyed" and "damaged" enemy aircraft, the fate of which cannot always be known over enemy territory. The average was as much as three to one after the first month of the fighting, but as the German warning system improved and his fighter pilots became more experienced and were reinforced, the fighting has become more even.

2. It varies tremendously. Sometimes we have good days, such as Saturday, August 16th, when we destroyed 16 Germans for a loss of three of our own [*author's note: actual German losses were one and five damaged*]. On the other hand we have bad days, such as the 21st August, when we had eleven aircraft missing [*author's note: fourteen lost in total*] and only destroyed one German aircraft, though in addition ten "probables" were accounted for, confirmation being difficult owing to thick cloud.

3. In fact sometimes we manage to surprise the Germans, or bring them to action on satisfactory terms, and sometimes we ourselves are outnumbered locally or have a number of our Fighters picked off without a general engagement. The occasions on which we do less well are usually when the conditions are cloudy, and visibility poor in haze, which have enabled concentrations of enemy Fighters to jump smaller numbers of our own Fighters who temporarily have lost touch with their Squadrons or Wings.

4. During August, 101 German Fighters have been destroyed, and 48 probably destroyed for the loss of 74 British fighter pilots. Over the period of these "CIRCUS" operations from the 14th June to the 3rd September, 437 German

Fighters have been destroyed, and 182 probably destroyed, for the loss of 194 British fighter pilots.

5. As regards the Bomber aspect of these operations, targets have been attacked mainly in the LILLE-LENS-BETHUNE industrial area. During 72 "Circuses" actually carried out since June 14th, 520 Bombers in all have been escorted, (BLENHEIMS, STIRLINGS and HAMPDENS). A total of 10 have been lost due to flak, and only 4 due to Fighter action. It is therefore evident that from the Bomber point of view the results of the "Circuses" have been highly satisfactory, and that under present circumstances we can take Bombers in to the limit of the Fighter endurance with comparative impunity from enemy Fighter attack whenever the weather is suitable.

6. With the assumption of the offensive we have thus gained the initiative over the Germans, with the result that they are forced to maintain a high state of "Readiness" while we are free to give our Squadrons adequate time for meals, recreation and rest. This, coupled with a reluctance to come and "mix it" with British Squadrons, even though the Germans are fighting over their own territory, must have a very adverse morale effect on their Fighter pilots. To maintain this morale ascendency is vitally important when considering future air operations, for it seems highly improbable that the German Fighter force will ever be prepared to fight harder over ENGLAND than they are now doing over FRANCE.

7. In considering "Circus" operations and the results obtained in air fighting, there are certain tactical factors to be borne in mind:-

(a) The 109F has a slightly superior performance to the SPITFIRE V, which in itself confers a certain tactical advantage on the Germans.

(b) As we are the attackers, the Germans know approximately where we are going and the height band within which our Bombers operate. They are thus able to climb away – to return to the attack at moments favourable to themselves, and come in only when they have attained an initial height and sun advantage.

(c) In all operations the moment comes when the formation has to turn for home. Owing to the fact that we are operating to the limit of our petrol endurance when over the LILLE-BETHUNE area, it means that on the homeward journey there is little scope for our Fighters to fight the Germans freely and follow them down, as they invariably break off and dive away south-east if they are not in a favourable position.

(d) In raids of deep penetration the chief fighting usually takes place near the target area and continues right back to the coast. Experience now shows that for these raids the proportion of Fighters accompanying the Bombers and their Escort Wing and Escort Cover Wing needs to be increased and other Wings should be located at a favourable point on the return route.

In raids of shallower penetration, however, it pays to give a number of Wings *carte blanche* to operate in loose formation with freedom to seek out and destroy the enemy.

(e) Diversions, e.g. a raid of shallow penetration carried out some 45 minutes before the main raid of deeper penetration, are very successful in that the enemy Fighters are caught refuelling, but they must not be practised too regularly or these will lose their effect.

(f) Generally the sun is unfavourable to us during the whole of the morning, as it is difficult to withdraw other than down–sun and that, of course, is the most favourable condition of light from the German's point of view.

(g) Any of our aircraft which are damaged by a lucky shot, (such as a bullet in the glycol tank from a long-range shot), are likely to be missing as we are fighting over enemy territory.

(h) The German warning system has improved out of all recognition since these operations commenced. In the earlier operations our formations were generally only reported as they crossed the coast, and the German Fighters were slow to take the air. Now German Fighter formations are generally plotted over the ST OMER, LILLE and BETHUNE areas as soon as our Fighters leave the English Coast, and the fact that they are plotted means that they have already gained a considerable amount of height. It is, therefore, more difficult for our formations to surprise the Germans and easier for them to surprise us.

(i) The Germans have withdrawn their Fighters from the coastal region and operate from such areas as AMIENS, ALBERT, LILLE, BRUGES and ST OMER. The only coastal aerodromes regularly in operation are LE CROTOY and LE TREPORT, and this has made it impossible for us to jump on his Fighters in the neighbourhood of their aerodromes as we could have done had they continued to occupy the group of aerodromes in the north–west corner of the PAS DE CALAIS.

(j) One of the chief essentials in these operations is for our formations not to be surprised. I consider that at present the training of the Wings is of a high standard, and it is a rare thing for any of the formations to be surprised in good weather conditions. However, it is far more difficult to avoid surprise, especially when the penetration is deep, and it is under these conditions that comparatively heavy casualties have occasionally been suffered.

(k) Failure of the Bombers to navigate direct to the target or to make the French landfalls selected on the outward and homeward journeys at points comparatively free from Flak, to bomb without waste of time, or to keep good formation and withdraw in cohesion have usually proved expensive to the bombers themselves, and to the Fighter escort who are thereby placed at a disadvantage. I do not wish to stress this point, for generally the co-operation of the Bombers has been good and they are occasionally embarrassed by unskilled leaders and crews. I would point out, however, that a small formation of Heavy Bombers is a far more powerful striking force, uses far less trained pilots, and is far easier to protect than a larger formation of BLENHEIMS.

8. This brings me to a point of the first importance, i.e. that unless the Bombers hit hard and well, the enemy Fighters are not forced to risk a direct and determined attack upon them in the face of the escort – but content themselves with pecking at our Fighters under conditions when, as para. 7 above shows, are generally advantageous to the enemy. There have been periods during these "Circus" operations when our Bombers have placed heavy loads on the right spot to such effect that the Germans have been forced to go for the Bombers themselves; on subsequent Circuses we have profited accordingly by this pinning down of German Fighters to medium altitude fighting at the bomber height. On the other hand, a succession of light or abortive bombings encourages the enemy to ignore the Bombers and to fight only when with tactical advantage it suits him to do so. Under these latter conditions the dispatch of some 200 of our Fighters over enemy territory is not so profitable.

9. Despite the difficulties referred to in paras. 7 and 8 above, however, experience has shown that we can take in and escort in comparative safety sufficiently powerful forces of bombers to the important industrial objectives in the LILLE – LENS – BETHUNE industrial area to compel the enemy to attack them and so give our Fighters the opportunity to fight on satisfactory terms and consequently with favourable results.

I realise that the general policy of the Air Council is to utilise every available heavy Bomber for bombing GERMANY rather than occupied territory, but I believe that the diversion of even say 5% of our heavy Bombers to regular "Circus" operations would enable our Fighters to maintain such a high toll of enemy Fighter pilots as to embarrass his Eastern Operations.

10. It is for consideration to what extent pressure should be maintained on the enemy by the use of "Circuses". It is clear that as the position becomes stabilized on the Eastern front it will no longer be essential to maintain our daily pressure, but it will still be necessary to maintain our present air superiority and moral ascendancy in Northern France and to continue to use this fighting for the training of our Squadrons which have such a high proportion of new pilots. Moreover, it is desirable to maintain such degree of disorganisation of industry as has been attained in Northern France, and to pin down the enemy Fighter Units. Further, I believe that occasional offensive operations will be essential during the winter months in order to maintain the morale of our own squadrons, as any fighting force tends to deteriorate if subjected to long periods of inactivity.

RECOMMENDATIONS

11. I therefore wish to make the following recommendations: –

(i) "Circus" operations should be continued but the best opportunities of weather only should be taken – rather than maintaining daily attacks.

(ii) The aim of "Circus" operations being to relieve enemy air pressure on the Eastern Front, the immediate object should remain that of exploiting to the full enemy reaction to the attack of his industrial targets by destroying enemy Fighters in Northern France.

(iii) To enable our Fighters to engage the enemy on satisfactory terms, a Squadron of Heavy Bombers – either STIRLINGS or HAMPDENS should be allotted until the end of October, 1941, and trained in formation bombing for regular day operations on "Circuses". After October bombers should be made available during spells of fine weather.

(iv) If possible these Bombers should be camouflaged in day colours to reduce their vulnerability to Flak.

(v) The efforts of these heavy Bombers should be supplemented by the use or substitution of HURRICANE Bombers on certain classes of "Circus" operations.

(vi) When this force of heavy Bombers trained for day operations begins to make their weight felt, they will force the enemy to the regular attack of the Bombers, as opposed to their present tendency to ignore the Bombers and to pick at our Fighters from a height advantage. "Circuses" should then alternate raids of deep and lesser penetration. The raids of deep penetration to areas such as LILLE – BETHUNE are essential to force the enemy into action, but these raids do not produce the most satisfactory conditions for our Fighters to engage and destroy the enemy. Raids of shallow penetration are, therefore, also necessary to enable our Fighters to engage the enemy on favourable terms.

(vii) Continued use should be made of both deliberate heavy attacks as well as diversionary attacks in the ROUEN – HAVRE area in order to force the enemy to spread out his Fighter forces and thus make it more difficult for him to concentrate his forces in the North-East areas of France.

12. In conclusion, to summarise my views, I submit that Circus Operations have enabled us to gain the initiative, to develop our offensive tactics, and to take Bombers with comparative impunity, in daylight, to the attack of important objectives heavily defended by enemy fighters. They have enabled us to train Squadrons which have been full of untried pilots to fight under difficult circumstances, and by so doing to train Flight Commanders and Wing Leaders of the future. In addition, they have been the means of disrupting war industry in an area where production is important to the Germans, and

as a result of these operations since 14th June of this year, we have destroyed over enemy country 437 German aircraft compared to the loss of 194 of our own pilots. In achieving these results we have established very marked moral ascendency over the German Air Force in that part of France close to England.

I consider that it is important to carry on with this work which has been to our own benefit and the detriment of the Germans.

T Leigh-Mallory
Air Vice-Marshal
<u>Air Officer Commanding No.11 Group</u>

11G/S.500/13/Ops.
<u>5th September 1941.</u>
Douglas mentions this memo in his memoirs: 'Leigh-Mallory doubted whether the sweeps were really paying their way.' so he was fully aware of the problems. In one of his despatches, Douglas wrote:

'It would be unwise to attach too much importance to statistics showing the claims made and losses suffered by our fighters month-by-month throughout the offensive. The experience of two world wars shows that in large-scale offensive operations the claims to the destruction of enemy aircraft made by pilots, however honestly made and carefully scrutinised, are a most inaccurate guide to true situations.'

* * *

A few days later Sholto Douglas received the following letter from Leigh-Mallory:

<u>SECRET</u>

From HQ 11 Group, Uxbridge.   11 September 1941

Dear Sholto,
1. Thank you very much for your D.O. letter of the 7th September regarding the results of "Circuses" and other offensive operations. I am very glad to learn that the losses inflicted on the German Fighters during "Circuses" and the continued threat to objectives in Northern France have combined to effect in our favour the German Fighter dispositions on the Eastern Front and in the Mediterranean.

2. At my request Gibbs[10] came up to see you yesterday and you were good enough to let him see the draft Chief of Staff paper to which you refer. I understand that in that draft the figures for "Circuses" gains and losses from January until the present date are given as: -

Our Fighter losses	273
Our Bomber losses	39
Enemy aircraft destroyed	460

My own figures for that period are: -

Our Fighters lost		218
Our Bombers lost		15 (of which only 5 are due to fighters)
Enemy fighters destroyed		444
(& e/fighter prob destroyed	192	
(& e/fighter prob damaged)		240

3. The differences would appear to be accounted for by the fact that you include under the heading of "Circus", the losses (and the small gains) incurred in operations such as the attacks on Brest and La Pallice, and certain bomber operations off the German coast.

4. I realise that you wish to present to the Chief of Staff a picture of the results of the day offensive operations as a whole, but I feel that incorrect deductions may arise from the inclusion of such operations under "Circuses" – which are conducted under entirely different conditions. "Circus" is the code name – I might almost say trade mark, which I do not want to see infringed – of the combined Fighter and Bomber offensive operations which have been carried out between Cherbourg and Lille. Operations in this area are carried out within normal Fighter range, and we employ very powerful forces – up to 200 or more fighters at a time. Consequently, this class of operation is entirely different from those carried out in other areas at long range with comparatively small fighter escort, and in fact these latter operations are not described as "Circuses" in operational orders.

5. No doubt, even using your present draft figures for "Circus" gains and losses, you would be able to get a recommendation from the Chief of Staff for the modified continuance of the daylight offensive – but I feel that an incorrect picture of what can be done within normal fighter range will be given unless you show separately the results of the "true" "Circuses", and once wrong impressions have taken root the results on future direction are incalculable.

---

10. Group Captain Gerald E. Gibbs MC**, SASO, No.11 Group, Fighter Command.

6. I hope you will agree with the foregoing, and be able to amend your draft paper accordingly, though I know what a nuisance it is to make yet another alteration to a paper which is about to be approved.

T Leigh–Mallory

After the war, the RAF would learn that between 14 June and 3 September 1941, the Germans had only lost 128 fighters with a further 76 damaged. Not all of these casualties were caused simply as a result of Circus operations.

* * *

Sholto Douglas presented the following policy directive three days later:

From: Headquarters, Fighter Command
To: HQ 10 Group, 11 Group and 12 Group
        Copies to HQ No.2 Group and Air Ministry (DF. Ops)

Date: 14th September 1941.

CIRCUS OPERATIONS – OFFENSIVE POLICY

1. In forwarding a copy of the memorandum by AOC No.11 Group on the subject of "Circus" Operations (circulated under No.11 Group ref 110/ S500/13/Ops, dated 5th September), I have informed Air Ministry that I am in agreement with the memorandum. In addition I have stressed the need for co-operation of a squadron of heavy bombers in these offensive operations.
2. I now wish to modify the policy which we have been applying to these Circus operations in the light of results which they have recently shown. We can no longer expect to maintain the highly satisfactory results achieved in our earlier offensive operations, since the enemy is prepared to engage us in strength only when conditions are in his favour. His defensive organisation, particularly in the Pas de Calais area, is much improved and he maintains there a large concentration of fighters at a high state of readiness.
3. It is my intention therefore that we should scale down the effort slightly against the Pas de Calais area by restricting our major efforts in that area to days in which the weather conditions are particularly in our favour. At the same time, in order to keep the enemy's fighter forces in this area at a high state of readiness we should, when occasion is suitable, make feint attacks using fighters only and without necessarily penetrating enemy territory.
4. It is my intention also to endeavour by undertaking more widespread attacks against suitable fringe targets along the broader front from Texel to Brest, to

force the enemy to disperse the fighter force now concentrated in the Pas de Calais area. Such attacks involve less penetration and meet with less opposition than those against the Lille district, and can be undertaken in smaller strength and in less favourable weather.

5. The spreading of attacks along the broader front of the enemy's coast will call for effective coordination between the Bomber and Fighter Groups concerned and I look to the Fighter Group Commanders to ensure that the necessary inter-Group liaison is maintained. A memorandum FC. /S.24752/ Air dated 14th September has already been issued on the organisation of these operations.

6. In regard to the employment of Hurricane bombers, which is mentioned in this memorandum, I do not at present intend these aircraft to be employed as bombers on raids of deep penetration against land targets. Supplies of aircraft of this type will be limited, at least for a time, and their primary task at first will be to engage enemy shipping in the Straits area. There is however, no objection to their use against suitable land targets in open country near the coast such as enemy aerodromes, provided they are not employed to the detriment of their more important anti-shipping role.

W S Douglas

The following extract from the memorandum Sholto Douglas refers to, was originated and sent out by Air Vice-Marshal Douglas Evill CB DSC AFC, at Fighter Command:

METHOD

8. Land Targets – The areas of Fighter Group responsibility for the support of bomber attacks of targets on land will be as defined in paras. 14, 15 and 16 below, extending to the depth of fighter range.

9. The daylight attack by bombers of land targets is the task primarily of No.2 Group; targets will therefore be selected as a rule by AOC No.2 Group and details of each operation will be decided in consultation between AOC No.2 Group and the Fighter Group Commander concerned. On occasions heavy bombers of No.5 Group or other Bomber Groups may be allotted for this purpose, and similar arrangements will then be made between the two Group Commanders concerned.[11]

---

11. Commanding 2 Group was ACM Sir James Robb GCB KBE DFC AFC. Both he and Gerald Gibbs had been successful fighter pilots during WW1.

10. The greater part of the offensive effort is likely to be directed against the Pas de Calais area, but it is most desirable that we should exercise and so wear down the enemy's defences along the whole of his front within range of our fighters between Den Helder and Brest. It is thus most essential to maintain a measure of co-ordination between the various operations undertaken.

11. It has been decided, therefore, that the Bomber sorties which No.2 Group can make available for these operations will be divided as between Fighter Groups concerned, and a basis that will be notified from time to time by this Headquarters after consultation with Bomber Command.

12. Fighter Groups are to ensure that fighter operations are carefully co-ordinated as between Groups.

13. Shipping Targets – Responsibility for attacking shipping with bomber or torpedo aircraft in the Channel and the North Sea has been allotted as follows:

(a) Between Cherbourg and Wilhelmshaven – No.2 Group.

(b) In other areas – Coastal Command.

14. In the case of attacks on shipping in the area west of 1° W. (Pte. De Barfleur incl.) fighter protection and support for bombers of No.2 Group and of Coastal Command will be provided by No.10 Group. Squadrons available in No.10 Group for this purpose will include one squadron of long-range fighters in the Portreath Sector.

15. In the case of attacks on shipping in waters between 1° W. and Ostend, fighter protection will be provided by No.11 Group. To this end No.2 Group maintain one squadron at Manston, of which one flight is maintained at 30 minutes notice for attacks on enemy shipping. A further striking force of one Blenheim squadron is maintained by No.2 Group standing by at one hour's notice to reinforce the Manston squadron when necessary. No.11 Group is to maintain one fighter squadron at Manston available to give close support to these bombers and is to provide adequate escort and cover according to the situation.

16. It is the intention in the near future to relieve No.2 Group of the task of engaging shipping in the vicinity of the Straits [of Dover] by employing two Hurricane bomber squadrons in Fighter Command against shipping targets in the area Manston – Ostend – Dieppe – Beachy Head; the bombers of No.2 Group will then only operate against shipping in the Straits if specially called upon by No.11 Group to do so.[12]

17. In the case of attacks on shipping in the Coastal waters between Texel and Ostend, fighter protection and support for bombers of No.2 Group will be

---

12. The two squadrons later employed on such operations would be 607 and 615.

provided by No.12 Group. To this end No.12 Group includes one squadron of long-range fighters in the Coltishall Sector and will give further support as necessary.

18. The areas of responsibility allocated to Fighter Groups as above are not intended to be rigid, but close liaison must be maintained between Fighter Groups regarding any operations encroaching upon other Group's areas.

* * *

A few days later, the Chief of the Air Staff, Air Chief-Marshal Sir Charles Portal KCB DSO MC, produced a memorandum covering aspects of the RAF's daylight raids over France.

MOST SECRET

DAYLIGHT RAIDS ON NORTHERN FRANCE AND GERMANY

Memorandum by the Chief of the Air Staff

1. The Chiefs of Staff at their 302nd meeting held on the 29th August discussed our losses in daylight operations over Northern France and Germany and invited the Air Staff to circulate a short note giving a comparison of daylight sorties flown and casualties sustained in relation to the military value of the attacks delivered.
2. The raids may be divided into two phases; a non-intensive phase from 5th January to 15th June, and an intensive phase from 15th June to 31st August. The following table gives the figures called for: –

	5th Jan–15th Jun	15th Jun–31 Aug
FIGHTER COMMAND		
Offensive Sorties	2,411	13,896
Aircraft Lost	40	265
Proportion of losses to sorties	1.6%	1.9%

These figures show that the casualty rate in Fighter Command is very low. The bomber casualties, although proportionately heavier, have not been serious except in certain particularly hazardous operations such as the daylight raids on Brest, Rotterdam and the Cologne Power Stations. It may be added that over the whole period the strength of Fighter Command has increased by nearly 50% and the strength of the bomber group principally concerned has remained practically constant.

3. Comparable figures for German effort and losses are not available but the following table illustrates the positions: -

	5th Jan	15th Jun	31st Aug
Establishment of German S/E [single engine] fighter Units in the West, excluding Reserve Training Units.	1,027	621	222

	5th Jan-15th Jun	15th Jun-31st Aug
Average establishment.	902	340
Aircraft lost (excluding probables and damaged)	30	at least 400

4. These operations have not succeeded in compelling the withdrawal of short-range fighters from the Eastern Front, principally because the area within range of the fighter escort does not include industrial objectives of vital importance to the enemy's war effort. It is certain that withdrawals of enemy aircraft from the East would follow heavy sustained daylight attacks upon objectives in Germany itself; we have demonstrated our ability to make such attacks deep into enemy territory, but this is beyond the range at which fighter cover can be provided and the losses inevitably incurred have been such as cannot at present be accepted in sustained operations.

5. The operations have nevertheless, been in other respects highly successful. In particular:

(i) Serious damage has been done to German warships, to MVs in harbour or under construction, and to industrial objectives in France, Belgium and Holland, and NW Germany. In particular, there is evidence that the output from the important coal producing area and steel industries in the Lille-Lens districts has [sic] been considerably reduced by the successful attacks on the principal power stations and plants in this region.

(ii) Greater losses in aircraft have been imposed on the German fighter force than we have ourselves incurred. There is as yet no sign of a shortage of aircraft, and many enemy pilots probably escaped by parachute. The cumulative effect on German morale is reported, however, to have been considerable, and the morale of our own forces is undoubtedly raised by taking the offensive.

(iii) The morale of the population in the occupied territories has been sustained.

(iv)   Although the enemy's fighter strength in the west has been greatly reduced, his policy in other theatres has been affected by the necessity of continuing operations on an intensive scale in Western Europe. For example:

   (a)   Reserve training units have been considerably used in operations in the West; some of these reserve units have belonged to first-time units operating in the East. This procedure inevitably has the effect of retarding the flow of reserve crews and aircraft.
   (b)   The existing German fighter forces in the East are known to have proved inadequate, and it has in the Southern sector been found necessary to use fighters from the Italian, Rumanian and Hungarian air forces. Thus even the limited number of fighters retained in the West would have been of substantial importance in the European campaign.
   (c)   It has not been possible for the Germans to maintain a fighter force in Sicily, in spite of the extreme urgency of providing convoy protection in that area and the number of German fighters in North Africa is barely adequate to the task.

6. Conclusions
   (i)   Daylight bombing of objectives in occupied territory has not been and is not likely to be effective in forcing the enemy to withdraw short-range fighters from the Eastern front.
   (ii)   In spite of this our offensive operations have shown a very substantial balance of advantage in our favour.
   (iii) The balance of fighter losses has recently tended to become less favourable to us than at the beginning of the intensive phase of operations, and weather conditions are also likely to be less favourable as winter approaches. It is, however, essential that daylight offensive operations should be maintained, although at a reduced level. In addition to the advantages enumerated in para.5, the continuance of these operations is necessary in order to keep the morale ascendency we now hold to provide fighting experience for the pilots of Fighter Command.

18th September 1941

* * *

There are any number of interesting extracts mentioned in these letters, memos and reports. Not the least, of course, is the assumption that Leigh-Mallory was either not privy to intelligence coming from the 'Y' Service or was ignoring it. And perhaps even

Sholto Douglas was not given access to it either. If they had they would presumably not have been happy to record the number of enemy fighters being claimed as destroyed.

Perhaps it was only those Air Force personnel above the position of Command and Group leaders who knew the facts. Churchill and the Chief of the Air Staff must have had some knowledge that, according to intercepted radio traffic, German fighter units were not requesting from the quartermasters anything like the number of aircraft needed to replace the reported losses indicated by Fighter Command claims.

If this is true it must have had something to do with maintaining morale amongst the RAF's fighter pilots. These pilots could see the empty chairs at meal times after operations and it would have been soul-destroying to think that the Germans were not suffering the losses that the claims indicated. Bomber crews of 2 Group might also be peeved if they thought that being bait for enemy fighters, with all the strain and danger that that entailed, was not producing some sort of positive result against the German Air Force.

There is also the question of decorations for the fighter pilot's efforts. If pilots were not actually inflicting the combat casualties against the Me109s, yet individual pilots were being credited with, quite often, a high number of victories, was it right to give decorations to them? Perhaps again, this was all part of the front to maintain morale in the face of Fighter Command losing more pilots and aeroplanes than the Germans were. Not that there is any question as to the bravery and courage of the RAF fighter pilots. During 1940 many of them had fought themselves to a standstill, not only during the Battle of France, but during the even more important defence of Britain throughout the summer and autumn of that year. Now they were being asked to fly over miles of unforgiving sea, then to fight an enemy that were more than happy to engage but only when in a favourable position. Once battle was joined the fighter pilots had to survive combat with that nagging thought that soon they would have to break away in sufficient time to reach England, with drying fuel tanks and, in all probability, either low or out of ammunition.

Yet the thought of those in charge of the 1941 offensive must have been that they were losing more pilots and aircraft than the Germans, and that if they thought all this was of any help in deflecting German efforts on the Russian Front, they must have known it was not. The intelligence boys knew almost exactly what the numbers were and how many Gruppen the Luftwaffe had in France and the Low Countries, and that no units were being withdrawn from the East in order to help the German pilots engaging the RAF's efforts over northern France. However, it was all that could be done. Britain simply did not have the operational strength to do more, and the demands coming from the Mediterranean and North Africa for more and more pilots and planes continued to drain Britain's aircraft industry and training abilities. Unknown to them as September 1941 began, was the fact that before the end of the year, events in the Far East was going to increase the pressure still further on the British fighter force.

Chapter 10

September

While all this correspondence was going on, Fighter Command and 2 Group of Bomber Command, continued with the 'season' as it was being called by the fighter pilots.

As Circus operations continued the RAF was increasingly flying other types of missions. Gudgeon operations had already been in evidence and so were Ramrods and Roadsteads. Ramrods were similar to Circuses, but with the emphasis being on the destruction of a specific target rather than merely putting up a threat to entice German fighters into combat. Roadstead was the name applied to anti-shipping operations. Enemy shipping in the North Sea and the Channel never seemed to slacken despite the efforts of Bomber and Coastal Command to stop them operating. Blenheims suffered more losses in these types of operations than they ever did flying a Circus. Two Hurricane squadrons operating from RAF Manston, 607 and 615, were flying what was called 'Channel Stop' missions, trying literally to stop enemy shipping from operating. They might not suffer the high casualty rate Blenheims did, but their hitting power was a little less, although four 20mm cannon had their effect.

As the month began the various 11 Group Wing Leaders were:

Biggin Hill	W/Cdr M. L. Robinson DSO DFC
Kenley	W/Cdr J. A. Kent DFC AFC
Hornchurch	W/Cdr F. S. Stapleton DFC
Tangmere	W/Cdr H. de C. A. Woodhouse AFC
North Weald	W/Cdr F. V. Beamish DSO DFC
Northolt	W/Cdr T. H. Rolski VM KW
Duxford (12 Gp)	S/Ldr R. R. S. Tuck DSO DFC & 2 Bars

These Wings comprised:

Biggin Hill	72, 92, 609 Squadrons
Kenley	452 RAAF, 485 RNZAF, 602 Squadrons
Hornchurch	54, 603, 611 Squadrons
Tangmere	41, 129, 616 Squadrons
North Weald	71, 111, 222, 402 RCAF Squadrons
Northolt	306, 308, 315 Polish Squadrons
Duxford	56, 266, 601 Squadrons

10 Group escorted a Roadstead to Cherbourg on the afternoon of the 1st, 118 Squadron losing a pilot. Leutnant Siegfried Schnell of 9./JG2 claimed a Blenheim for his forty-seventh victory, although none were lost.

The next day saw two fairly uneventful fighter sweeps and a Roadstead to Ostend. 452 Squadron escorted the Blenheims on the latter and, as Me109s came in to attack, two pilots engaged them and claimed two shot down, although in the event only one pilot of JG26 was lost.

Circus No.93 – 4 September

The first Circus of the month called for twelve Blenheims to attack the power station at Mazingarbe. North Weald got the Close Escort slot, Biggin the Cover. Target Support went to Kenley and Hornchurch, Forward Support to Northolt and Rear Support, Tangmere. Low cloud over the Channel became hazy over France with just fragments of cloud.

The bombers, all from 18 Squadron, operated in two boxes of six, and made RV over Manston at 10,000 feet at 1800. Seventeen minutes later they were crossing the French coast at Mardyck and reached Mazingarbe ten minutes after that. Bombs from the first box all overshot, but the second six saw their bombs fall on the Ammonia Plant, on the coking ovens and across the nearby rail line. However, on the way in a single Me109 dived on the rear section near Hazebrouck and opened fire on one which pulled out with black smoke pouring from its starboard engine. It then burst into flames and just before it blew up, one of the crew baled out. The attacking pilot was none other than Adolf Galland who thus achieved his eighty-second victory.

The Escorts became embroiled in fights with Me109s going to and returning from the target and while 222 Squadron lost two pilots, the Wing claimed 2-3-1 before the 109s broke off. Both NCO pilots ended up 'in the bag'. 111 Squadron also had one pilot forced to bale out over the Channel, but he was later rescued. This was Sgt T. R. Caldwell's second bale out, having done so back on 23 July. Of the three Blenheim crew, only the pilot survived, joining the two fighter pilots in captivity.

The Biggin Hill Wing was similarly engaged, flying between 17 and 20,000 feet. 92 Squadron lost a Canadian pilot, another prisoner of war, but three 109s were claimed as probables. One 609 pilot had his Spitfire damaged in combat and then, running out of fuel, had to crash-land at Detling, further damaging his machine which was consequently written off. Kenley's Wing was up at 25–26,000 feet and had no encounters until coming back. They saw several 109s but no engagement took place.

Hornchurch, however, flying higher, became engaged with 109s. During numerous dogfights, four 109s were claimed destroyed, with three more probables and two damaged. Two pilots did not get home and another (Sgt G. W. McC. Neil of 603) returned wounded in the left shoulder and foot. The two lost were from 54 Squadron, both being killed.

The Poles also had some scraps, claiming one Messerschmitt with a second damaged, but lost a pilot from 308 Squadron, who ended up a prisoner. Tangmere engaged a few 109s, 129 Squadron claiming one as damaged, while 616 claimed a probable for no loss.

Total claims came to seven destroyed, ten probably destroyed and five damaged for the loss of six pilots and another wounded. Eight Spitfires were lost in total. Apart from Galland and his Blenheim, JG26 claimed eight or nine Spitfires, with Priller gaining his forty-seventh kill, Müncheberg his fifty-first and fifty-second, and Schmid his twenty-seventh, twenty-eighth and twenty-ninth. JG2 claimed three Spitfires, one credited to Maj. Walter Oesau – victory number ninety-seven. The only casualty to either Geschwader was one FW190 pilot damaging his fighter's undercarriage in a hard landing at Moorsele.

No mention has yet been made by RAF pilots about the arrival of the new Focke-Wulf 190 fighter, but JG26 had been using them for several weeks, mostly during conversion flights from the trusty old Me109s. They had yet to make an impact in air actions, but that would soon come. Once RAF pilots began to return with reports of seeing a radial-engined fighter, as opposed to the in-lined engine of the 109s, it was thought the Germans were using old French Curtiss Hawks, captured in 1940. They quickly discovered the new fighter was far superior to the old Hawk 75.

This day also saw another Gudgeon IV operation, with Westland Whirlwinds of 263 Squadron escorting 2 Group Blenheims to attack a tanker observed in Cherbourg Harbour. One report says the tanker was hit, another that it was missed and the bombs fell on the south end of the harbour. Me109s of JG2 intercepted the formation and several pilots became engaged. Feldwebel Erwin Philipp shot down one Whirlwind for his first victory. As one might expect, JG2 erroneously claimed a total of four other Whirlwinds and a Hurricane. Leutnant Schnell claimed two Whirlwinds and the Hurricane, to bring his score to a nice round fifty!

This date also saw Knight's Crosses awarded to two of JG2's aces, Kurt Bühligen and Josef Wurmheller, both Oberfeldwebels (Senior Warrant Officers), with scores of twenty-one and twenty-four victories.

* * *

Back in 1969 (was it that long ago!?) I had the pleasure of meeting Galland in Manchester when he was giving a talk to aviation enthusiasts. My main reason in doing so was to follow up on correspondence we had had about a specific Hurricane he had shot down in late 1940. However, I managed to slip in a question of how he felt about the early operations by the RAF over France in 1941. He said he had admired the way Fighter Command quickly developed their tactics in protecting the small bomber formations, and also admired the way the majority of fighters were not tied to the close protection flights as the Luftwaffe had been in 1940. He rarely was able to use all of his three Gruppen in these actions, generally sending up just one at a time, or even just sections of staffel strength. What he and Oesau had devised, when possible, was for their pilots to try to engage and divert the close escorting fighters leaving the more expert pilots (aces) to take advantage of any gap created to dash in and have a crack at the bombers. Sometimes, he said with a smile, it worked.

Circus No.94

In the two weeks between Circuses 93 and 94, at least two Roadstead missions had been carried out, some sweeps and Rhubarbs. On the 7th, 71 Eagle Squadron got caught in the grinder that was JG26 and had three Spitfire pilots shot down, two killed and one taken prisoner. A fourth got back slightly wounded. One of those killed was F/O E. Q. Tobin. 'Red' Tobin and had been among the first American volunteer pilots to see action with the RAF in 1940. Galland had led his pilots into the attack and in all six Spitfires were not only claimed but credited. Galland (eighty-third victory), Müncheberg (fifty-three) and Schmid (thirty) were the 'big hitters'. Should anyone think that it was only JG2 and sometimes JG26 that over-claimed, I./JG52 reported shooting down four Spitfires off Den Helder on the afternoon of the 12th. One 12 Group Hurricane failed to return from an escort to some Blenheims attacking a target in Holland.

As for Circus 94, the records appear particularly lacking in clarity. One states that eighteen Blenheims attacked Le Trait ship-yards on either 16 or 17 September, although the more accurate reference probably lies in an undated 2 Group document which states that six bombers each from 88 and 114 were recalled after an 1100 take-off due to unsatisfactory weather.

On the 16th the Polish Wing flew a sweep and near Boulogne was attacked by Me109s of JG2 and JG26. 306 and 315 each lost a pilot killed, and this attracted claims of one Spitfire by JG26, and one Hurricane and two Spitfires by JG2. Müncheberg of JG26 thereby got his fifty-fourth kill, while Oblt. Egon Mayer of JG2 claimed two Spitfires for victories twenty-two and twenty-three.

Circus No.95 – 17 September

There were two operations this day, the first calling for twenty-four Blenheims to bomb the synthetic petrol plant and power station at Mazingarbe. Twelve of the bombers came from 114 Squadron, six from 82 – although one had to abort – plus another six from another un-named squadron but they may not have joined in. There was only slight cloud over the Channel.

As a prelude to this operation, one fighter squadron from Manston (615) and one from Debden (403 RCAF) made rendezvous over Hastings at 1310 with one Blenheim in order to carry out a diversionary operation. Manston's 607 Squadron was to have taken part but they were late at the RV so flew direct to Le Touquet. The formation crossed the French coast south of Berck at 14,000 feet, swept from Frevant to St Pol then came out just north of Le Touquet without interference. More than twenty Me109s were observed climbing as the RAF headed out. In all an estimated fifty to sixty enemy fighters had risen to investigate.

The main event was for twenty-three bombers, escorted by North Weald, Northolt and Biggin Wings with Target Support supplied by Kenley and Hornchurch. Forward and Rear Wings came from Tangmere and 12 Group. They headed in over Dunkirk at 1430 and bombs went down from 12,000 feet, setting fire to a large tank and a hangar-like building in the middle of the target. Several explosions were seen on the north and south-east corners and explosions continued in another spot. The bombers made the French coast but flak caught one Blenheim, blowing off a propeller, and it went down in flames. It was an 82 Squadron machine from which nobody survived.

The first thing the Escort Wing noticed at the RV was that the bombers were in two boxes of six rather than the expected four boxes of three, so had to rapidly re-deploy their positioning. Over the French coast they came under sporadic AA fire but most of it exploded behind the bombers. To and from the target several 109s made attacks either singly or in pairs but did not linger to press home these passes but dived away after a quick squirt. In these encounters the Wing claimed two 109s probably destroyed and another damaged but lost two pilots, both from the Eagle Squadron. One was killed, the other baled out and was rescued from the sea by the Germans.

The Northolt Wing was stepped up above and behind the main formation from between 14 and 16,000 feet. All three Polish squadrons became involved with small groups of 109s during which three 109s were destroyed and another damaged, but 306 lost one pilot, who was taken prisoner, and 308 Squadron, P/O C. Budzalek, collided with a 109 from JG26, piloted by Obfw. Max Martin. Budzalek did not survive but Martin successfully baled out although he was injured. Two of the 109s were credited to 306's CO, S/Ldr S. F. Skalski, bringing his score to eighteen. Stanislaw Skalski had flown against the Germans in Poland in 1939 and been successful during the Battle of Britain. His two victories today were his last until 1942 and 1943, by which time he would bring his score to around twenty-four. His decorations included the DSO, DFC and two Bars, the Polish *Virtuti Miltari*, and the Cross of Valor (KW) with three Bars.

The German pilots kept up similar sniping attacks against the Biggin Hill squadrons that were stepped up from 18 to 23,000 feet. The RAF boys split up into fours and although one 109 was claimed as a probable, 92 Squadron had one pilot killed and another returned wounded.

Kenley reached the target at 1440 and orbited up to 30,000 feet. Some 109s were seen above but they did not come down, therefore at the briefed time the bombers should have started back, the Wing headed north too. The Hornchurch Wing, on the other hand, did get into action. They too were stepped up to 30,000 feet and 54 Squadron became engaged with several 109Fs while 611 saw others and dived to attack. 603 Squadron lost contact with the other two squadrons and headed back towards Le Touquet where they spotted fifty 109s in several formations. In numerous air fights, the Wing claimed two 109s probably destroyed and two damaged but lost three pilots, all from 54 Squadron, with another wounded. He crash-landed back at Hornchurch. Among those killed was the CO, S/Ldr N. Orton DFC & Bar. 'Fanny' Orton, as mentioned previously, was a veteran of the Battle of France, and at the time of his death he had achieved some seventeen combat victories with others unconfirmed and damaged. This was another severe loss to Fighter Command.

Tangmere Wing had some skirmishes, 616 Squadron damaging one 109, while P/O J. H. Whalen of 129, claimed two destroyed and damaged a third. Jimmy Whalen, from Vancouver would score three victories in 1941 and in 1942, flying in the defence of Colombo against the Japanese, and would bag three dive bombers in one action with 30 Squadron. He would die in 1944 over Burma and be awarded a belated DFC after the war's end.

The 12 Group Wing saw plenty of 109s up high but none came down to engage and quickly flew away. Once the operation ended and the squadrons began to land back at their bases, several ASR boats were out, covered by Spitfires, to search for downed pilots in the Channel.

This operation cost Fighter Command six pilots killed, two taken prisoner, plus three wounded. Nine Spitfires lost too. Among the German pilots, Priller gained his forty-eighth victory and Siefert his twentieth, while the 306 Squadron loss was credited to Adolf Galland's brother Paul, his third victory. RAF claims seem to be in the region of eight destroyed, five probables and five damaged.

Circus No.96 – 17 September

No sooner had Circus 95 set off than six Hampdens from 408 Squadron were starting out to bomb the Shell factory at Marquise, escorted by North Weald and covered by Hornchurch and Kenley. 408 was led by S/Ldr W. J. Burnett DFC RCAF, who had earlier been with 49 Squadron. Target Support went to Biggin and Tangmere, plus support from 12 Group's Wing. There was good visibility over France but ground haze made things difficult up to 3,000 feet.

They reached the area of Marquise in one box formation but the bomber leader was unable to identify the factory and his formation was also being harassed by heavy flak and fighters. Five of the bombers were damaged. Burnett's aircraft was among them and he lost his hydraulics, so was unable to open his bomb doors. In the end the bombers aborted the attempt and brought their bombs home. An air gunner claimed a 109 damaged.

All the escorting fighters had been turned round in record time to take part in this second Circus of the afternoon, which is probably why North Weald again got the Close Escort slot. They had made RV over Dungeness at 1730 hours and headed out; the target area was reached at 1751. The Hampdens were flying so slowly the Wing had trouble keeping behind them and had to weave continually. Added to this, they had already been warned over the radio that a number of 109s were waiting for them long before they reached the French coast! They were not disappointed. Some pilots counted up to fifty enemy fighters in small formations and most began to adopt the now familiar hit and run tactics, diving out of the sun, firing, then continuing to head down, knowing (but hoping) the Spitfires would not follow and leave their charges. They too received their share of flak, but not much fighting took place, in fact only one 109 was claimed as damaged.

The Hornchurch Wing too was heavily engaged once they entered France and its pilots were involved in numerous dogfights, and for once it appeared the Luftwaffe pilots were keen to get involved. 54 Squadron claimed a damaged but Sgt F. L. Preece collided with a Messerschmitt, and had to ditch in the Channel, from where he was later rescued. 603 and 611 Squadrons had fights but no losses or claims.

The Kenley Wing was made up of 485 (New Zealand), 452 (Australian) and 602 Squadrons, together with 123 Squadron. Some 109s came down on 602 Squadron but 602 shot one of them down, although they lost one of 123's pilots, who was killed. 452 and 485 were both attacked but no damage was inflicted by either side.

Spitfires of the Biggin Hill Wing reached St Omer at 1745 at 25,000 feet and above. Some red marker AA puffs were seen some way behind them when they were ten miles in from the coast. The Wing turned back towards Boulogne where many 109s could be seen and some fights developed. One enemy fighter was damaged but 609 had one pilot shot up and forced to bale out over the Channel, from where he was rescued later. This was P/O J. A. Atkinson, one of the longest serving pilots on 609 – in fact it seems that the postings people had forgotten all about him. He went on to be a flight commander and receive the DFC on Typhoons. He later became Sir Alec Atkinson KCB, a wonderful and helpful gentleman whom I met on a few occasions at his home.

Tangmere and 12 Group Wings were not engaged although they too saw many 109s in the areas of France they had been covering. Both reported heavy AA fire.

Total claims came to two destroyed, five probables and two damaged, with one pilot missing and two rescued from the sea. JG26 had two aircraft downed and one shot down into the Channel. Another had baled out over St Omer. One pilot, flying one of the new FW190s, chased the RAF formation back over the Channel and claimed a Spitfire. JG2 claimed three for no loss, which was added to a single claim against the first Circus. German claims for the day amounted to the four by JG2 and ten by JG26, with JG26 losing three pilots killed and two wounded.

Group Captain Bouchier mentioned in his report the fact that the Hampdens had caused problems for their escort by flying too slowly, at perhaps 120 mph. It was requested that in future operations the bombers fly at a minimum, between 140–145 mph indicated air speed.

Circus No.97 – 18 September

Hampdens were again the bomber of choice on the 18th, six from 408, and led by its CO, W/Cdr N. W. Timmerman DSO DFC RCAF, who, like Burnett, had also been with 49 Squadron earlier, assigned to go for the marshalling yards at Abbeville. Five mixed Spitfire and Hurricane squadrons were providing the Close Escort position, 402 from Hornchurch, 607 from Debden, plus 41, 129 and 616 from Tangmere. The Polish Wing gave Escort Cover, with Target Support provided by North Weald and the other three squadrons of the Hornchurch Wing. 12 Group gave Forward Support.

The weather was not good. 10/10th cloud with fog or mist over the English coast and Channel that gave way to ground haze over France although it was clear above. RV had been planned above Hastings and the bombers reported their arrival had been right on time, although no fighters appeared. After circling for twenty-five minutes the Hampdens broke off and went home.

Things did not improve. The five squadrons of Close Escort fighters met up near Tangmere and then Beachy Head where they found eleven Blenheims in two boxes of six and five respectively, but apparently no escort. 607 Squadron attached themselves to the box of five, 402 to the box of six, and headed south. They had mixed themselves in with Circus 99, with 18 and 139 Squadrons bound for the power station at Rouen. Meantime, the Close Escort Wing to Circus 99, Kenley, came to the RV to find the two Hurricane squadrons attached to the Blenheims.

The Tangmere pilots made the correct RV time but found Hastings covered in cloud. After a short wait they headed south, even seeing more RAF fighters below but eventually the Wing was recalled, when they spotted the Hampdens flying away north.

The Poles arrived over Hastings too at 1430, and saw the Blenheims turning to fly out to sea. Unable to comprehend why they were seeing Blenheims and not Hampdens, they decided to go with them but even though they got as far as the north of Rouen, they then received the recall. As they headed back a few 109s were surprised below but their pilots took rapid evasive action when the Spitfires made a turn to engage.

The Target Support Wings reached the target just on 1500 but could not see any bombers, so orbited for eight minutes in case they should show. North Weald saw a few 109s and a single 109 that dived down in front of 71 Squadron was claimed shot down by F/Lt C. G. Peterson. Chesley Peterson was to become a leading light with the Eagle Squadron with a victory score of 6-3-6 and receiving the DFC. When the Eagle squadrons became the American 4th Fighter Group in late 1942, he became the Executive Officer. He added two more victories to his tally in 1943, by which time the British had awarded him the DSO. Colonel Peterson was later Combat Operations Officer with the US 9th Army Air Force and added to his decorations by receiving the American DSC DSM, Legion of Merit and Air Medal.

The three Hornchurch squadrons all made attacks on scattered 109s, 603 Squadron probably destroying two. Otherwise, both Wings headed for home, still wondering where the bombers had got to. Meanwhile 12 Group Wing patrolled their assigned area and had ten 109s circle above them and although four or five dived towards them they did not press home an attack.

All that this operation achieved was two 109s destroyed, three probables and two damaged, for the loss of one Hurricane pilot of 607 Squadron. He was picked off by Joachim Müncheberg, for his fifty-fifth victory, timed at 1605 (German time).

Group Captain Bouchier's report did not make for comfortable reading. He said it had not been anticipated that the rendezvous would have to be made above 10/10th cloud, and that things were further complicated because the second Circus (99) had been arranged for the same time and in roughly the same place, just fifteen to twenty miles further along the coast. In future, when two operations have targets in the same areas, the RVs will be chosen with enough space to ensure this sort of thing did not happen again and thereby confuse the escorts. All very well, but it should not have happened in the first place.

Circus No's 98 and 99 – 18 September

Circus 98 called for an attack upon the Lille railway repair shops but it never materialised. As we read above, Circus 99 became entangled with Circus 97. The eleven Blenheims had proceeded to the target and bombed with 22 x 250lb instantaneously-fused bombs and 21 x 250lb delayed-action bombs. Some fell on the target, others over or undershooting. Flak and fighters were a problem, with one bomber being damaged by AA fire. One air gunner claimed hits on a 109.

With the two Hurricane squadrons of Circus 97 horning in, 452 Squadron of the Kenley Wing had difficulty in carrying out their Close Escort role, forcing them to fly in two sections in line astern either side of the bombers. The Kenley Wing encountered an estimated fifty Me109s that tried to get to the bombers all the way to the target as well as on the return, to some halfway out across the Channel. 54 Squadron saw much of the action and claimed four 109s shot down. One was seen to explode in the air and two more to crash inland. However, four of 452's Australians did not make it back. Two were killed and two became prisoners of war. The New Zealanders of 485 were similarly engaged, losing one pilot killed but claiming three 109s destroyed. 602 Squadron suffered no losses and damaged one 109.

The Biggin Hill Wing, who had been assigned as Escort Cover, arrived at the RV above Beachy Head but could see no sign of the bombers. They orbited for five minutes before the Wing Leader was told by the Controller that the Blenheims had already started out so he led his fighters towards St Valery. Reaching a position twelve miles from Rouen without sighting any bombers, and deciding they must have turned back, the Wing reversed course too. Then they spotted a large gaggle of 109s and turned towards them but whether or not the German pilots saw them isn't known as they headed off in the direction of Abbeville, so Biggin's pilots headed for home too. Seven 109s had been claimed destroyed with three more damaged on this Circus but it had cost the RAF five pilots.

It had been Müncheberg's 7th Staffel of JG26 that had ploughed into the Australians, Müncheberg himself claiming his fifty-sixth kill, and Oblt. Klaus Mietusch his eleventh. Another pilot scoring over the Channel was Hptm. Schmid, bringing his personal score to thirty-one, while Priller achieved his forty-ninth.

JG2 got into the mix and claimed four Spitfires, which brought the German total to twelve – for no loss to either Geschwader – on this afternoon, despite the RAF's asserted claims of 16-8-7.

* * *

Earlier on this day, a Roadstead had been flown to Ostend by Blenheims of 88 Squadron and Hurribombers of 615 Squadron, escorted by 41 Squadron's Spitfires. They were engaged by Me109s and FW190s from JG26 and P/O C. F. Babbage found a radial-engined fighter in front of him and shot it down. He reported it as a Hawk 75, although he later remarked: 'No Hawk ever had the performance of that brute!' In fact it was a Focke-Wulf, the first one shot down by the RAF. The pilot had been Hptm. Walter Adolph, who had taken over from Rolf Pingel after he had been captured during Circus 42 back in July. Adolph went straight into the sea. He had flown in Spain and with JG1 and JG27 in WW2 before taking command of JG26's II Gruppe. He had achieved twenty-eight victories and been awarded the Knight's Cross.

Cyril Babbage DFM was an experienced fighter pilot, having flown with 602 Squadron in the Battle of Britain. Adolph was his eighth victory, and he ended the war as a wing commander.

While off Ostend, 41 Squadron's pilots claimed two 109s and a probable, also a Hs123, and a Ju52, although in fact they were a Gotha 145 and a JuW34 respectively. Two Blenheims were shot down with all six crewmen killed. One was brought down by Ltn. H-H König of 5./ZG 76, the other by Obfw. W Röth of JG26, for his twelfth victory. A pilot from 2./JG52 also claimed a Blenheim. It was while circling the crashed Blenheim that Adolph had been surprised by Babbage and killed. 615 had two pilots brought down; one baled out and was later rescued, but the other was killed. 41 Squadron also had a pilot ditch off Freeston, through combat damage, but he too was rescued by HSL 145 rescue launch.

Circus No's: 100A, 100B and 100C - 20 September

As can be seen over the last few operations, the commanders of 11 and 2 Groups had obviously got together in the light of recent directives from Sholto Douglas, *et al*. The use of Hampdens had recommenced, with the help of 5 Group's commander, AVM J. C. Slessor DSO MC, and diversion tactics had been employed. Diversion tactics were going to be used today, although it does seem a little curious, because if the aim overall was to bring German fighters to battle, why was the RAF trying to get enemy fighters into the air in order that they would be back on the ground when the main attack began?

However, today saw a new innovation. Three Circuses were to be flown, the first being 100A, employing three Blenheims of 88 Squadron, taking off from RAF Manston to bomb – as a diversion – the Hazebrouck marshalling yards, escorted by the Hornchurch Wing, with North Weald as Cover, while 12 Group provided a Wing in support.

The Blenheims did not cross the French coast until 1534 hours, reaching the target to drop 12 x 250lb bombs and 12 x 25lb incendiaries from 14,000 feet. Many explosions were seen in the target area and several sheds appeared to be hit and burning as the bombers withdrew. Several formations of 109s were seen high above, either in pairs, fours or sixes, and they started to dive prior to the bombers' approach to the target, during their attack, and on the way out, and up to five miles out to sea. They mostly dived and tried to come up underneath the main formation. All the time flak fire came up and all the close escort fighters were engaged, especially by a group of around ten 109s that came in from the west at 18,000 feet. By the time the 109s broke off, one pilot from 611 Squadron had been shot down, while just one Me109 was thought to have been probably destroyed.

The missing pilot was another Battle of Britain veteran, F/Lt R. G. A. Barclay DFC. By this time, George Barclay had been reasonably successful and flying with 249 Squadron had achieved some six victories with another six probables and four damaged. After a rest he had been made a flight commander with 611, in August 1941. The weather was cloudless with good visibility, and Barclay was flying No.3 to W/Cdr Stapleton, with Sgt Ormiston as his wingman. Over St Omer Barclay spotted half a dozen 109s diving in behind the Squadron and called a warning, but apparently his R/T had gone u/s and nobody had heard his call. One 109 attacked his No.2 and as it flew over, Barclay took a squirt at it but saw no results. Then bullets began to hit his Spitfire and in taking evasive action fell behind the others. But his engine had been hit and he was unable to increase speed.

Me109s began attacking Barclay, but he managed to evade despite losing height. In his diary, Barclay recorded:

'I was immediately confronted by high tension cables – I had no speed to fly over them so flew between two trees underneath them. I missed most of the cables but hit one with more sag than the others – there was a flash and bang and the cable wrapped around the nose and then dropped. I put the flaps down and made a normal wheels-up landing in a very large field.

'I sat in the cockpit of poor FY-K [W3816] and pretended to be dead while the 109 circled around at 150 feet. It was the first time I had heard the noise a 109 makes – a mixture of a Spitfire's whistle, some stones in a tin can and a harsh grinding sound. It circled about three times and then flew off south-west. I got out, leaving my flying kit in the aeroplane and began to run eastwards.'

George Barclay, helped by French civilians, eventually received assistance from the French Underground, and was passed along to Spain, then Gibraltar, flying home by Catalina in December. He later returned to operations in North Africa but was killed in action in July 1942.

The North Weald Wing began encountering 109s as soon as they reached the French coast and concentrated attacks began as the main formation turned left at Hazebrouck, allowing the enemy pilots to get up-sun. Around fifty 109s were reported and the vast majority came down to engage, 111 Squadron receiving the brunt of this assault. Two of its pilots were shot down, one Spitfire exploding in mid-air. This was probably F/Lt L. S. Pilkington DFM who was killed. Lionel Pilkington, yet another experienced fighter pilot, had won his DFM in France with 73 Squadron. In the Battle of Britain he was an instructor with 7 OTU, and in September 1940 he had shot down a Ju88 over North Wales flying an armed Spitfire.

The other loss was Sgt D. G. Harwood, who survived as a prisoner. One Me109 was claimed as destroyed by F/Lt M. Kellett. Mike Kellett had got in on the tail end of the Battle of Britain and would survive the war as a squadron leader and be awarded the DFC. Four more 109s were thought to have been damaged.

In direct contrast, the 12 Group Wing saw just one hostile fighter during its sweeping patrol and no flak was encountered either. Thus the results remained at three pilots missing for claims of 1-1-5.

* * *

Circus 100B, consisting of six Hampdens from 5 Group's 408 Squadron, again led by its CO, W/Cdr Timmerman, going for the Abbeville marshalling yards, escorted by the Biggin Hill Wing, plus one squadron from Debden, with Kenley flying Cover. Visibility over France was good despite ground haze. The bombers released 1,900lbs of ordnance (six bombs), five of which were seen to burst in the centre of the target.

If the first Circus had been flown to divert enemy fighters, then it worked for the bombers had no trouble with either flak or fighters and bombed successfully. However, 109s began nibbling at 92 Squadron of the Close Escort halfway to the target and some dogfights developed. 72, 609 and 607 Squadrons flew on and had no problems with enemy opposition of any kind. 92 meantime claimed one 109 destroyed (but may only have been credited with a probable) but lost Sgt G. P. Hickman to a German prison camp.

Kenley got the bad luck. Stepped up above 20,000 feet they were engaged by a large number of 109s at the French coast, coming down in fours from above. Massive dogfights began in which six 109s were claimed destroyed but three pilots were lost. 602 Squadron had two pilots killed, while 452 had Sgt I. A. L. Milne rescued from the sea by the Germans and taken prisoner. The main claimants were 452 Squadron, with Paddy Finucane and Bluey Truscott claiming three destroyed and two destroyed and one damaged respectively. Truscott now had five official victories, Finucane twenty, including shares. Sergeant K. B. Chisholm got the sixth. This was Keith Chisholm's seventh victory (five and two shares) and he was about to be the first RAAF pilot to receive the DFM. Figures for Circus 100B came to 7-1-1 for the loss of three pilots.

* * *

Circus 100C saw twelve Blenheims from 82 and 114 Squadrons heading for the Rouen shipyards, with three Tangmere squadrons and one Hornchurch squadron providing Close Escort, leaving Northolt's Poles to fly Cover. RV was to be made over Shoreham but no sooner had this been achieved than one box of six bombers was seen to turn inland into some haze at 13,000 feet. The other box of six proceeded to the target with their escort. Reaching the target, 24 x 250lb bombs went down, together with 12 x 25lb incendiaries. Explosions could be seen on buildings immediately south of the shipyards and south of the paper mills there. Other bombs fell on what was thought to be a cellulose factory, from which enormous smoke clouds were produced. No flak was experienced on the way in and only some inaccurate AA fire came from the target area.

Over the RV, 402 Squadron left the formation to follow the Blenheims seen to fly inland, but when the leader decided he was following the wrong formation, turned back out to sea but failed to contact the main body so he was ordered to return to base. The others all went with the bombers and also experienced little flak except near the target. Then a large number of 109s began circling round the Wing at all heights and during attacks by them, three were claimed destroyed without loss.

Northolt formed up above and behind the main force as it crossed the Channel at 1520 hours. About thirty miles out the Wing was ordered to orbit, but the leader decided to ignore the order as he was still in sight of the main body of bombers and fighters, and crossed into France stepped up from 22–24,000 feet. No sooner had the bombing been completed than 308 Squadron became heavily engaged with numerous 109s during which four 109s were claimed destroyed for no loss. This made it seven enemy casualties to nil. One was credited to the CO, S/Ldr Marian Pisasrek:

'On the way back to the Channel flying at 20,000 feet I was leading the Squadron – the whole formation was retiring. I saw an Me. attacking P/O Zbierzchowski from close range; he was flying in my group of four. I warned him to turn to the left and as he did so, I approached the Me. giving 5 short bursts from 100 yards, closing to 50 yds from behind, to port and above. The Me. broke away sharply. Later the same Me. attacked me from above and a dogfight ensued. I lost height in tight turns, and then suddenly shot up so the Me. overshot me and found itself below me. I then got on to his tail, and putting my nose down gave a long burst from 50 yds. The e/a belched smoke and getting into a steep dive, plunged into the Channel. I was then at 3,000 feet. I claim this Me109F as destroyed.'

Pisarek was an experienced fighter pilot, having flown during the Polish campaign and in the Battle of Britain with 303 Squadron. By the end of 1941 he had achieved twelve victories, been awarded the British DFC and the Cross of Valour and three Bars. He was killed in action as a Wing Leader in April 1942, being awarded a posthumous *Virtuti Militari* in 1947.

Group Captain Bouchier was very pleased with the results of this combined 'three-ringed' Circus, which, according to reports, netted fifteen Me109s destroyed, two probables and six damaged. One of his comments was: 'The dearth of 'Y' messages during the progress of this operation (from German ground control to German fighter patrols in the air) confirm the impression gained that the confusion it was hoped to create in the mind of the enemy as to where our main thrust was coming was, in fact, satisfactorily achieved.'

Why the two Blenheim boxes got into trouble was thought to be because both boxes were some way apart at the RV and in orbiting, one had turned left, the other to the right, increasing the distance between them. With such a delay and confusion it reduced the chance of them forming up, so one had aborted.

While Bouchier may well have been pleased with the results, the Germans were probably much happier. JG26 and JG2 had been in combat, JG2 with the Blenheims. According to the Germans, JG26 had claimed eight Spitfires, two by Adolf Galland (eighty-four and eighty-five), and one to Schmid for his thirty-second. JG2 had claimed a total of thirteen victories for the loss of just one pilot killed (Uffz. Heinz Hoppe), and another 109 damaged. Among the high-scorers were Erich Rudorffer who got his thirty-sixth, and Hptm. Karl-Heinz Greisert, his 20th. JG26 hadn't lost anyone! In addition the Einsastz-staffel, JFS 5 claimed three Spitfire shot down off Fécamp, although other records note this unit with nine Spitfires and Hurricanes shot down, with three more unconfirmed. JFS 5 suffered one loss and another 109 damaged.

Something within the confirmation system employed by Fighter Command was going seriously awry. The Germans too, with twenty-five claims against seven known RAF losses appeared more than a little over-confident too.

* * *

On anti-shipping sorties this day, 18 Squadron lost one Blenheim and crew during an attack on a convoy off Zandvoort, Holland, while 226 Squadron lost two more with their crews, off the Hook of Holland. One of these was caught in the blast of its own bombs, the other shot down by flak.

Circus No.101 – 21 September

On this Sunday afternoon 2 Group supplied twelve Blenheims, six each from 18 and 139 Squadrons, to attack the power station at Gosnay, the bombers taking off at 1411 hours. Close Escort went to Tangmere's 41, 129 and 616 Squadrons, accompanied again by Hurricanes from Debden. Cover went to Kenley's 452, 485 and 602 Squadrons, while Support came from the Polish Wing at Northolt, 306, 308 and 315. It was planned to coincide with Circus 102, six Hampdens attacking the Lille Railway Repair Shops.

Jack Rae of 485 Squadron noted in his log-book: '12 a/c led by F/Lt Wells to take part in Circus 101 to Gosnay. Very large numbers of E/A were seen. The Squadron was heavily engaged and became split up. 3 E/A were destroyed, 2 by F/Lt Wells and one by P/O Francis and one probably destroyed by P/O Compton. Pilot Officer Knight failed to return and presumably landed in France. One a/c crash-landed in vicinity of Bagshot. Telegram from International Red Cross Society that Sgt Russell is a PoW and has had his arm amputated.' [Russell went missing on 12 August.]

The fighters began taking off at 1530 and made RV without too many problems, although Kenley Wing failed to pick up the bombers, and within ten minutes, German fighters were starting to take off too. This quick start allowed the 109s to intercept for once, before the target was reached rather than on the way back. JG26 was well to the fore, and even though Joachim Muncheberg's new FW190s took longer to get airborne, their greater speed soon had them joining their 109 comrades high above the Pas de Calais. The Kenley Wing headed over alone and as it crossed the French coast was attacked by Me109s that shot down two Spitfires of 129 Squadron. Before the operation was over they lost another, while 616 also took a loss. The 8th Staffel lost Ltn. Ulrich Dzialas to the incoming Spitfires.

Meantime, Northolt came under attack from JG26's II Gruppe, whose pilots bagged two Spitfires of 315 Squadron, one pilot killed, one captured. The pilot captured was the CO, S/Ldr S. Pietraszkiewicz who had to make a forced-landing. The other was F/O Tadeusz Nowak. Nowak had seen action over Poland, and once in England, flew in the Battle of Britain with 253 Squadron, and later 303 Squadron. He moved to 315 upon its formation at the beginning of 1941. He had claimed five victories and received the KW and two Bars, the latter two posthumously. 6./JG6 claimed the Spitfires from 315 including Nowak. He was heard to give a Mayday call and survived a ditching in the Channel but rescuers failed to locate him,

Stanisław Pietraszkiewicz was 35-years-old and had been in the Polish Air Force since 1926. Once Poland had fallen he moved to France and then to Britain where he helped form 307 Squadron before flying with 303 Squadron late in 1940. He had just begun to get into his stride when he was shot down, remaining a PoW for the duration. He was awarded the VM and KW with two Bars.

The Polish pilots of 308 claimed five 109s destroyed, plus two probables and two damaged, and 315 put in claims for four, two 109s and two 190s. Pietraszkiewicz's pilots confirmed two for him upon their return. This equates with their claims for radial-engined fighters, a French MB151 and an Italian Mc200! Meanwhile, JG26's First Gruppe managed to get into the main Close Escort fighters, which lost five, another from 129 Squadron who had to bale out into the Channel, where he was later rescued by friendly forces. 607 also lost a pilot who ended up as a guest of the Germans.

Finucane and Truscott were scoring again – Finucane with two destroyed, Truscott one, while other Aussies claimed a further two and two damaged. 485 claimed three destroyed plus a damaged, and 602 just a modest one damaged. 485 had one pilot shot down and captured and 602 had a pilot killed (Sgt A. R. Hedger) and one bale out over France. A third Spitfire was written off in a crash back in England but the pilot was OK. Sergeant P. H. Bell was the one down in France. He successfully evaded to Spain and Gibraltar, with the help of the French Resistance, and was back home in the first week of January 1942. Sadly he was killed in July 1943 with 19 Squadron.

JG 26 claimed a total of fifteen victories but only lost one pilot. Fighter Command claimed twelve plus probables and damaged. Adolf Galland scored his eighty-sixth kill, Schöpfel his thirty-fourth, Schmid his thirty-third and thirty-fourth, Oblt. Klaus Mietusch his twelfth and thirteenth, and Walter Schneider his eighteenth and nineteenth. JG2 put in claims for thirteen Spitfires, while pilots from 5.Erg./Staffel claimed three Spitfires for one loss near Fécamp. Don Caldwell, in his splendid history of JG26, *The JG26 War Diary* (Vol 1) included the following regarding this day:

'F/O Franciszek Surma of No.308 Squadron had a long, inconclusive dogfight over the Channel with an experienced German pilot. His opponent was almost certainly from JG2, but these comments from his combat report are pertinent: "From my experience on this Circus I have formed the opinion that the Me109F is superior to the Spitfire V in both speed and climbing power. The German pilots' ... tactics have changed as they did not attack from high above, but mostly on the same level." This was a prescient observation. The superiority of the Spitfire in turning combat was drummed into the German pilots from flight school, especially by instructors who had been withdrawn from the Western Front for a rest. The pilots of the Kanalgeschwader now had enough confidence in the 109F to take on the Spitfires on the latter's own terms.'

Circus No.102 – 21 September

This operation was timed to coincide with Circus 101 and there is no doubt that a number of German pilots were back on the ground and in the process of re-arming etc., when the alarm came. The Hampdens of 408, led by S/Ldr Burnett, escorted by North Weald, plus one squadron from Debden, with Hornchurch and Biggin Hill as Cover, flew high above the low haze and in good visibility reached and attacked the Lille target, dropping 1,900lb and 500lb bombs from 15,000 feet, some of which exploded around the target but others went into nearby fields. Flak was heavy and all six bombers received some sort of minor damage. One Me109 dived on the formation but sheered off when met by return fire from the Hampdens' gunners.

Escort fighters made RV at 1550 over Manston, reaching Lille at 1626 where the flak was equally heavy for them. Shortly after turning for home, fifteen to twenty Me109s came into the attack, heading in from all directions. In the fighting that took place to the coast, three 109s were claimed destroyed but two 111 Squadron aircraft were lost, one falling to Galland for number eighty-seven.

Hornchurch had a slight rendezvous problem which left them one minute late and in trying to make it up, reached Lille five minutes early. The Wing made a right-hand circuit short of the target and positioned themselves up-sun of the bombers as they began to withdraw. Some 109s were seen but they appeared unwilling to engage. While not mentioned in the report, 603 Squadron had a pilot bale out over the Channel after an attack by a 109. He was rescued by a HSL. 609 had a pilot injured. He ran out of fuel trying to land at Gravesend, crashed, and wrote off his machine.

These two operations cost Fighter Command five pilots killed, five taken prisoner, one lost but evading, plus two more Spitfires lost over the Channel, with two others written off in crashes. Fifteen fighters in total.

JG2 had only managed to claim two RAF fighters in Circus 102. Total claims for JG2 for the day came to twenty-two, so with JG26's ten, made it thirty-two altogether, for one loss.

According to 408 Squadron's records, six Hampdens, led by S/Ldr Altman, took off to bomb Mazingarbe on the 22nd but were recalled after 1½ hours. Whether it was meant to be a Circus operation is unclear.

Circus No.103A and 103B – 27 September

The commanders of 2 and 11 Group were obviously putting their heads together now in order to try and confuse the enemy, for today they mounted a further two-pronged operation. Both were afternoon raids, the first – 103A – was for eleven Blenheims (originally twelve) from 110 and 226 Squadrons to attack the Amiens marshalling yards. Close Escort came from Kenley, Cover from Tangmere, with High Cover provided by Northolt.

Weather was hazy over the Channel and France up to 2,000 feet but visibility was fine above that although with some 5/10ths cumulus cloud at 5,000 feet over the target area. With one bomber having dropped out, the other eleven placed bombs and incendiaries all over the target while above, RAF fighters were busy with enemy fighters.

The Escorts made RV over Hastings at 1403, flying at 14,000 feet but the leader of Kenley Wing had to return owing to an injured back, and three pilots of 602 followed him. Several 109s were seen, a couple of which made attacks but were driven off, so the Wing returned home with nil claims and nil losses.

Tangmere also encountered 109s, although they had been slightly split up due to 41 Squadron's heavy weaving. Four 109s made an attack after which one Spitfire was seen to glide away trailing smoke. The Wing now became completely split-up as dogfights developed. One Me109s was claimed but two pilots failed to return, one from 129 and one from 616. Another pilot from 616 got as far as the south coast of England before he was forced to bale out, to be rescued off Bexhill by ASR. The pilot was New Zealander Sgt J. G. West DFM.[13]

---

13. When the author of this book first moved to Bexhill in 1998, there were pieces of Jeff's Spitfire in the window of a small shop used by the local RAFA Club, the pieces having been dredged up from the sea.

Northolt's Polish squadrons were up at 22–24,000 feet and became heavily engaged with enemy fighters on reaching the French coast, becoming split up. Again they saw radial-engined opposition, noting they were probably captured French Bloch 151s. One pilot in 315 Squadron opened up on one of these and saw it break up and go down. 308 Squadron was also engaged, one pilot calling to say he had just shot down one enemy fighter but had been hit himself and was baling out. This was Sgt E. Watolski, who became a prisoner. 306 became involved with a large number of fighters over Amiens, and they claimed a number of Germans shot down, Sgt S. Krzyzagerski claiming 1-1-2. In all, the Wing claimed 6-2-3 for the one loss.

JG2 was mainly involved in these actions and claimed six or seven Spitfires. Hans Hahn thereby achieved victory number forty-five, Erich Rudorffer his fortieth, and Hptm. Greisart his twenty-first. JG2 had had two pilots force-land with combat damage during the first operation.

* * *

Meantime, Circus 103B, with another eleven Blenheims from 114 Squadron (again quickly reduced from twelve), went for the Bully power station at Mazingarbe. Hornchurch did the Close Escort job, with 402 Squadron from Debden, North Weald the Cover, Biggin the High Cover and 12 Group took on the Forward Support.

Rendezvous was made over Manston at 1415 hours, ten minutes later than scheduled, so presumably the plan had been for both bomber formations to head out within a couple of minutes of each other. This was followed by an error in navigation which caused the bombs to be dropped on a railway station, one mile south-west of La Bassée. It looked like two sheds were hit but several bombs fell into nearby fields. Despite something like forty to fifty 109s waiting for the formation not a single bomber was touched and all landed back between 1550 and 1600 hours.

The link up with the bombers had failed, due to the haze but the formation stuck to the flight plan and crossed the French coast at Mardyck. Some ten miles inland two large formations of Me109s made determined attacks coming in from below and from the same level. A second bunch of 109s headed down from the sun. 403 Squadron and half of 603 Squadron were split up and forced away from the main formation. Flak was heavy and several RAF fighters were hit. Claimed victories came to nine destroyed, four probables and five damaged, but five Spitfires did not return. 402 Squadron lost one, 611 one, 403 one, and 603 two. 403 Squadron also had a pilot wounded by flak but he got home. This same squadron had its CO, S/Ldr R. A. Lee Knight DFC, as one of the casualties. A Blenheim fighter pilot in 1940, he had converted to single-seaters and before taking command of 403 had seen action with 91 and 610 Squadrons in 1941, claiming several victories.

North Weald also believed this large formation of 109s had been waiting for them up-sun as they crossed into France, for they immediately came into the attack from above and behind. The attacks continued intermittently all the way to the target and back again. Several pilots of 222 Squadron were able to fire short bursts, making no claims, but the main assault was upon the Eagle pilots of 71 Squadron, although they did not suffer any casualties and were able to claim 2-1-2 victories.

Biggin Hill's squadrons were also attacked inland, north-west of St Omer by a great number of 109s, continually trying to get in behind the Spitfires. This did split the Spitfires and many dogfights ensued. Claims of 3-4-6 were made for the loss of two pilots of 72 Squadron, both killed. Another pilot, the Belgian Vicki Ortmans of 609, was so heavily engaged by two 109s he ran out of fuel and had to bale out off Dover, where he was picked up by HSL 147. This was the second time he had baled out and been rescued, the first being on 19 August.

The 12 Group Wing was not immune to assault by this large armada of 109s, flying at 25–28,000 feet over the Montreuil region. In a chase and scrap with fifteen 109s, they claimed one damaged but they lost one Spitfire to AA fire. The pilot almost got back to the English coast before he was forced to bale out over Dungeness. He survived but was injured.

Total claims came to 14-10-13 for the loss of seven pilots. Thirteen Spitfires were lost. This made a grand total of claims for the day of 20-12-16. Among the Wing Leaders who made claims were W/Cdr Jamie Rankin, one destroyed, two damaged; W/Cdr T. H. Rolski, one probable, and G/Capt Harry Broadhurst, one destroyed.

Circus 103B had been engaged by JG26, whose pilots put in claims for ten Spitfires and one Blenheim! JG26 had just one loss when Uffz. Gottfried Dietze was shot-up, slightly wounded, and forced to bale out near Clairmarais. The pilot who claimed he had shot down a Blenheim [none lost] was Johann Schmid, who had also shot down two Spitfires shortly beforehand, so had brought his score to thirty-seven. Gerhard Schöpfel had gained his thirty-fourth victory in the action.

Chapter 11

Autumn

September had seen much action, but by now the 'shooting season' was nearing its end. So what had been achieved during September 1941? Certainly Fighter Command's statistics looked very different to earlier months. Eighty-three German aircraft had been claimed as destroyed for the loss of forty-nine pilots killed, prisoners or missing during Circus operations. Overall, taking in fighter sweeps, anti-shipping sorties, Rhubarbs, etc, these totals grew to 114 enemy aircraft destroyed for the loss of sixty-three pilots. A more accurate figure overall is forty-three killed, twenty-five taken prisoner, ten wounded, two evading capture in France, and a possible total of at least ninety-four fighters lost.

As October began the front-line Wing Leaders were:

Biggin Hill	W/Cdr J. Rankin DSO DFC & Bar
Kenley	W/Cdr E. N. Ryder DFC & Bar
Hornchurch	W/Cdr F. S. Stapleton DFC
Tangmere	W/Cdr H. de C. A. Woodhouse AFC
North Weald	W/Cdr F. V. Beamish DSO DFC AFC
Northolt	W/Cdr T. H. Rolski VM KW
Duxford	W/Cdr R. R. S. Tuck DSO DFC & 2 Bars

The Wings comprised:

Biggin Hill	72, 92, 609 Squadrons
Kenley	452 RAAF, 485 RNZAF, 602 Squadrons
Hornchurch	54, 603, 402 RCAF, 611 Squadrons
Tangmere	41, 65, 129 Squadrons
North Weald	71, 111, 222 Squadrons
Northolt	303, 308, 315 Polish Squadrons
Duxford	266, 411 RCAF, 412 RCAF Squadrons

Circus No.104

This operation appears to have been requested to take place on 30 September, but in fact was postponed till 2 October. However, the bombers, from 88 Squadron, failed to meet up at the rendezvous and so the fighter escort Wings from North Weald,

Hornchurch and Biggin Hill carried out a fighter sweep instead. Whether it was cloud or just 'finger' trouble is unclear, but after the six bombers had circled Shoreham four times, they were ordered to return to base.

A new tactic this day was a Diversionary Fighter Sweep by nine squadrons from North Weald, Hornchurch and Biggin Hill, but with all the mix-up over Shoreham it turned into being the main operation. North Weald ran into 109s over Abbeville and during a turn, 71 Squadron was placed on the inside and came directly over some 109s. The Wing Leader ordered them to be engaged, so the Eagles dived and claimed four shot down. None of the 109s took evasive action and the general feeling by the Americans was that they had run into a training unit.

Several more Me109s were engaged by Biggin's pilots and the Spitfires claimed eight enemy fighters for the loss of three pilots of 92 Squadron killed, with a fourth shot-up and forced to crash-land near Ashford, Kent, its pilot injured. JG2 had done the damage and managed to claim eight Spitfires, although the combat times might indicate five claims between 1503 and 1514, but with another at 1643, and two more at 1850 and 1852.

Hauptmann Hans Hahn was the 'big hitter' with one at 1505 and those two late ones, which brought his score to forty-eight. Egon Mayer claimed his twenty-fifth and Ltn. Walter Höhler his eleventh. Hauptmann Schmid of JG26 appears to have had a hand in this combat although his timing too is rather late, but he was credited with his thirty-ninth victory. Despite the RAF's claims, JG2 had just two of their fighters make belly-landings after these combats.

A further, smaller scale, Fighter Sweep by Tangmere and Kenley Wings also resulted in combat claims. Two 109s destroyed and one damaged for no loss.

Circus No.105 – 3 October

Despite their losses on the 2nd, 92 Squadron was part of the Biggin Hill Wing on the 3rd, to escort six Blenheims making for the Ostend power station. Close Escort went to North Weald, Cover to Biggin, Forward Support to Kenley and Northolt, while Rear Support was assigned to Hornchurch.

The weather gave slight cumulus at 6–7,000 feet with some haze up to 4,000 feet, otherwise, visibility very good. RV was made above Clacton at 10,000 feet at 1400 and the force headed for Nieuport on the Belgian coast. Penetrating inland some fifteen miles it then turned towards the target, where 23 x 250lb HE bombs went down along with 24 incendiaries. The bombs that were seen to explode did so, on the far side of the nearby canal and the other side of the power station, although some buildings or perhaps warehouses were hit and set on fire. Some of the North Weald pilots thought some bombs had hit the target however.

Flak was experienced almost the whole way across the Belgian coast in addition to some flak ships positioned off Ostend, but no enemy fighters were seen until leaving the coast again, although they did not attack. The Biggin Hill pilots were amazed at the amount of AA fire that came up, especially from around the target area, with shells bursting as high as 17,000 feet. 609 Squadron had become separated prior to the target, so when the force turned for home, 92 saw a dozen aircraft where 609 should have been and thought they were them. However, these aircraft were 109s, therefore 92 was 'jumped' as the coast was crossed and two of their Spitfires were shot down before it was realised they were German. Both pilots were killed. Finally realising what was happening the Wing Leader turned back, leading his section into some 109s, and F/Sgt D. E. Kingaby DFM claimed one 109 destroyed.

Kenley and Northolt saw virtually no signs of enemy fighters, and those that were seen did not come near. Meantime, the Rear Support Wing headed over in three formations of eight aircraft to Ruytingen Lightship, fifteen miles north of Mardyck, flying at between 15–20,000 feet. After flying a circuit to the north and then south-east they met the returning bombers ten miles out to sea. As they were turning to the left to follow the main 'beehive' of aircraft, 54 Squadron made rather a wide circuit and got themselves 'jumped' by six 109s. Two of them seemed to act as decoys by diving in front of the Squadron and almost immediately one of the remaining two pairs dived on the Spitfires to port while another pair came in from starboard. At the same time two radial-engined fighters, with three 109s behind them, were seen above, with another six 109s hovering above those. The majority of the Wing's pilots extricated themselves from the danger, however, one Spitfire failed to make it back. Sergeant J. C. Ward went into the sea, his body later being washed ashore several days later. The final count was one claim for the loss of three pilots.

All three Spitfires were claimed by JG26. 92's losses went to Hptm. Siefert, his twenty-first victory, the other to Ltn. Paul Schauder for victory number seven. Ward fell to Johannes Schmid, bringing his score to a round forty. While there are no recorded losses, the 109 claimed by Don Kingaby brought his score to sixteen plus numerous probables and damaged. He was the only RAF fighter pilot to receive the DFM and 2 Bars, and later would receive the DSO and raise his score to twenty-three.

Circus No.106

Two operations were given the numbers 106A and 106B, planned for attacks on Boulogne and Dunkirk Docks for 7 October, but no such operations took place so they must have been cancelled, probably due to adverse weather. The autumn weather was now starting to affect operations over the French coast, and in any event, according to a letter from Sholto Douglas to Leigh-Mallory, he wanted Circuses to be scaled down. This letter is dated 7 October:

My Dear Mallory,
1. I am under the impression – possibly an erroneous impression – that you are still not fully seized of the position with regard to 'Circus' ops. Your request to use No.402 Squadron on 'Circus' ops is a 'straw in the wind'. I do most definitely want you to scale down on your 'Circus' effort.

2. Let me say at this point (lest you should think that I am ungrateful) that I am most appreciative of the way you have conducted these 'Circus' ops. The organisation of them and the careful planning that you have put into them are first rate, and they have been a most valuable contribution to our war effort this summer. All the same I do seriously want the effort scaled down, quite apart from the restrictions of weather.

3. I had thought of putting a definite limit of, say, four to six 'Circus' ops per month until further notice. I do not want to do this however, since obviously weather conditions must to some extent control the number of ops; but I do want you to turn your mind away to some extent from 'Circus' ops in other directions. My reasons are as follows:

   (a) We are going to be desperately short of fighters for the next six months and we cannot afford heavy losses, however large the gain.

   (b) During the next few weeks the Russian campaign will be temporarily decided one way or the other until the spring, so that whatever we do will have little effect on the enemy's air effort in Russia.

4. What I want you to concentrate on for the next few months are:

   (a) Rhubarb ops. These are far more suitable to winter weather and are less expensive in casualties. We ought to make a definite plan for 'Rhubarb' ops and carry them out against specific targets. A directive with a list of suitable targets is being got out for you.

   (b) Night-Fighting. There is little doubt that the enemy will within the next month or two, transfer a suitable proportion of his bomber force back to the Western Front, with a view to conducting bombing ops at night against our shipping, commercial ports and possibly industrial centres. It is of supreme importance that we should be able to meet this effort and inflict heavy casualties.

5. I should be grateful therefore if you would bend your mind in these directions.
6. I am ready to discuss these questions with you at any time if you wish.

Yours,
WSD

So, things were about to change now that the 'shooting season' was nearing its end. What exactly Douglas knew, or thought he knew, about events on the Russian front are unclear, but it seems certain that he was beginning to realise, even if he had not already been aware, that Fighter Command was losing more fighters over France than his pilots were scoring victories. And it is still unclear if he was privy to the German losses as might be indicated via the 'Y' Service. The effort had been a progression following the defensive battles of 1940, and it had given the RAF a chance to hit back. Had the cost been fully realised or even envisaged, air operations in 1941 might have proved very different. In any event, at least the Russians, and Joseph Stalin in particular, knew that Britain was at least trying to ease pressure on his country by the Germans, even if there could be no promise of an early invasion from the West. The phrase 'leaning into France' had been formulated to indicate the RAF's effort of hitting back, and it was a phrase referred to by Sholto Douglas in his book *Years of Command*, published by Collins in 1966. Douglas wrote:

> *In addition to night bombing being done by Bomber Command, it continued to be the task of Fighter and Bomber Commands to carry out strikes by day at objectives which were within range of the escorting fighters; and from the point of view of the fighters it quite often went beyond leaning into France and became almost a stretching into France.*
>
> *The industrial area around Béthune, Lens and Lille – which was so well known to all the senior commanders in the RAF from our own flying over it in the first war – was considered to be the most sensitive spot for attack by air in daylight from England, and we hoped that these daylight raids would induce the Germans to concentrate their own fighters in north-eastern France. These combined Circus operations led our fighters to the limit of their endurance, and one of the serious problems in our planning was that such long flights did not allow much time for actual fighting over the area once it was reached. The fighters always had to make sure that they had enough fuel left to get back to their bases in England.*
>
> *In the introduction of new aircraft with improved performance it was still, as always, a see-saw, with first one side and then the other gaining the upper hand. With our improved Spitfires we had caught up with the Me109F. The struggle had remained on a fairly equal footing until towards the latter part of the summer of 1941; and then we were caught flat-footed. My pilots reported seeing over Amiens a new type of radial-engined fighter. It was in the course of one of the Circus operations, and there were some particularly experienced pilots flying in the wings from Kenley, Tangmere and Northolt. Our Intelligence people ridiculed the idea. But what the pilots reported was correct; they were seeing for the first time the Focke-Wulf 190.*

Circus operations did begin to scale down, but a spot of reasonable weather on the 12 and 13 of October, gave Leigh-Mallory the chance to mount three more.

Circus No.107 – 12 October

With the target being the docks at Boulogne, this operation was clearly replacing Circus 106A originally scheduled for the 7th. A force of twenty-four Blenheims was sent, twelve from 110 Squadron and six each from 21 and 226. They began taking to the air at 1115 am and had Hornchurch as Close Escort, North Weald as Cover, Biggin Hill High Cover, Kenley and Northolt as Target Support and Tangmere as Rear Support. In total nineteen fighter squadrons.

Despite some cloud at 5,000 feet and with some haze below, the bombers found a clear patch over Boulogne itself. One bomber pilot found it impossible to keep up with the rest and eventually turned back, but the other twenty-three all bombed and most of the explosions occurred in the target area, between Docks 4 and 6 and some south of Dock 4. Flak was again heavy and two Blenheims received some damage but no crew members were hit. By 1217 the bombers were heading for home.

As far as the Close Escort was concerned it was a completely uneventful operation, although its pilots did see an estimated sixty Me109s well below and astern of them as they headed back across the Channel. Similarly, the Escort Cover Wing saw very little, just one lone 109 that was chased inland and got away. Biggin Hill had nothing to report either.

However, the Target Support boys did see some action, with 452 Squadron getting into a running fight with numerous 109Fs between Le Touquet and mid-Channel. About thirty 109s were seen to the starboard side and when combat was joined, a further twenty came down out of the sun from the port side. These succeeded in getting between Northolt and Kenley Wings. When the fight ended the pilots could only claim just one 109 destroyed with another damaged but had lost two of their number. Sergeant K. B. Chisholm DFM of 452 and Sgt A. Meredith of 602, had both been shot down and captured. Finucane of 452, claimed the destroyed, while Truscott in fact claimed one probable and one damaged.

Keith Chisholm came down in the sea off Berck sur Mer. He was rescued by the Germans but later he escaped from prison camp, or to be exact, from an outside working party. This was only the start of many adventures by this Australian, and it took him till August 1944 to finally return to England. For his escaping activities he received the Military Cross.

The Northolt Wing crossed into France at Gravelines upwards to 28,000 feet then flew south and after passing St Omer made their way to Le Touquet, at which point the Controller warned them of 109s south of Boulogne. The Wing wheeled in that direction and 308 Squadron encountered enemy fighters, claiming two destroyed without loss. 303 Squadron became engaged too, and a 109 was shot off the tail of one 308 pilot. 315 came to the aid of both the other units, found four 109s chasing two Spitfires but when they were engaged, the 109s dived away and escaped.

Rear Support did their job although the Tangmere pilots saw no action but covered the withdrawal of the bombers and escorting Spitfires, then continued along their patrol line but no 109s were chasing anyone out of France. Total for the day, four 109s destroyed and one damaged according to the Circus report, for the loss of those two pilots already mentioned.

JG26 had claimed the two Kenley Wing Spitfires without loss, but it seems that JG2 was also in action at this time, and also claimed two Spitfires, and suffered one loss. The JG26 claimants were Priller, his fifty-second, and Seifert, his twenty-second. Leutnant Jakob Augustin claimed both of JG2's victories, his eighth and ninth kills.

A few hours later Ltn. Seigfried Schnell of JG2 claimed two Spitfires for his fifty-third and fifty-fourth victories, and Fw. Erwin Philipp claimed a third flying with 1.Erg./JG2, but there are no record of any losses this day other than the two referred to above. 118 Squadron, of 10 Group, was flying an armed reconnaissance over Jersey where it came into contact with JG2 over Cap de la Hague, but they suffered no loss. 118 Squadron did, however, claim three 109s and a damaged. Leutnant Rolf Byer of Erg.Gr./JG2 was shot down and killed in this action, flying a 109E.

Circus No.108A and 108B – 13 October

This was another two–Circus operation, 108A, to the Arques ship lift, and 108B to the Mazingarbe chemical works. 139 Squadron provided six Blenheims for each raid and Circus 108A began at 1215 hours, while 108B started fifty minutes later. Close Escort went to Kenley, Cover to a 10 Group Wing (501, 118 and 234 Squadrons). Northolt flew High Cover, Target Support went to Tangmere, while 12 Group fielded 266, 411 and 412 Squadrons as Rear Support Wing. There was no cloud and visibility was noted as being exceptional.

Manston was the RV point and from here they headed out but two bombers were unable to keep up and had to drop out. Over the French coast at Gravelines by 1316, height 13,000 feet, some 109s came down through cloud to attack one Blenheim that fell to the ground. Flight Lieutenant R. J. Chamberlain DFC and his crew all died. Richard Chamberlain had received his DFC following the massive raid on Cologne on 12 August. The raid had seen participating aircrew receive two DSOs, ten DFCs and three DFMs. Adolf Galland was the pilot who downed this Blenheim, having already, according to the timing of his combats, shot down a Spitfire, thus raising his score to eighty-nine. A second Blenheim was credited to his wingman, Ltn. Peter Göring, he was hit by return fire from the Blenheim gunner and crashed to his death. The crediting of this victory to young Göring was merely a 'courtesy' claim.

The remaining three bombers attacked the target at 1321 but the crews were unable to observe results due to the presence of more enemy fighters, but they got away and back, although two were slightly damaged by AA fire.

Both Escort Wings were subjected to continuous attacks by 109s into and back out of France. They were in large formations, some pilots estimating anything up to sixty 109s, and 485 Squadron reported that some thirty of these pressed home their attacks on both bombers and escorts. In some heavy fighting, six Me109s were claimed shot down, with two more probably destroyed and seven more damaged, but three pilots failed to return. 452 had one pilot killed, while another baled out over the Channel from where he was rescued. 602 lost two, one killed and one taken prisoner, so four Spitfires lost in total. Among the Australian Squadron pilots claiming was Paddy Finucane with two destroyed and one damaged, while Bluey Truscott claimed two more destroyed. 602, led by veteran S/Ldr A. C. Deere DFC, claimed a more modest five damaged. 485 claimed 1-0-1. Al Deere's combat report noted:

'I was leading 602 Squadron as close escort to 4 Blenheims. My section of 4 aircraft were on the port side and slightly above the bombers. Other than 452 Squadron there was absolutely no cover as protection to either the bombers or my section from the port side. We were attacked repeatedly, by pairs of Me109s, and had no alternative but to fight back. I was unable to warn Sgt Brayley, Red 2, (as my transmitter was U/S) that he was about to be attacked, and saw him go down with smoke and glycol coming from his machine. I also saw another Spitfire (I think Sgt Ford, Yellow 4) go down in similar manner, and a 109 spinning out of control. I was by now alone, and had to ward off repeated attacks on my return. I managed a short burst at two 109Fs, the second from about 150 yards and above. I feel sure his hood disintegrated and caved in, as if hit by a cannon shell. (I cannot definitely confirm this.) He went onto his back and then vertically down from 13,000 feet.'

The 10 Group Wing's first jaunt with an 11 Group Circus, gave cover to the escort and over the target area they too became involved with 109s and fought them all the way back to the coast. They claimed one destroyed and two damaged. The Poles were up between 21–26,000 feet and over the target at 1322; they saw some twenty 109s below them but most of the pilots were unable to attack. However, 308 went for seven 109s halfway between Gravelines and the target and destroyed three for no loss. By this time the Squadron had lost considerable height and one pilot attacked the airfield at St Omer/Fort Rouge, shooting up a hangar, while another pilot strafed a heavy AA gun post in the Gris Nez area. One 303 Squadron pilot also claimed a Bloch fighter damaged – in reality a FW190. In fact, Sgt M. Adamek appears to have been credited with a destroyed, but in any event, the evidence from his camera gun finally gave some solid confirmation of the FW190 in action.

The Tangmere Wing gave support to the operation, heading into France to approach the target from the north-west, before turning right to withdraw. As they did so small formations of 109s appeared from all directions and a series of engagements followed, resulting in the Wing becoming split up for a time. 129 Squadron, at 23,000 feet, was attacked by four 109s and then two sections went down on six radial-engined fighters with square wing-tips. In other actions, one 109 was destroyed and another probably so but two RAF pilots were missing when they reformed. Both pilots were killed.

The top Squadron, 41, at 25,000 feet was assailed by numerous formations of 109s and in the fighting one of these was probably destroyed but again, two RAF pilots were shot down, both being killed. 65 Squadron had seven 109s come down on them shortly after leaving the target area, and a fifth pilot from the Wing was killed.

Meantime, Rear Support by 12 Group patrolled as instructed and they were soon starting to see formations of 109s milling about them, some pilots counting up to forty.

In combats, three 109s were claimed destroyed, with two more and one unidentified fighter claimed as damaged. Although the Circus Report does not mention it, 411 Squadron had one of its Canadian pilots shot down. Pilot Officer R. W. McNair took to his parachute and injured his back as he splashed down into the Channel, from where he was rescued by a High Speed Launch. Buck McNair would later become a leading Canadian ace with the DSO, DFC and 2 Bars, seeing action over Malta and later again over France.

Flying what was termed a 'Spotting Patrol', Spitfires of 91 Squadron were engaged in looking out for downed pilots and they did indeed find one, and giving a fix, helped direct a rescue boat to the man. Whether this was P/O R. W. McNair or Sgt J. R. H. Elphick of 452 Squadron is unclear.

Today's action had been costly, for quite apart from one Blenheim shot down, 10 RAF fighters were lost, resulting in seven pilots killed, one taken prisoner, with two rescued from the sea. The Circus Report only noted eight pilots missing, but it did record the following claims. Fifteen Me109s destroyed, four probably destroyed, plus twelve 109s, one Bloch and one unidentified fighter damaged.

Circus 108B. As Circus 108A was ending, 108B was on its way to bomb the power station at Mazingarbe with eighteen Blenheims, six from 139 and twelve from 114 Squadrons. This had begun fifty minutes after the first show, with North Weald Wing and one Hornchurch squadron (412) acting as Close Escort, Hornchurch taking flying Cover with Biggin Hill up at High Cover.

Rendezvous was above Manston at 1350 hours and heading for the target, all bombed the power station and adjoining Coking Ovens and Synthetic Petrol Plant. Bombs were seen to explode on the power station and among the condensers, two cooling towers, nearby marshalling yards and on slag heaps. Intense flak fire hit and damaged no fewer than fourteen of the bombers but there were no personnel casualties. No enemy fighters were seen either.

However, there were some around, North Weald seeing several on the return journey, just after they had survived the gauntlet of AA fire. This fire had hit and brought down a Hurricane pilot of 402 Squadron, who was captured. As the 109s started to nibble at the RAF fighters, one pilot of 71 Squadron was shot down and wounded, baling out into the sea. His pals saw him get into his dinghy about five miles off Boulogne, but in the event he was picked up by the Germans and made a prisoner. This was P/O G. C. Daniel RCAF, who was in fact a Native American, having been born on an Osage Indian Reservation. When he joined the RCAF his birth certificate recorded his birth as November 1921, but he looked much younger than his eighteen years. After the war it was discovered he had been born in 1925, so was still a month from his sixteenth birthday when he was shot down.

Hornchurch also went through much AA fire and then some 109s attacked, shooting down one pilot of 603 Squadron, who was killed. 54 Squadron claimed a 109 shot down into the sea near Boulogne. 611 Squadron was attacked by two 109s but were driven off without injury to either side.

Biggin Hill's squadrons also became engaged with a few 109s, 609 Squadron claiming one destroyed and one damaged. A pilot of 92 Squadron returned alone from St Omer because of an oxygen leak. However, upon his return to base, he claimed three 109s destroyed, two of them colliding when he attacked, and damaged a fourth. The pilot was the CO, S/Ldr R. M. Milne DFC, and this mission was rewarded by a Bar to his DFC. A report noted:

'S/Ldr Milne of 92 Squadron broke away from the wing owing to a bad oxygen leak and continued into France at a lower level. When S.E. of St. Omer, S/Ldr Milne was attacked by a 109F which made off when the S/Ldr got round onto the e/a's tail. Finding himself alone, he proceeded homeward and was able to attack two 109Es, shooting one down in flames and damaging the other. A little later, S/Ldr Milne spotted two 109Fs in time to evade their stern attack and swung round quickly. He was able to get in a burst from about 70 yards on one which then emitted smoke and crashed into the other e/a. Pieces flew off and both a/c went down together, the pilot of one baling out.'

So, in all, five 109s destroyed and two damaged for the loss of one Spitfire pilot killed, one taken prisoner, plus a Hurricane pilot taken prisoner. This brought the total for both Circuses to twenty destroyed, four probables and sixteen damaged (or by another count, 22-2-18), for the loss of thirteen RAF pilots shot down, two of whom were safe after rescue. Apart from Galland's two kills, JG26 claimed a further seven Spitfires, one by Priller for his fifty-third, one by Müncheberg for his fifty-seventh, and two more for Schmid, for his forty-first and forty-second. JG2 claimed eleven Spitfires for no loss! The big names of JG2 to claim were Oesau, his ninety-eighth and ninety-ninth, Erich Leie his twenty-eighth and twenty-ninth, and Rudi Pflanz his twenty-fifth.

Despite the RAF's claims, only young Göring had been lost, and that to a Blenheim gunner, with one FW190 having to make a crash-landing on Moorsele airfield. Oberleutnant Klaus Mietusch of JG26 landed at St Omer with only slight combat damage to his 109F-4.

Pilot Officer Truscott, of 452 Squadron, reported that he had fired at a German pilot who was descending in his parachute, an action met with much disapproval by his fellow Australians. However, as no German pilots were shot down in combat, let alone baling out, Truscott must have been firing at an RAF pilot!

* * *

On 15 October 10 Group mounted Ramrod 69 at midday, twelve Blenheims going for an oil tanker at Le Havre. The bombers and their Spitfire escort were intercepted by Me109s that shot down two Blenheims, with all six men aboard being lost. One Spitfire and its pilot were also lost. Claims by the escorting Spitfires came to 5-1-5.

The Germans who made the interception were from 4.(Eins.)/JFS 5, and while two pilots did claim the two bombers, six Spitfires were claimed, although probably only three were credited. Two of these went to Uffz. Peter Gerth, for his tenth and eleventh victories. Losses were one pilot wounded, two 109s lost and another damaged.

It was another bad day for the Blenheim boys, for 139 Squadron lost three during anti-shipping operations, while 114 Squadron lost another two. 5./ZG76 claimed at least two.

On the 21st anti-shipping sorties cost 2 Group another three Blenheims, one to flak and two to fighters of 3./JG53 off the Dutch coast.

Things were now about to change. Circus operations for the year were about to stop, and Sholto Douglas issued in letter form his views on policy for future operations, dated 21 October. This letter was sent to 10, 11 and 12 Groups within his Command, and the HQs of Bomber and Coastal Command:

OFFENSIVE OPERATIONS – POLICY

1. With reference to my memorandum FC/S.21552 dated 12th October 1941, I now wish to lay down for guidance a statement as to approximately the amount of fighter effort that may be expended upon the operations in support of bomber aircraft referred to in paras. 3 and 4 of that memorandum.

2. Such a statement can only be an approximate guide to Group Commanders as to my intentions, and will be subject to alteration from time to time. The fact also that the effort is expressed in terms of sorties per week does not mean that these figures can or should be closely adhered to. On the contrary, variations in the nature and the scale of our operations from week to week are necessary in order to surprise the enemy and keep his defences on full tension.

3. Subject to these remarks, the general measure of effort should be as follows:-

Circus Operations by 11 Group

[Only] One full scale operation per week or a maximum of six in one month, each operation comprising approximately 18 to 24 squadrons.

Ramrod Operations

These are fighter escorted bomber attacks on fringe targets, the strength of escort varying according to the target involved and being anything from one up to nine squadrons. Such operations can be accompanied by feint attacks by other fighter formations to draw off the enemy defences without committing our fighters to heavy engagements. The scale of effort envisaged for these operations is roughly:-

10 Group	–	10 squadron sorties per week
11 Group	–	18 squadron sorties per week
12 Group	–	6 squadron sorties per week

Roadstead Operations

These are attacks on shipping by bombers with fighter support which is provided for the purpose of engaging flak ships and providing light overhead cover during the attack. It is not contemplated that these operations will be pressed against strong fighter defences. The effort expended per week on these operations may be additional to that allotted to Circus and Ramrod Operations and is left to the discretion of Fighter Group Leaders.

4.   Occasions may arise from time to time when fighter support is called for at short notice in support of bombing attacks against important fleeting targets. In these circumstances there is no question of refusing support on the grounds that this additional fighter effort exceeds for the current week the scales laid down in para 3 of this letter. The effort should, however be averaged out over a period, and in case of doubt, reference should be made to Fighter Command Headquarters.

WSD
Air Marshal
Air Officer Commanding–in–Chief
FIGHTER COMMAND, ROYAL AIR FORCE

This edict was later scaled down, on 24 November 1941, from one full–scale Circus operation per fortnight to a maximum of three per month. From some of the wording it certainly seems that Sholto Douglas was appreciating that his losses were no way comparable to enemy losses, despite the exaggerated claims by his fighter pilots. So while these operations were not being totally cancelled, the defensive element had overtaken the desire to 'bring the enemy to battle'.

* * *

So, with this scaling down of offensive actions, certainly of the Circus variety, and with the winter weather fast approaching, the types of operations laid down in Douglas's letter began to exercise the RAF's daytime planning and thinking. As October drew to a close 11 Group became more active by flying Low Ramrods, such as the one flown on Friday 31 October, sending six Hurribombers of 607 Squadron to attack the Transformer Station at Holque, accompanied by one flight of 615 Squadron for anti-flak, plus Spitfires as escort. Later that afternoon, 607 and 615 flew a similar operation to knock out barges at Bourbourgville.

On 1 November it was twelve Blenheims on a 10 Group Rodeo (No.15) against the German airfield at Morlaix, although nearby Lannion was attacked in error. Further east, Low Ramrods 3A and 3B went for German army huts at Neuchatel, and Berck

Aerodrome. These sorts of operations continued during the first week of November and it was not until the 8th that the next – and last – Circus was flown in 1941.

* * *

There appears to be no record of a Circus 109 and it can only be assumed that it was either cancelled or perhaps Circus 108B had been mistakenly recorded as the missing 109.

Circus No.110 – 8 November

This day was to see the final Circus of the year and not surprisingly, with all the letters and talk about all those that had gone before, this one stood out as something completely different. Circus 110 would be flown in three parts, and be made up of one Circus, one Rodeo and one Ramrod - Parts I, II and III.

The weather for this combined show consisted of a thin layer of 5/10ths cloud at 4,000 feet with good visibility below. The Rodeo part was an attack against the area of Dunkirk, on this Saturday morning, with three fighter squadrons, 71 and 222 from North Weald, and 111 from Debden, otherwise the Debden Wing. They made rendezvous over Manston at 1100 hours stepped up from 15 to 18,000 feet. After orbiting Manston for five minutes they headed south and made a sweep to a point five miles north of Dunkirk, which they reached at 1120. They then flew back towards Deal but when about halfway across the Channel they returned in the direction of Dunkirk and continued their patrol until 1142 before heading for home. They began landing back by 1205 without incident or action.

The Ramrod was against an alcohol distillery plant at St Pol – normally a rhubarb target. Eight Hurribombers from 607 Squadron, with another four Hurricanes from 615 Squadron as anti-flak aircraft, made the attack. Close escort to these was provided by 65 and 41 Squadrons from Tangmere, while Biggin Hill's 72, 401 and 609 Squadrons gave Escort Cover.

The eight Hurribombers and their flak suppression friends, plus escorts, made RV over Dungeness, at 10,000 feet at 1102, headed south and crossed the French coast just to the south of Baie D'Authie. 615 Squadron was leading, 607 in the middle and the Spitfires to the rear. Once over the coast the formation went into a shallow dive, passing over Hesdin by which time they were down to 5,000 feet, so that just before they reached the target, they were more or less on the deck. 615 flew in from the west-south-west and fired at the still tower, from which dense blue and yellow smoke arose. 607 followed in from the west, with their machine guns blazing as they approached their target and all pilots dropped their bombs on or near to the distillery building and the surrounding factory. One bomb was seen to lodge in the base of the still tower and another passed clean through it, knocking great lumps of debris from it. The Hurricanes made two left turns and came out at low level back along the same route.

As they flew away the still tower was seen to break into pieces, while the whole factory appeared to be a mass of smoke and falling debris.

On the way to the coast several pilots machine-gunned a factory south-west of Hesdin which may also have been a distillery building but results were not observed. The only flak experienced came from a single machine-gun post on some high ground north-east of Vron and inaccurate fire from the Port of Mahon. The factory itself seemed totally undefended. Once again, no casualties, and no encounters with enemy fighters.

Meanwhile, the Close Escort, after covering the Hurricanes to the target, saw three Me109s flying in from the north-east, making a half-hearted attack on the Hurricanes but two were turned away, one by a pilot of 41 Squadron and another from 65 Squadron. However, one Czech pilot from the latter squadron failed to return, and must have been hit by the third 109. His death was later confirmed.

The Cover Wing, however, ran into 109s of JG2 that began to menace them, with some 109s diving on the top squadron from up-sun, and continued to do so until the Wing was way off the French coast. They then orbited, so that stragglers could catch up, and at this time the Wing Leader went down to 3,000 feet in pursuit of some 109s that were attacking a Spitfire. He shot down one and damaged another before he was himself engaged. Several other pilots were jumped by enemy fighters and while four pilots failed to get home, the rest did, but were pretty much scattered, landing at five different aerodromes in southern England.

In fact, the Wing lost five Spitfires. 72 Squadron had three pilots shot down. One baled out over the Channel – probably due to engine trouble – and was rescued, but the other two missing men were killed. 401 Squadron had one pilot killed with another taken prisoner. So in all, five pilots were reported missing, with a sixth rescued, for claims of 1-1-1.

German fighter pilots filed seven Spitfire claims. The early sweep had alerted the fighters which were already aloft and at a good height when the Hurricanes arrived; further, the sun's glare helped to shield the German fighters whilst it silhouetted the Hurricanes and Spitfires against the ground haze. JG26 claimed the two Canadian pilots of 401 Squadron.

* * *

The last part of the operation saw twelve Blenheims, six each from 21 and 82 Squadrons, start out at 1050 hours to bomb the railway repair shops at Lille. They were escorted by the Northolt Wing, 315, 308 and 303 Squadrons, covered by fellow Poles from 10 Group's 302, 316 and 317 Squadrons, while Kenley took the High Cover slot with 452, 485 and 602 Squadrons. Rear Support was provided by 12 Group's 411, 412 and 616 Squadrons, plus 54 Squadron from Hornchurch. Unfortunately, and in retrospect surprisingly, it was led by a wing commander who had not flown any operational missions, much less led one! Another problem was fog which caused one of the support wings to remain stuck on the ground.

The 12 Group Wing arrived over the French coast in good order, but it was early and the leader began to circle the formation rather than proceed towards Lille. The orbit became too tight and some of the outside sections became spread out. AA fire from Dunkirk did not help and the formation disintegrated. Seen by Hauptmann Müncheberg's II Gruppe FW190s, they began picking off three 412 Squadron stragglers of the high squadron. The Leader, Wing Commander D. R. Scott AFC did not return. The last anyone heard of him was over the radio, saying: 'I guess I'm too old for this, boys.' He was 33-years-old and the Germans buried him at Dunkirk.

Six of the bombers turned back early due to R/T failure in one leading Blenheim and another failed to take off. The others carried on, but somehow they did not locate their target and bombed another instead. The report noted that this target was unknown at the time and the photographs had not been identified by the time this report was written. We now know it was Gosnay. Whatever the factory was thought to be at the time, several bombs hit it. Flak was heavy and accurate, causing the bombers to take evasive action on several occasions.

As the Northolt Wing joined up with the bombers and headed south, they were thrown into confusion by the 10 Group Wing, which was flying ahead of the bombers when they turned, but once sorted out they all headed into France. Several 109s were seen below and these tried to engage the bombers and then started nibbling from behind. The CO of 315 Squadron called to say he was running short of fuel when near Dunkirk on the way back and no more was heard from him. Squadron Leader W. Szczęśniewski failed to return and was later reported a prisoner. He had seen action over Poland and France before arriving in England, where he participated in the Battle of Britain with 307 and 303 Squadrons. In February 1941 he was made flight commander with 315 and CO in September.

308 Squadron had tried to catch up to the bombers after becoming separated over Manston but did not find them. They patrolled over Dunkirk-Calais and later fought some 109s and one pilot was shot down and killed by Hptm. Sieffert, of JG26, the German's twenty-third victory. The Poles damaged two 109s. Meantime the other Poles from 10 Group had flown into France, seen the bombs going down and then, on the way back, became involved with 109s and Focke-Wulfs. In an intense dogfight, one FW190 was claimed shot down and seen to crash about five miles south-east of Dunkirk, while a 109 went down in flames between St Omer and Hazebrouck. However, 302 Squadron lost a pilot (captured), and 316 Squadron lost its CO, S/Ldr W. Wilczewski, who was badly wounded and also became a guest of the Germans. Adolf Galland was in this action and, while Wilczewski thought he had been hit by flak, it is probable that Galland shot him down. Galland in fact, claimed two Spitfires this day, bringing his score to ninety-five. Priller was also involved and was credited with his fifty-seventh and fifty-eighth victories. The Wing claimed 2-1-1 for the loss of two pilots.

Over Manston, the Kenley Wing, having arrived shortly ahead of schedule, did not see bombers or fighters so headed south after delaying some minutes. Over France they still did not see any sign of the main formation so headed for Lille, orbiting there at 1155. Seeing AA fire to the south-west they finally picked up the bombers but also saw numerous 109s in the distance. As the Wing approached the French coast again several 109s started to make attacks which lasted till well out to sea. 452 was particularly engaged but they shot down one 109F and probably another – both by Bluey Truscott. However, the Australian was eventually forced to bale out east of Ramsgate from where he was later rescued along with another 452 pilot, who was also running short of petrol.

Rear Support Wing became depleted due to fog, which kept all but 54 Squadron who managed to take off, on the ground. The 12 Group Wing was therefore short of cover but headed over France, although at a different height than briefed, dictated by the loss of Hornchurch's other two squadrons. The Wing was flying at between 20–23,000 feet and came under heavy AA fire which caused the Wing to split up somewhat just as many 109s were spotted. Nobody seemed fully aware if the 109s were going to attack and later, when four pilots failed to return it was supposed that flak may have been the major factor in their downfall, for no major engagements had been reported. It appears, however, that 412 Squadron was hit by JG26 and all four missing men were killed, including the CO, S/Ldr C. Bushell. Overall this day, the three operations had netted claims of 3-2-4 but at the cost of eight pilots missing, with another three rescued from the sea. However, the cost was a little higher than the report suggests, with nine killed, four captured, plus the three rescued – sixteen fighters lost. German losses were one pilot killed from JG26 and one severely injured during a crash-landing. Three more fighters sustained damage that also resulted in crash-landings. Among the aces Müncheberg had brought his score to fifty-nine with two kills, Obfw. Mayer had got his twelfth and Oblt. Kurt Ebersberger, his sixteenth.

* * *

On the 9th, Trafford Leigh-Mallory wrote the following report on Circus 110:

<u>SECRET</u>
Report on 11 Group Operations – "Circus 110"
Part I, II and III – 8/11/41

1. These operations were carried out in 2 phases. The first phase consisted of an attack by 8 Hurricane Bombers, assisted by 4 Hurricanes for anti-flak work. This force was covered by 2 Spitfires squadrons from Tangmere which acted as escort, and the Biggin Hill Wing which acted as high cover.
2. The squadrons for this attack rendezvoused at Dungeness, and approached the French coast between Berck and Le Touquet.

3. At the same time as this attack, a diversionary operation was carried out by the North Weald Wing, which rendezvoused at Manston and approached the French coast east of Dunkirk, and then flew back towards England again. These two operations were intended partially as a diversion to get the German fighters into the air before the main attack which was to take place 30 minutes after the first operation.

4. The main attack was directed against the locomotive works at Lille, and was to be undertaken by 12 Blenheims with 3 Wings in immediate attendance, and two other Wings located to cover the withdrawal.

5. The first two operations worked out very well with the exception of the Biggin Hill Wing, which suffered 4 casualties for one EA destroyed. The attack of the Hurricane Bombers accompanied by the anti-flak aircraft of 615 Squadron, was particularly successful. It was the first time that we had attempted a diving attack from the coast into the target. They crossed the coast at 10,000 feet and dived right down to ground level into the target area, accompanied by the 2 Tangmere squadrons. The attack was entirely successful. Only a few enemy aircraft were encountered on the way out, but these did not press their attack. One sergeant pilot of the Tangmere Wing was missing, but cannot be accounted for.

6. Meanwhile the Biggin Hill Wing had crossed the coast and arrived at Hesdin, where it orbited twice. There is evidence to show that the Wing got split up during this process which indicates a lack of judgement on the part of the Wing Leader as to the speed or size of circuits with which he carried out these manoeuvres. This resulted in the loss of 4 pilots for only one EA destroyed. It is most unfortunate that the normal Wing Leader, WC Rankin, had been given 48-hours leave owing to indisposition, and was not leading the Wing.

7. The operation of the North Weald Wing passed off without incident. It is estimated that these 2 actions brought up some 60 EA, which was exactly the kind of reaction hoped for when the operation was planned.

8. In the main operation 12 Blenheims rendezvoused at Manston at 11.30 hours with the Northolt Wing as close escort, the 10 Group Polish Wing escort cover and the Kenley Wing as high cover. The Northolt Polish Wing arrived at the rendezvous about 10 minutes early. The bombers also appeared early, and I think there is no doubt that the bombers left the rendezvous 5 minutes before the time laid down. This was apparent at the time and in the plotting which appeared on the table. The Kenley Wing arrived at the rendezvous one minute before the rendezvous time, and they could see no trace of the bombers, the escort and the escort cover. They orbited for 3 minutes, and then set course. In the meantime, the Flight Commander of one of the flights of Blenheims experienced trouble with his aircraft and turned back; unfortunately the remainder of his flight accompanied him. This upset the escort wing as it took place just after they were setting course for the French coast, and one of the

Northolt squadrons accompanied the box of 6. This squadron later realised its mistake, went back over France and eventually picked up the bombers in the Béthune area when the bombers were on their homeward journey, thus 6 Blenheims started off for the French coast accompanied by 2 squadrons of the escort wing, and the escort cover wing. The high cover wing was not in contact.

9. The bombers were due to cross the coast 5 miles east of Dunkirk. They actually crossed the coast between Calais and Gravelines. Instead of going to Lille they went to Arras, turned over Arras and consider they bombed Gosnay on the homeward journey. As the bombers turned over Arras, 10 Group Wing turned inside them and got in front of them and at this time caused some confusion of the 2 close escort squadrons. The 10 Group Wing continued in front of the bombers throughout the journey home.

10. From this time onwards, the 2 Polish squadrons of the close escort were engaged frequently.

11. In the meantime the Kenley Wing had made straight for the target, and then wheeled westwards as they saw AA bursts some way to the south-west of them. They picked up the bombers and their escort somewhere in the Béthune area, and from that time onwards fulfilled their role as high cover. Their top squadron was continuously engaged, and owing to this some of their pilots ran out of petrol, three of them actually landing in the Channel and being subsequently picked up.

12. Altogether in this part of the operation we had 4 casualties which, considering the penetration and the fact that our forces were incomplete most of the time, can only be regarded as extremely fortunate. In this phase 3 EA were destroyed, 2 probables and 3 damaged.

13. At 11.40 hours the 12 Group Wing were due to rendezvous at Manston and proceed to patrol 5 miles south-east of Dunkirk. This Wing was ordered to patrol at 24,000 feet to 27,000 feet. They did, in fact, patrol at 20–23,000 feet. It must be pointed out that this was the original height that they were ordered to patrol when a complete wing was available to patrol above them. Owing to the fog at Hornchurch this arrangement had to be altered when it appeared it would not be possible to supply any high cover for this wing. The height was accordingly altered, and this was not telephoned by GC Beamish to WC Scott. The Wing reports that it was broken up by flak in the Dunkirk area. It would appear that the Wing did not get together again after its initial break up, as they lost the Wing Leader, one Squadron Leader and 2 pilots. No definite engagement is reported, and only one EA is claimed as being damaged.

14. As the weather at Hornchurch improved slightly one squadron was despatched rapidly to fly above the 12 Group Wing at between 28–30,000 feet. This squadron finally escorted the bombers out, and reports seeing attacks on the

tail of the main formation; they dived down and drove off the EA but made no claim.

15. In conclusion, it appears that on the main penetration the casualties were not high but the Germans were able to deliver their attacks with much fewer casualties to them than if our higher wings had been in position to exploit the tactical advantage which the high escorting wings usually have. Still it could not be regarded as one of the more successful operations as we lost 4 aircraft for only 3 of the enemy destroyed. The casualties which appear unjustifiable are those in the Biggin Hill and 12 Group Wings. In the Biggin Hill Wing I consider that this was in no small measure due to the poor judgement on the part of the Leader. In the case of 12 Group, it would appear from the information available that the Wing flew at a lower height than it was ordered to, thereby giving the EA a tactical advantage, they flew over the flak area which was not necessary in carrying out their role, and by doing so got split up, enabling the enemy to make use of his height advantage by diving on stragglers.

16. During the second operation the enemy fighter reaction appeared to be on a moderate scale only, but it is difficult to gauge their numbers owing to lack of enemy plots during the operation.

17. The weather was fairly good but there was some haze. The Kenley Wing Commander reports that he could see St Omer from the coast, and had no difficulty in finding his way to Lille.

Trafford Leigh-Mallory - 9/11/41
Air-Vice-Marshal
Commanding No.11 Group

On this same date, Sholto Douglas replied to a call from Air Commodore J. Whitworth Jones at Air Ministry concerning this operation. He wrote:

1. You asked me this morning to let you have a report on yesterday's Circus Operation. I attach a report by AOC No.11 Group.

2. There is one factor which the AOC does not mention but which, I think, had an appreciable effect on the high casualty rate. Whilst the wind on the ground was only about 5 mph, there was a wind at 35,000 feet of 75 mph, from the north-west. This means that formations returning to the English coast took appreciably longer than usual to get away from enemy fighters and flak. Moreover, the wind undoubtedly caused a shortage of petrol, which again would have the effect of causing pilots to run for home instead of staying and fighting it out. At least 2 pilots (both of No.452 Squadron) ran out of petrol on the way home, after being heavily engaged at full throttle, and force-landed

in the sea. Fortunately both were picked up, but this factor may have been responsible for some of the other casualties.

3. In view of the results of this operation and of the need for conserving our resources in order to form new squadrons in replacement of those sent overseas, I have told the AOC 11 Group to scale down still further the number of Circus and other big operations that he does. I now propose to do not more than two, or at the outside three, Circuses per month for the time being.

Yours, WSD.

They were not only scaled down, but stopped, at least for 1941. They returned in 1942, a year that saw a further 130 flown with 11 Group fighters, while 10 Group put on at least ten more and several Ramrods.

By that time the Japanese war had begun, resulting in even more men and machines being needed overseas. Malta, North Africa, Burma – it was going to be a long war.

Chapter 12

Aftermath

While Circus 110 was the last of the type flown in 1941, other operations continued for the remaining few weeks of the year. Circuses did not come to an end; Circus No.111 was mounted on 11 February 1942. The operations flown in these latter weeks were mostly called Low Ramrods, which had been around for some time. There was obviously some numbering system for them because one flown on 15 October 1941 is shown as Ramrod 69, while 10 Group had their own system too. On this same date 10 Group noted their Ramrod No.12. Towards the end of October there were Ramrods numbered in Roman numerals, IVA and IVB on 4 November for instance, with Ramrod V on 6 November, followed by VIA and VIB on the 7th.

With the deteriorating weather more Rhubarbs were being flown, but they were no safer than they had been earlier. Some Rodeos are recorded too, and fighter sweeps. Strangely there is reference to two Circuses on 8 December, but they did not feature in Bomber Command's list of Circus Ops. In the afternoon Ramrod XV, with Hurricanes attacking Hesdin produced a lot of action, as had some morning sorties. Eight fighter pilots were killed on these missions, and two lost to captivity, including one Air Sea Rescue Spitfire pilot killed by FW190s. JG26 claimed six Spitfires between 1255 and 1515 for the loss of two fighters, a FW190 shot down by a Spitfire, while a 109 pilot hit the ground during a low manoeuvre and had to belly-land at St Omer-Arques. Müncheberg brought his personal score to sixty in these actions. JG2 put in claims for another three Spitfires and one Hurricane although no Hurricane was lost.

On the 13th, two Hampdens of 44 and 144 Squadrons failed to return from early evening 'Gardening' missions – laying mines off Brest. Both fell to Me109s of JG2. It had been a good day for JG2, for around noon they had shot down two Curtiss P40 Tomahawks of Army Co-operation Command off the Somme Estuary.

Shortly before Christmas there was Rodeo II on the 18th, the same day that Operation 'Veracity' was mounted – an attack on the German battleships *Scharnhorst* and *Gneisenau* in Brest. JG2 engaged the bombers, claiming four Stirlings and one Manchester, plus two Spitfires. Number 7 and 15 Squadrons lost five Stirlings. A Halifax of 35 Squadron, also on this raid, was crippled by flak and its pilot (and Squadron CO) W/Cdr B. V. Robinson DFC, had to ditch his bomber sixty miles off the English coast – and survived. 97 Squadron lost one of its Avro Manchesters to fighter attack off Brest, while the Squadron CO, W/Cdr D. F. Balsdon, had to return with his aircraft severely damaged, only to stall and crash at RAF Coningsby. All eight crewmen died.

Operation 'Veracity' (II) was conducted on 30 December, by 10 Group. Nine Spitfires squadrons escorted bombers to Brest again, losing three fighters with all pilots listed as missing. One was killed, and the other two were taken prisoner. This raid also cost the RAF three Halifax aircraft, one each from 10, 35 and 76 Squadrons. JG2 claimed all three although AA fire seems to have done the major damage. Oberleutnant Erich Leie claimed one of the bombers for his thirty-second victory. Three Spitfires also failed to return. One of the pilots, Sgt A. E. Joyce of 234 Squadron, was captured, ending up in the famous Stalag Luft III prison camp. However, he was shot during an escape attempt in June 1943 and died on the operating table before doctors could save him. One of the others, from 306 Squadron, may have been hit by flak as it was seen to lose a wing over Brest while engaged in combat. Another Polish pilot, from 317 Squadron, ended up as a prisoner of war.

The escorting Spitfire pilots put in claims for seven destroyed, seven probably destroyed and three damaged, later revised to 8-6-3, most claims coming from the Polish Wing. JG2 lost two Me109s with one pilot killed.

* * *

The year of 1941 had been a desperate one for the Allies on all fronts. Allied armies in North Africa were on a see-saw of operations back and forth across the desert, Malta was being pounded by Italian and German aircraft, German U-boats were decimating ships bringing supplies across the Atlantic, Russia had been invaded, and in early December Japan had brought America into the war by attacking Pearl Harbor. There had been one or two high spots, such as the sinking of the German battleship *Bismarck* in May, and the London *Blitz* had come to an end that same month, but everything seemed to be going rapidly downhill. Bomber Command was doing its best to strike back, but without the navigational aids and target identification methods that were to come, the damage inflicted was less than supposed, or hoped for.

Fighter Command, along with light bombers from 2 and 16 Groups, and later with Stirlings and Hampdens from 3 and 5 Groups, had taken the air war into the skies of northern France and Belgium, but at what cost? If success was being thought to be made because losses were far less than German aircraft shot down, then success was elusory. In the beginning, the idea was merely to take the air war to the Germans following the hard fought actions during the Battle of Britain. It helped morale if the RAF fighter pilots could hit back and feel they were 'dishing it out' rather than constantly 'taking it'.

After the Germans moved on Russia in mid-June, there was another incentive in taking this air war to the enemy. Russia wanted Britain to harass the Germans in the West in the hope that the pressure in the East could be eased somewhat. Britain's war leaders thought that by keeping up attacks over northern France, it would force the Germans to reduce the number of aircraft being used on the Eastern Front. As we now know this did not happen, and leaving just two fighter Gruppen in France and the Low Countries was more than enough to cope with these RAF incursions.

The idea that massed fighter sweeps by Fighter Command would encourage Luftwaffe fighters to rise and do battle was very naïve. While many German pilots were keen to engage in dogfights, if for no other reason than to increase personal victory scores, their leaders saw no percentage in shooting down a few Spitfires or Hurricanes while risking perhaps a similar number of losses. The RAF had found this out in late 1940, knowing that fighter sweeps, or *Frei Jagd* as the Germans called them, posed no threat to military or civilian targets, and were mostly left alone, thereby eliminating the loss of valuable pilots and aircraft. The Germans had countered by using their bomb-carrying *jabo* staffels to make it difficult for RAF interceptors to ignore. Now, in 1941, the Germans had to be encouraged to engage by using small formations of bombers as bait, and when this started to pall, the RAF introduced four-engined Stirlings to entice air combat.

As 1941 progressed, the RAF was encouraged by the number of German fighters that were being shot down, or in truth, being 'claimed' as shot down. Even in the 1914–18 war it was known that fighter claims bore little or no relation to the number of enemy aircraft that were actually destroyed. In that conflict, the RFC, RNAS and then the RAF, were constantly over the German side of the lines in France, and the chances of a German falling on the Allied side were few and far between. In order to produce some measure of success, the only guide to what damage was being inflicted was by corroborated reports by the pilots themselves.

This was all very well, but put simply, the conditions that prevailed made this a very hit and miss affair. Aeroplanes, and therefore airmen, flying at high speed, and, if they were not stupid, constantly looking out for danger, had very limited access to a clear picture of what was happening around them. Certainly if they were firing upon a hostile aeroplane and it burst into flames in front of them, or perhaps a wing or two came adrift, then it was fairly certain the aircraft was destroyed. Even seeing it go down and strike the ground resulted in making a good claim, but it could rarely, if ever, be known with absolute certainty if the crashing aircraft was in fact the one you had shot at. Several pilots shooting at several aircraft, and as the whirling and turning continued, looked down when an opportunity occurred, and saw an aircraft crash, believed it was the one they had been firing at moments before. In this way, one crashing aircraft produced two or three claims by the squadron as a whole.

Cloudy or misty conditions did not help in the claiming game either. Firing at and seeing an opponent go spinning down into cloud, could never be turned into a confirmed kill, so it was frustrating for the fighting pilots not to be able to claim a definite scalp. Therefore, it was not long before these sorts of actions resulted in what was termed as an 'out of control' claim. That is to say, someone else saw the action and confirmed that their colleague had indeed hit an enemy aircraft so badly that it had gone down 'out of control' (adding the word completely also helped). Pilots were supposed to understand the difference between an aircraft really out of control, rather than one with a pilot simply spinning out of the fight, and once below the cloud into which he was seen spinning, flattened out and went home, a better and a wiser man. This inevitably became, what in WW2 would be known as a 'probable' victory. Of course, the 'ooc' aircraft might well have continued down through the cloud or ground mist, to smash to pieces over the French countryside, but unless it was near enough to the lines for an Allied soldier to witness it, the 'victorious' pilot could only report one enemy aircraft 'out of control'.

As things progressed, the word 'victory' became synonymous with 'destroyed', and the armchair historians in later years, added confirmed victories together with these 'ooc' aircraft (or probables) in order to create a total victory list for the man. Therefore, if the pilot was given credit for three enemy aircraft destroyed and four 'out of control' his score became seven. In citations for medals this separation was not always recorded and the journalists of the time, and then the pulp fiction writers of the 1920–30s invariably ignored (or did not fully understand) the two types of claims, and listed the victory scores as enemy aircraft destroyed. This in itself didn't matter a hoot, but this is why many WW1 pilots appear to have achieved a considerable number of victories – of which some, in reality, were merely probables.

In WW2 this did not happen. Fighter pilots could claim an enemy aircraft destroyed, probably destroyed or damaged. If confirmed as destroyed it had to have been witnessed by an independent person and seen to crash, crash in flames, break up in the air, or the pilot take to his parachute. If it merely fell or spun away out of sight trailing smoke or flame but not actually seen to crash, blow up or its pilot bale out, then it was a probable. Even if the victorious pilot reported it had crashed but had no witnesses to the event, the squadron intelligence officer could only give credit for a probable, although it became obvious that certain pilots – those with a track record for shooting down enemy machines – were often given credit. Whatever the result, only those aircraft confirmed as destroyed were credited as victories, and were not, like WW1, added to probables to show an overall score. As camera guns were fitted to day fighter aircraft, often a confirmed victory could be given if the pictures showed the enemy aircraft being destroyed, or at least, so heavily damaged that it was more than probable that it was destroyed. Anything less, even if the attacker saw the aircraft crash after he had stopped firing, was more often than not given as a probable or even a damaged.

The German pilots had similar categories of victory credits, especially the confirmation by another pilot or ground observer. However, neither side, obviously, kept to these rules, as witnessed by the number of claims and credits against actual losses. It was generally a case of the head seeing what the eye did not. If a pilot was convinced that his opponent had been destroyed, even if he had to admit to himself he had not actually seen it, he might easily report it destroyed because he could not believe it could have survived the damage he had inflicted.

If the problem of speed in WW1 contributed to over-confidence in claiming a victory because, having fired at an opponent, then taking his eyes from it to check his own safety, then having turned or banked looked back and saw what he assumed to be the aircraft he had just attacked crash, it was easy to assume it was his. In the Second World War, the speed of combat compared with World War One meant that a pilot very quickly exited the immediate combat zone. It was this more than anything else, especially in a fight where there were several aircraft of both sides involved, that one falling aircraft could become the 'victory' of several pilots. And if an aircraft was seen to fall into the sea or crash several thousand feet below, it was easy to say that it was a German aircraft when in fact it might well have been a British one.

What of course becomes very clear from the earlier chapters in this book, is that both sides were claiming vastly more of their opponents as destroyed, than were actually lost or even damaged. On Circus operations during 1941, the RAF's own score of enemy fighters destroyed came to 556, which added to other types of operations that showed 219 victories, the total then became 775. Of the 219, eighty-two were under the heading of 'fighter sweeps' and often these sweeps were in support of Circuses, so one could argue that Circuses had accounted for well over 600 victories. As the Germans only lost 103 fighters between 14 June and 31 December on the Western Front in 1941, it does not take a mathematical genius to see that the RAF pilots were vastly over-claiming. Often in good faith one has to say. To say otherwise would not be very gallant. However, there are some examples of pilots being credited with a confirmed victory with untruthful combat report narratives.

Today's Internet figures record that the Germans lost 236 fighters from all causes, 103 of them in combat. RAF claims, however, amounted to 711 [another source says 731] enemy aircraft, while the RAF lost approximately 411 Spitfires and ninety-three Hurricanes [or about 505 in total].

It is only human nature to discover that if the intelligence officer was not keen in giving a confirmed victory or if a pilot's report did not mention a realistic demise of enemy aircraft or pilot, that an extra couple of words would make the difference. There is the case of one successful British pilot who claimed a 109 shot down, and ended his report by saying he saw it dive into the sea. We now know from German evidence that this particular German pilot, while heading for the sea, did not crash but pulled out and went home. But as the RAF pilot's report said it dived into the sea, it helped his claim for a confirmed victory. Don't forget that most of these RAF pilots were little more than boys and with the adrenalin flowing, heart pumping and breathing heavy, it is all too easy to guild the lily, and come home a champion rather than an also-ran.

It happened on the German side too. One has only to compare RAF losses with German claims to see that the same was just as true as with the RAF, especially on the rare occasions when Blenheims survived the fighter onslaught and *all* returned home, yet some were claimed as destroyed anyway. Despite the assumed strict confirmation rules, it has to be said that those German aces with growing scores, appear to be among the most prolific over-claimers. Their carrot was the award of the Knight's Cross for approximately twenty victories, it was a definite aim.

Luftwaffe claims according to one report noted almost 1,500, broken down into 850 Spitfires, 100 Hurricanes, 161 Blenheims, 149 Wellingtons and 1 Lancaster (but no Stirlings).

* * *

We armchair historians are great at levelling judgements long after the events, but there are questions to be asked, even if they cannot be answered now by those who were 'running the show'. One question is where does wishful thinking end and common sense (logic) begin?

As already mentioned in earlier chapters, was Air Ministry – that is to say, the top brass who were over-seeing the day to day, week to week, month to month activities of the offensive operations being carried out – blinkered to common sense, or did they just go along with everything? Did they really think that Fighter Command was actually inflicting so such damage on the Luftwaffe? Surely Intelligence gathering sources could reveal that there was a vast difference between claims of losses and actual losses?

At the end of August 1941 for instance, Fighter Command gave an analysis of enemy casualties during that month. Total enemy losses attributed to RAF fighters was 146 with another seventy-seven as probables. While this did include some sixteen Me110s, He111s, Do17s and Ju88s, it still made 131 Me109s lost by the enemy. Staying with the fighter losses, these figures estimated (and assumed) personnel losses of the same number, i.e. 131, plus a possible sixty-eight more casualties in the probable category, making 199 pilot casualties. This analysis also estimated, by adding total and probable losses together, that the Luftwaffe had suffered a possible loss of 227 during the month.

We imagine that the Chief of the Air Staff and his immediate inner circle read these figures and jumped up and down with joy, believing the war was not far off being won if their fighter pilots could inflict such pain on the enemy. However, there had to be some officers questioning the 'intelligence' reports. Presumably everyone looked with less favour on RAF losses. During the year the figure of lost pilots recorded by Fighter Command who had been on Circus operations totalled 296 killed, taken prisoner or were still missing. Another fifty-five had become casualties on fighter sweeps, while overall, for all operations (including Rhubarbs, anti-shipping escorts, etc.), pilot losses were 462.

A good number of these losses were veterans of the Battle of Britain, in fact over 200 pilots that had seen action in the defence of Britain in the summer and autumn of 1940 had become casualties from late 1940 and during 1941 – some eighty-two being killed in action with twenty-six others taken prisoner. Some, naturally, had lost their lives in flying accidents – about fifty-three – while about twenty others had been lost or shot down after being sent to Malta or North Africa, but that still meant that over 100 had become casualties, mainly over France and the Channel, while 'taking the war to the enemy'. A number had also been wounded, some never to return to operational flying. A few had also been brought down, evaded capture and eventually managed to return to England.

During the second half of the 1941 'offensive', the RAF lost around 600 fighters, as opposed to some 920 in the Battle of Britain. Luftwaffe records seem to indicate around 100 Me109s lost.

The two main Geschwaders, JG26 and JG2, generally had around 250 fighters on strength, although serviceability often reduced this overall figure – sometimes by up to a third. After Rolf Pingel was interrogated following his capture in early July, it became clear to Fighter Command leaders that their task of reducing Luftwaffe effort on the Eastern Front so as to counter the offensive over France was not working. It also became clear that German losses were not in accord with RAF claims. Following a conference on 29 July, it was decided to reduce somewhat the intensity of the offensive. Ironically, the RAF failed to realise that their efforts were in fact having some impact on Luftwaffe fighter serviceability which was at this time down to 70 per cent. More ironically, the respite enabled the serviceability to increase to around 80 per cent by August. However, this brief lull was over by mid-August and Circus operations returned to normal. In late August the question of continuing with these operations was still being considered.

This book records what occurred during this momentous year of 1941 and brings into clear focus the very great trial imposed on Fighter Command. Yet, as we like saying today, it gave the leaders of the day - 'lessons to be learned'. Everything is new every day in war. The trick is to keep going, take the blows and fight on. There is no doubt that in Fighter Command, the Wing and Squadron commanders, in the main, learnt the lessons and continued the fight, and the youngsters that followed them helped achieve ultimate victory for the British people.

Circus Operations flown during 1941

No.	Date	Target	Target Code	Bombers	
1	10 Jan	Forêt de Guines		6 Blenheims	114 Sqn
2	2 Feb	Boulogne docks		6 Blenheims	139 Sqn
3	5 Feb	St Omer A/F		12 Blenheims	114 & 139 Sqn
4	10 Feb	Dunkirk		6 Blenheims	114 Sqn
5	10 Feb	Boulogne		6 Blenheims	59 Sqn
?	10 Feb	Calais		6 Blenheims	59 Sqn
6	26 Feb	Calais		12 Blenheims	139 Sqn
7	5 Mar	Boulogne		6 Blenheims	139 Sqn
8	13 Mar	Calais-Marck		6 Blenheims	139 Sqn
9	16 Apr	Berck-sur-Mer		6 Blenheims	21 Sqn
10	21 May	Gosnay		18 Blenheims	21, 82, 110 Sqn
11	21 May	St Omer Cancelled			
12	14 Jun	St Omer/Longuenesse		12 Blenheims	105 & 110 Sqn
13	17 Jun	Chocques	Z302	18 Blenheims	110, 107, 139, 18 Sqn
14	16 Jun	Boulogne		6 Blenheims	59 Sqn
15	18 Jun	Bois de Licques		6 Blenheims	107 Sqn
16	21 Jun	St Omer		6 Blenheims	21 Sqn
17	21 Jun	Desvres A/F		6 Blenheims	110 Sqn
18	22 Jun	Hazebrouock M/Y	Z437	10 Blenheims	18 & 139 Sqn
19	23 Jun	Chocques	Z220	24 Blenheims	21, 105, 110 Sqn
20	23 Jun	Mardyck A/F		6 Blenheims	107 Sqn
21	24 Jun	Comines	Z195	17 Blenheims	18, 107, 139 Sqn
22	25 Jun	Hazebrouck M/Y	Z437	12 Blenheims	21 & 110 Sqn
23	25 Jun	St Omer/Longuesesse		12 Blenheims	18 & 139 Sqn
24	26 Jun	Comines	Z195	28 Blenheims	105, 107, 226 Sqn
25	27 Jun	Lille	Z184	24 Blenheims	18, 21, 139, 226 Sqn
26	28 Jun	Comines	Z195	23 Blenheims	18 & 21 Sqn
27	30 Jun	Pont-à-Vendin	Z303	18 Blenheims	18 & 139 Sqn
28	1 Jul	Chocques	Z229	12 Blenheims	18 & 226 Sqn
29	2 Jul	Lille	Z246	12 Blenheims	21 & 226 Sqn
30	3 Jul	Hazebrouck M/Y	Z437	6 Blenheims	139 Sqn
31	3 Jul	Hazebrouck M/Y	Z437	6 Blenheims	18 Sqn
32	4 Jul	Chocques & Abbeville	Z220/440	12 Blenheims	21 & 226 Sqn
33	5 Jul	Lille	Z183	3 Stirlings	15 Sqn
		Abbeville sidings		1 Stirling	15 Sqn
34	6 Jul	Le Trait/Yainville	Z363/453	3 Stirlings	7 Sqn
35	6 Jul	Lille	Z183	6 Stirlings	15 Sqn
36	7 Jul	Hazebrouck M/Y	Z437	1 Stirling	15 Sqn
37	7 Jul	Meaulte	Z189	4 Stirlings	7 Sqn
38	7 Jul	Chocques	Z220	3 Stirlings	15 Sqn
39	8 Jul	Lens & Mazingarbe	Z562/301	3 Stirlings	7 Sqn

40	8 Jul	Liille	Z245/246	3 Stirlings	15 Sqn
41	9 Jul	Mazingarbe	Z562	3 Stirlings	15 Sqn
42	10 Jul	Chocques	Z220	3 Stirlings	7 Sqn
43	11 Jul	Yainville & Le Trait	Z453/363	3 Stirlings	7 Sqn
44	11 Jul	Diversion for C45		1 Blenheim	60 Group
45	11 Jul	Lille	Z183	3 Stirlings	15 Sqn
		(in the event, bombed Hazebrouck M/Y, Z437)			
46	12 Jul	Arques	S5513	3 Stirlings	15 Sqn
47	12 Jul	Diversion for C46		1 Blenheim	60 Group
48	14 Jul	Hazebrouck M/Y	Z437	6 Blenheims	21 Sqn
49	14 Jul	Cancelled			
50	14 Jul	Aborted			
51	19 Jul	Lille (bombed Dunkirk)	Z246	3 Stirlings	15 Sqn
52	20 Jul	Hazebrouck M/Y	Z437	3 Stirlings	15 Sqn
		Aborted due to cloud			
53	20 Jul	Abandoned – weather			
54	21 Jul	Lille – aborted - flak	Z565	3 Stirlings	15 Sqn
55	21 Jul	Mazingarbe – aborted, cloud		3 Stirlings	15 Sqn
56		Cancelled			
57	22 Jul	Le Trait	Z368	6 Blenheims	114 Sqn
58	22 Jul	Diversion by fighters			
59	23 Jul	Forêt de Eperlecques		6 Blenheims	114 Sqn
60	23 Jul	Mazingarbe	Z562	6 Blenheims	114 Sqn
61	24 Jul	Diversion for *Sunrise* Op		9 Blenheims	59 Sqn
62	7 Aug	Lille	Z246	6 Blenheims	107 Sqn
		(Two bombed Gravelines			
63		Cancelled			
64		Cancelled			
65	5 Aug	St Omer/Longuenesse		6 Blenheims	226 Sqn
66	7 Aug	St Omer/Longuenesse		6 Blenheims	107 Sqn
67	7 Aug	Lille (bombed barges instead)		6 Blenheims	
68	9 Aug	St Omer/Longuenesse		5 Blenheims	226 Sqn
69	12 Aug	St Omer		6 Hampdens	408 Sqn
		(not located, bombed alternate target)			
70	12 Aug	Gosnay		6 Hampdens	106 Sqn
71	12 Aug	Le Trait	Z363	6 Blenheims	226 Sqn
72	14 Aug	E-Boats at Boulogne		12 Blenheims	107 & 114 Sqn
73	14 Aug	Marquise (aborted)		6 Blenheims	
74	16 Aug	Marquise		6 Blenheims	82 Sqn
75	16 Aug	St Omer/Longuenesse		6 Blenheims	21 Sqn
76	17 Aug	Le Havre Docks	(aborted)	6 Blenheims	139 Sqn
77	17 Aug	Cancelled			
78	18 Aug	Lille	Z246	9 Blenheims	110 & 226
79	18 Aug	postponed to the 19th.			
80	18 Aug	Marquise		5 Blenheims	18 Sqn
81	19 Aug	Gosnay		6 Blenheims	18 Sqn
82	19 Aug	Hazebrouck M/Y	Z437	6 Blenheims	107 Sqn
83	21 Aug	Chocques	Z220	6 Blenheims	18 Sqn
84	21 Aug	Chocques	Z220	6 Blenheims	88 Sqn
85	27 Aug	Diversion for C 86 – aborted		5 Blenheims	139 Sqn
86	27 Aug	Lille	Z246	9 Blenheims	18 Sqn

87	26 Aug	St Omer/Longuenesse		6 Blenheims	18 Sqn
88	29 Aug	Hazebrouck M/Y	Z437	6 Blenheims	139 Sqn
89		Cancelled			
90	31 Aug	St Omer (Diversion for C91) (three bombed railway W. of Audricq)		6 Blenheims	21 & 82 Sqn
91	31 Aug	Lille	Z246	12 Blenheims	18 & 114 Sqn
92	31 Aug	Le Trait	Z363	6 Blenheims	139 Sqn
93	4 Sep	Mazingarbe		12 Blenheims	18 Sqn
94		Cancelled			
95	17 Sep	Mazingarbe		24 Blenheims	82, 114 Sqn
96	17 Sep	Marquise		6 Hampdens	408 Sqn
97	18 Sep	Abbeville M/Y		6 Hampdens	408 Sqn
98	18 Sep	Cancelled			
99	18 Sep	Abandoned			
100A	20 Sep	Hazebrouck M/Y	Z437	3 Blenheims	88 Sqn
100B	20 Sep	Abbeville M/Y		6 Hampdens	408 Sqn
100C	20 Sep	Rouen shipyard		12 Blenheims	82 & 114 Sqn
101	21 Sep	Gosnay		12 Blenheims	18 & 139
102	21 Sep	Lille		6 Hampdens	408 Sqn
103A	27 Sep	Amiens M/Y	Z446	11 Blenheims	110 & 226 Sqn
103B	27 Sep	Bully	Z301	11 Blenheims	114 Sqn
104	2 Oct	Le Havre (aborted)	Z218	6 Blenheims	88 Sqn
105	3 Oct	Ostend	Z871	6 Blenheims	88 Sqn
106A	7 Oct	Cancelled			
106B	7 Oct	Cancelled			
107	12 Oct	Boulogne		24 Blenheims	21, 110, 226 Sqn
108A	13 Oct	Arques	Z563	6 Blenheims	139 Sqn
108B	13 Oct	Mazingarbe	Z301	18 Blenheims	114 & 139 Sqn
109		No Record – possibly confused with 108B			
110	8 Nov	1 Lille	Z185	12 Blenheims	21 & 82 Sqn

Appendix B

Single-seat Day Fighters
Order of Battle January 1941

11 Group

Sqn	Type	Station	Commanding Officer
1	Hurricane I	Northolt	S/Ldr M. H. Brown DFC
601	Hurricane I	Northolt	S/Ldr J.A. O'Neill DFC
41	Spitfire IIa	Hornchurch	S/Ldr D. O. Findlay DFC
64	Spitfire I/IIa	Hornchurch	S/Ldr A. R. D. Macdonald DFC
611	Spitfire I	Hornchurch	S/Ldr E. R. Bitmead
66	Spitfire IIa	Biggin Hill	S/Ldr A. S. Forbes DFC
74	Spitfire IIa	Biggin Hill	S/Ldr A. G. Malan DSO DFC
92	Spitfire I	Biggin Hill	S/Ldr J. A. Kent DFC
253	Hurricane I	Kenley	S/Ldr P. R. Walker DFC
615	Hurricane I	Kenley	S/Ldr R. A. Holmwood
605	Hurricane IIa	Croydon	S/Ldr G. R. Edge DFC
65	Spitfire I	Tangmere	S/Ldr G. A. W. Saunders DFC
145	Hurricane I	Tangmere	S/Ldr J. R. A. Peel DFC
302	Hurricane I	Westhampnett	S/Ldr P. Łaguna
610	Spitfire I	Westhampnett	S/Ldr J. Ellis DFC
56	Hurricane I	North Weald	S/Ldr E. N. Ryder DFC
249	Hurricane I	North Weald	S/Ldr R. A. Barton DFC
17	Hurricane I	Debden	S/Ldr A. G. Miller
85	Hurricane I	Debden	S/Ldr P. W. Townsend DFC
242	Hurricane I	Debden	S/Ldr D. R. S. Bader DSO DFC
91	Spitfire IIa	Hawkinge	S/Ldr C. P. Green DFC

10 Group

87	Hurricane I	Charmy Down	S/Ldr I. R. Gleed DFC
501	Hurricane I	Exeter	S/Ldr E. Holden DFC
504	Hurricane I	Exeter	S/Ldr J. Sample DFC
32	Hurricane I	Middle Wallop	S/Ldr M. N. Crossley DSO DFC
152	Spitfire I	Warmwell	S/Ldr D. P. A. Boitel-Gill DFC
609	Spitfire I	Warmwell	S/Ldr M. L. Robinson DFC
238	Hurricane I	Chilbolton	S/Ldr H. A. Fenton
234	Spitfire I	St Eval	S/Ldr M. V. Blake DFC
79	Hurricane I	Pembrey	S/Ldr J. H. Hayworth
247	Hurricane I	Roborough	S/Ldr P. G. StG. O'Brian

12 Group

19	Spitfire IIa	Duxford	S/Ldr B. J. Lane DFC
310	Hurricane I	Duxford	S/Ldr J. Jeffries DFC

213	Hurricane I	Church Fenton	S/Ldr D. S. MacDonald DFC
303	Hurricane I	Church Fenton	S/Ldr A. Kowalczyk
222	Spitfire I	Coltishall	S/Ldr R. C. Love DFC
257	Hurricane I	Coltishall	S/Ldr R. R. S. Tuck DFC
151	Hurricane I	Wittering	S/Ldr J. S. Adams DFC
266	Spitfire I	Wittering	S/Ldr P. G. Jameson DFC
71	Hurricane I	Kirton in Lindsay	S/Ldr M. W. Churchill DSO DFC
616	Spitfire I	Kirton in Lindsay	S/Ldr H. F. Burton DFC
46	Hurricane IIa	Digby	S/Ldr A. C. Rabagliati DFC
2 RCAF	Hurricane I	Digby	S/Ldr G. R. McGregor DFC
308	Hurricane I	Baginton	S/Ldr B. G. Morris

Appendix C

Single Seat Day Fighters
Order of Battle 1 June 1941

11 Group

145	Spitfire IIa/IIb	Merston	S/Ldr P. S. Turner DFC
616	Spitfire IIa	Westhampnett	S/Ldr H. F. Burton DFC
610	Spitfire IIa	Westhampnett	S/Ldr H. de C. A. Woodhouse AFC
312	Hurricane IIb	Kenley	S/Ldr E. Gizak
258	Hurricane IIb	Kenley	S/Ldr W. G. Clouston DFC
1	Hurricane IIa	Redhill	S/Ldr R. P. Brooker DFC
609	Spitfire IIa	Biggin Hill	S/Ldr M. L. Robinson DSO DFC
92	Spitfire Vb	Biggin Hill	S/Ldr J. Rankin DFC
601	Hurricane IIb	Manston	S/Ldr E. J. Gracie DFC
91	Spitfire Vb	Hawkinge	S/Ldr C. P. Green DFC
74	Spitfire IIa/Vb	Gravesend	S/Ldr J. C. Mungo-Park DFC
603	Spitfire Vb	Hornchurch	S/Ldr F. M. Smith DFC
54	Spitfire IIa/Vb	Hornchurch	S/Ldr R. F. Boyd DFC
611	Spitfire Va	Hornchurch	S/Ldr F. S. Stapleton DFC
56	Hurricane IIb	North Weald	S/Ldr E. N. Ryder DFC
242	Hurricane IIb	Stapleford Tawney	S/Ldr W. Whitney Straight MC
3	Hurricane II/IIc	Martlesham	S/Ldr S. F. Godden
71	Hurricane IIa	Martlesham	S/Ldr W. E. G. Taylor
303	Spitfire IIb	Northolt	S/Ldr W. Łapkowski VM
306	Hurricane IIa	Northolt	S/Ldr T. H. Rolski VM KW

10 Group

32	Hurricane IIa	Angle	S/Ldr R. A. B. Russell
316	Hurricane I	Pembrey	S/Ldr C. J. Donovan
79	Hurricane I	Pembrey	S/Ldr G. D. Haysom
152	Spitfire IIa	Portreath	S/Ldr J. Darwen
247	Hurricane I	Portreath	S/Ldr P. G. StG. O'Brian
66	Spitfire IIa	Portreath	S/Ldr A. S. Forbes DFC
501	Spitfire IIa	Colerne	S/Ldr A. H. Boyd DFC
87	Hurricane I	Charmy Down	S/Ldr I. R. Gleed DFC
504	Hurricane I	Exeter	S/Ldr M. Rook
118	Spitfire IIa	Ibsley	S/Ldr F. J. Howell DFC
234	Spitfire IIa	Warmwell	S/Ldr M. V. Blake DFC

12 Group

19	Spitfire IIa	Fowlmere	S/Ldr R. G. Dutton DFC
310	Hurricane IIa	Duxford	S/Ldr F. Weber
222	Spitfire IIa/IIb	Coltishall	S/Ldr R. C. Love DFC
257	Hurricane IIb/IIc	Coltishall	S/Ldr R. R. S. Tuck DSO DFC

151	Hurricane I	Wittering	S/Ldr J. S. Adams DFC
266	Spitfire IIa	Collyweston	S/Ldr T. B. de la P. Beresford
401 RCAF	Hurricane IIa	Wellingore	S/Ldr A. D. Nesbit
402 RCAF	Hurricane IIa	Coleby Grange	S/Ldr V. B. Corbett
65	Spitfire IIa	Kirton in Lindsay	S/Ldr G. A. W. Saunders DFC
452 RAAF	Spitfire IIa	Kirton in Lindsay	S/Ldr R. W. Bungay
485 RNZAF	Spitfire I	Leconfield	S/Ldr M. W. B. Knight

Appendix D

Statistics Relating to Day Offensive Operations by Fighter Command, 1941

Key:
a = No. of Sorties
b = No. of enemy aircraft claimed as destroyed
c = No. of fighter pilots lost (killed, PoW or missing)

Month	*Circus*			*Fighter Sweeps*			*Rhubarbs*		
	a	b	c	a	b	c	a	b	c
January	9	2	–	7	–	–	4	–	2
February	45½	7	12	18	–	2	2	–	2
March	18	2	5	21½	3	1	2	–	–
April	5	1	2	25	4	5	8	3	3
May	16	4	6	20½	2	–	8	3	–
June	267	161	39	39	4	5	3	1	1
July	404	161	84	39	6	6	5	–	1
August	321	100	72	117	18	8	16	–	3
September	152	83	49	45	7	7	9	5	3
October	75	31	19	77	27	16	20	7	5
November	13	4	8	30	11	5	17	2	6
December	–	–	–	19	–	–	7	–	1
Totals:	1,325½	556	296	458	82	55	101	21	27

In addition, fighter pilots lost on - anti-shipping sorties = 23
Some 404 sorties were flown in addition covering operations where the following losses were incurred:

> – other bombing ops = 50
> – miscellaneous ops = 5
> – recce missions = 5
> (Total = 83)

These figures were issued by Fighter Command HQ, and on the face of it there does seem to be some discrepancies, so they are shown here for information.

In total, the Command had flown 2,288½ operational sorties, claimed a total of 775 enemy aircraft destroyed (including 156 on other operations), while acknowledging fighter pilot losses of 461.

Bibliography

The JG 26 War Diary (Vol One), by Donald Caldwell, Grub Street, 1996
Bomber Command Losses, 1941, by W. R. Chorley, Midland Counties/(Ian Allan), 1993
Spitfire into Battle, by G/Capt Duncan Smith, John Murray, 1981
The First and the Last, by Adolf Galland, Methuen, 1955
Fighter Pilot, by William R. Dunn, University Press of Kentucky, 1982
Kiwi Spitfire Ace, by Jack Rae, Grub Street, 2001
Nine Lives, by G/Capt Alan C. Deere, Hodder & Stoughton, 1959
Spitfire Patrol, by G/Capt Colin Gray, Hutchinson, 1990
With the Wind in my Face, by W/Cdr J. P. Falkowski, Privately Published, c1967
Fighter Command, by Peter Wykham, Putnam, 1960
Fighter Pilot's Summer, by Norman Franks & W/Cdr Paul Richey, Grub Street, 1993
The War Diaries of Neville Duke, edited by Norman Franks, Grub Street, 1995
One of the Few, by G/Capt J. A. Kent, William Kimber, 1971
Aces High, by Christopher F. Shores & Clive Williams, Grub Street, 1994
Those Other Eagles, by Christopher Shores, Grub Street, 2004
Commanders of the Polish Air Force Squadrons in the West, by Józef Zieliński and Tadeusz Krzystek, Posnań, 2002
The Canadian Years (242 Sqn), by Hugh Halliday, Midland Counties, 1982
Years of Command, by MRAF Lord Douglas of Kirtleside, Collins, 1966
Die Ritterkreuzträger der Luftwaffe, by Ernst Obermaier, Verlag Dieter Hoffmann, 1966
RAF Evaders, by Oliver Clutton-Brock, Grub Street, 2009

Index